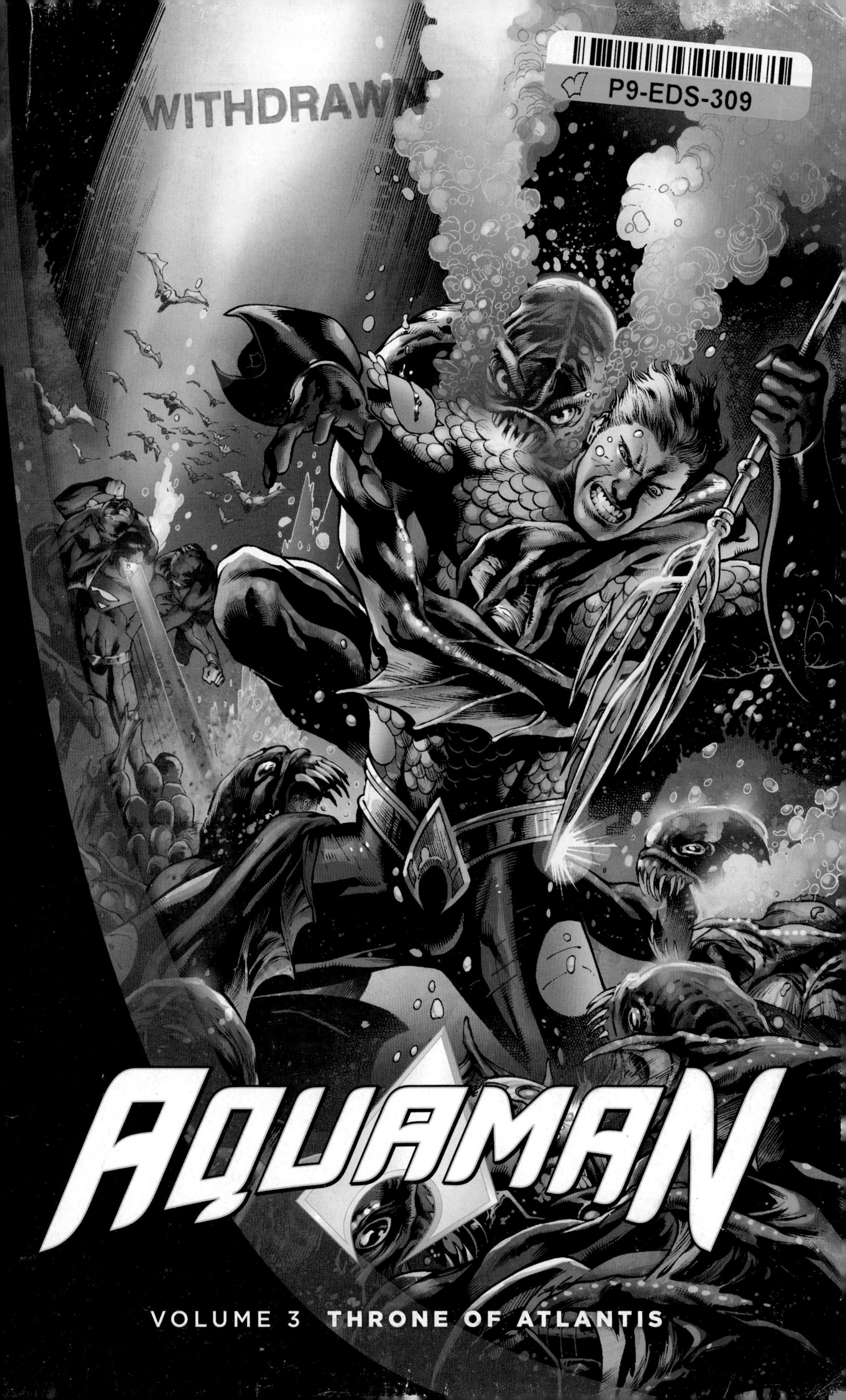

AQUAMAN

VOLUME 3 **THRONE OF ATLANTIS**

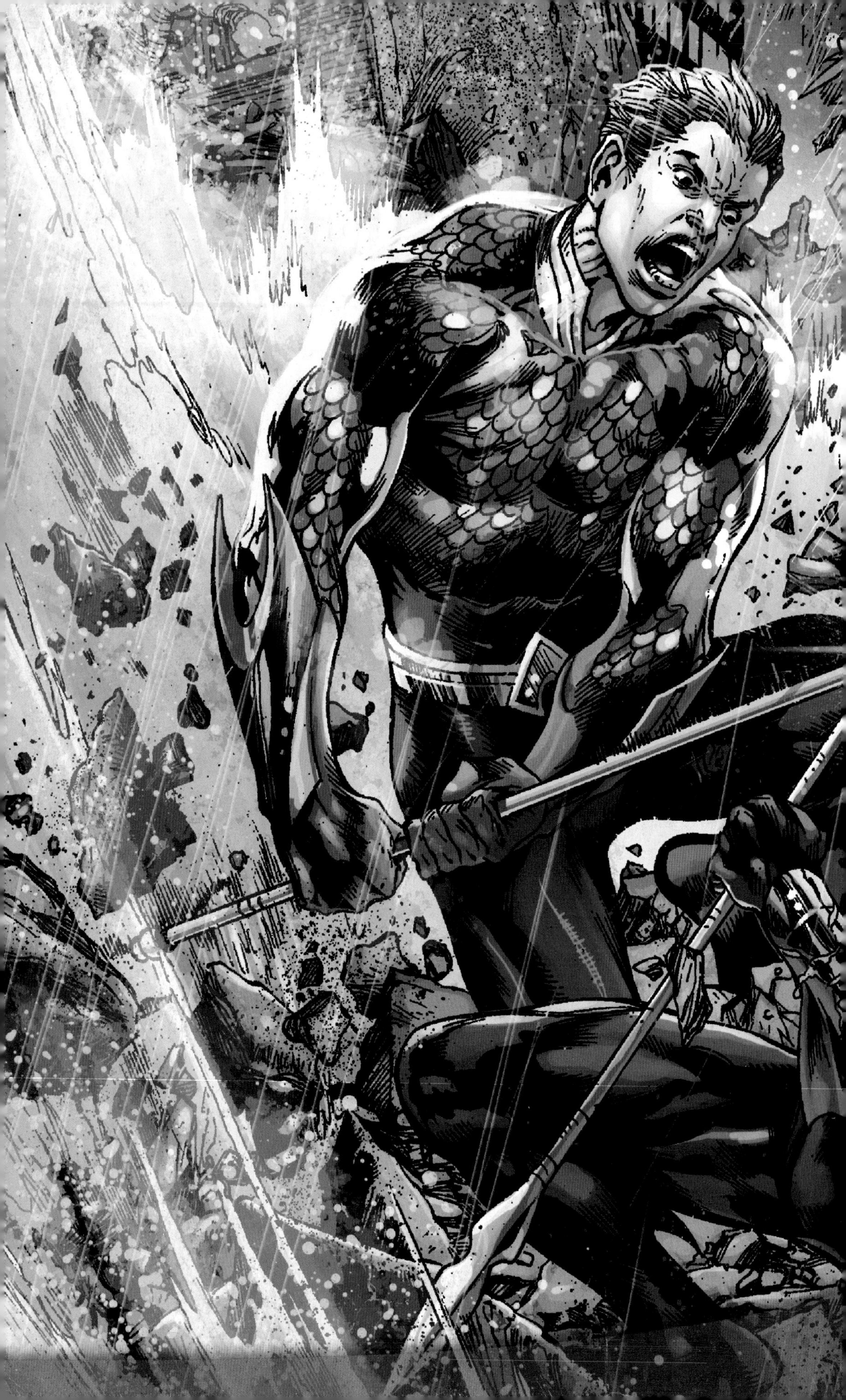

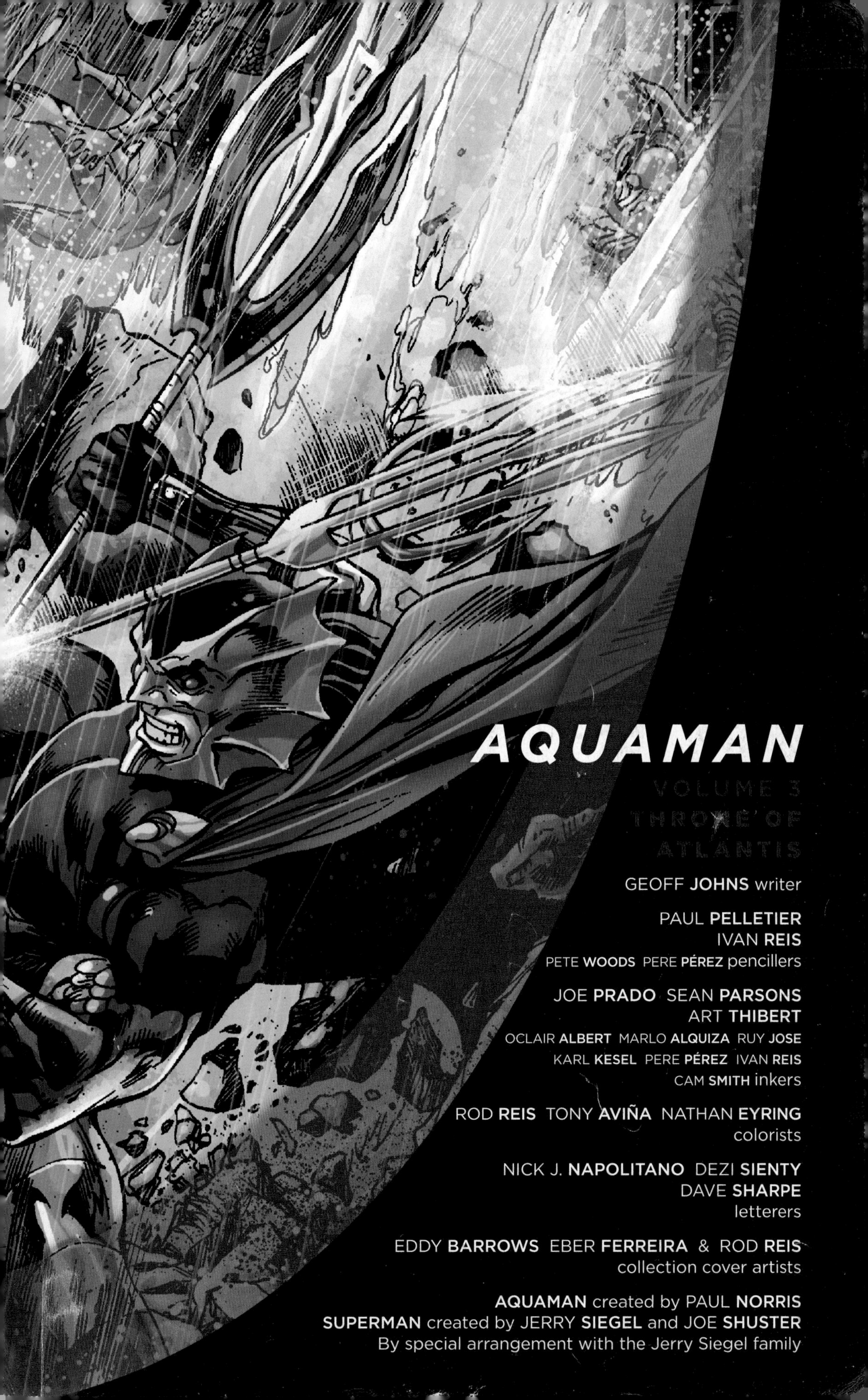

AQUAMAN

VOLUME 3
THRONE OF ATLANTIS

GEOFF **JOHNS** writer

PAUL **PELLETIER**
IVAN **REIS**
PETE **WOODS** PERE **PÉREZ** pencillers

JOE **PRADO** SEAN **PARSONS**
ART **THIBERT**
OCLAIR **ALBERT** MARLO **ALQUIZA** RUY **JOSE**
KARL **KESEL** PERE **PÉREZ** IVAN **REIS**
CAM **SMITH** inkers

ROD **REIS** TONY **AVIÑA** NATHAN **EYRING**
colorists

NICK J. **NAPOLITANO** DEZI **SIENTY**
DAVE **SHARPE**
letterers

EDDY **BARROWS** EBER **FERREIRA** & ROD **REIS**
collection cover artists

AQUAMAN created by PAUL **NORRIS**
SUPERMAN created by JERRY **SIEGEL** and JOE **SHUSTER**
By special arrangement with the Jerry Siegel family

BRIAN CUNNINGHAM PAT McCALLUM Editors – Original Series KATIE KUBERT CHRIS CONROY Associate Editors – Original Series
KATE STEWART Assistant Editor – Original Series ROBIN WILDMAN Editor
ROBBIN BROSTERMAN Design Director – Books ROBBIE BIEDERMAN Publication Design

BOB HARRAS Senior VP – Editor-in-Chief, DC Comics

DIANE NELSON President DAN DIDIO and JIM LEE Co-Publishers GEOFF JOHNS Chief Creative Officer
JOHN ROOD Executive VP – Sales, Marketing and Business Development
AMY GENKINS Senior VP – Business and Legal Affairs NAIRI GARDINER Senior VP – Finance
JEFF BOISON VP – Publishing Planning MARK CHIARELLO VP – Art Direction and Design
JOHN CUNNINGHAM VP – Marketing TERRI CUNNINGHAM VP – Editorial Administration
ALISON GILL Senior VP – Manufacturing and Operations HANK KANALZ Senior VP – Vertigo and Integrated Publishing
JAY KOGAN VP – Business and Legal Affairs, Publishing JACK MAHAN VP – Business Affairs, Talent
NICK NAPOLITANO VP – Manufacturing Administration SUE POHJA VP – Book Sales
COURTNEY SIMMONS Senior VP – Publicity BOB WAYNE Senior VP – Sales

AQUAMAN VOLUME 3: THRONE OF ATLANTIS

Published by DC Comics. Copyright © 2013 DC Comics. All Rights Reserved.

Originally published in single magazine form as AQUAMAN 0, 14-16, JUSTICE LEAGUE 15-17 Copyright © 2012, 2013 DC Comics.
All Rights Reserved. All characters, their distinctive likenesses and related elements featured in this publication are trademarks
of DC Comics. The stories, characters and incidents featured in this publication are entirely fictional.
DC Comics does not read or accept unsolicited ideas, stories or artwork.

DC Comics, 1700 Broadway, New York, NY 10019
A Warner Bros. Entertainment Company.
Printed by RR Donnelley, Salem, VA, USA. 4/11/14. First Printing.

ISBN: 978-1-4012-4695-2

Library of Congress Cataloging-in-Publication Data

Johns, Geoff, 1973- author.
Aquaman. Volume 3, Throne of Atlantis / Geoff Johns, Paul Pelletier, Ivan Reis.
pages cm
"Originally published in single magazine form as AQUAMAN 0, 14-16, JUSTICE LEAGUE 15-17."
ISBN 978-1-4012-4309-8
1. Graphic novels. I. Pelletier, Paul, 1970- illustrator. II. Reis, Ivan, illustrator. III. Title. IV. Title: Throne of Atlantis.
PN6728.A68J66 2013
741.5'973—dc23
2013026273

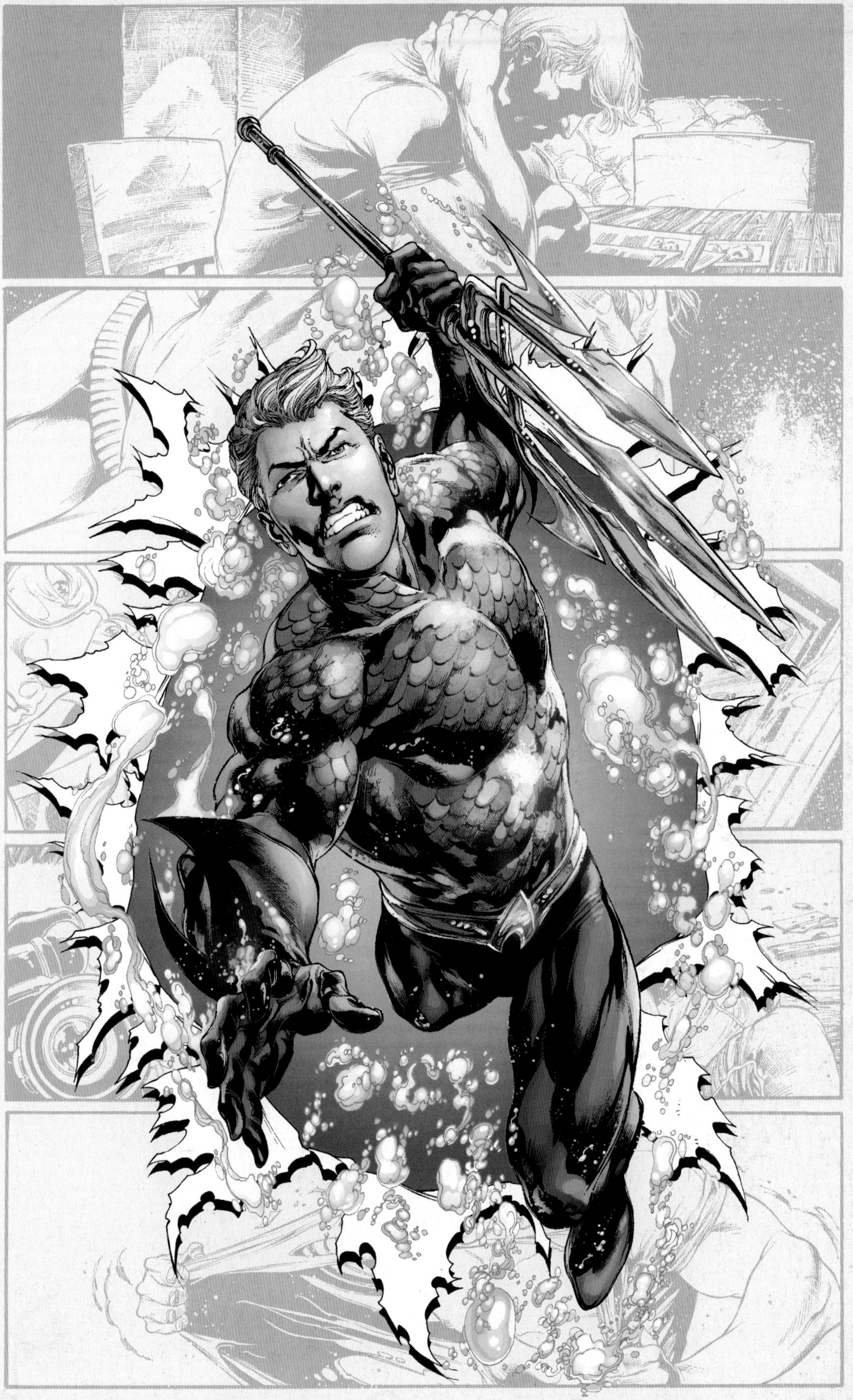

GEOFF JOHNS writer **IVAN REIS** penciller **JOE PRADO** inker cover by **IVAN REIS, JOE PRADO & ROD REIS**

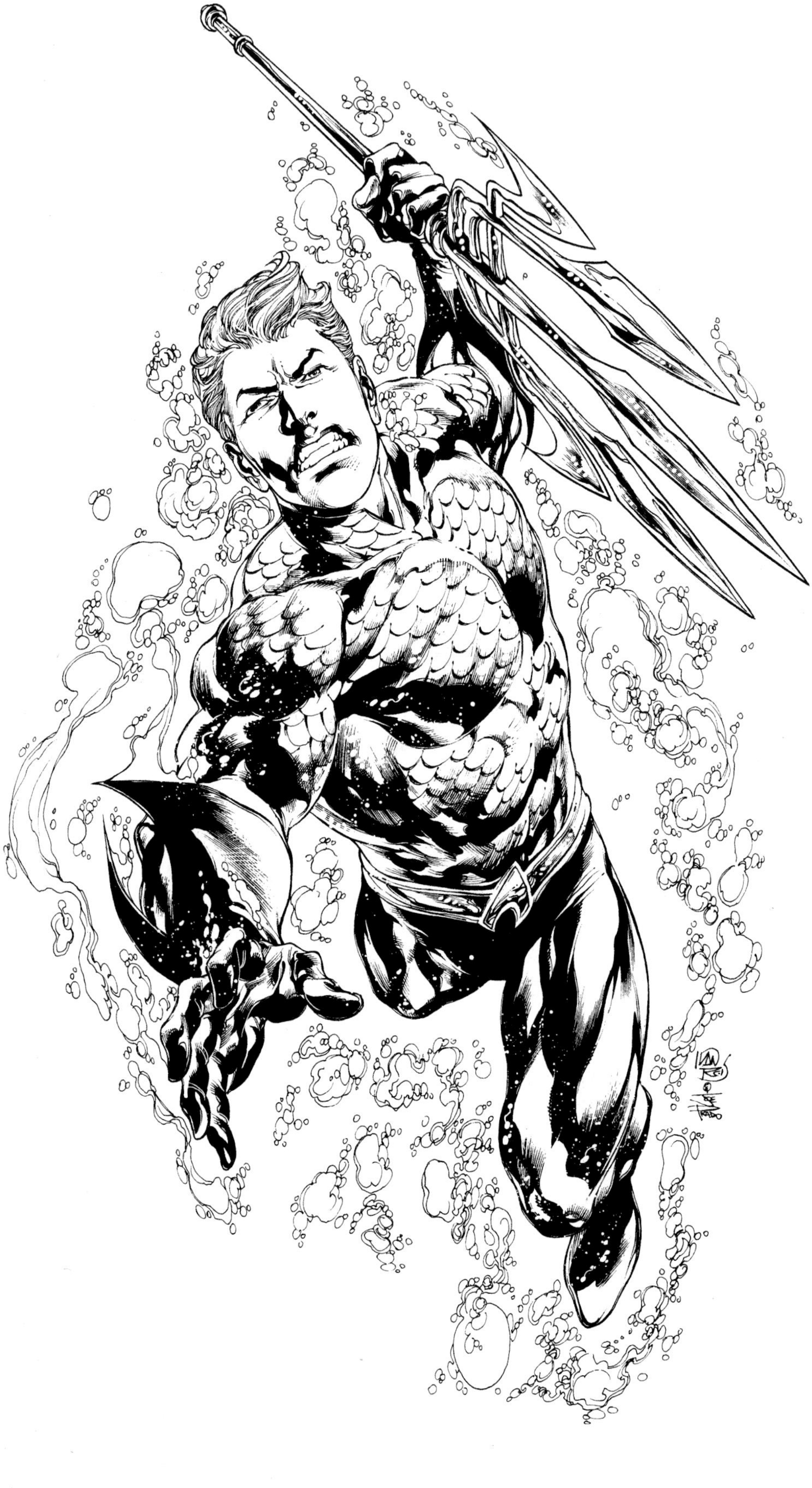

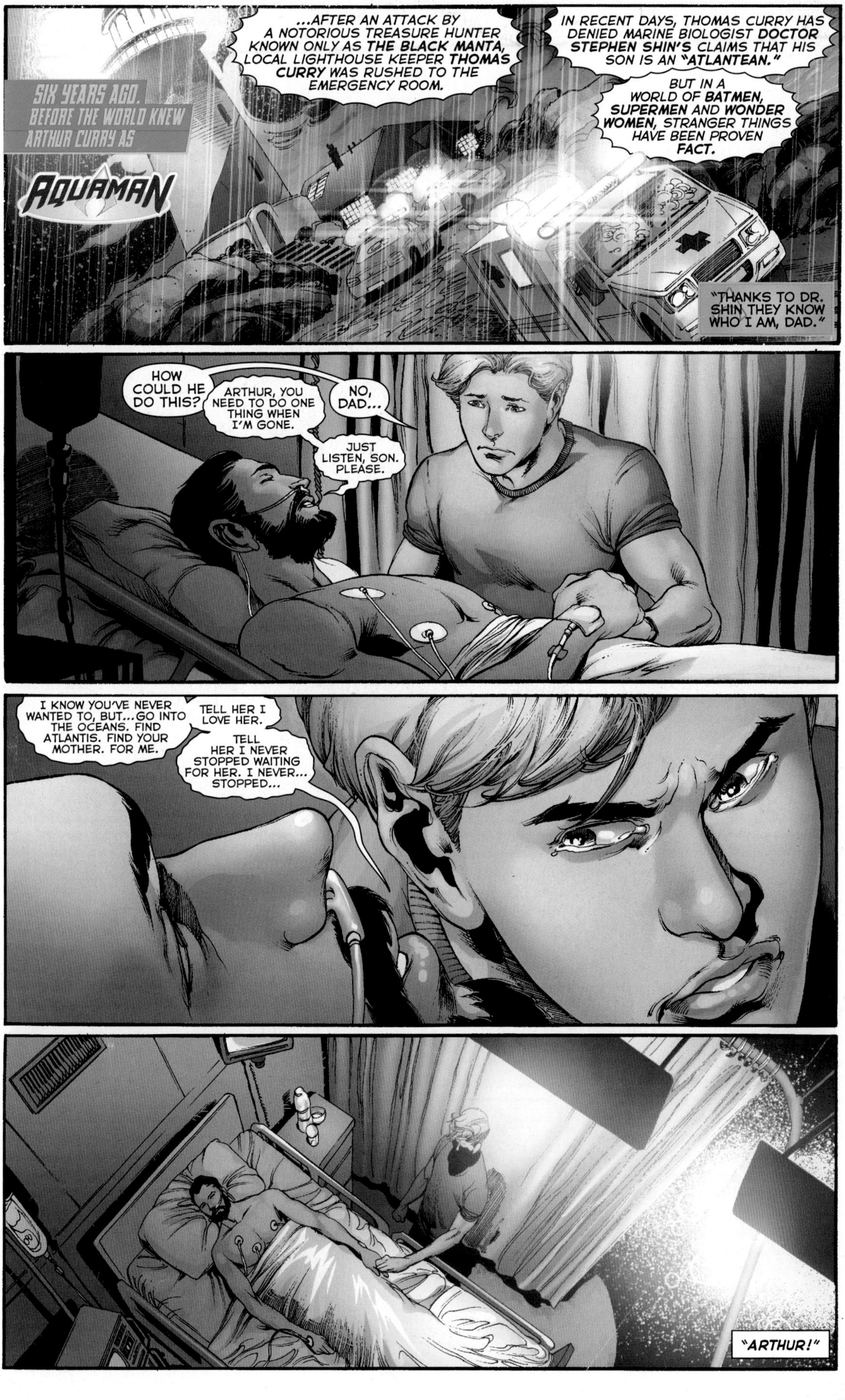
SIX YEARS AGO. BEFORE THE WORLD KNEW ARTHUR CURRY AS
AQUAMAN
...AFTER AN ATTACK BY A NOTORIOUS TREASURE HUNTER KNOWN ONLY AS THE BLACK MANTA, LOCAL LIGHTHOUSE KEEPER THOMAS CURRY WAS RUSHED TO THE EMERGENCY ROOM.
IN RECENT DAYS, THOMAS CURRY HAS DENIED MARINE BIOLOGIST DOCTOR STEPHEN SHIN'S CLAIMS THAT HIS SON IS AN "ATLANTEAN."
BUT IN A WORLD OF BATMEN, SUPERMEN AND WONDER WOMEN, STRANGER THINGS HAVE BEEN PROVEN FACT.
"THANKS TO DR. SHIN THEY KNOW WHO I AM, DAD."
HOW COULD HE DO THIS?
ARTHUR, YOU NEED TO DO ONE THING WHEN I'M GONE.
NO, DAD...
JUST LISTEN, SON. PLEASE.
I KNOW YOU'VE NEVER WANTED TO, BUT...GO INTO THE OCEANS. FIND ATLANTIS. FIND YOUR MOTHER. FOR ME.
TELL HER I LOVE HER.
TELL HER I NEVER STOPPED WAITING FOR HER. I NEVER... STOPPED...
"ARTHUR!"

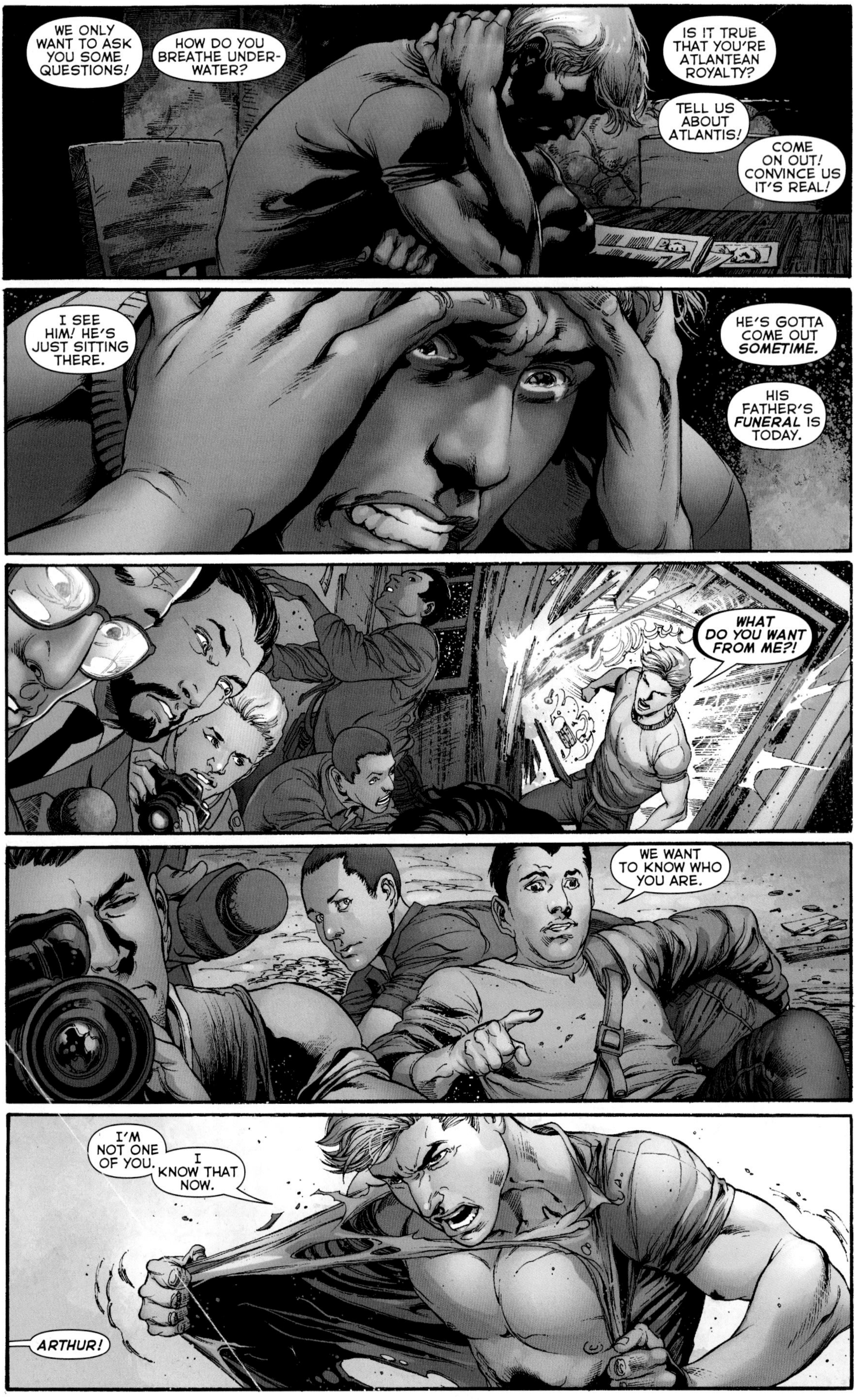
WE ONLY WANT TO ASK YOU SOME QUESTIONS!
HOW DO YOU BREATHE UNDER-WATER?
IS IT TRUE THAT YOU'RE ATLANTEAN ROYALTY?
TELL US ABOUT ATLANTIS!
COME ON OUT! CONVINCE US IT'S REAL!
I SEE HIM! HE'S JUST SITTING THERE.
HE'S GOTTA COME OUT *SOMETIME.*
HIS FATHER'S *FUNERAL* IS TODAY.
WHAT DO YOU WANT FROM ME?!
WE WANT TO KNOW WHO YOU ARE.
I'M NOT ONE OF YOU.
I KNOW THAT NOW.
ARTHUR!

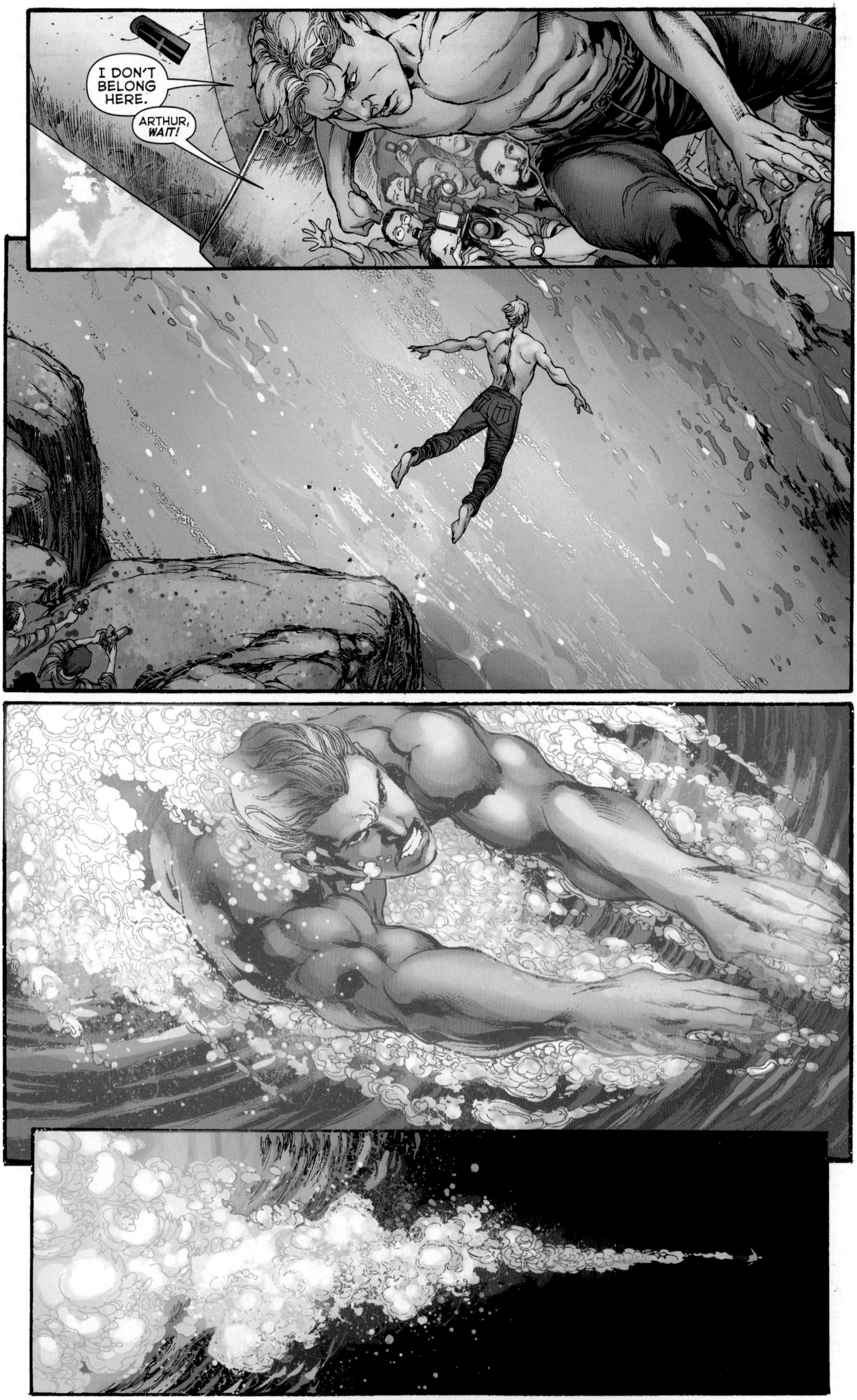
I DON'T BELONG HERE.
ARTHUR, *WAIT!*

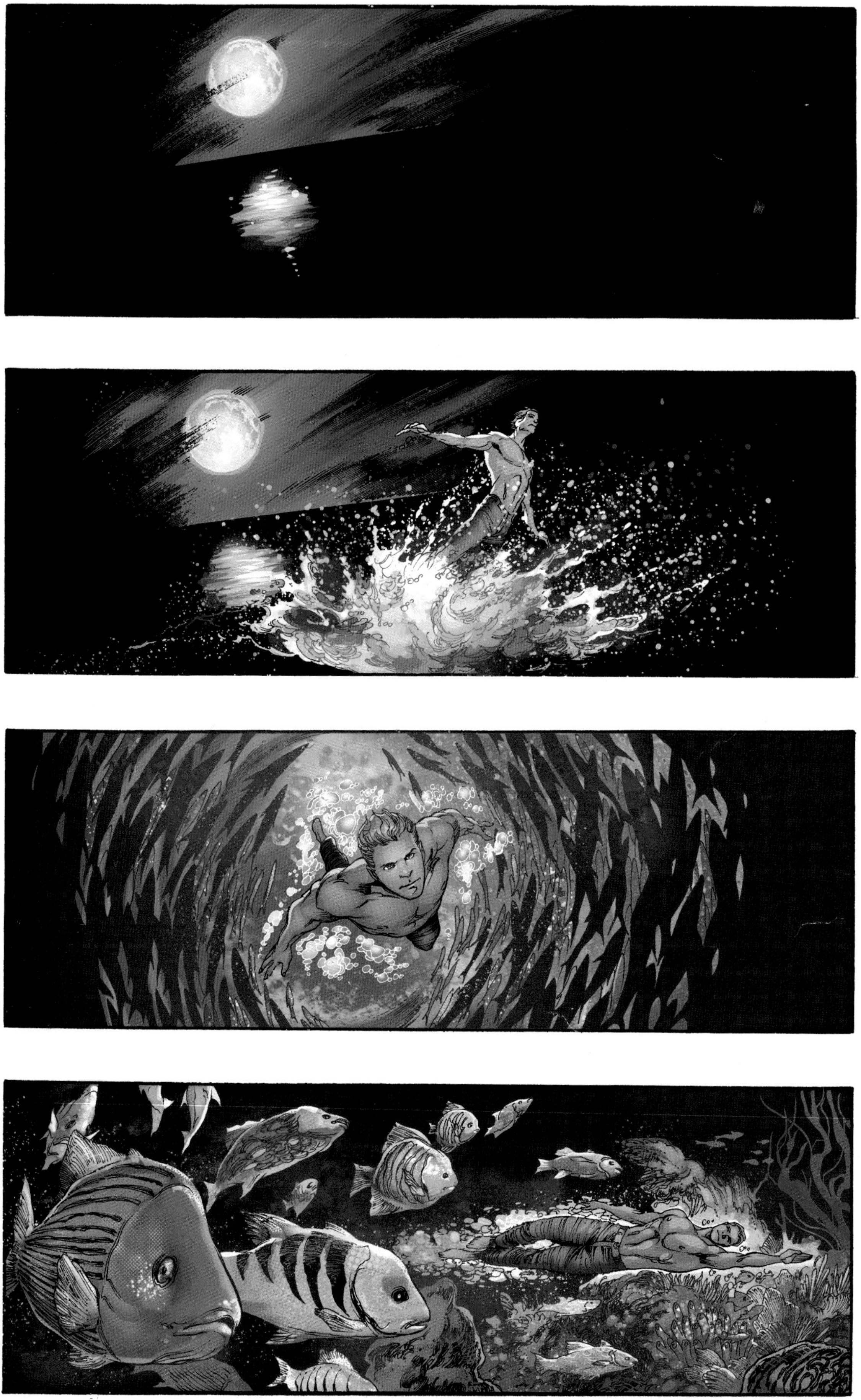

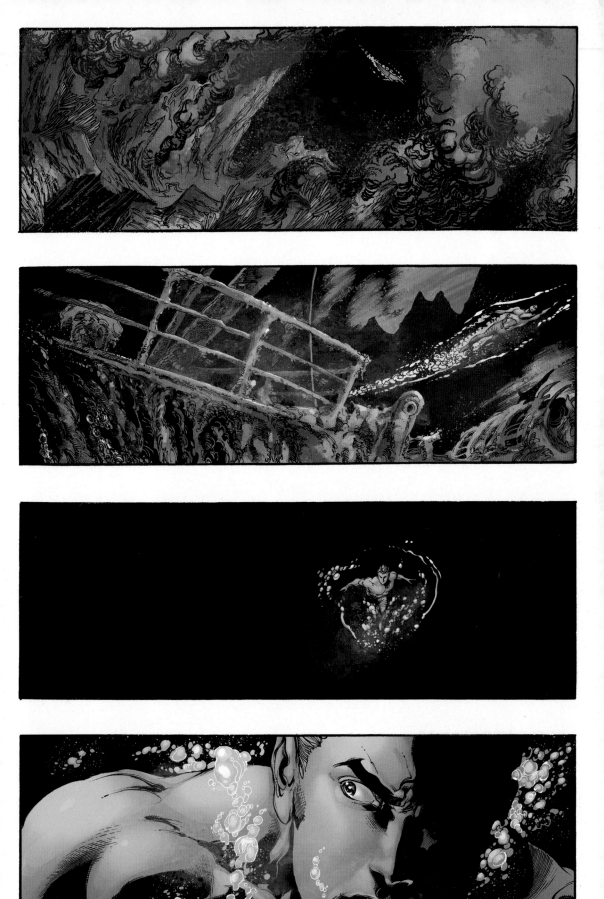

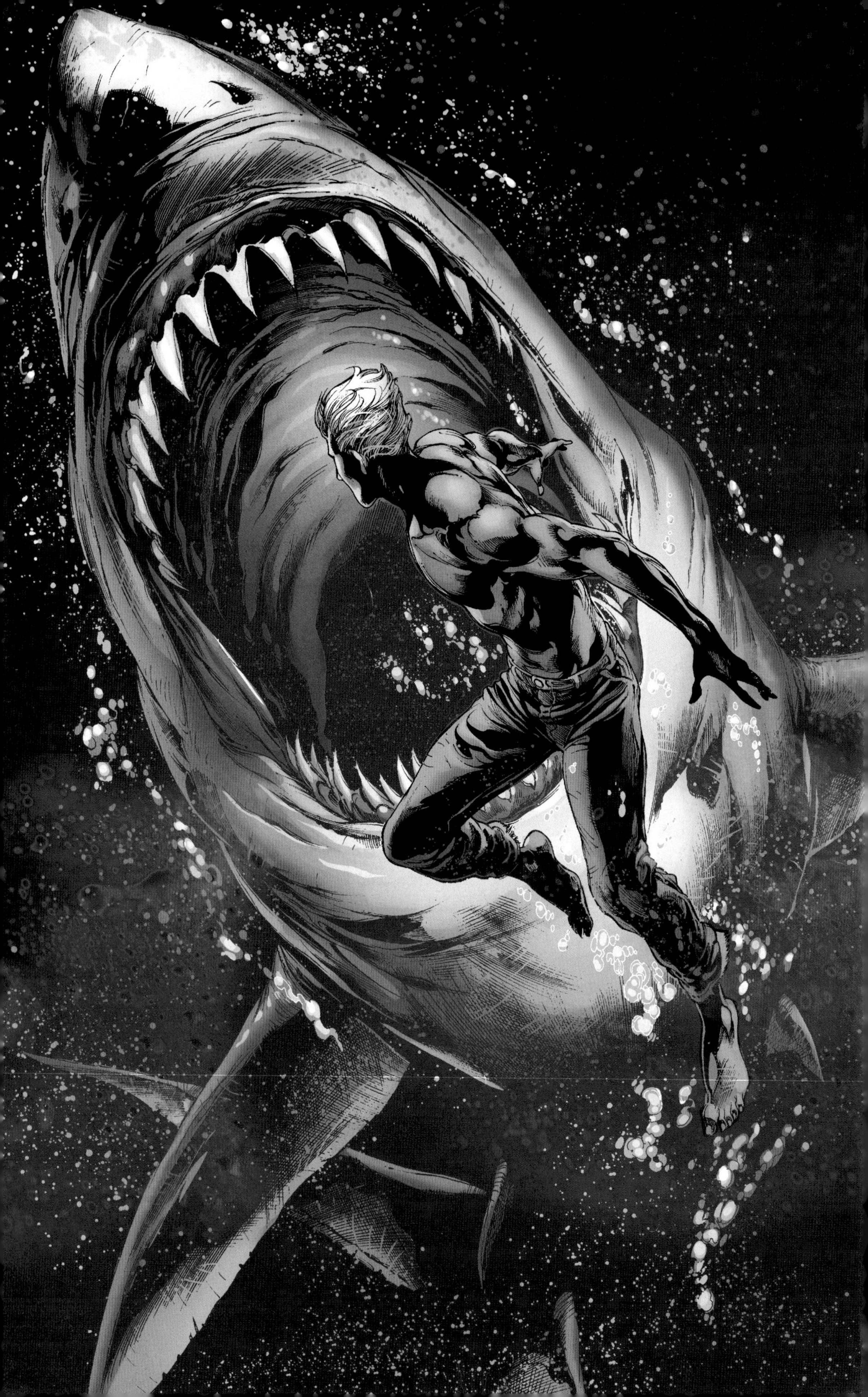

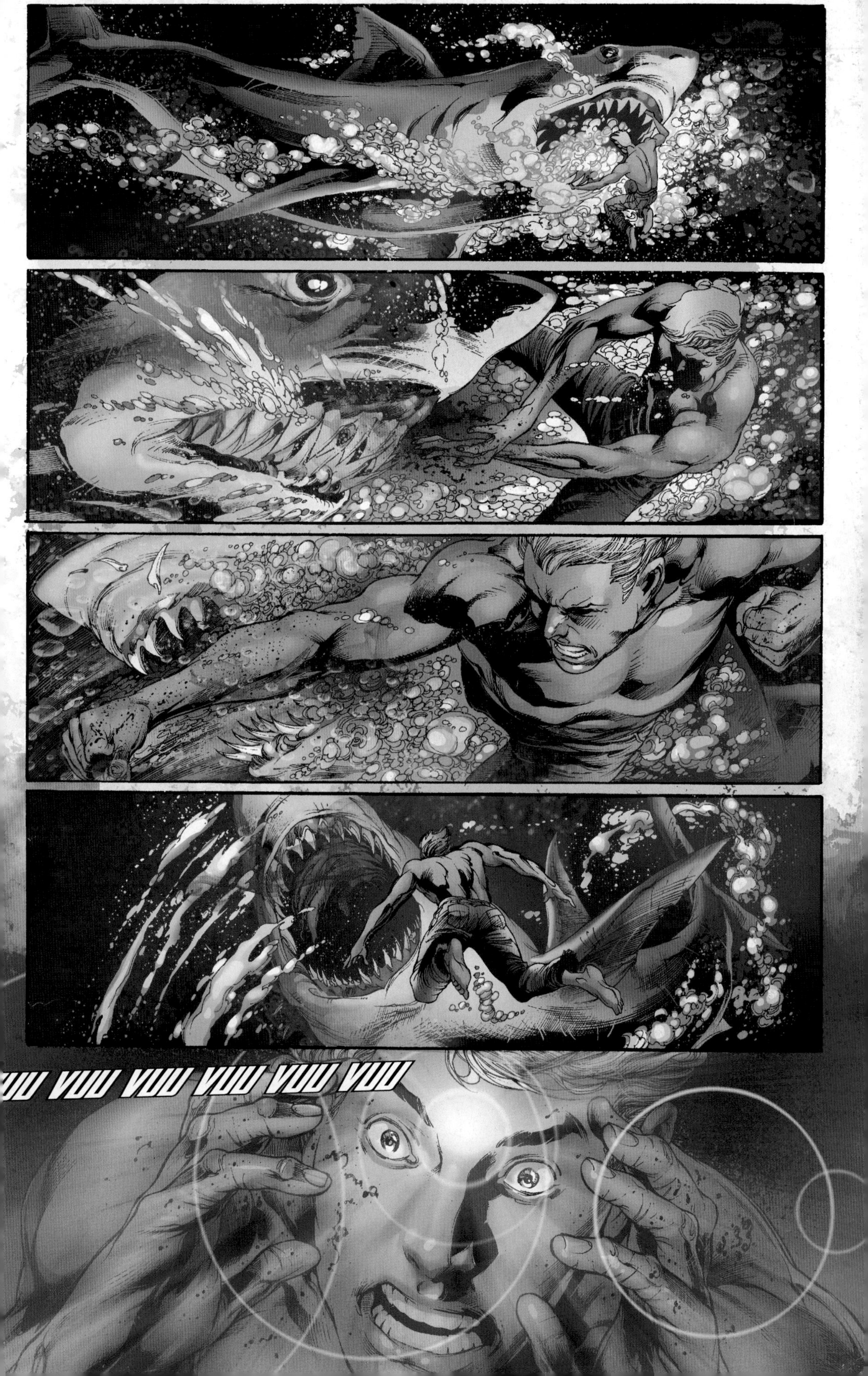
VUU VUU VUU VUU VUU VUU VUU

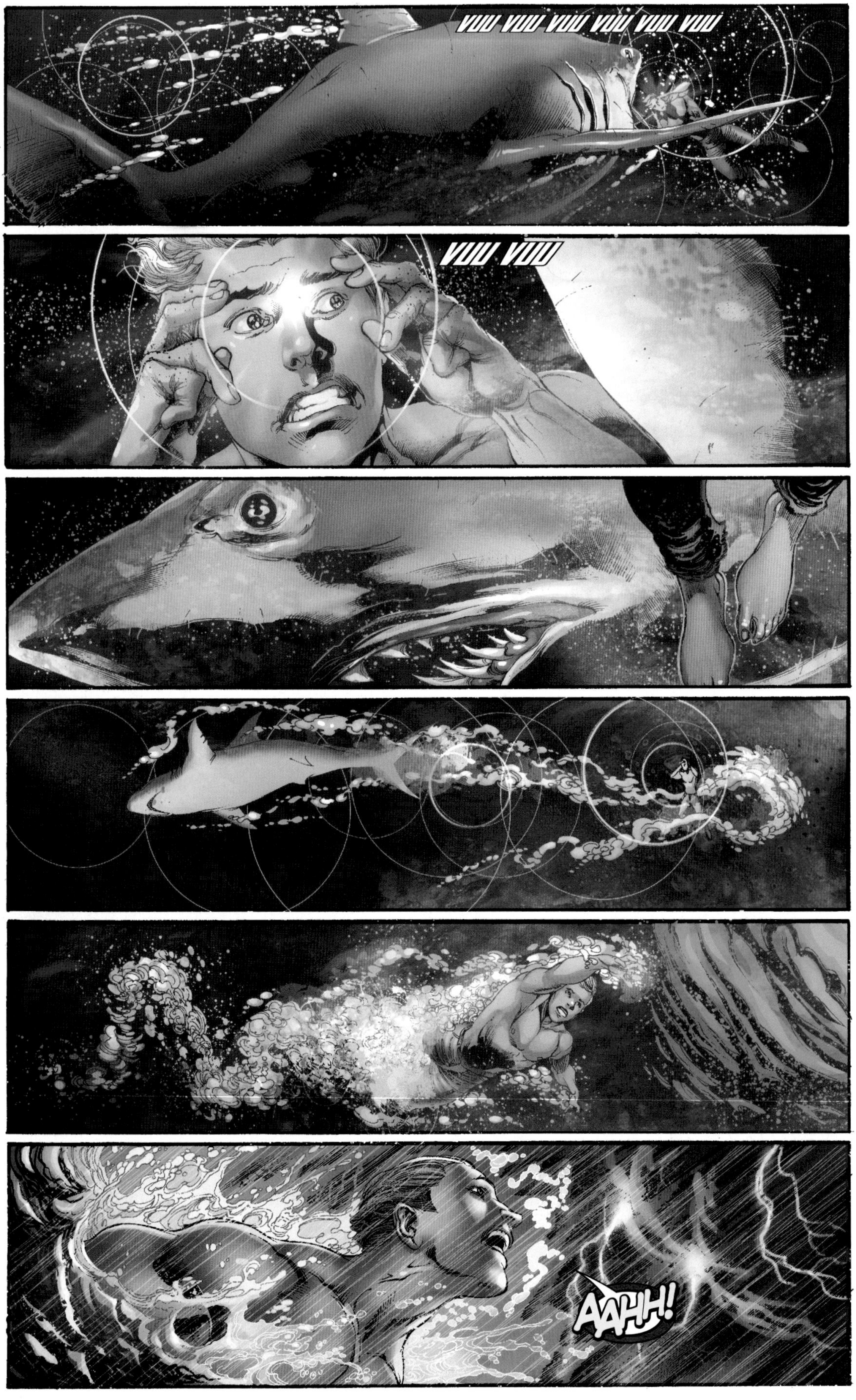
VUU VUU VUU VUU VUU VUU
VUU VUU
AAHH!

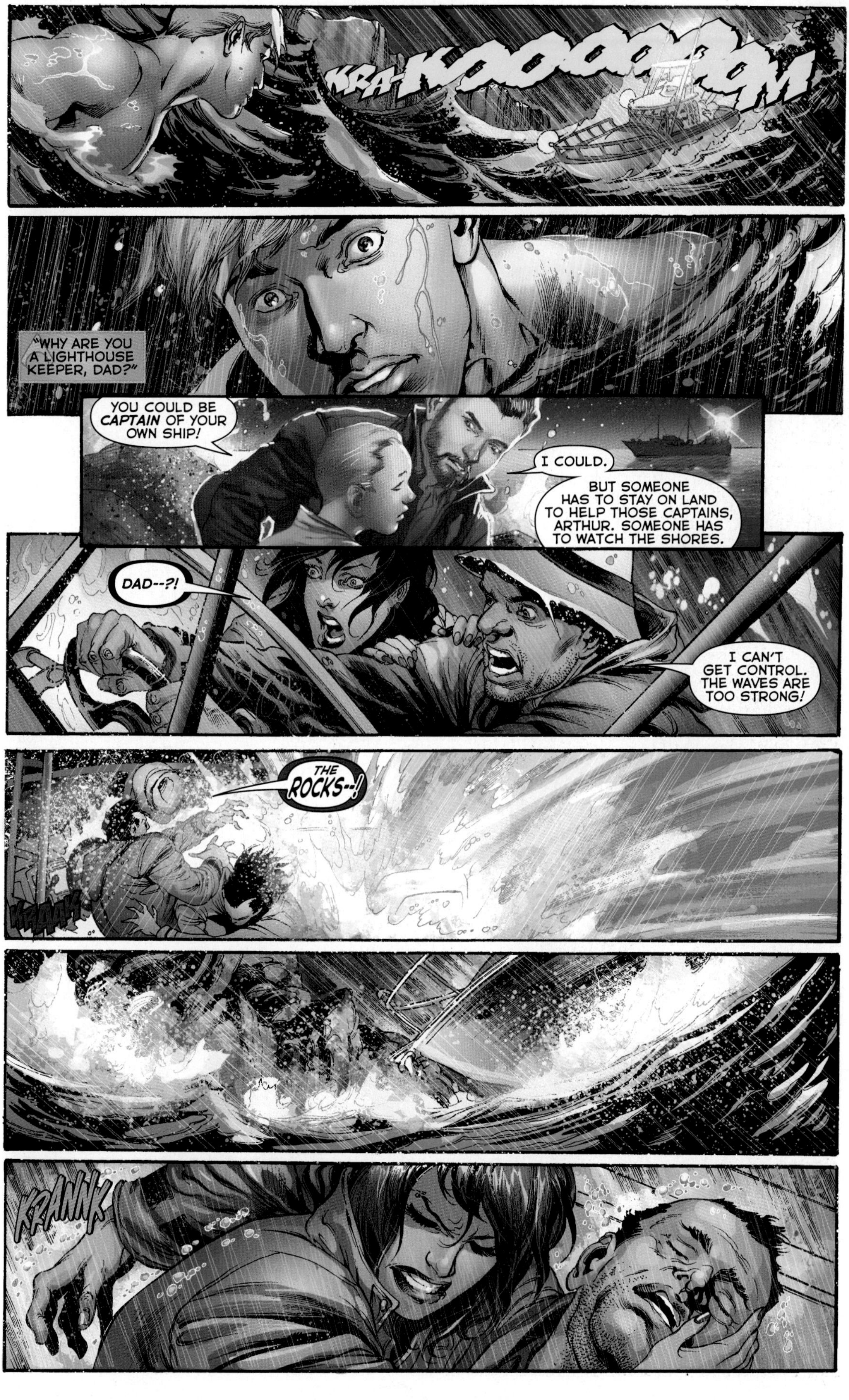
KRA-KOOOOOOOM
"WHY ARE YOU A LIGHTHOUSE KEEPER, DAD?"
YOU COULD BE CAPTAIN OF YOUR OWN SHIP!
I COULD.
BUT SOMEONE HAS TO STAY ON LAND TO HELP THOSE CAPTAINS, ARTHUR. SOMEONE HAS TO WATCH THE SHORES.
DAD--?!
I CAN'T GET CONTROL. THE WAVES ARE TOO STRONG!
THE ROCKS--!
KRANNK

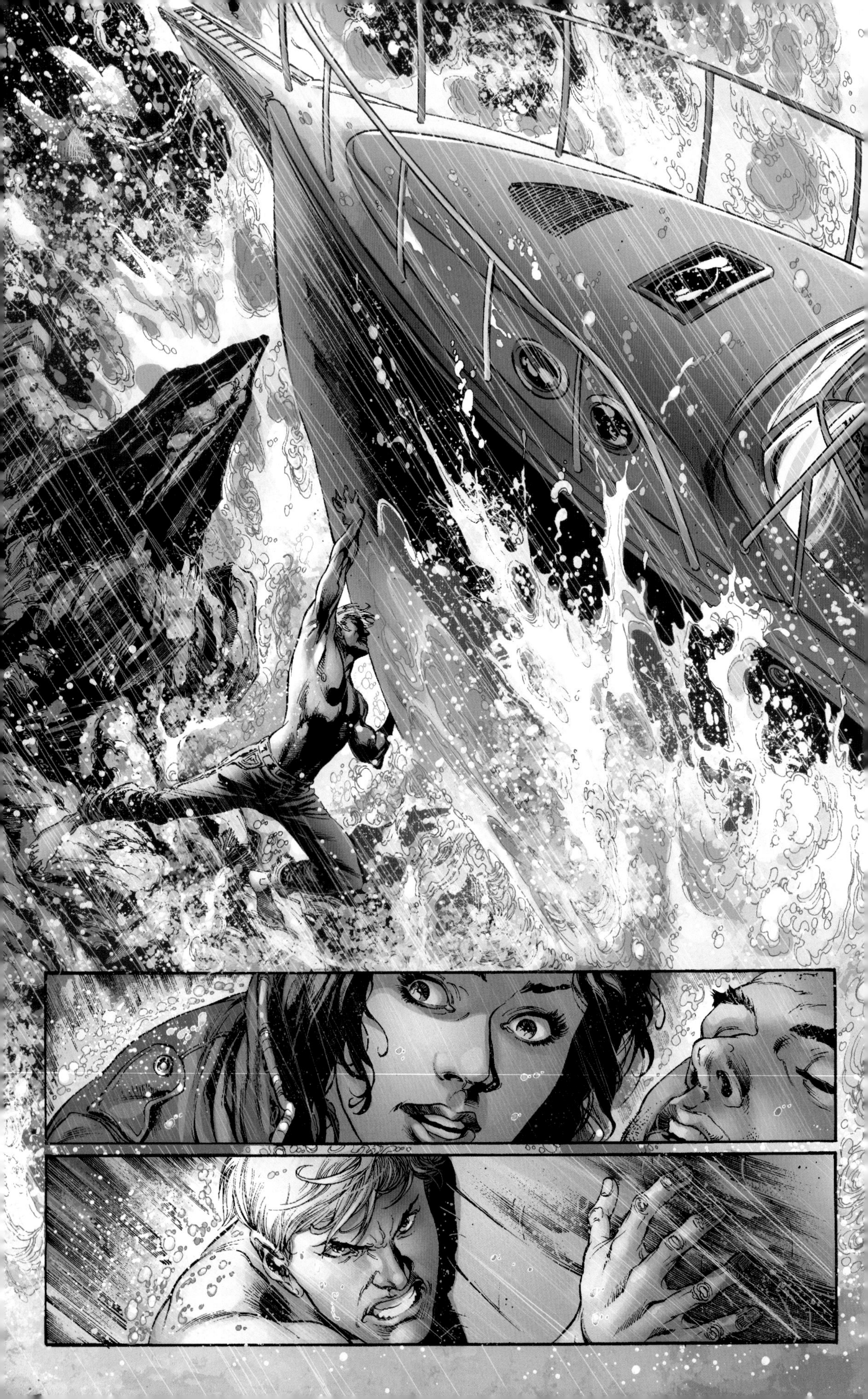

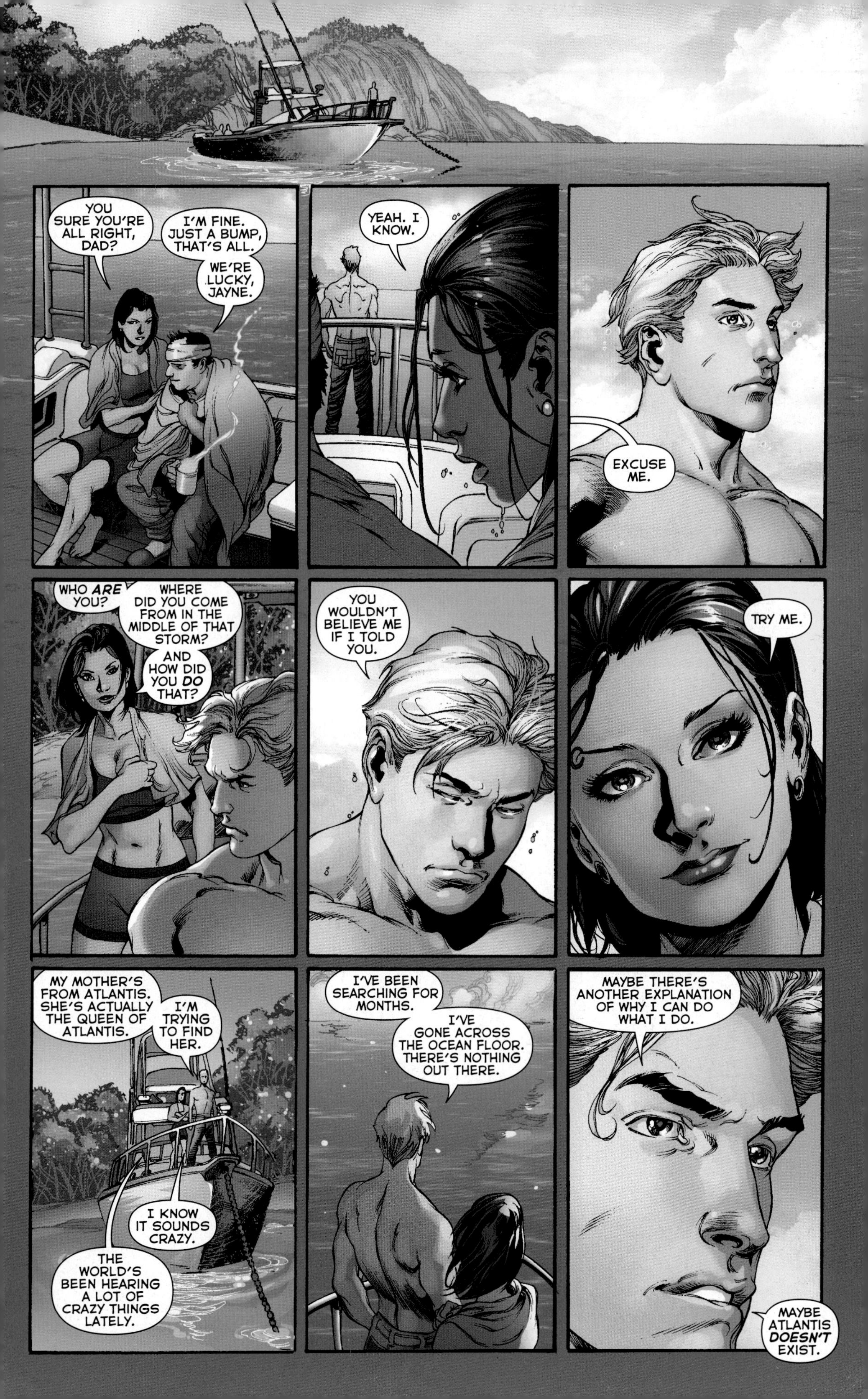
YOU SURE YOU'RE ALL RIGHT, DAD?
I'M FINE. JUST A BUMP, THAT'S ALL.
WE'RE LUCKY, JAYNE.
YEAH. I KNOW.
EXCUSE ME.
WHO *ARE* YOU?
WHERE DID YOU COME FROM IN THE MIDDLE OF THAT STORM?
AND HOW DID YOU *DO* THAT?
YOU WOULDN'T BELIEVE ME IF I TOLD YOU.
TRY ME.
MY MOTHER'S FROM ATLANTIS. SHE'S ACTUALLY THE QUEEN OF ATLANTIS.
I'M TRYING TO FIND HER.
I KNOW IT SOUNDS CRAZY.
THE WORLD'S BEEN HEARING A LOT OF CRAZY THINGS LATELY.
I'VE BEEN SEARCHING FOR MONTHS.
I'VE GONE ACROSS THE OCEAN FLOOR. THERE'S NOTHING OUT THERE.
MAYBE THERE'S ANOTHER EXPLANATION OF WHY I CAN DO WHAT I DO.
MAYBE ATLANTIS *DOESN'T* EXIST.

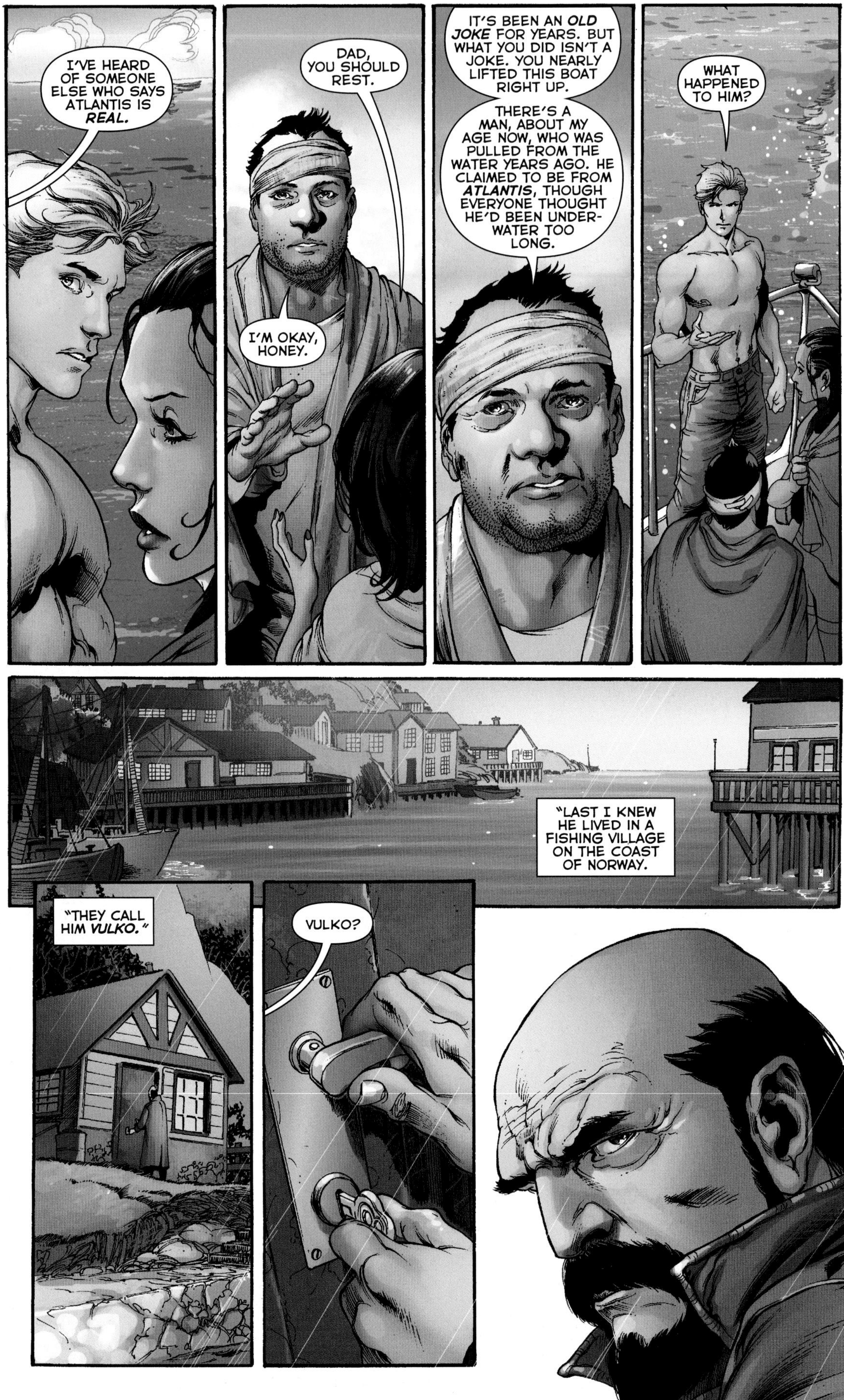
I'VE HEARD OF SOMEONE ELSE WHO SAYS ATLANTIS IS ***REAL.***
DAD, YOU SHOULD REST.
I'M OKAY, HONEY.
IT'S BEEN AN ***OLD JOKE*** FOR YEARS. BUT WHAT YOU DID ISN'T A JOKE. YOU NEARLY LIFTED THIS BOAT RIGHT UP.
THERE'S A MAN, ABOUT MY AGE NOW, WHO WAS PULLED FROM THE WATER YEARS AGO. HE CLAIMED TO BE FROM ***ATLANTIS,*** THOUGH EVERYONE THOUGHT HE'D BEEN UNDER-WATER TOO LONG.
WHAT HAPPENED TO HIM?
"LAST I KNEW HE LIVED IN A FISHING VILLAGE ON THE COAST OF NORWAY.
"THEY CALL HIM ***VULKO.***"
VULKO?

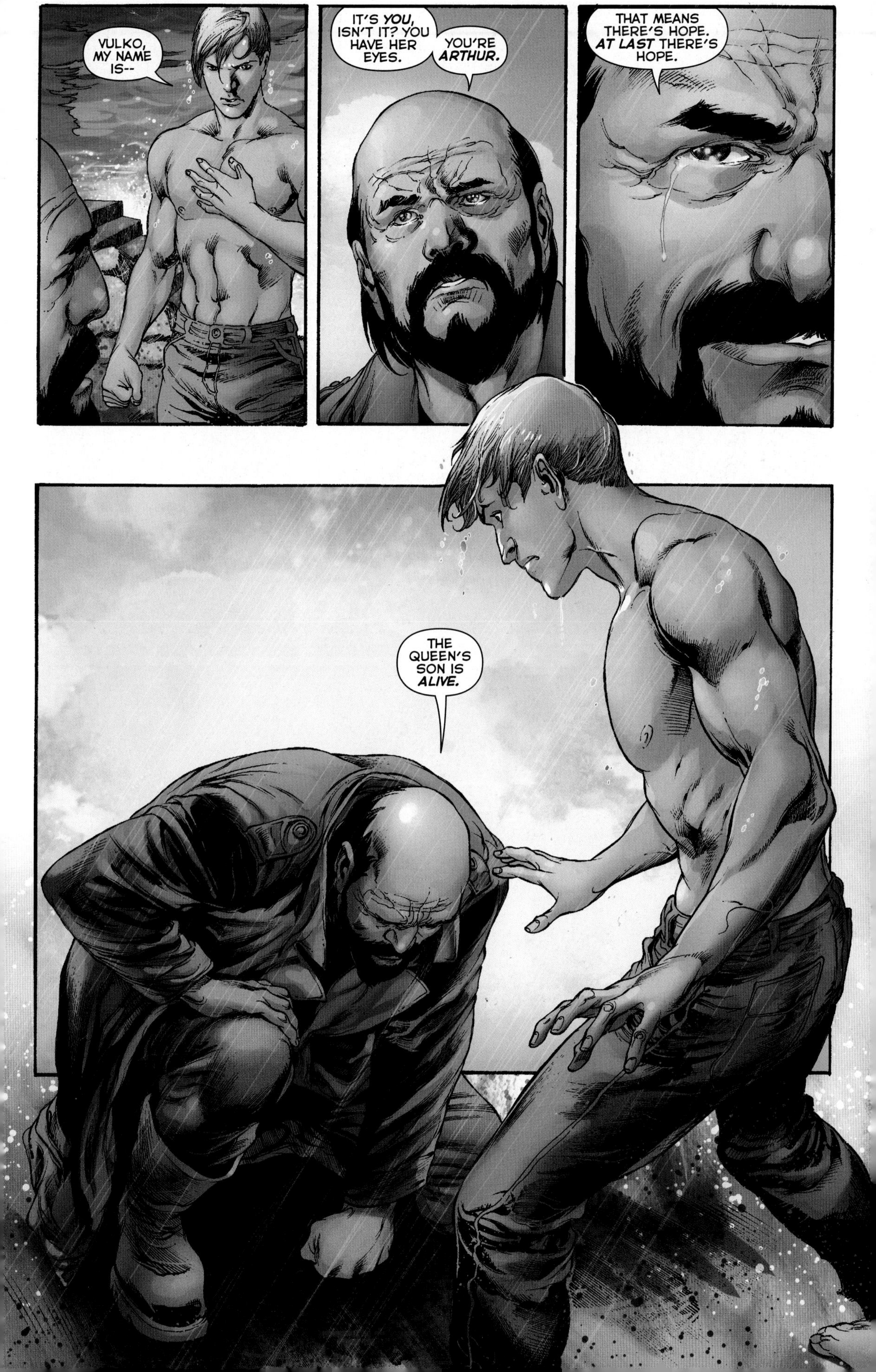
VULKO, MY NAME IS--
IT'S YOU, ISN'T IT? YOU HAVE HER EYES.
YOU'RE ARTHUR.
THAT MEANS THERE'S HOPE. AT LAST THERE'S HOPE.
THE QUEEN'S SON IS ALIVE.

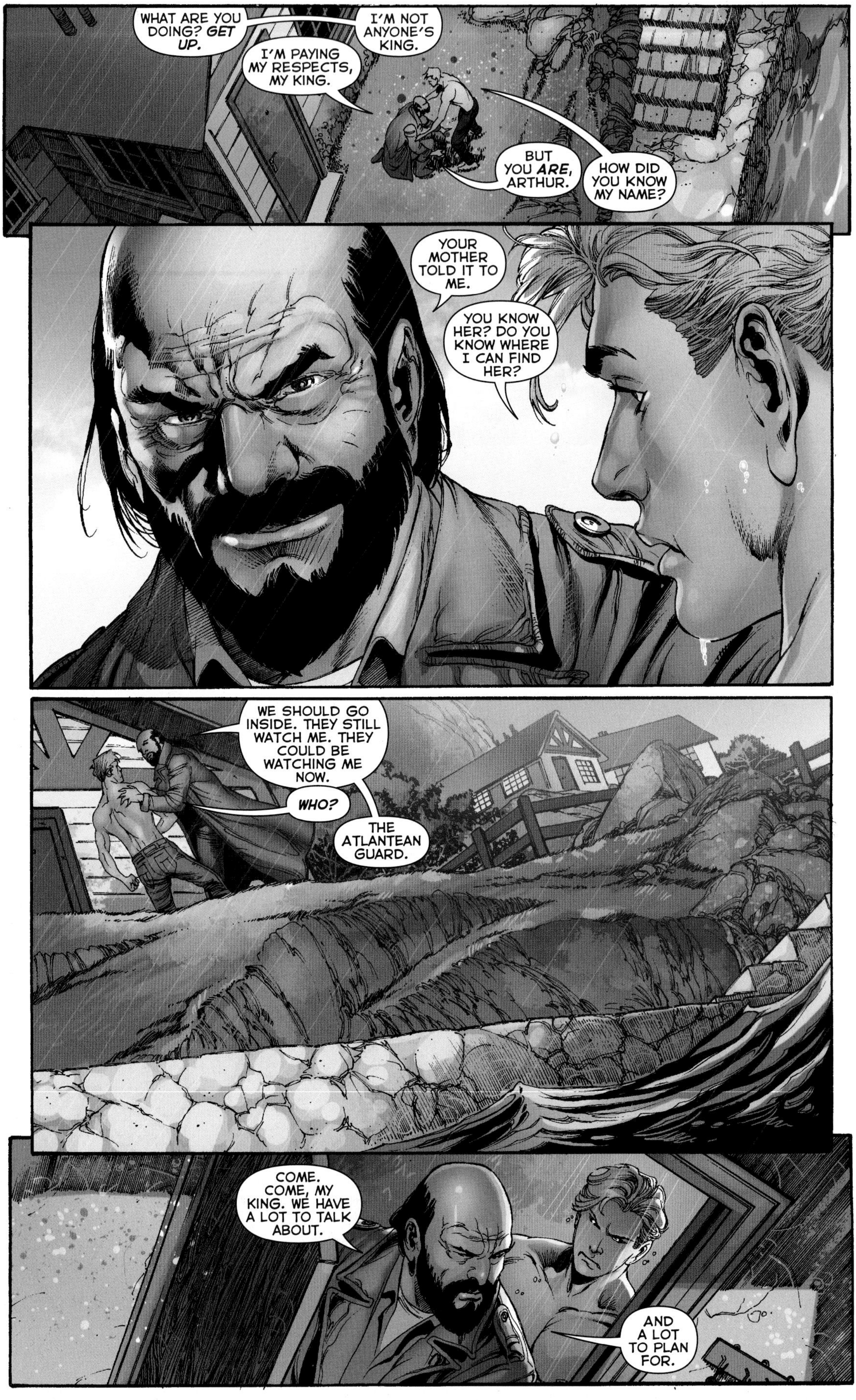
WHAT ARE YOU DOING? ***GET UP.***
I'M PAYING MY RESPECTS, MY KING.
I'M NOT ANYONE'S KING.
BUT YOU ***ARE,*** ARTHUR.
HOW DID YOU KNOW MY NAME?
YOUR MOTHER TOLD IT TO ME.
YOU KNOW HER? DO YOU KNOW WHERE I CAN FIND HER?
WE SHOULD GO INSIDE. THEY STILL WATCH ME. THEY COULD BE WATCHING ME NOW.
WHO?
THE ATLANTEAN GUARD.
COME. COME, MY KING. WE HAVE A LOT TO TALK ABOUT.
AND A LOT TO PLAN FOR.

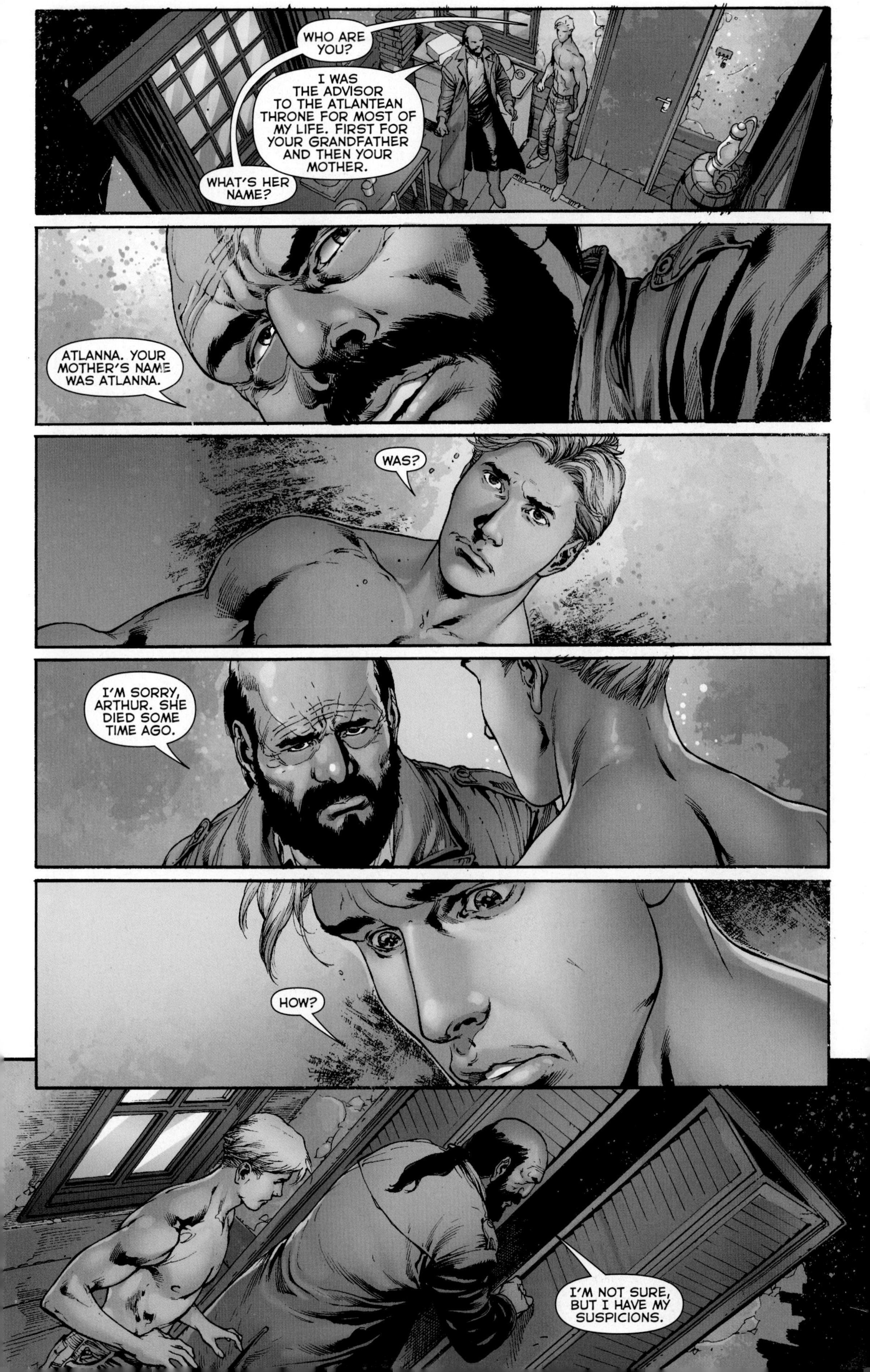
WHO ARE YOU?
I WAS THE ADVISOR TO THE ATLANTEAN THRONE FOR MOST OF MY LIFE. FIRST FOR YOUR GRANDFATHER AND THEN YOUR MOTHER.
WHAT'S HER NAME?
ATLANNA. YOUR MOTHER'S NAME WAS ATLANNA.
WAS?
I'M SORRY, ARTHUR. SHE DIED SOME TIME AGO.
HOW?
I'M NOT SURE, BUT I HAVE MY SUSPICIONS.

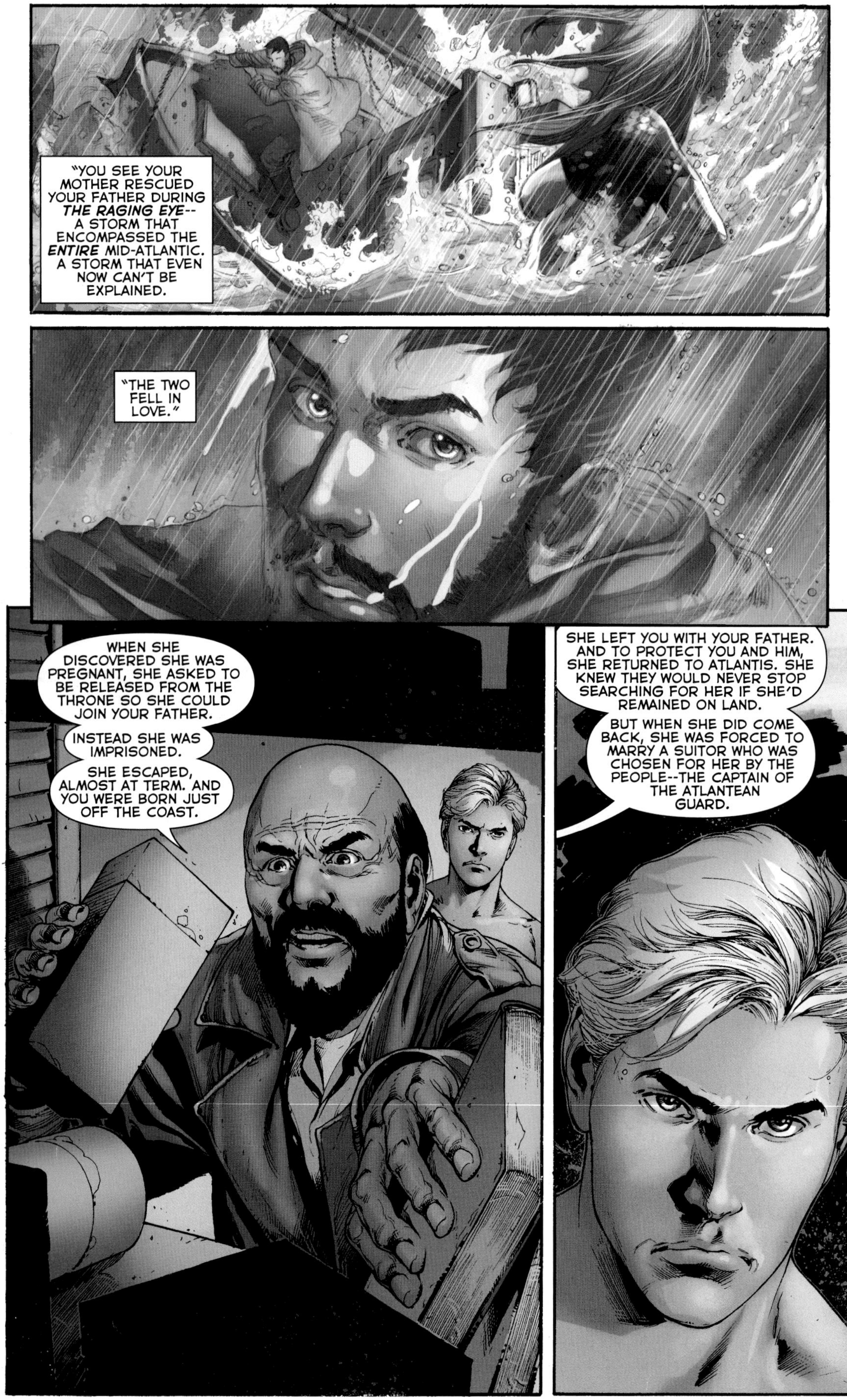
"YOU SEE YOUR MOTHER RESCUED YOUR FATHER DURING *THE RAGING EYE*-- A STORM THAT ENCOMPASSED THE *ENTIRE* MID-ATLANTIC. A STORM THAT EVEN NOW CAN'T BE EXPLAINED.
"THE TWO FELL IN LOVE."
WHEN SHE DISCOVERED SHE WAS PREGNANT, SHE ASKED TO BE RELEASED FROM THE THRONE SO SHE COULD JOIN YOUR FATHER.
INSTEAD SHE WAS IMPRISONED.
SHE ESCAPED, ALMOST AT TERM. AND YOU WERE BORN JUST OFF THE COAST.
SHE LEFT YOU WITH YOUR FATHER. AND TO PROTECT YOU AND HIM, SHE RETURNED TO ATLANTIS. SHE KNEW THEY WOULD NEVER STOP SEARCHING FOR HER IF SHE'D REMAINED ON LAND.
BUT WHEN SHE DID COME BACK, SHE WAS FORCED TO MARRY A SUITOR WHO WAS CHOSEN FOR HER BY THE PEOPLE--THE CAPTAIN OF THE ATLANTEAN GUARD.

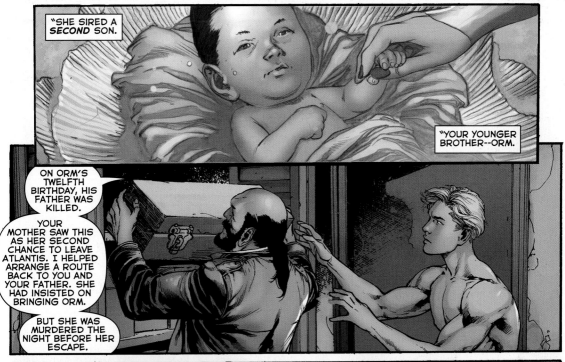

"SHE SIRED A *SECOND* SON.

"YOUR YOUNGER BROTHER--ORM.

ON ORM'S TWELFTH BIRTHDAY, HIS FATHER WAS KILLED.

YOUR MOTHER SAW THIS AS HER SECOND CHANCE TO LEAVE ATLANTIS. I HELPED ARRANGE A ROUTE BACK TO YOU AND YOUR FATHER. SHE HAD INSISTED ON BRINGING ORM.

BUT SHE WAS MURDERED THE NIGHT BEFORE HER ESCAPE.

WHO KILLED HER?

I BELIEVE IT WAS YOUR BROTHER. HER OWN SON.

AFTER HER DEATH HE BECAME THE *KING* OF *ATLANTIS*.

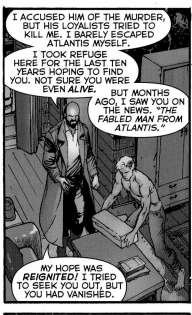

I ACCUSED HIM OF THE MURDER, BUT HIS LOYALISTS TRIED TO KILL ME. I BARELY ESCAPED ATLANTIS MYSELF.

I TOOK REFUGE HERE FOR THE LAST TEN YEARS HOPING TO FIND YOU. NOT SURE YOU WERE EVEN *ALIVE.*

BUT MONTHS AGO, I SAW YOU ON THE NEWS. "*THE FABLED MAN FROM ATLANTIS.*"

MY HOPE WAS *REIGNITED!* I TRIED TO SEEK YOU OUT, BUT YOU HAD VANISHED.

ONLY TO APPEAR HERE BEFORE ME.

THIS IS A MAP TO THE DEAD KING'S ARMORY, WHERE THE MOST POWERFUL OF ATLANTEAN ARTIFACTS ARE HELD.

INCLUDING HIS *INDESTRUCTIBLE* TRIDENT.

AND THESE ARE THE ATLANTEAN STONES THAT ONCE SAT UPON THE DEAD KING'S CROWN BEFORE IT WAS DESTROYED.

THE DEAD KING?

THE *CREATOR* AND *FIRST* KING OF ATLANTIS. BEFORE IT SANK INTO THE SEA.

YOU ARE HIS DESCENDANT AND RIGHTFUL HEIR OF THE GREATEST SOCIETY TO HAVE EVER EXISTED.

YOUR BROTHER IS AS SMART AND AS CHARISMATIC AS YOUR MOTHER, BUT AS VICIOUS AND CRUEL AS HIS FATHER.

FINALLY, HIS *HARSH* AND *VIOLENT* RULE IS OVER. THE *TRUE* KING IS HERE!

EVEN IF I THOUGHT I WAS, THEY'D NEVER ACCEPT ME.

YOU ARE THE ELDEST SON OF THE QUEEN. BY LAW, YOU ARE OUR KING. AND THE LAWS OF THE DEAD KING ARE THE ONLY ONES THE ATLANTEANS TRULY OBEY.

YOU ARE ATLANTIS'S SAVIOR AND MINE, ARTHUR.

OUR PEOPLE CAN BE *GREAT* AGAIN WITH A *GREAT* LEADER.

I WAS ONLY SEARCHING FOR MY MOTHER, VULKO. TO GIVE HER A MESSAGE FROM MY FATHER.

YOU CAN STILL GIVE HER THAT MESSAGE.

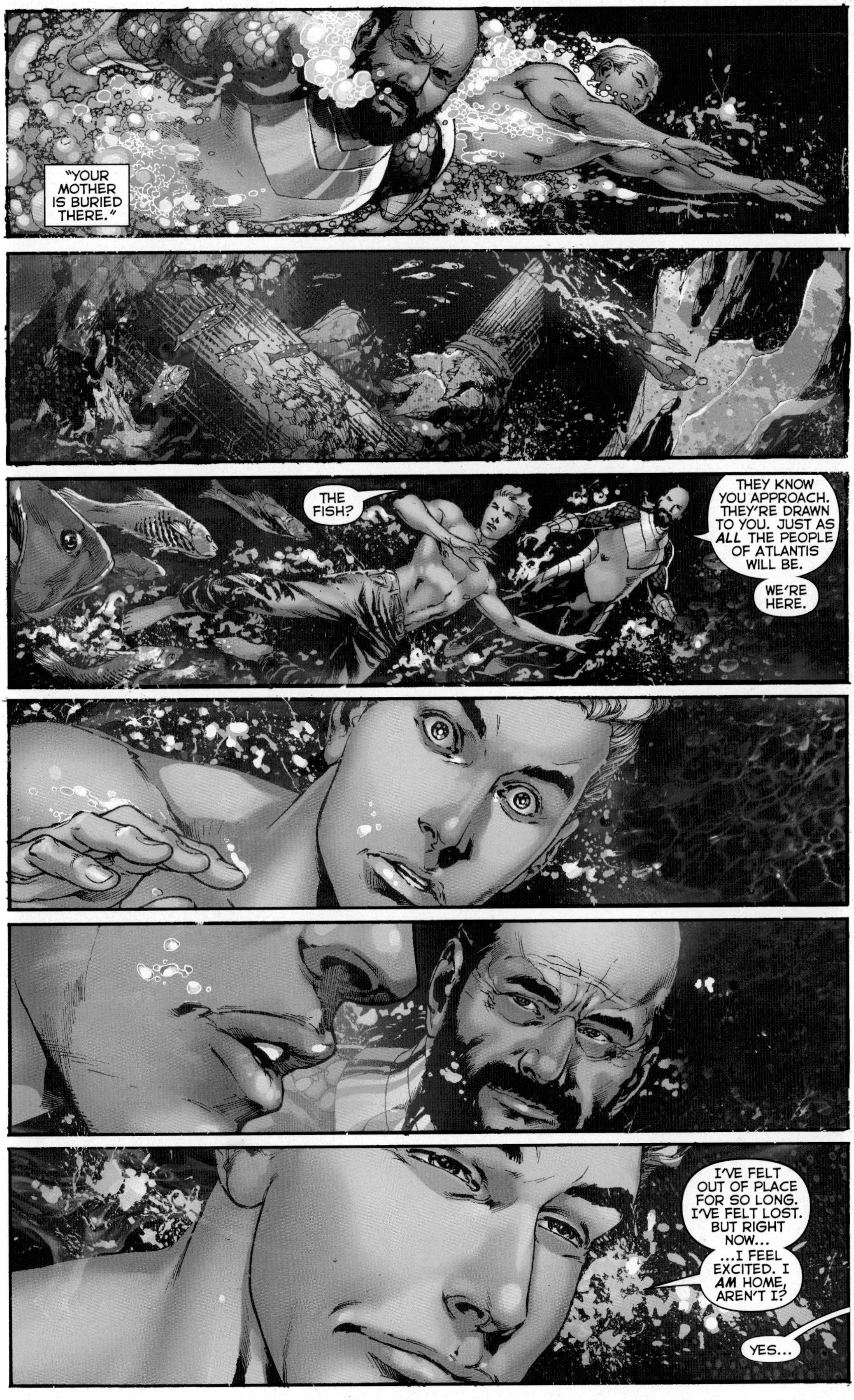
"YOUR MOTHER IS BURIED THERE."
THE FISH?
THEY KNOW YOU APPROACH. THEY'RE DRAWN TO YOU. JUST AS ALL THE PEOPLE OF ATLANTIS WILL BE.
WE'RE HERE.
I'VE FELT OUT OF PLACE FOR SO LONG. I'VE FELT LOST. BUT RIGHT NOW...
...I FEEL EXCITED. I AM HOME, AREN'T I?
YES...

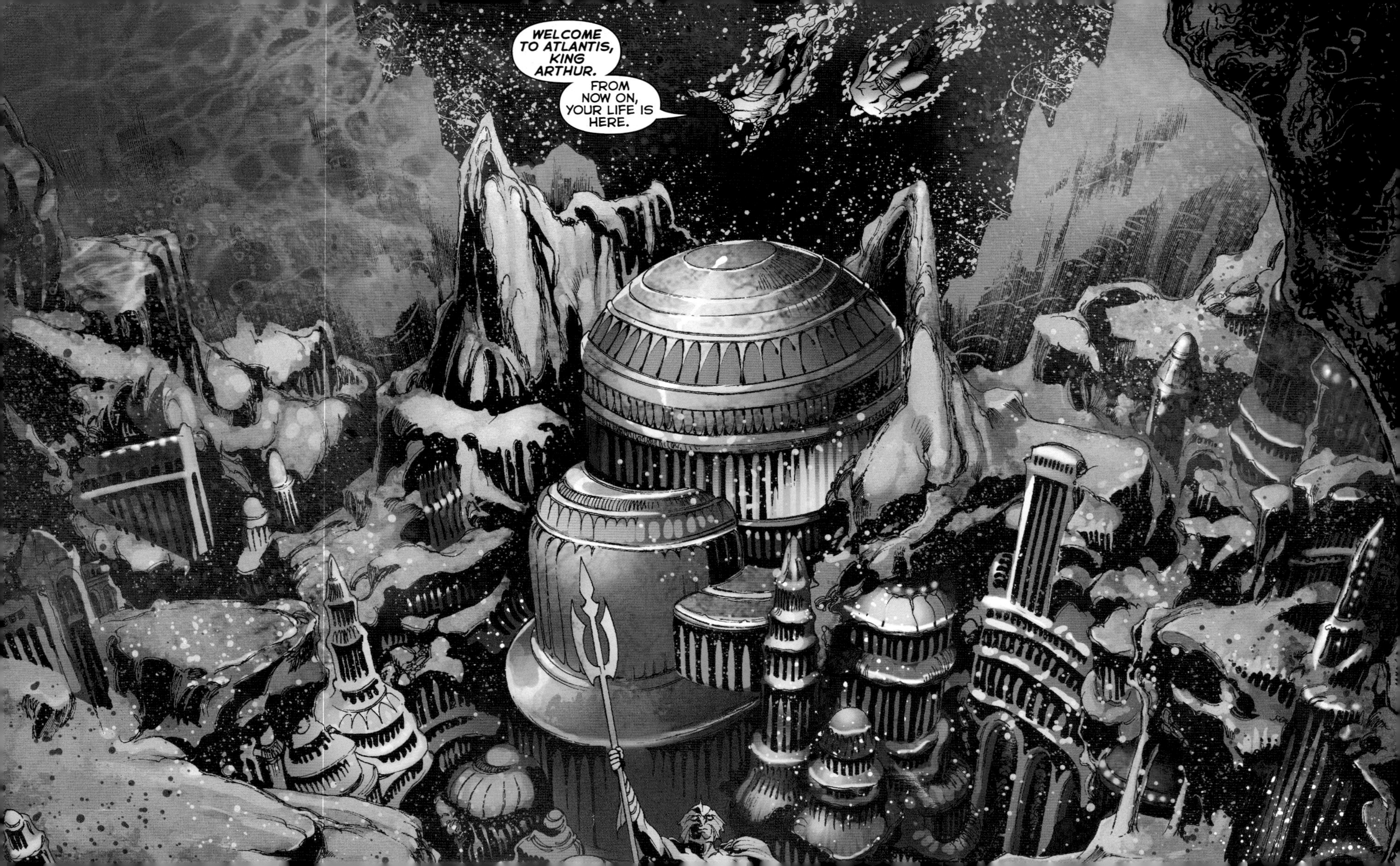
WELCOME TO ATLANTIS, KING ARTHUR.
FROM NOW ON, YOUR LIFE IS HERE.

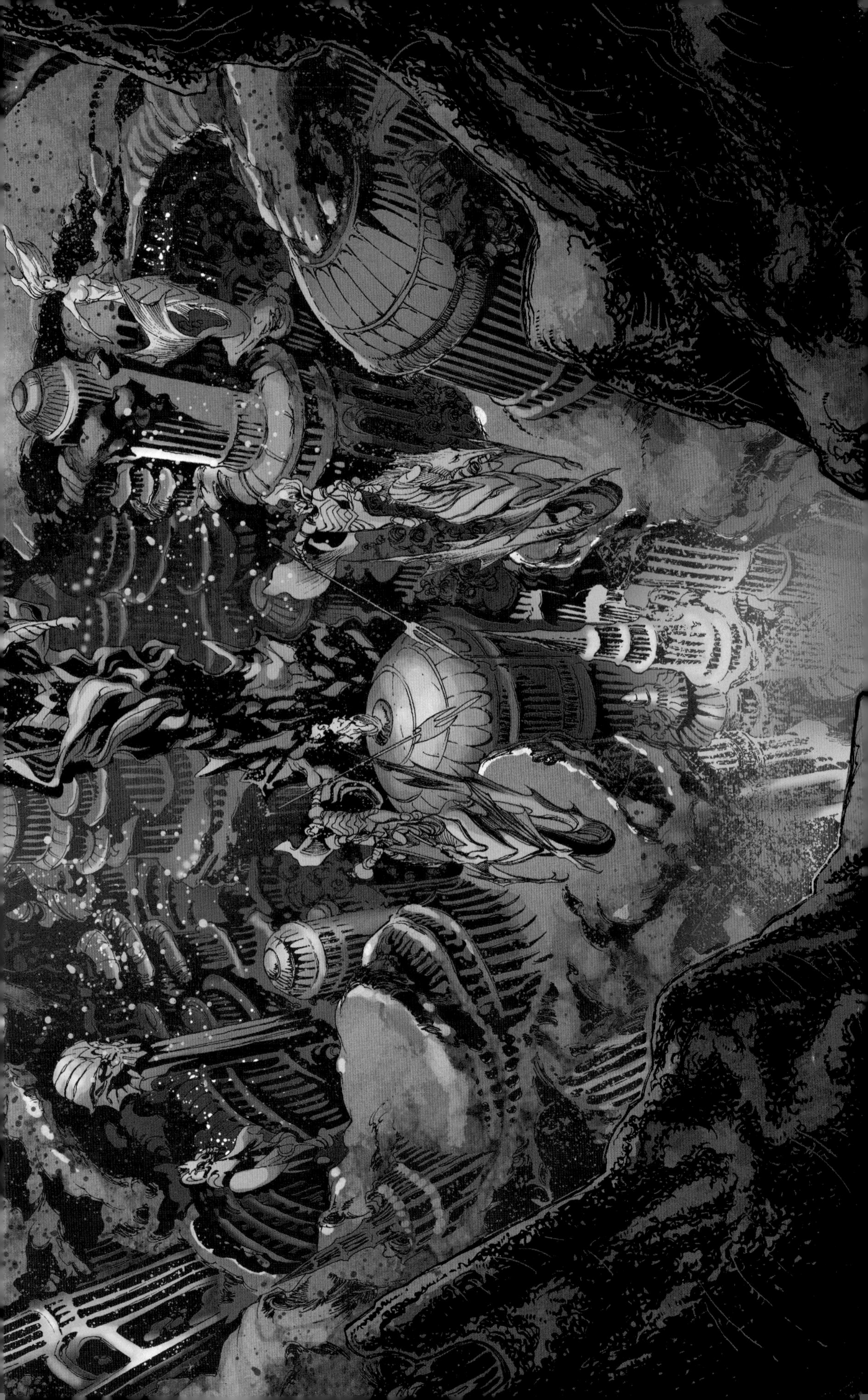

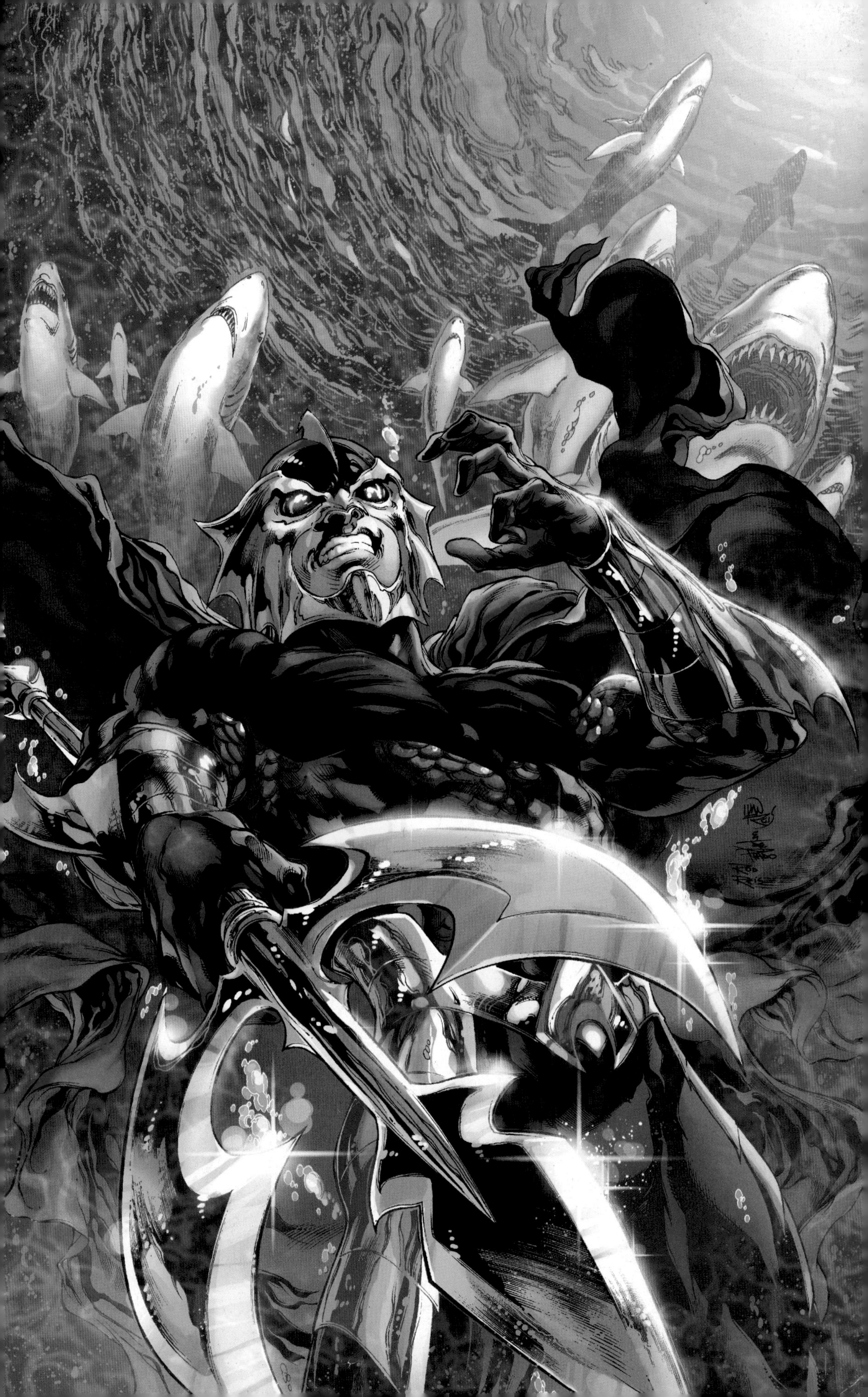

cover by IVAN REIS, JOE PRADO & ROD REIS

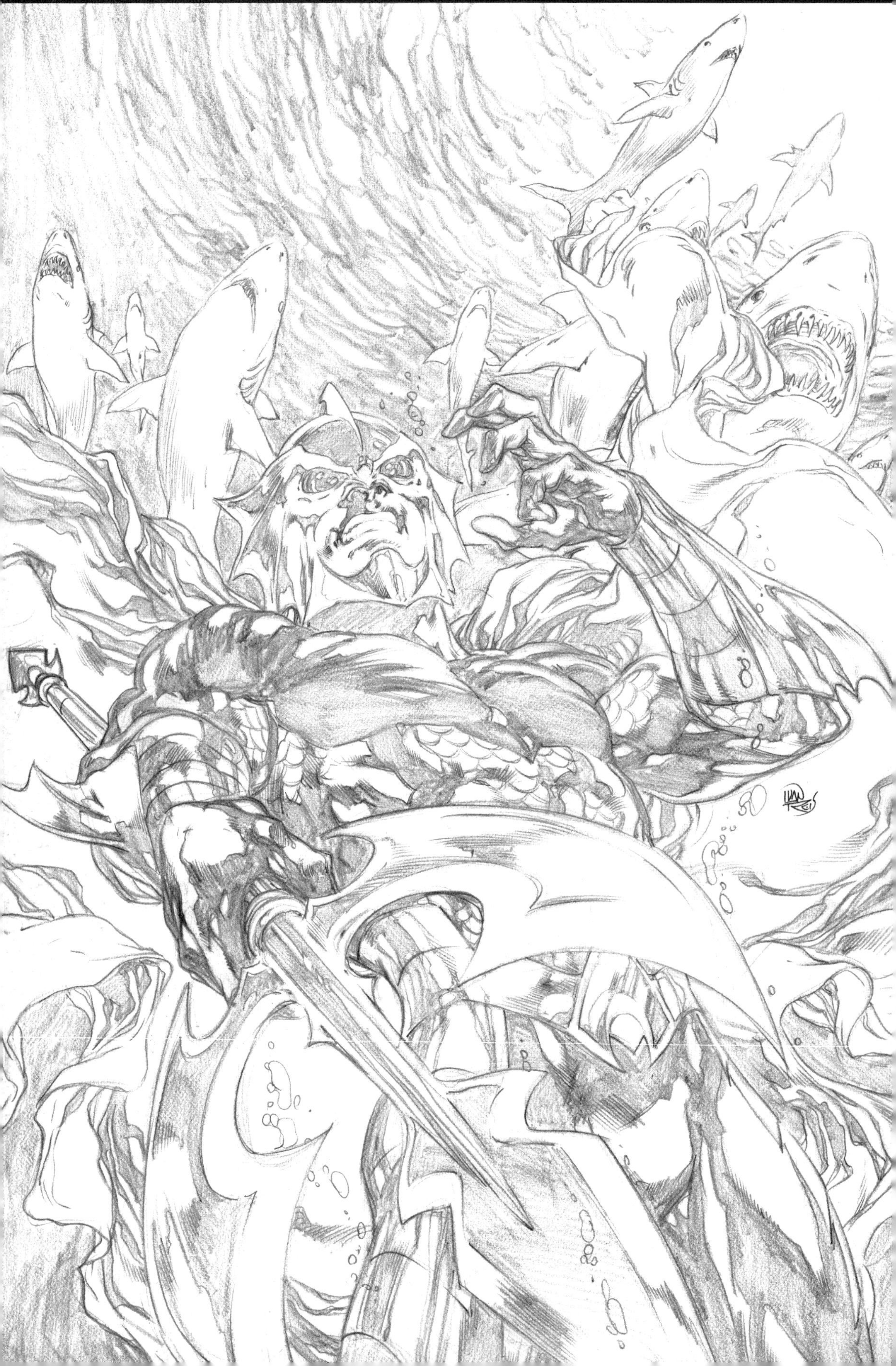

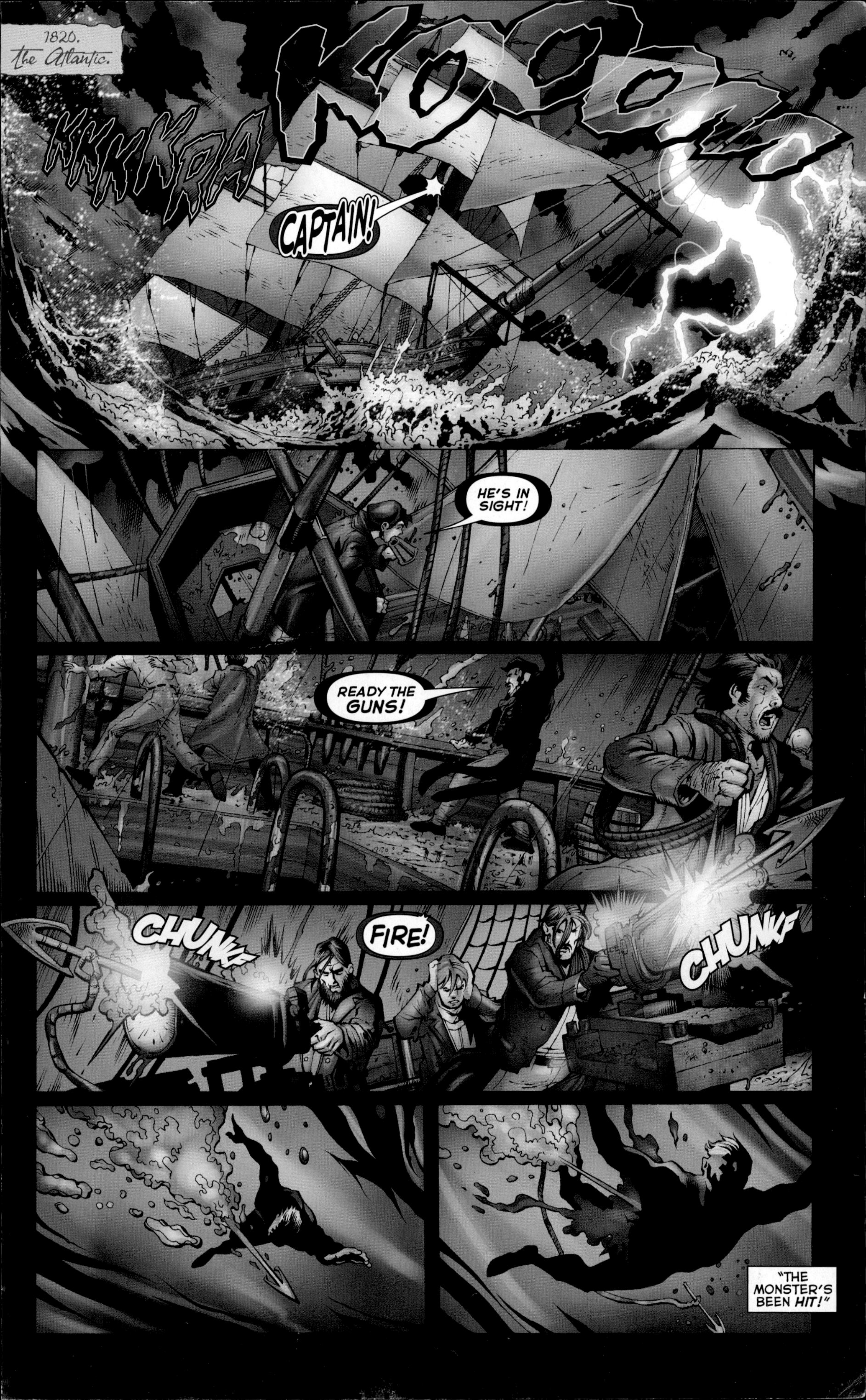
1820.
the Atlantic.
KKKKKRA
KOOOOOM
CAPTAIN!
HE'S IN SIGHT!
READY THE GUNS!
CHUNKF
FIRE!
CHUNKF
"THE MONSTER'S BEEN HIT!"

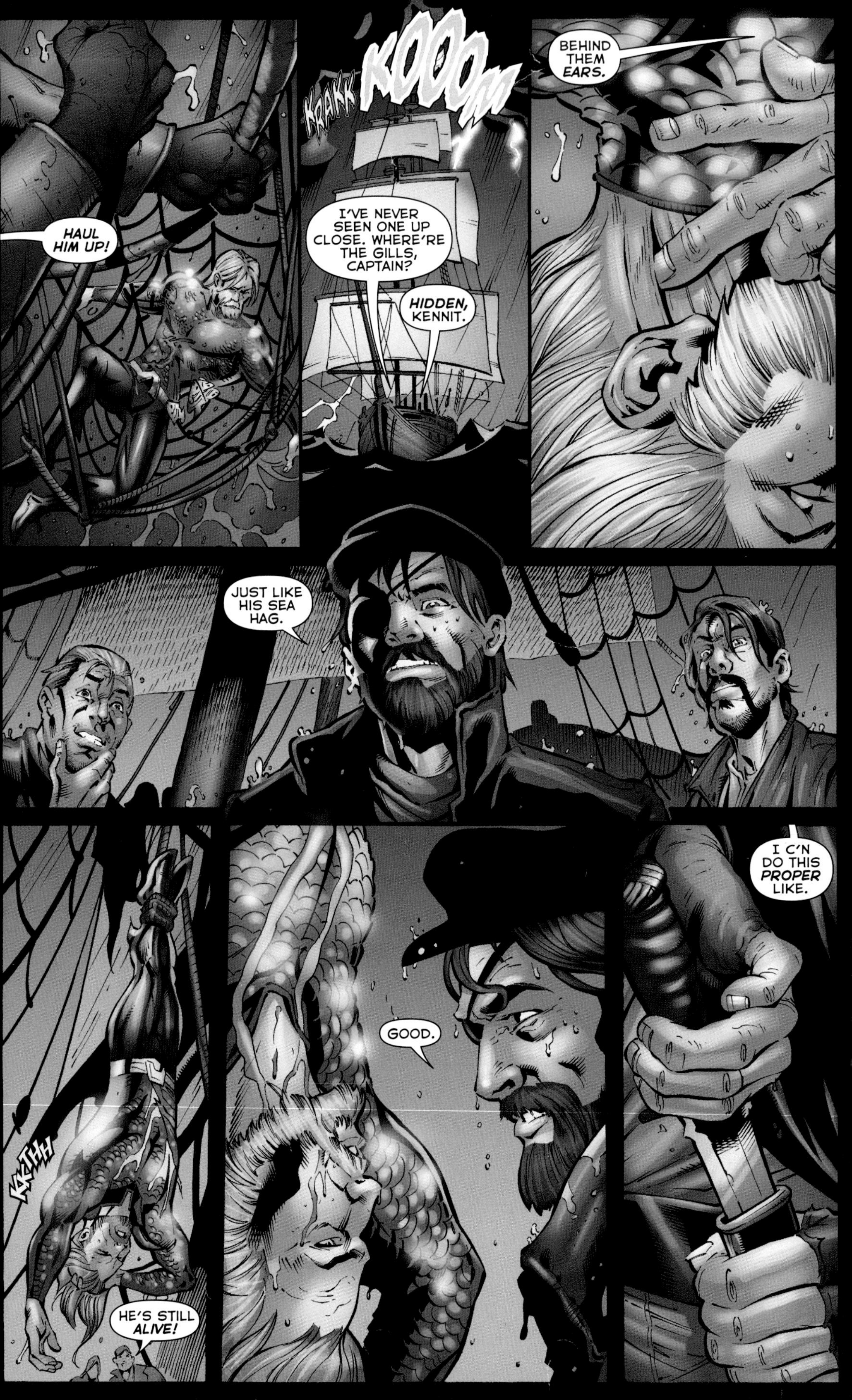
HAUL HIM UP!
KRAKK KOOOM
I'VE NEVER SEEN ONE UP CLOSE. WHERE'RE THE GILLS, CAPTAIN?
HIDDEN, KENNIT.
BEHIND THEM EARS.
JUST LIKE HIS SEA HAG.
KRTHH
HE'S STILL ALIVE!
GOOD.
I C'N DO THIS PROPER LIKE.

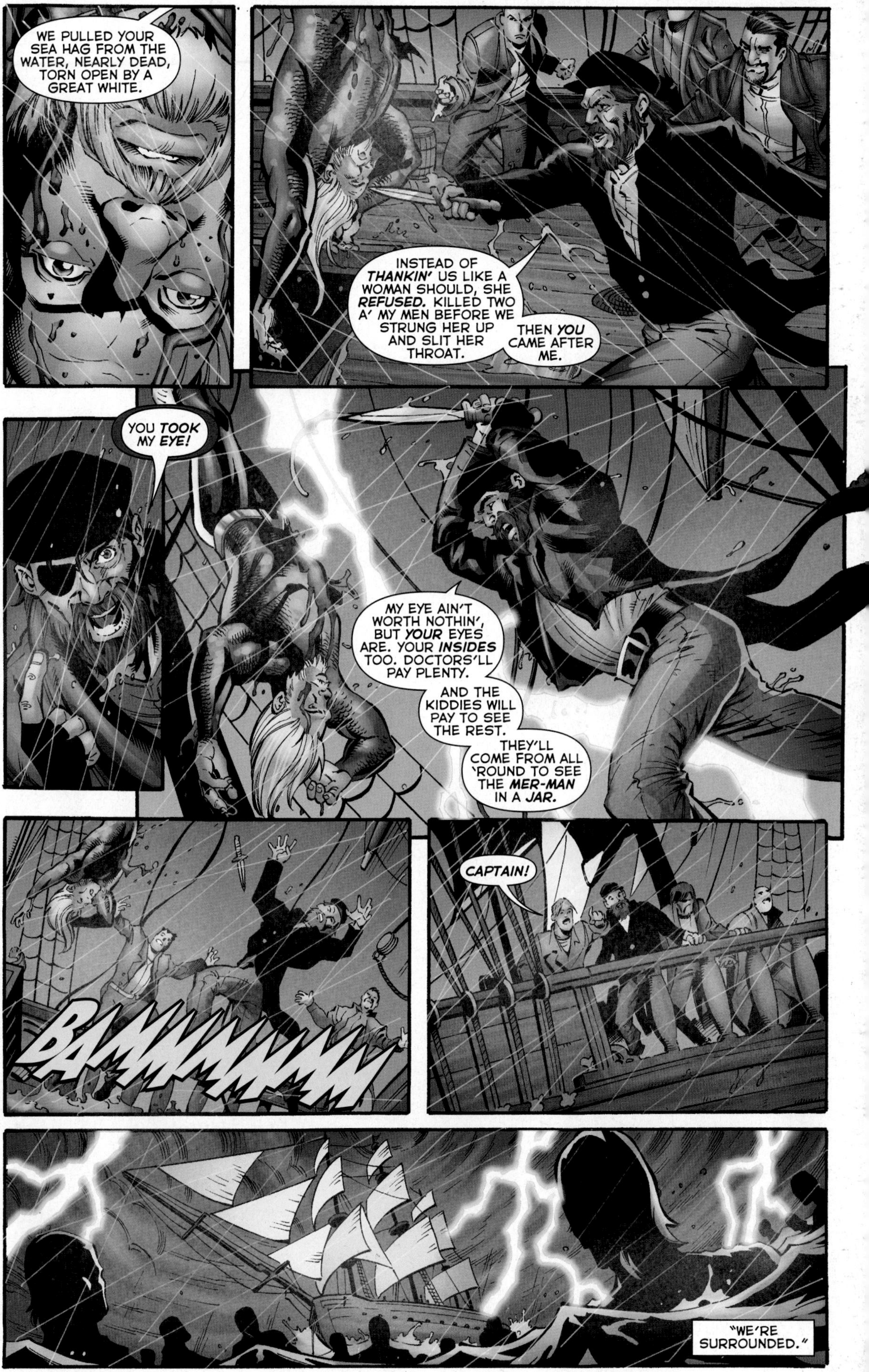
WE PULLED YOUR SEA HAG FROM THE WATER, NEARLY DEAD, TORN OPEN BY A GREAT WHITE.
INSTEAD OF *THANKIN'* US LIKE A WOMAN SHOULD, SHE *REFUSED.* KILLED TWO A' MY MEN BEFORE WE STRUNG HER UP AND SLIT HER THROAT.
THEN *YOU* CAME AFTER ME.
YOU *TOOK* MY *EYE!*
MY EYE AIN'T WORTH NOTHIN', BUT *YOUR* EYES ARE. YOUR *INSIDES* TOO. DOCTORS'LL PAY PLENTY.
AND THE KIDDIES WILL PAY TO SEE THE REST.
THEY'LL COME FROM ALL 'ROUND TO SEE THE *MER-MAN* IN A *JAR.*
BAMMMMMM
CAPTAIN!
"WE'RE SURROUNDED."

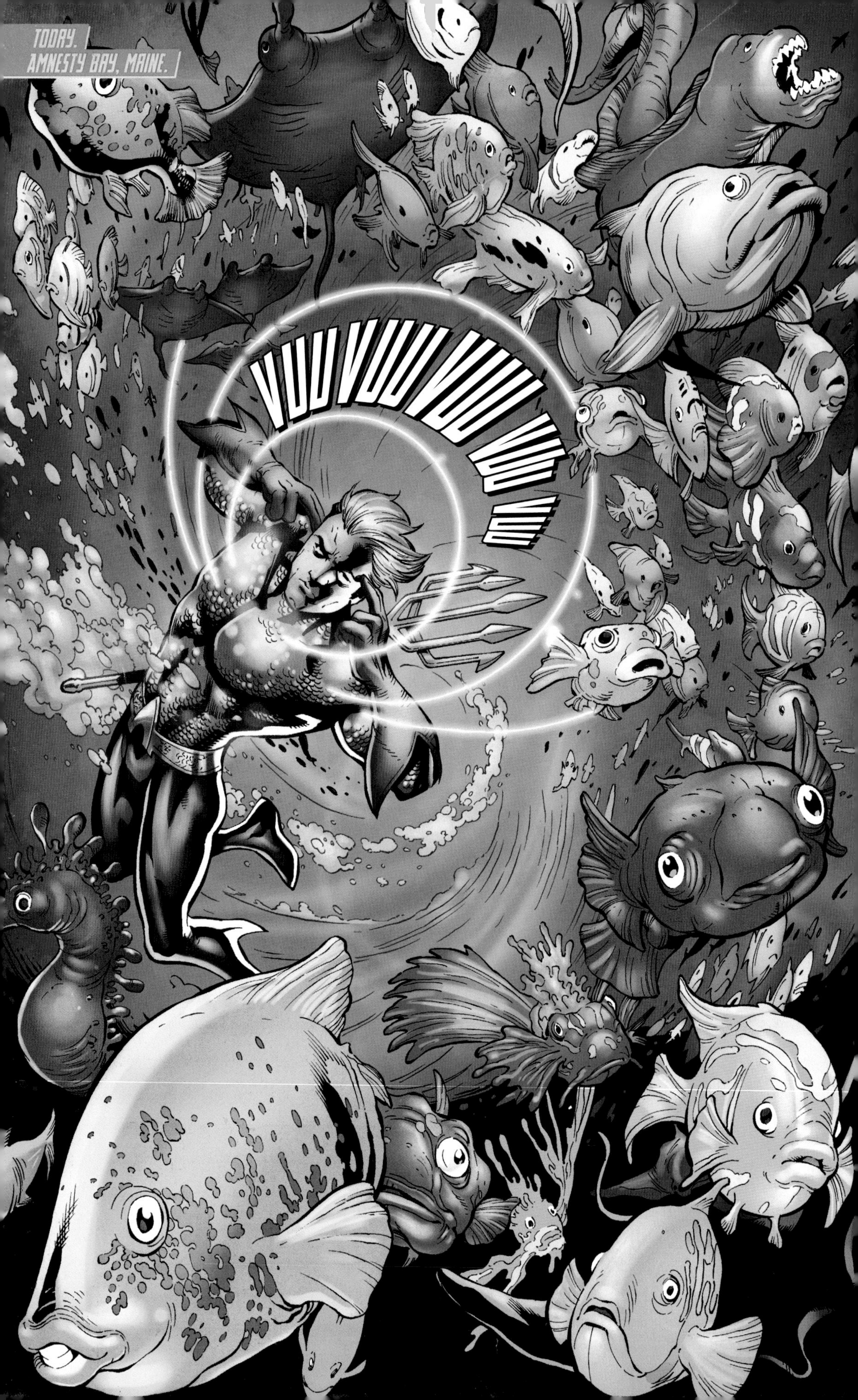
TODAY.
AMNESTY BAY, MAINE.
VUUVUUVUUVUUVUU

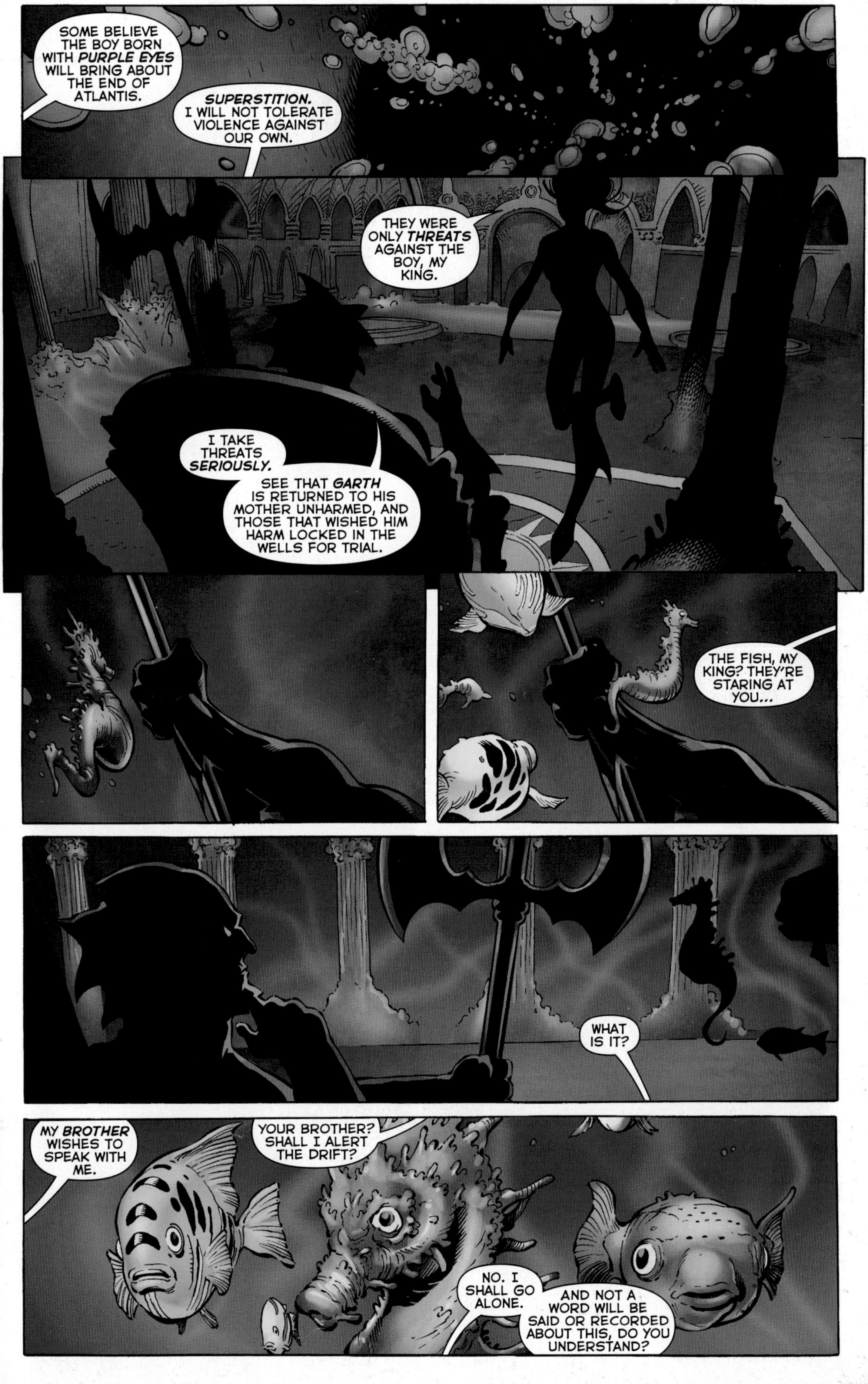
SOME BELIEVE THE BOY BORN WITH *PURPLE EYES* WILL BRING ABOUT THE END OF ATLANTIS.
SUPERSTITION. I WILL NOT TOLERATE VIOLENCE AGAINST OUR OWN.
THEY WERE ONLY *THREATS* AGAINST THE BOY, MY KING.
I TAKE THREATS *SERIOUSLY.*
SEE THAT *GARTH* IS RETURNED TO HIS MOTHER UNHARMED, AND THOSE THAT WISHED HIM HARM LOCKED IN THE WELLS FOR TRIAL.
THE FISH, MY KING? THEY'RE STARING AT YOU...
WHAT IS IT?
MY *BROTHER* WISHES TO SPEAK WITH ME.
YOUR BROTHER? SHALL I ALERT THE DRIFT?
NO. I SHALL GO ALONE.
AND NOT A WORD WILL BE SAID OR RECORDED ABOUT THIS, DO YOU UNDERSTAND?

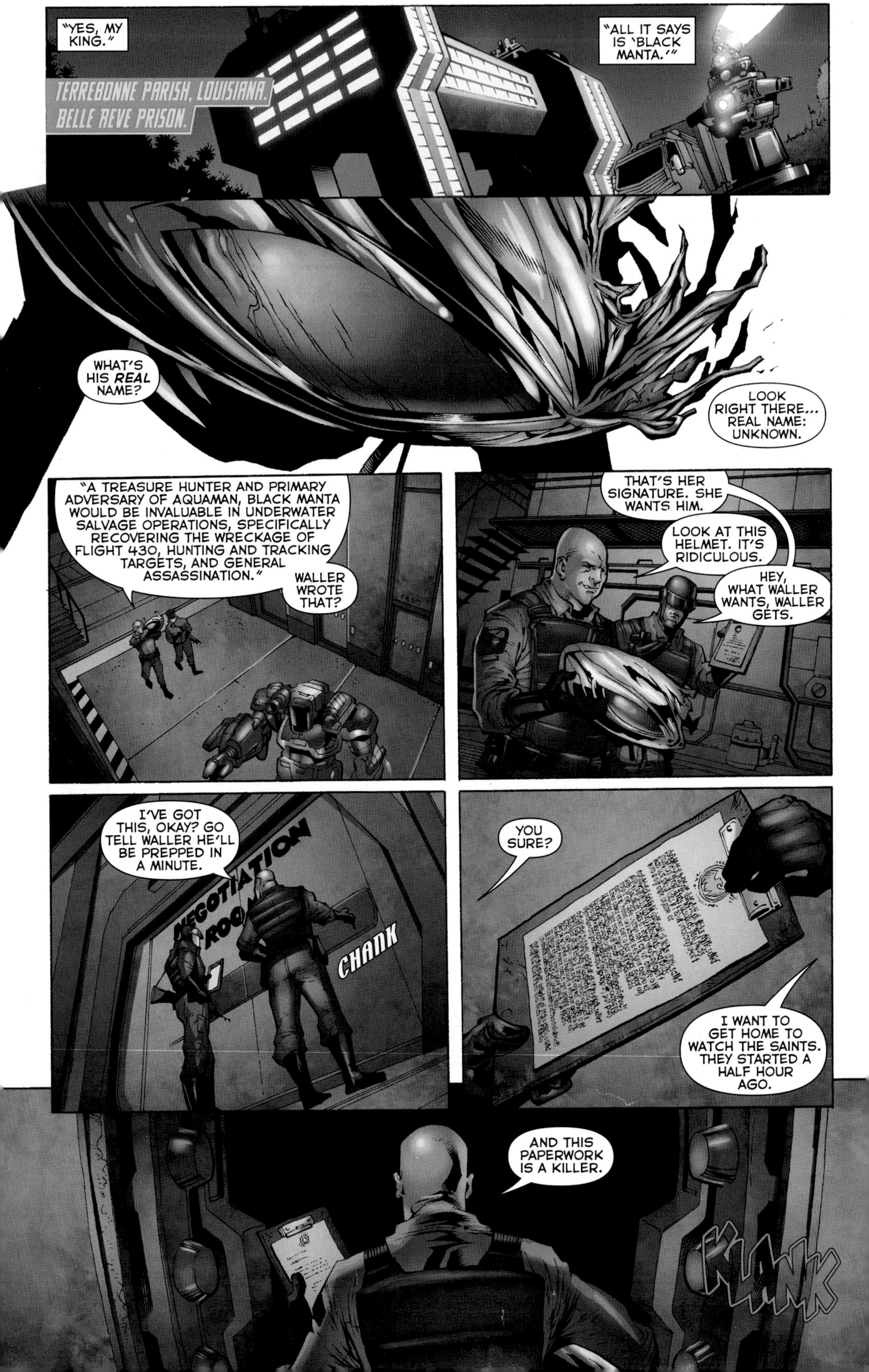

"YES, MY KING."
TERREBONNE PARISH, LOUISIANA. BELLE REVE PRISON.
"ALL IT SAYS IS 'BLACK MANTA.'"
WHAT'S HIS *REAL* NAME?
LOOK RIGHT THERE... REAL NAME: UNKNOWN.
"A TREASURE HUNTER AND PRIMARY ADVERSARY OF AQUAMAN, BLACK MANTA WOULD BE INVALUABLE IN UNDERWATER SALVAGE OPERATIONS, SPECIFICALLY RECOVERING THE WRECKAGE OF FLIGHT 430, HUNTING AND TRACKING TARGETS, AND GENERAL ASSASSINATION."
WALLER WROTE THAT?
THAT'S HER SIGNATURE. SHE WANTS HIM.
LOOK AT THIS HELMET. IT'S RIDICULOUS.
HEY, WHAT WALLER WANTS, WALLER GETS.
I'VE GOT THIS, OKAY? GO TELL WALLER HE'LL BE PREPPED IN A MINUTE.
NEGOTIATION ROOM
CHANK
YOU SURE?
I WANT TO GET HOME TO WATCH THE SAINTS. THEY STARTED A HALF HOUR AGO.
AND THIS PAPERWORK IS A KILLER.
KLANK

WHEN THEY FIRST BROUGHT YOU IN, WE DIDN'T KNOW IF YOU NEEDED TO BE IN A *FISH TANK* OR NOT.

BUT APPARENTLY, YOU DON'T BREATHE UNDERWATER LIKE YOUR AQUATIC PLAYMATE.

TELL ME SOMETHING, "BLACK MANTA."

HE REALLY THAT TOUGH?

YOU KNOW, YOU *CAN* GET OUT OF HERE. THERE'S AN OPTION. YOU'RE GOING TO HEAR ALL THE DETAILS IN A MINUTE, BUT IF YOU SIGN RIGHT--

YOU'RE TALKING ABOUT THE *SUICIDE SQUAD?*

WE KNOW ABOUT IT.

WE DON'T *LIKE* IT.

QUEIMADURA.

VEEE

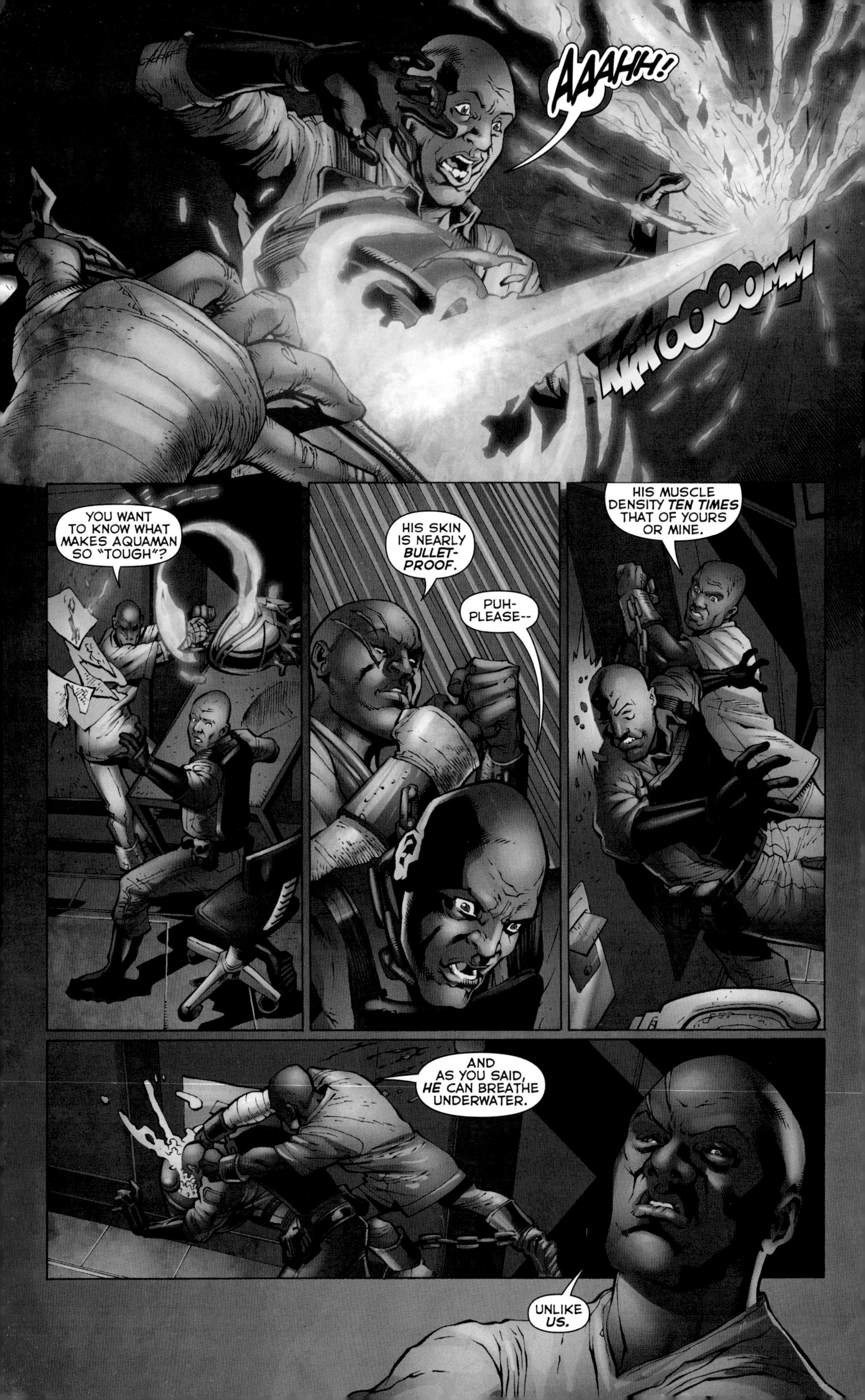

AAAHH!
KKKOOOOMMM
YOU WANT TO KNOW WHAT MAKES AQUAMAN SO "TOUGH"?
HIS SKIN IS NEARLY BULLET-PROOF.
PUH-PLEASE--
HIS MUSCLE DENSITY TEN TIMES THAT OF YOURS OR MINE.
AND AS YOU SAID, HE CAN BREATHE UNDERWATER.
UNLIKE US.

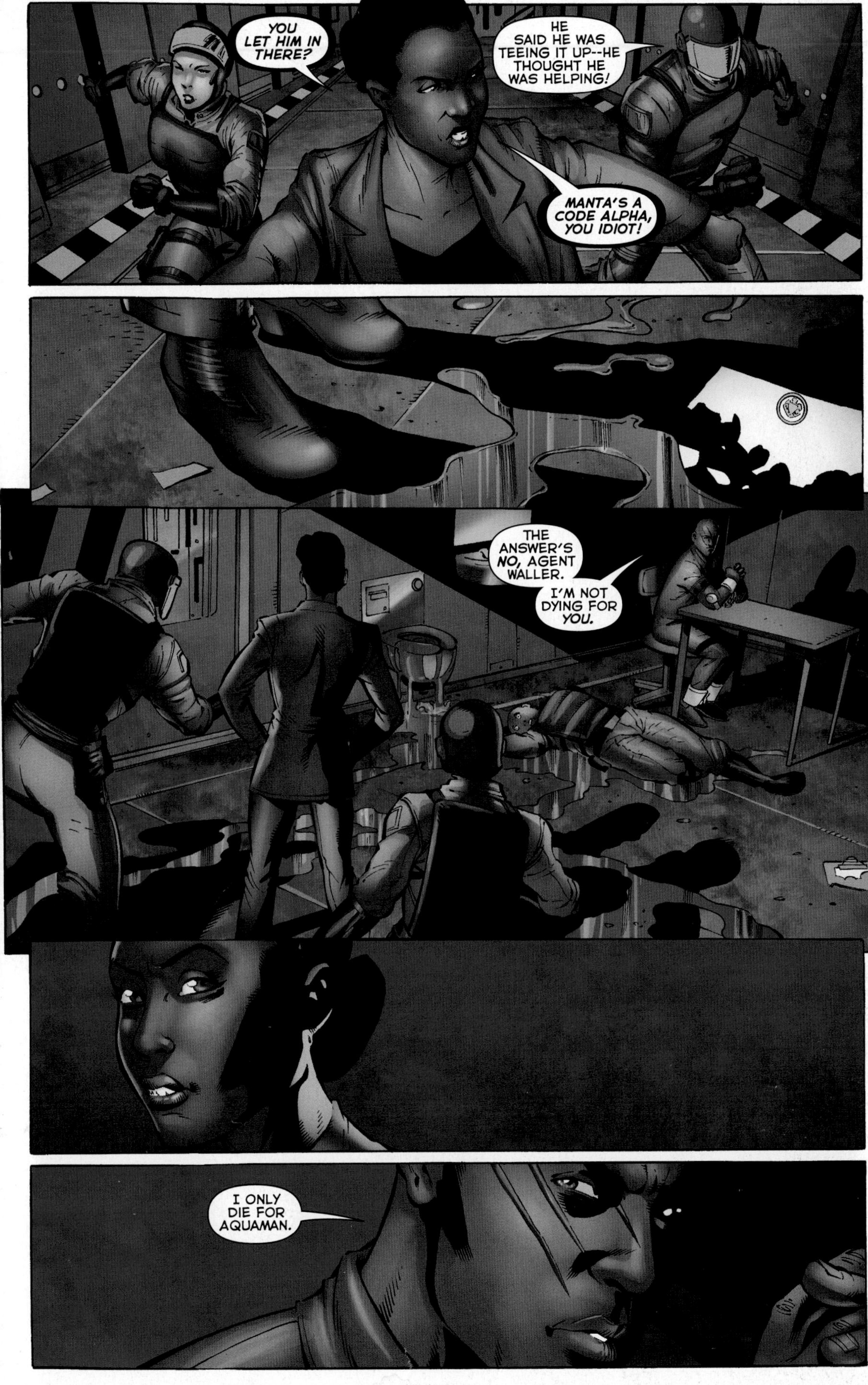
YOU LET HIM IN THERE?
HE SAID HE WAS TEEING IT UP--HE THOUGHT HE WAS HELPING!
MANTA'S A CODE ALPHA, YOU IDIOT!
THE ANSWER'S NO, AGENT WALLER.
I'M NOT DYING FOR YOU.
I ONLY DIE FOR AQUAMAN.

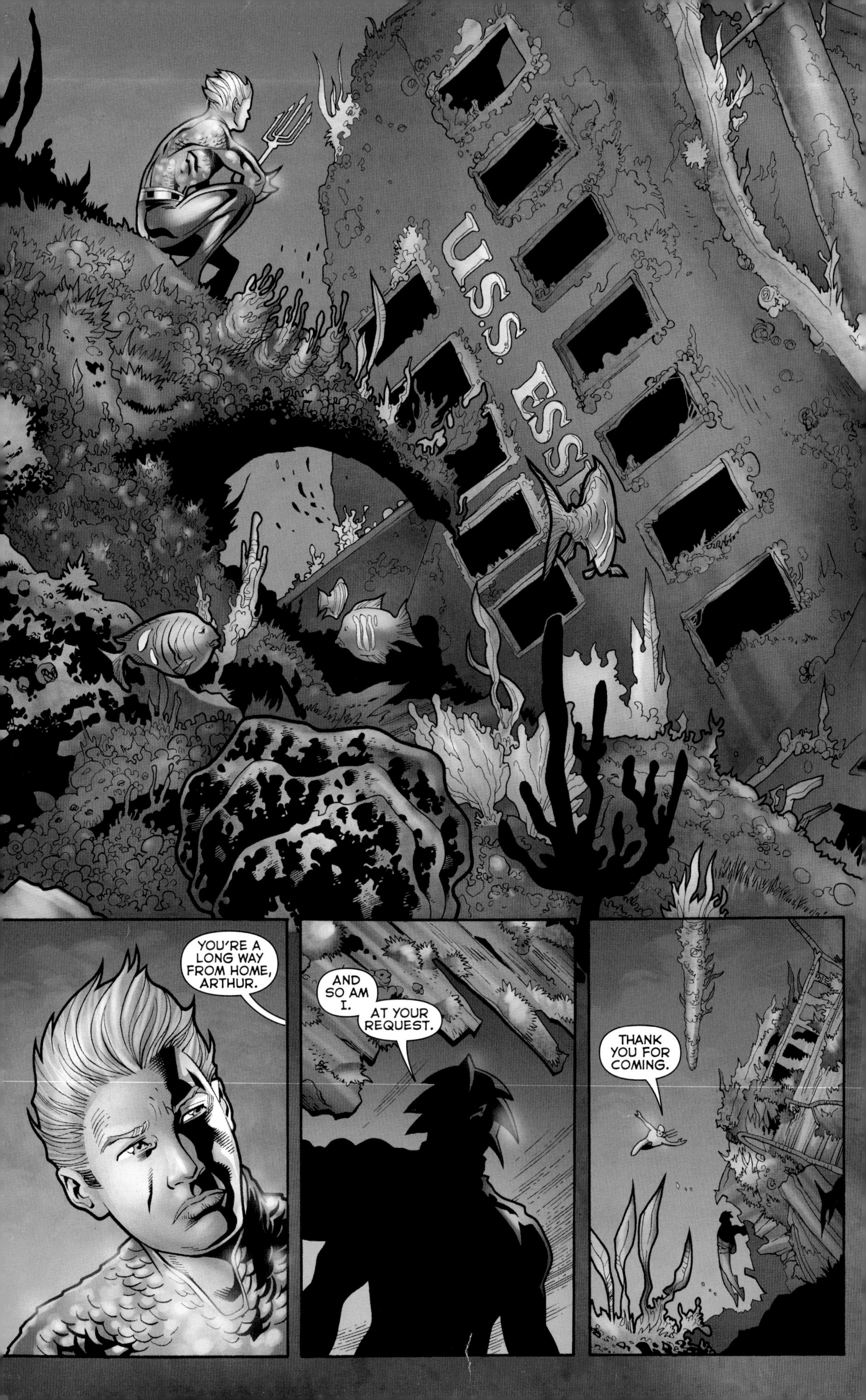
U.S.S. ESS
YOU'RE A LONG WAY FROM HOME, ARTHUR.
AND SO AM I.
AT YOUR REQUEST.
THANK YOU FOR COMING.

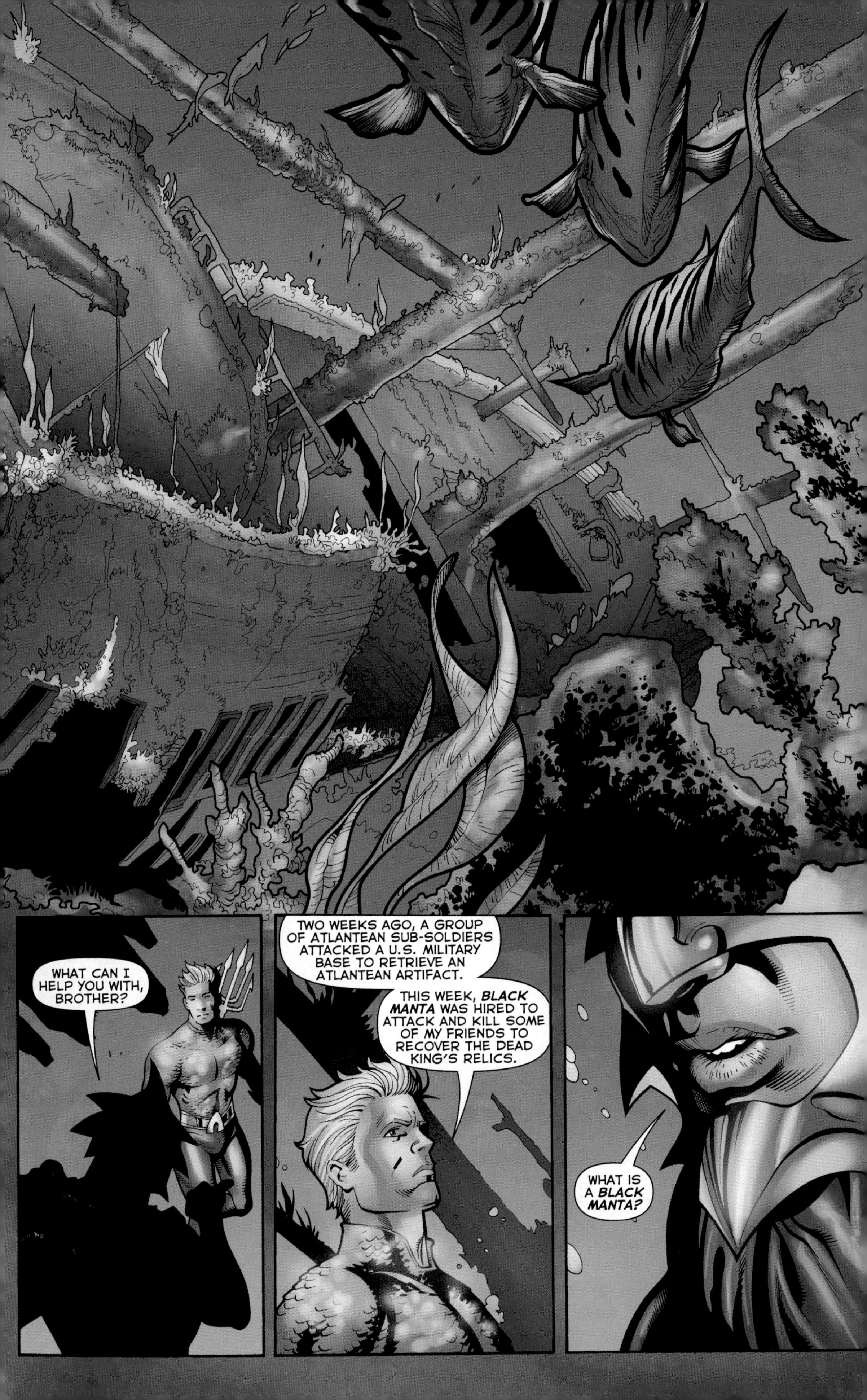
WHAT CAN I HELP YOU WITH, BROTHER?
TWO WEEKS AGO, A GROUP OF ATLANTEAN SUB-SOLDIERS ATTACKED A U.S. MILITARY BASE TO RETRIEVE AN ATLANTEAN ARTIFACT.
THIS WEEK, BLACK MANTA WAS HIRED TO ATTACK AND KILL SOME OF MY FRIENDS TO RECOVER THE DEAD KING'S RELICS.
WHAT IS A BLACK MANTA?

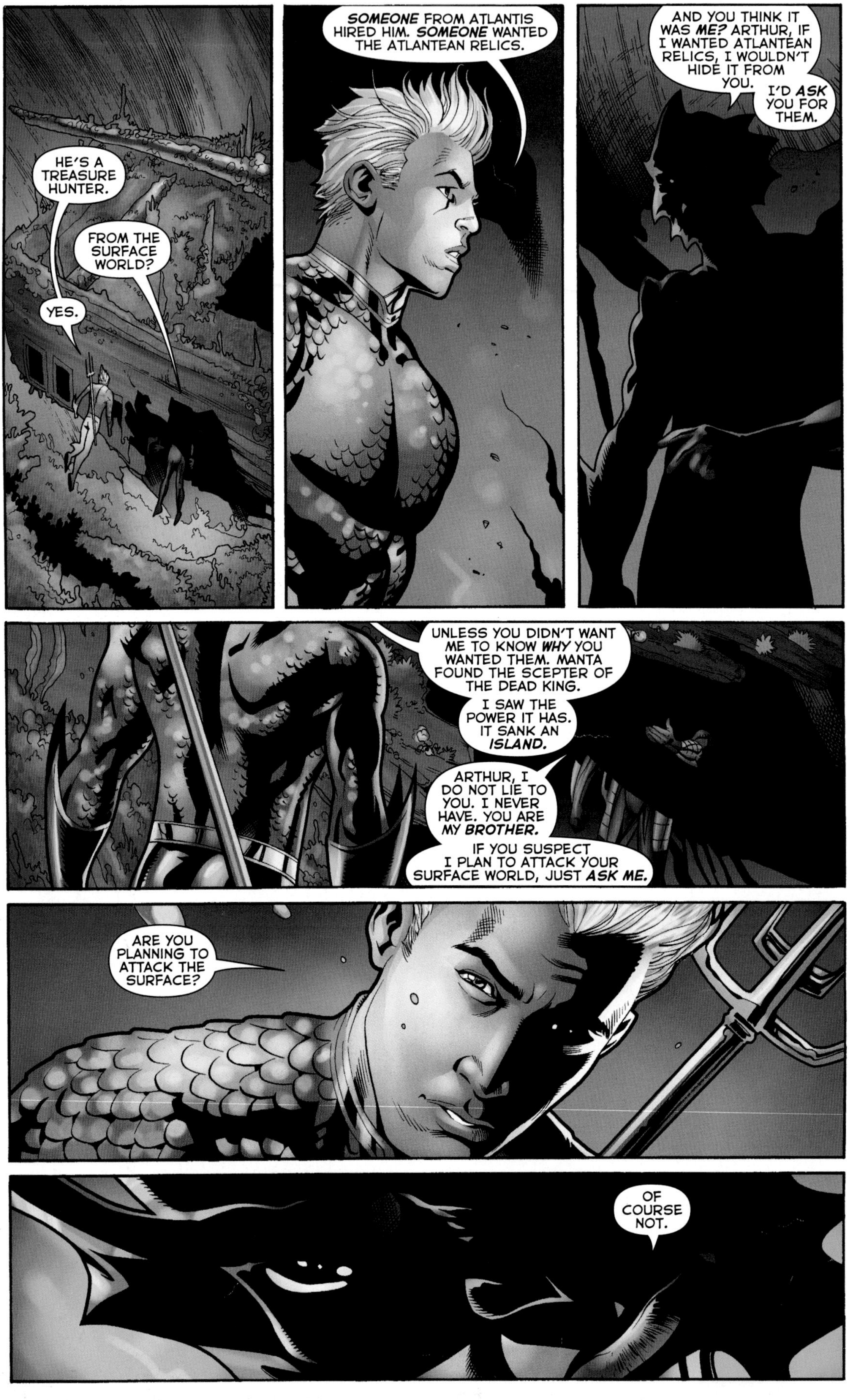
HE'S A TREASURE HUNTER.
FROM THE SURFACE WORLD?
YES.
SOMEONE FROM ATLANTIS HIRED HIM. SOMEONE WANTED THE ATLANTEAN RELICS.
AND YOU THINK IT WAS ME? ARTHUR, IF I WANTED ATLANTEAN RELICS, I WOULDN'T HIDE IT FROM YOU.
I'D ASK YOU FOR THEM.
UNLESS YOU DIDN'T WANT ME TO KNOW WHY YOU WANTED THEM. MANTA FOUND THE SCEPTER OF THE DEAD KING.
I SAW THE POWER IT HAS. IT SANK AN ISLAND.
ARTHUR, I DO NOT LIE TO YOU. I NEVER HAVE. YOU ARE MY BROTHER.
IF YOU SUSPECT I PLAN TO ATTACK YOUR SURFACE WORLD, JUST ASK ME.
ARE YOU PLANNING TO ATTACK THE SURFACE?
OF COURSE NOT.

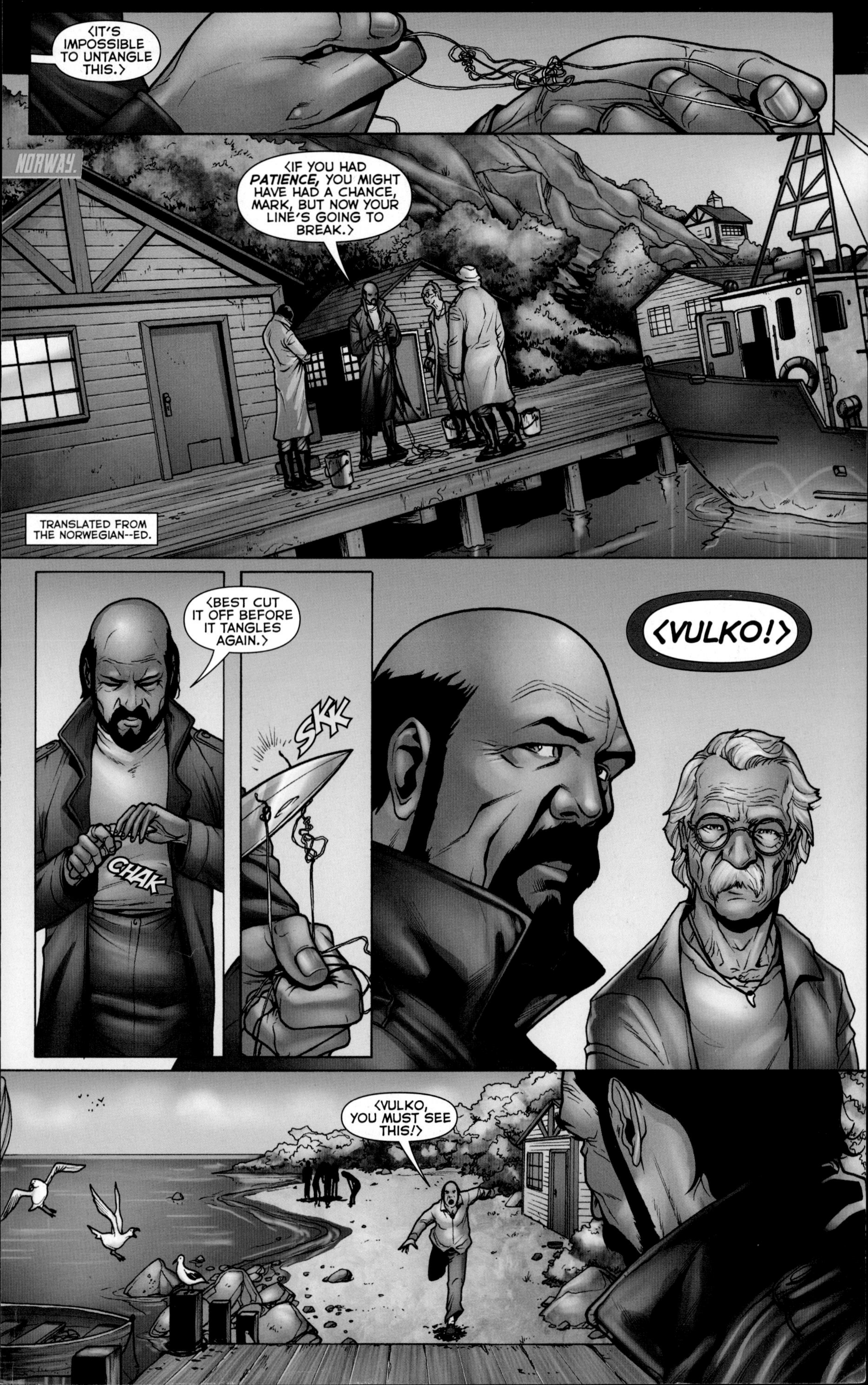

<IT'S IMPOSSIBLE TO UNTANGLE THIS.>
NORWAY.
<IF YOU HAD PATIENCE, YOU MIGHT HAVE HAD A CHANCE, MARK, BUT NOW YOUR LINE'S GOING TO BREAK.>
TRANSLATED FROM THE NORWEGIAN--ED.
<BEST CUT IT OFF BEFORE IT TANGLES AGAIN.>
CHAK
SKK
<VULKO!>
<VULKO, YOU MUST SEE THIS!>

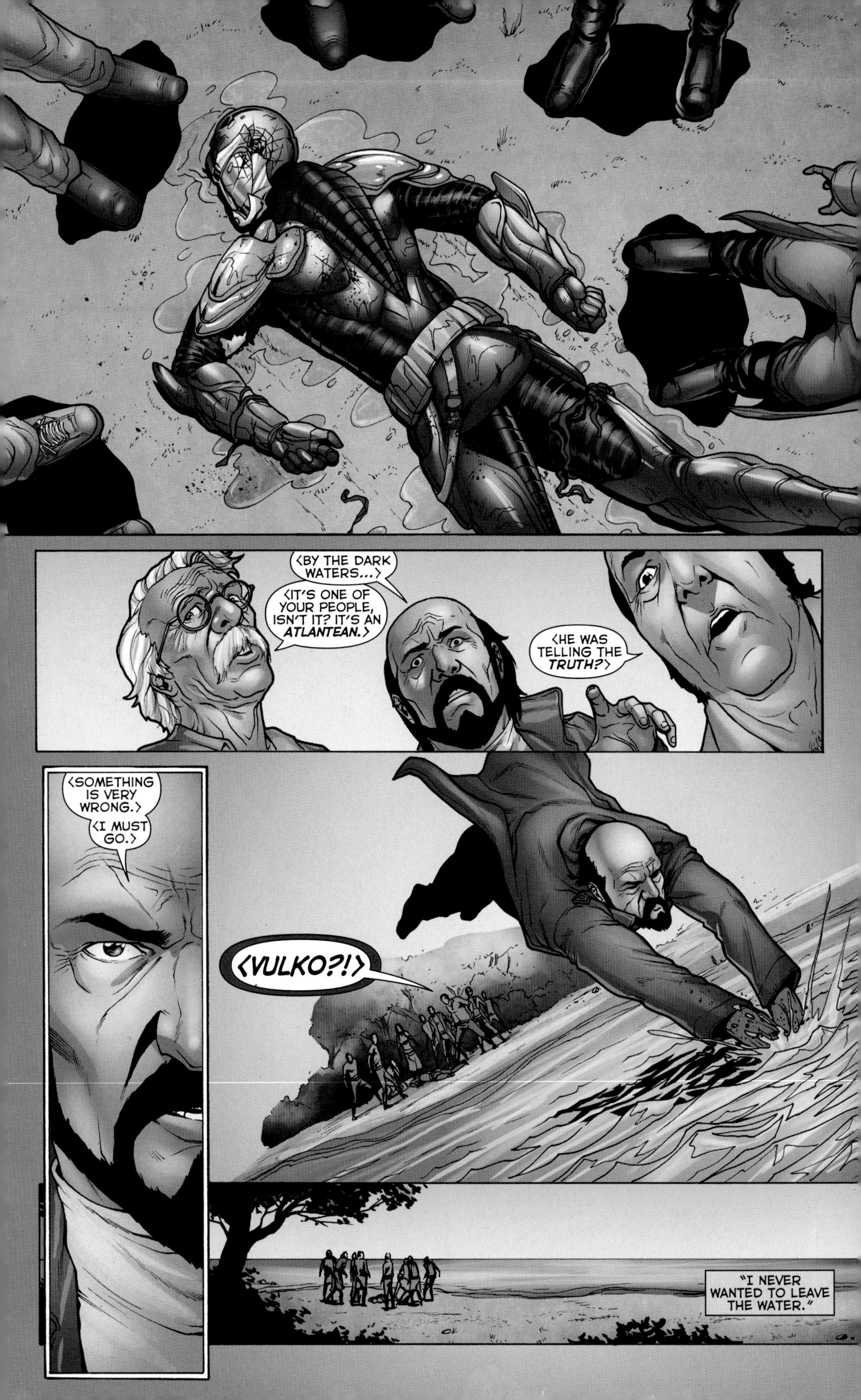

<BY THE DARK WATERS...>
<IT'S ONE OF YOUR PEOPLE, ISN'T IT? IT'S AN ATLANTEAN.>
<HE WAS TELLING THE TRUTH?>
<SOMETHING IS VERY WRONG.>
<I MUST GO.>
<VULKO?!>
"I NEVER WANTED TO LEAVE THE WATER."

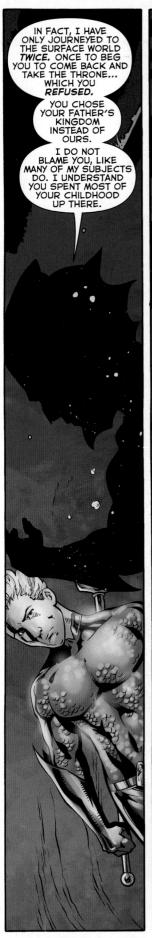

IN FACT, I HAVE ONLY JOURNEYED TO THE SURFACE WORLD *TWICE.* ONCE TO BEG YOU TO COME BACK AND TAKE THE THRONE... WHICH YOU *REFUSED.*

YOU CHOSE YOUR FATHER'S KINGDOM INSTEAD OF OURS.

I DO NOT BLAME YOU, LIKE MANY OF MY SUBJECTS DO. I UNDERSTAND YOU SPENT MOST OF YOUR CHILDHOOD UP THERE.

BREATHING THAT AIR.

PINNED TO THE GROUND.

HOW HORRIBLE IT MUST HAVE BEEN.

THE WORLD UP THERE ISN'T THE NIGHTMARE YOU THINK IT IS.

I AM SURE YOU HAVE IMPROVED IT, ARTHUR. JUST AS I HAVE IMPROVED ATLANTIS.

I ONCE THOUGHT WE WOULD DO THAT *TOGETHER.* NOW WE ARE LITERALLY WORLDS APART.

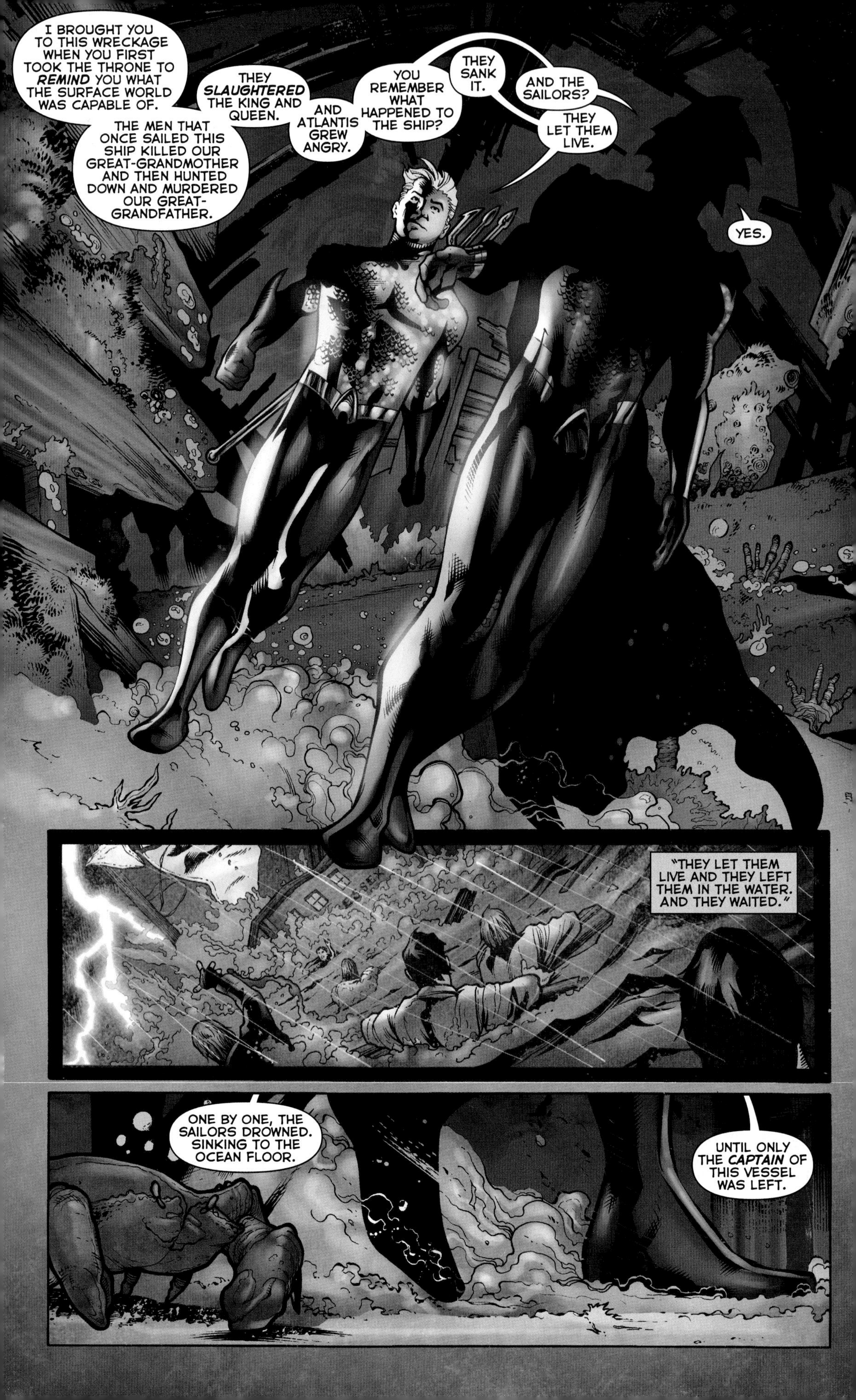
I BROUGHT YOU TO THIS WRECKAGE WHEN YOU FIRST TOOK THE THRONE TO *REMIND* YOU WHAT THE SURFACE WORLD WAS CAPABLE OF.
THE MEN THAT ONCE SAILED THIS SHIP KILLED OUR GREAT-GRANDMOTHER AND THEN HUNTED DOWN AND MURDERED OUR GREAT-GRANDFATHER.
THEY *SLAUGHTERED* THE KING AND QUEEN.
AND ATLANTIS GREW ANGRY.
YOU REMEMBER WHAT HAPPENED TO THE SHIP?
THEY SANK IT.
AND THE SAILORS?
THEY LET THEM LIVE.
YES.
"THEY LET THEM LIVE AND THEY LEFT THEM IN THE WATER. AND THEY WAITED."
ONE BY ONE, THE SAILORS DROWNED. SINKING TO THE OCEAN FLOOR.
UNTIL ONLY THE *CAPTAIN* OF THIS VESSEL WAS LEFT.

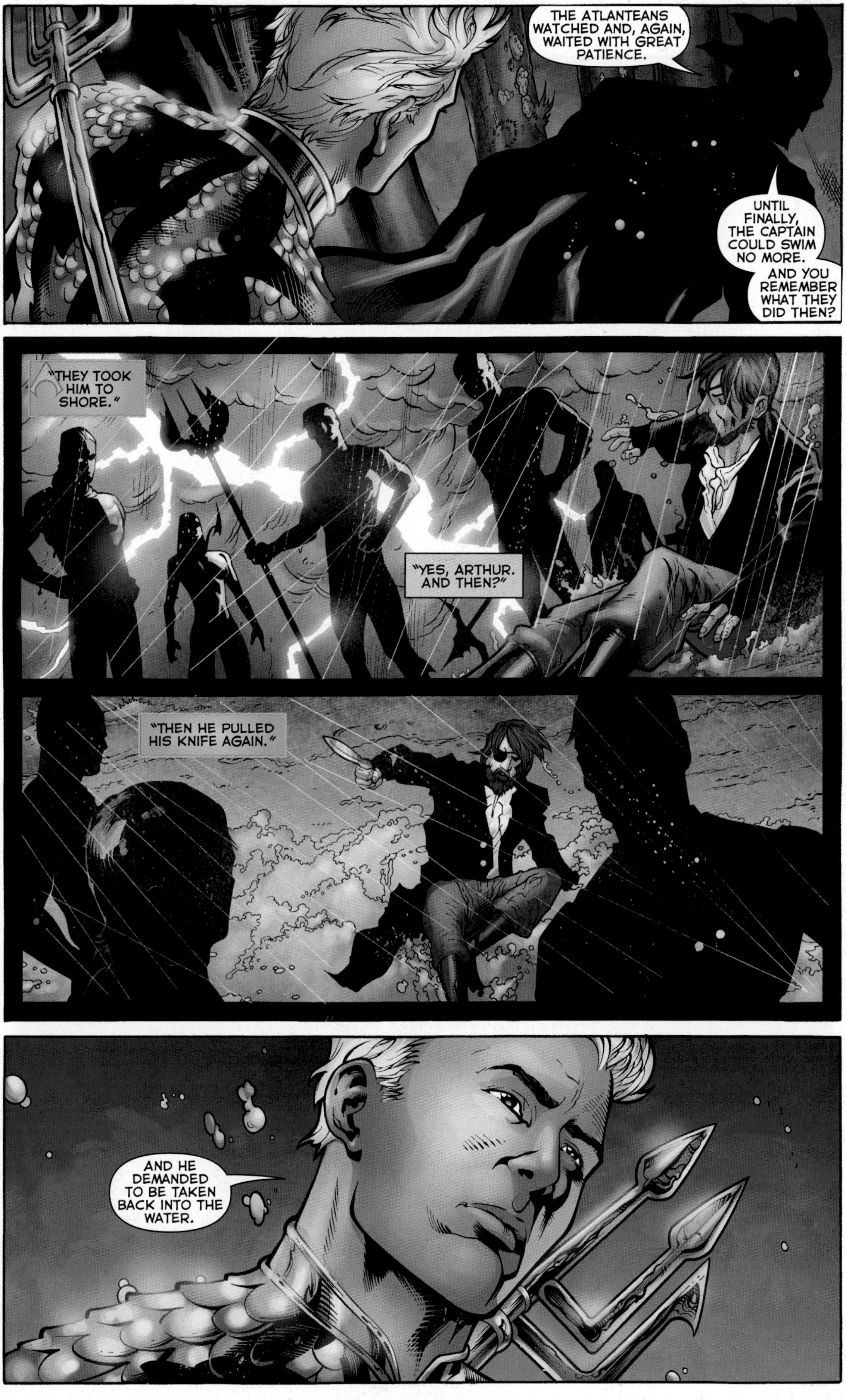
THE ATLANTEANS WATCHED AND, AGAIN, WAITED WITH GREAT PATIENCE.
UNTIL FINALLY, THE CAPTAIN COULD SWIM NO MORE.
AND YOU REMEMBER WHAT THEY DID THEN?
"THEY TOOK HIM TO SHORE."
"YES, ARTHUR. AND THEN?"
"THEN HE PULLED HIS KNIFE AGAIN."
AND HE DEMANDED TO BE TAKEN BACK INTO THE WATER.

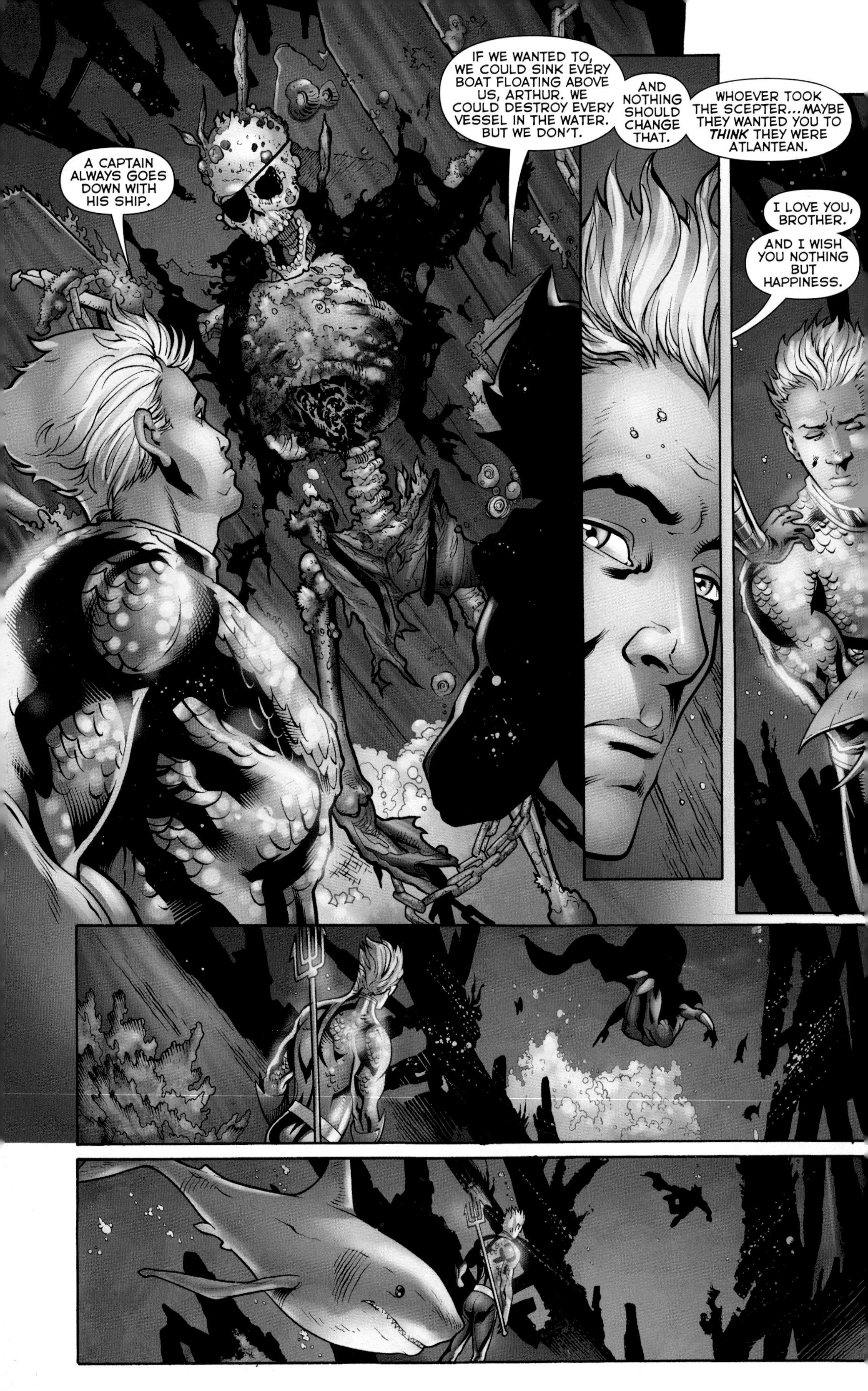
A CAPTAIN ALWAYS GOES DOWN WITH HIS SHIP.
IF WE WANTED TO, WE COULD SINK EVERY BOAT FLOATING ABOVE US, ARTHUR. WE COULD DESTROY EVERY VESSEL IN THE WATER. BUT WE DON'T.
AND NOTHING SHOULD CHANGE THAT.
WHOEVER TOOK THE SCEPTER...MAYBE THEY WANTED YOU TO *THINK* THEY WERE ATLANTEAN.
I LOVE YOU, BROTHER.
AND I WISH YOU NOTHING BUT HAPPINESS.

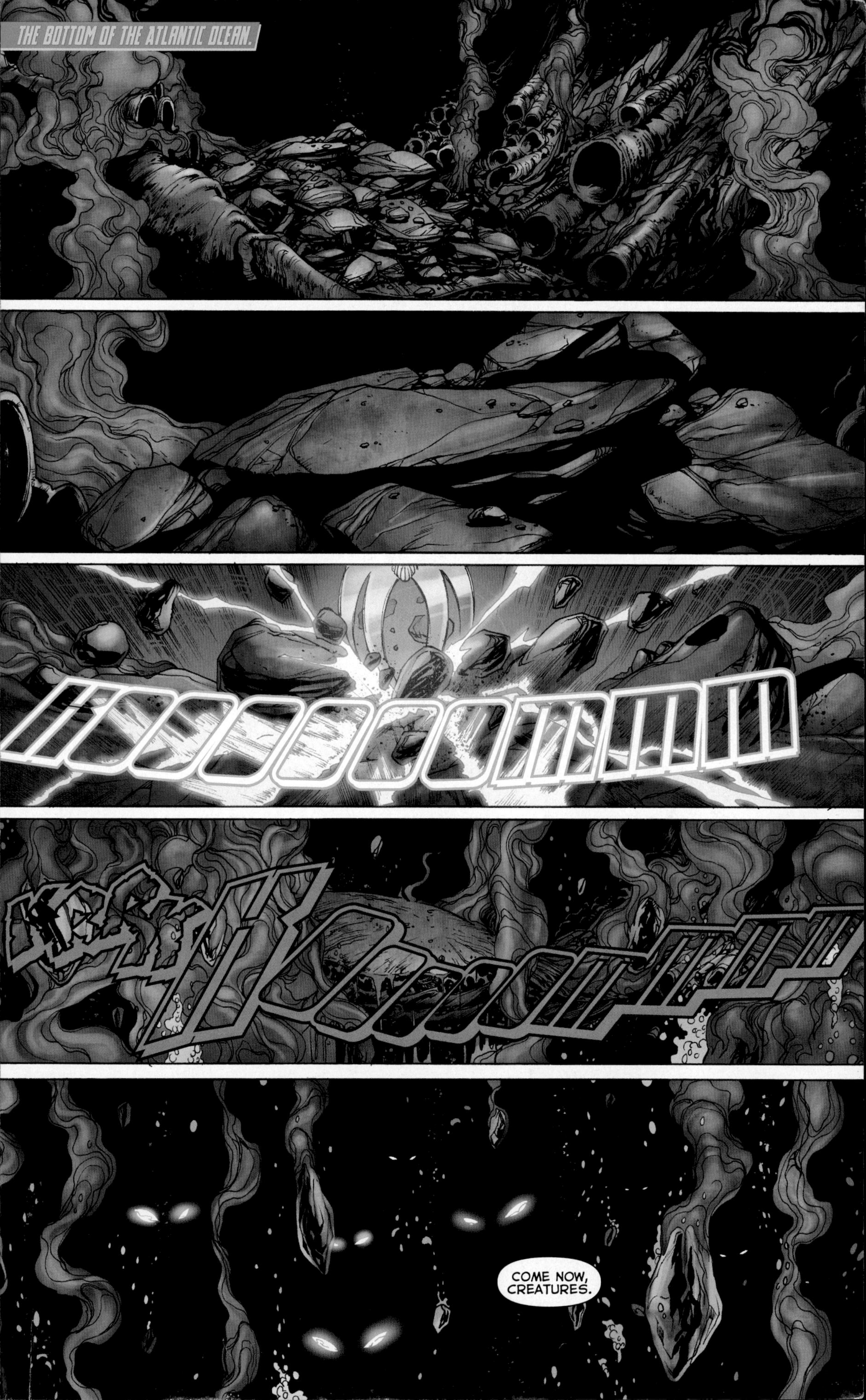
THE BOTTOM OF THE ATLANTIC OCEAN.
COME NOW, CREATURES.

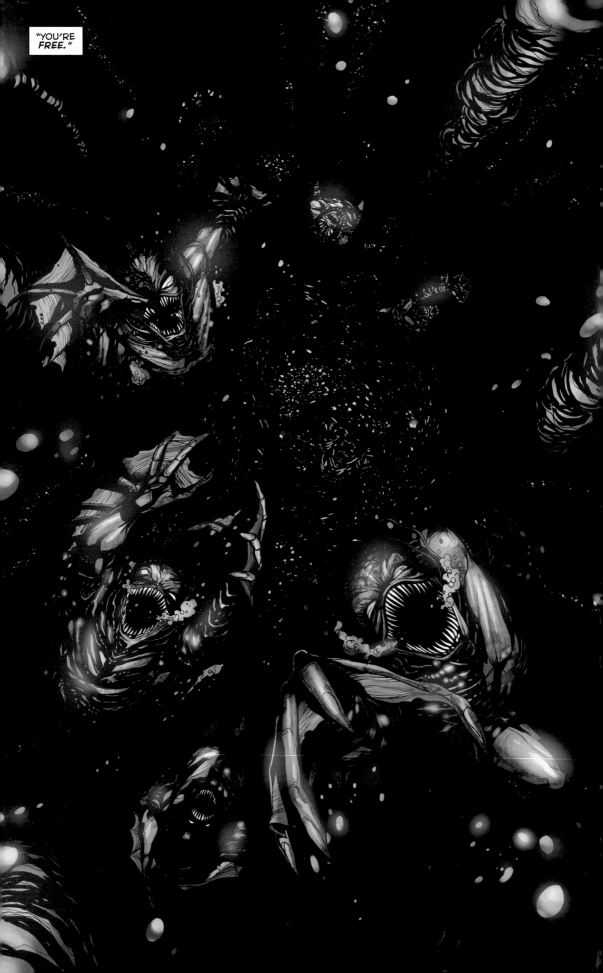

"YOU'RE FREE."

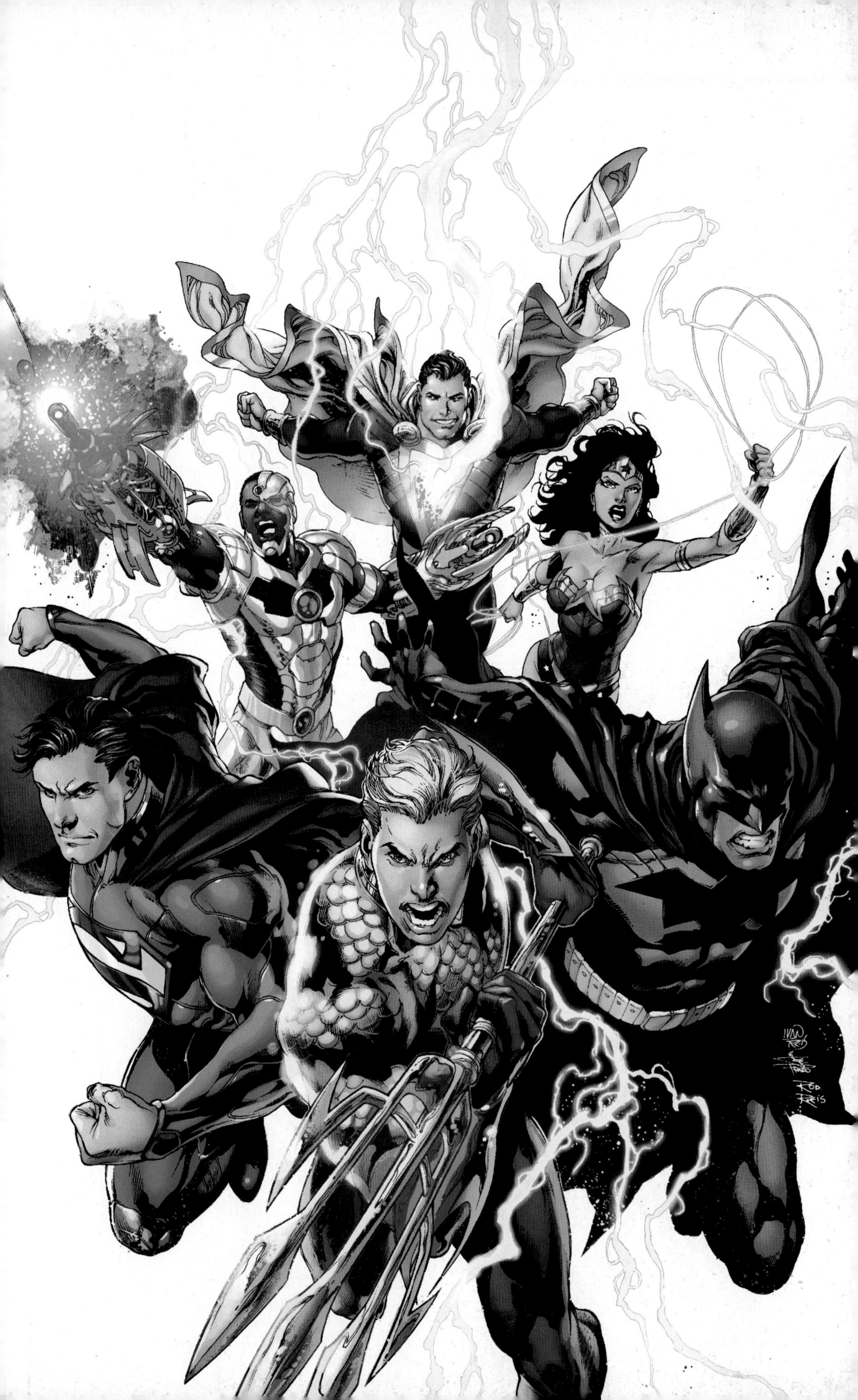

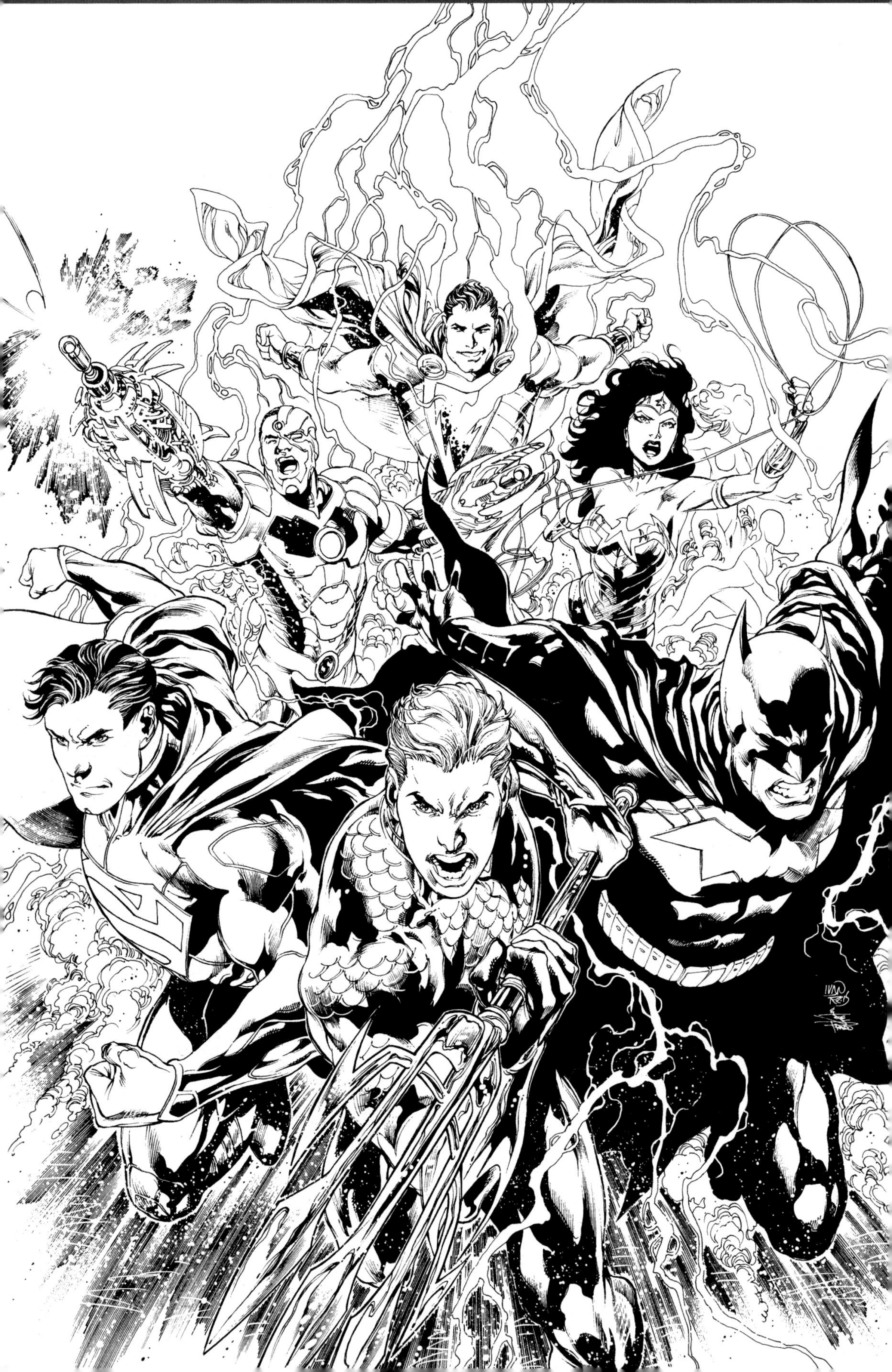

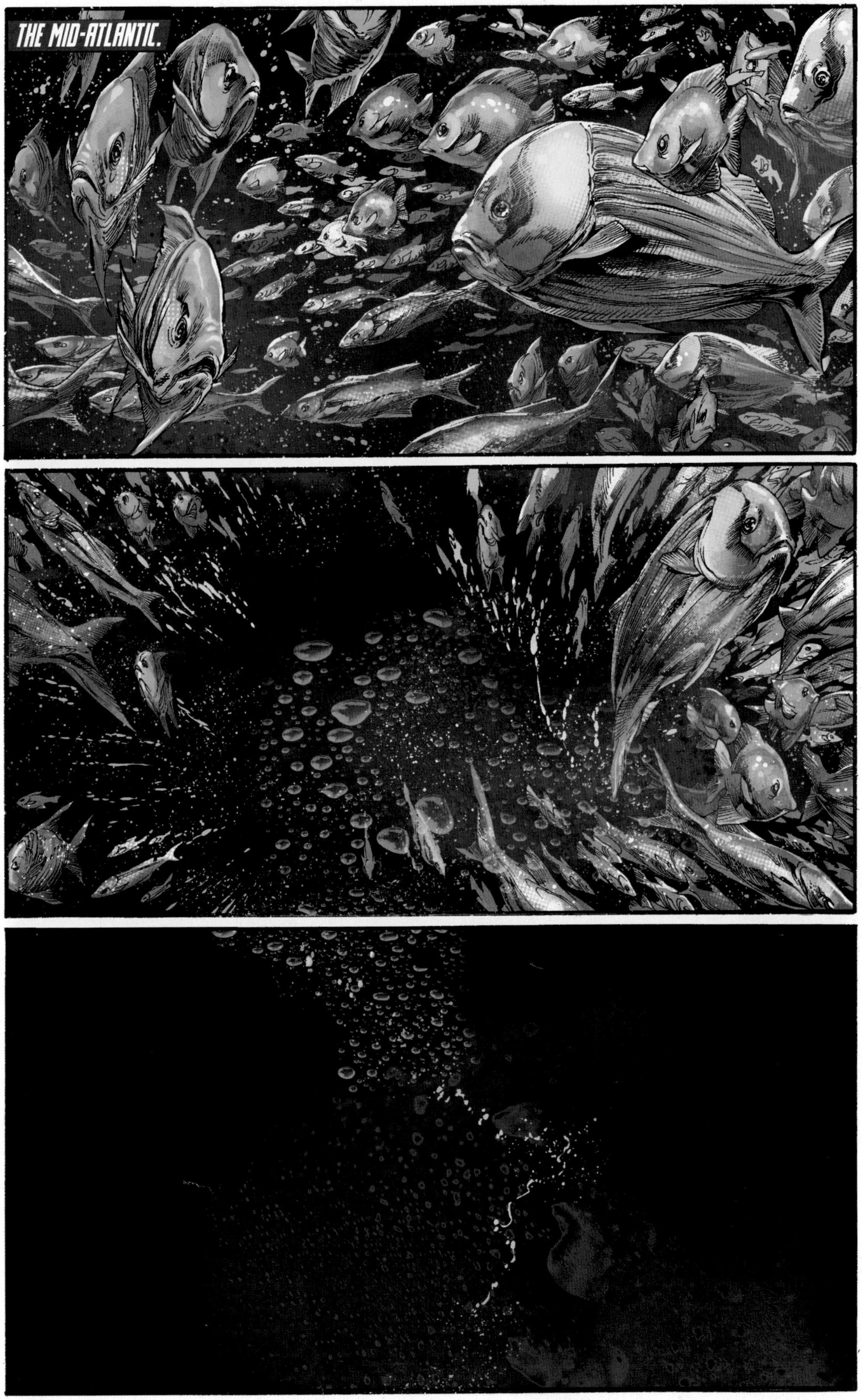
THE MID-ATLANTIC.

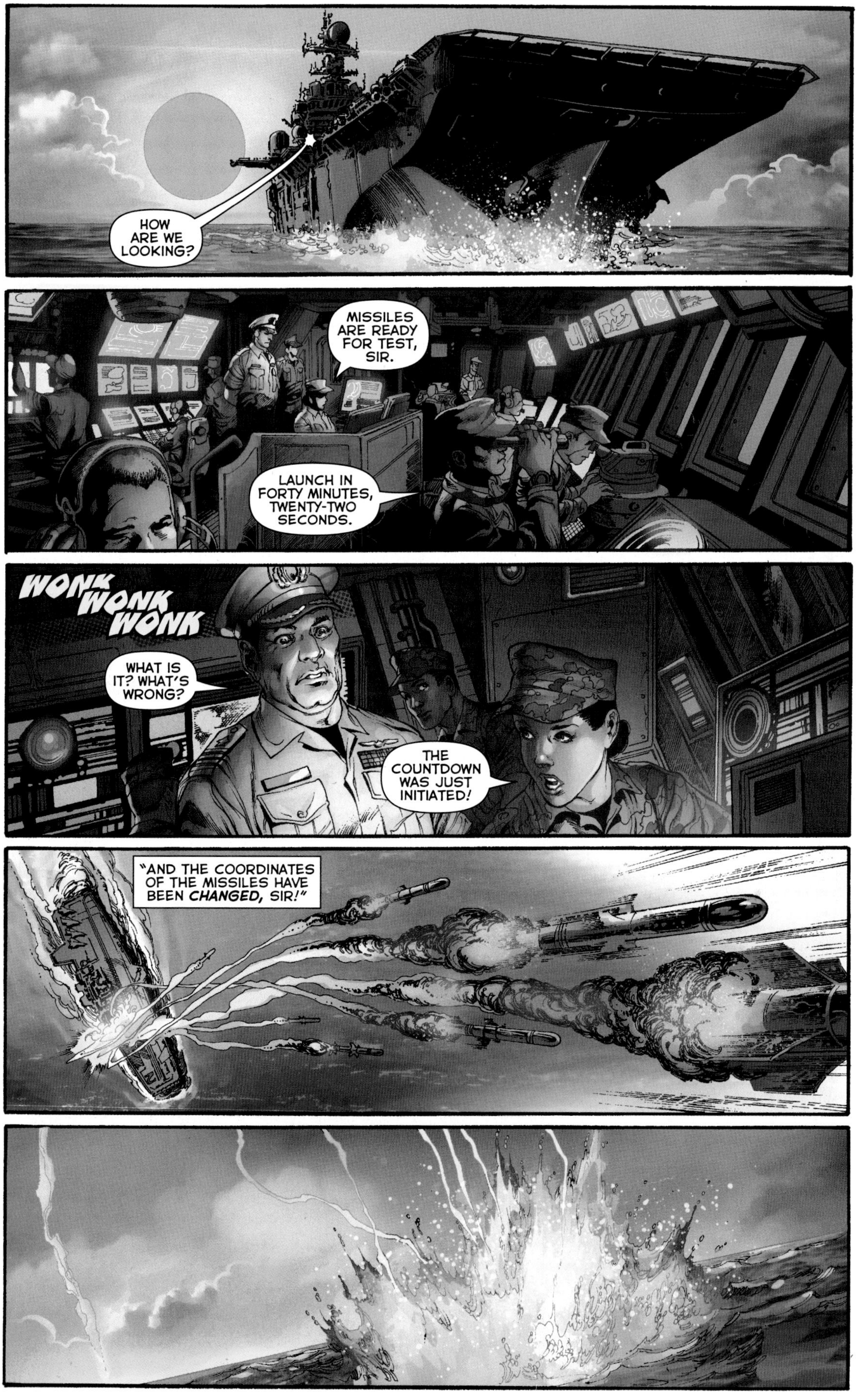
HOW ARE WE LOOKING?
MISSILES ARE READY FOR TEST, SIR.
LAUNCH IN FORTY MINUTES, TWENTY-TWO SECONDS.
WONK WONK WONK
WHAT IS IT? WHAT'S WRONG?
THE COUNTDOWN WAS JUST INITIATED!
"AND THE COORDINATES OF THE MISSILES HAVE BEEN CHANGED, SIR!"

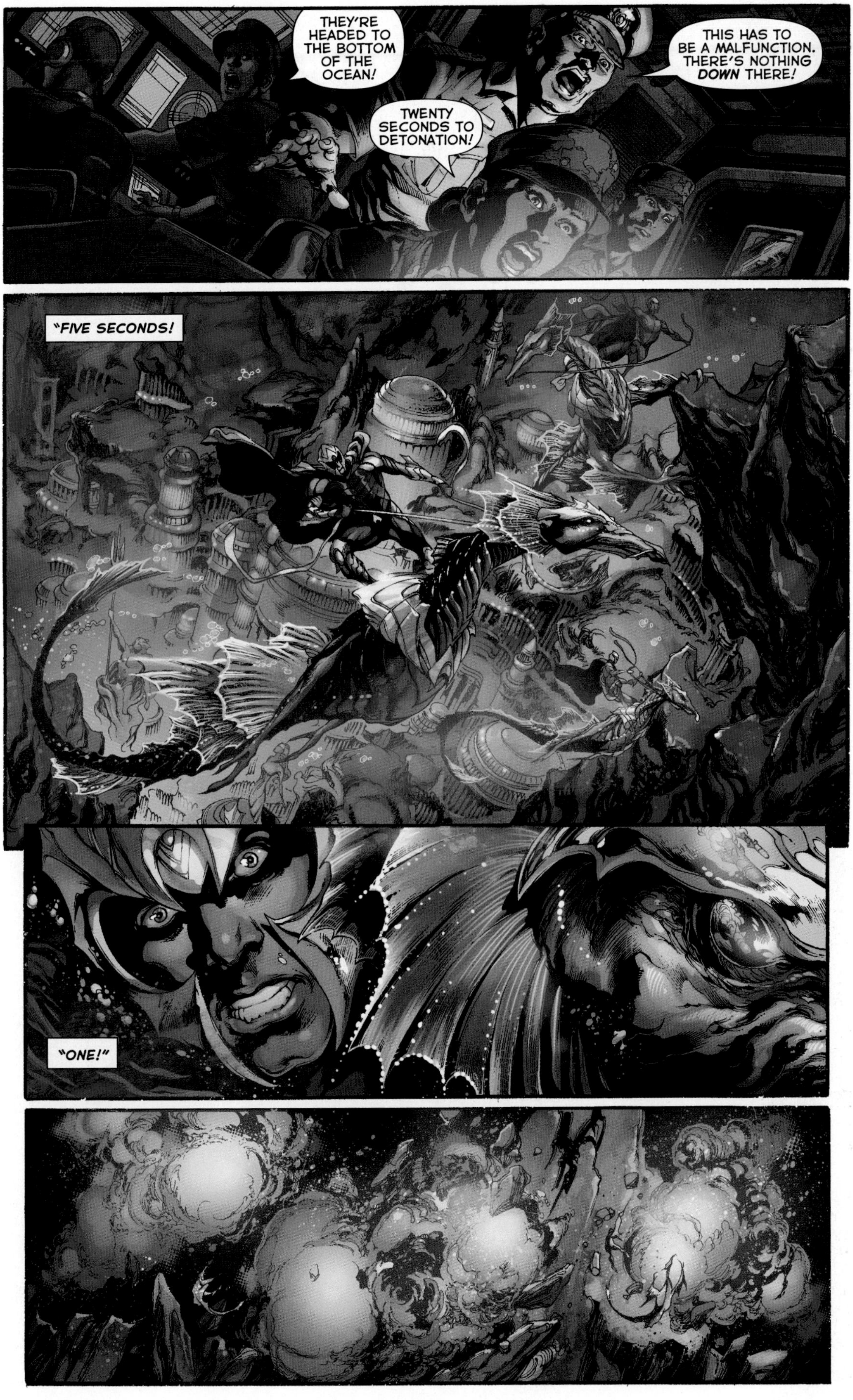
THEY'RE HEADED TO THE BOTTOM OF THE OCEAN!
THIS HAS TO BE A MALFUNCTION. THERE'S NOTHING *DOWN* THERE!
TWENTY SECONDS TO DETONATION!
"FIVE SECONDS!
"ONE!"

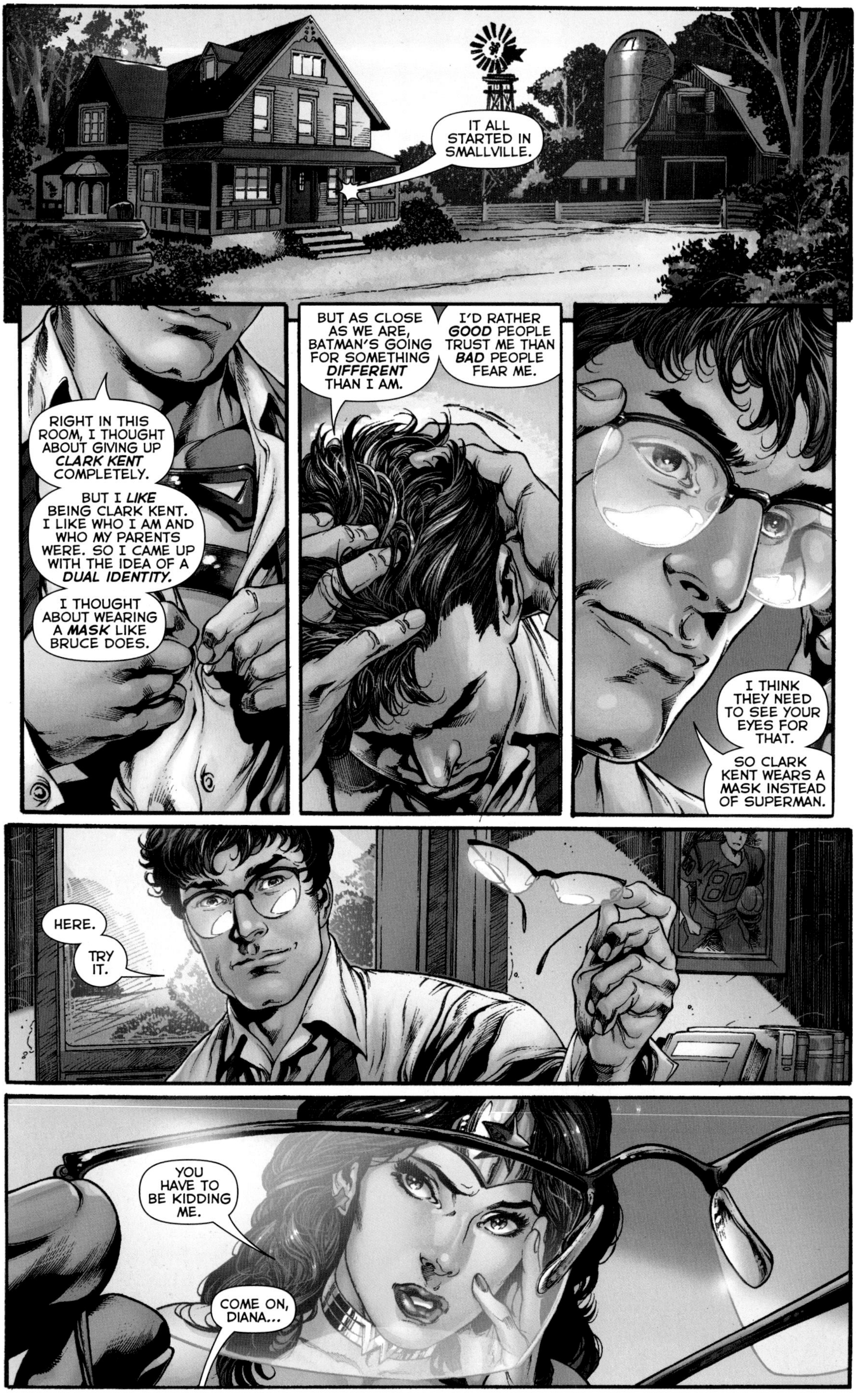
IT ALL STARTED IN SMALLVILLE.
RIGHT IN THIS ROOM, I THOUGHT ABOUT GIVING UP *CLARK KENT* COMPLETELY.
BUT I *LIKE* BEING CLARK KENT. I LIKE WHO I AM AND WHO MY PARENTS WERE. SO I CAME UP WITH THE IDEA OF A *DUAL IDENTITY.*
I THOUGHT ABOUT WEARING A *MASK* LIKE BRUCE DOES.
BUT AS CLOSE AS WE ARE, BATMAN'S GOING FOR SOMETHING *DIFFERENT* THAN I AM.
I'D RATHER *GOOD* PEOPLE TRUST ME THAN *BAD* PEOPLE FEAR ME.
I THINK THEY NEED TO SEE YOUR EYES FOR THAT.
SO CLARK KENT WEARS A MASK INSTEAD OF SUPERMAN.
HERE.
TRY IT.
YOU HAVE TO BE KIDDING ME.
COME ON, DIANA...

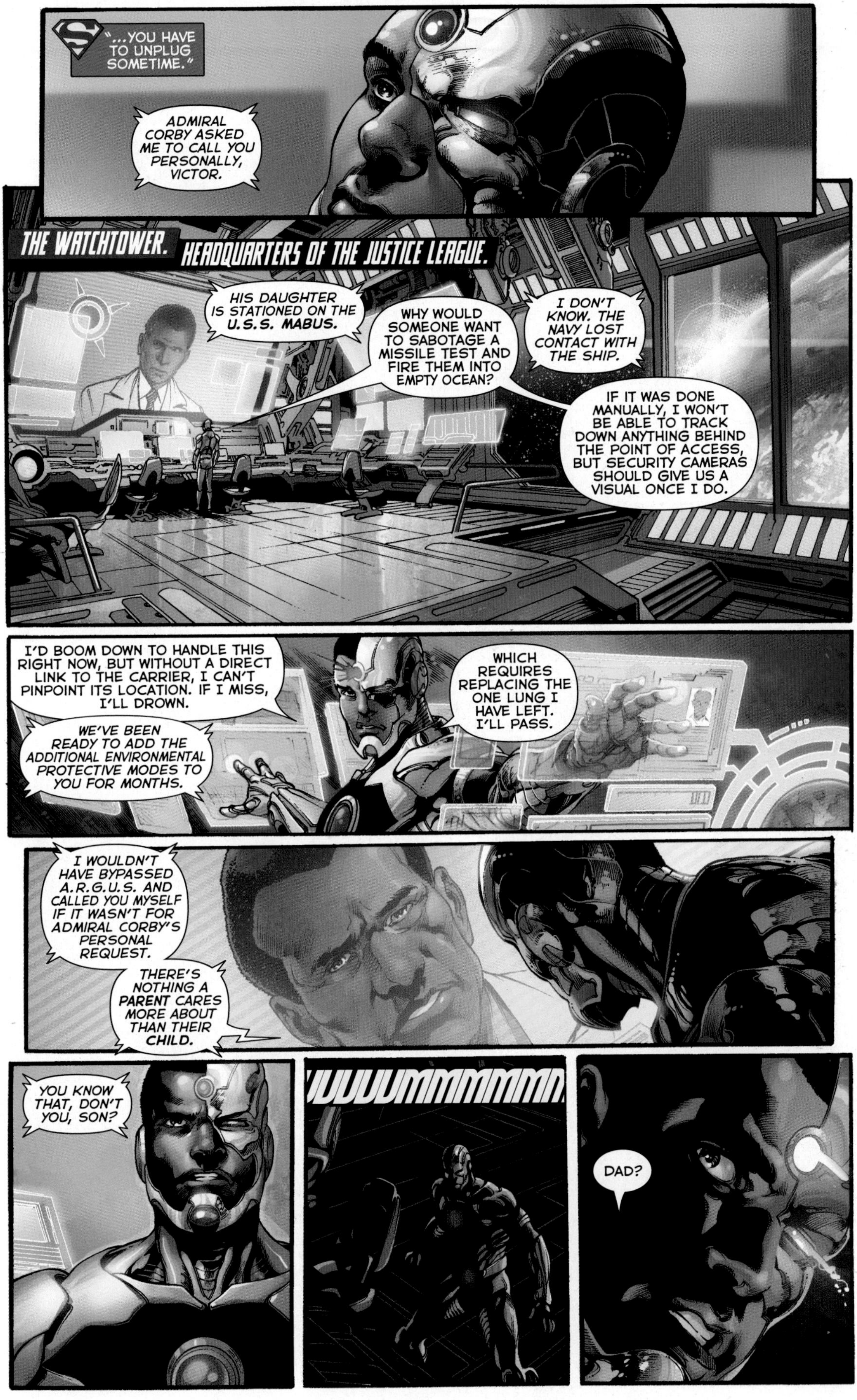
"...YOU HAVE TO UNPLUG SOMETIME."
ADMIRAL CORBY ASKED ME TO CALL YOU PERSONALLY, VICTOR.
THE WATCHTOWER.
HEADQUARTERS OF THE JUSTICE LEAGUE.
HIS DAUGHTER IS STATIONED ON THE U.S.S. MABUS.
WHY WOULD SOMEONE WANT TO SABOTAGE A MISSILE TEST AND FIRE THEM INTO EMPTY OCEAN?
I DON'T KNOW. THE NAVY LOST CONTACT WITH THE SHIP.
IF IT WAS DONE MANUALLY, I WON'T BE ABLE TO TRACK DOWN ANYTHING BEHIND THE POINT OF ACCESS, BUT SECURITY CAMERAS SHOULD GIVE US A VISUAL ONCE I DO.
I'D BOOM DOWN TO HANDLE THIS RIGHT NOW, BUT WITHOUT A DIRECT LINK TO THE CARRIER, I CAN'T PINPOINT ITS LOCATION. IF I MISS, I'LL DROWN.
WE'VE BEEN READY TO ADD THE ADDITIONAL ENVIRONMENTAL PROTECTIVE MODES TO YOU FOR MONTHS.
WHICH REQUIRES REPLACING THE ONE LUNG I HAVE LEFT. I'LL PASS.
I WOULDN'T HAVE BYPASSED A.R.G.U.S. AND CALLED YOU MYSELF IF IT WASN'T FOR ADMIRAL CORBY'S PERSONAL REQUEST.
THERE'S NOTHING A PARENT CARES MORE ABOUT THAN THEIR CHILD.
YOU KNOW THAT, DON'T YOU, SON?
VVVVVMMMMMMM
DAD?

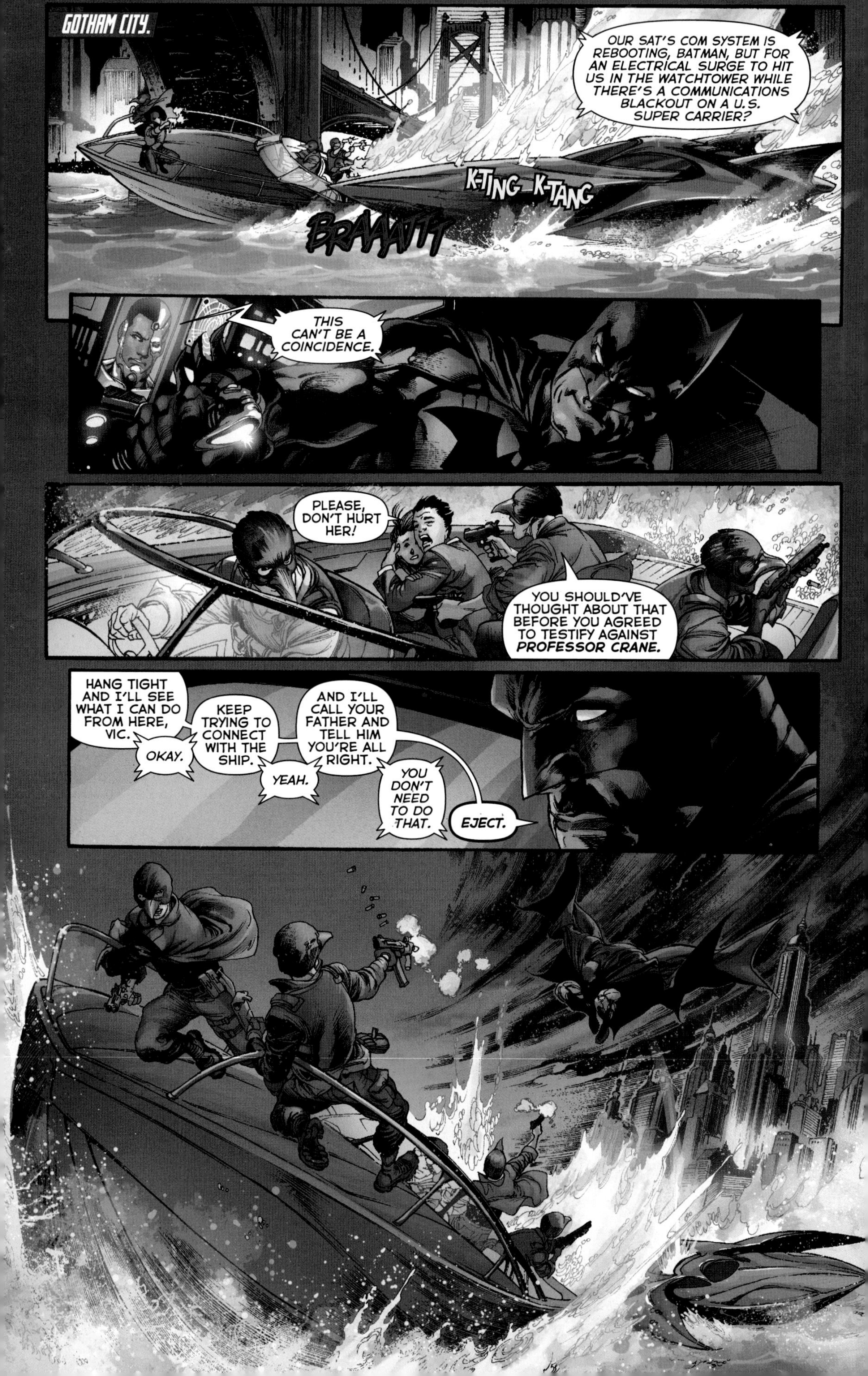
GOTHAM CITY.
OUR SAT'S COM SYSTEM IS REBOOTING, BATMAN, BUT FOR AN ELECTRICAL SURGE TO HIT US IN THE WATCHTOWER WHILE THERE'S A COMMUNICATIONS BLACKOUT ON A U.S. SUPER CARRIER?
K-TING K-TANG
BRAAATTT
THIS CAN'T BE A COINCIDENCE.
PLEASE, DON'T HURT HER!
YOU SHOULD'VE THOUGHT ABOUT THAT BEFORE YOU AGREED TO TESTIFY AGAINST *PROFESSOR CRANE.*
HANG TIGHT AND I'LL SEE WHAT I CAN DO FROM HERE, VIC.
OKAY.
KEEP TRYING TO CONNECT WITH THE SHIP.
YEAH.
AND I'LL CALL YOUR FATHER AND TELL HIM YOU'RE ALL RIGHT.
YOU DON'T NEED TO DO THAT.
EJECT.

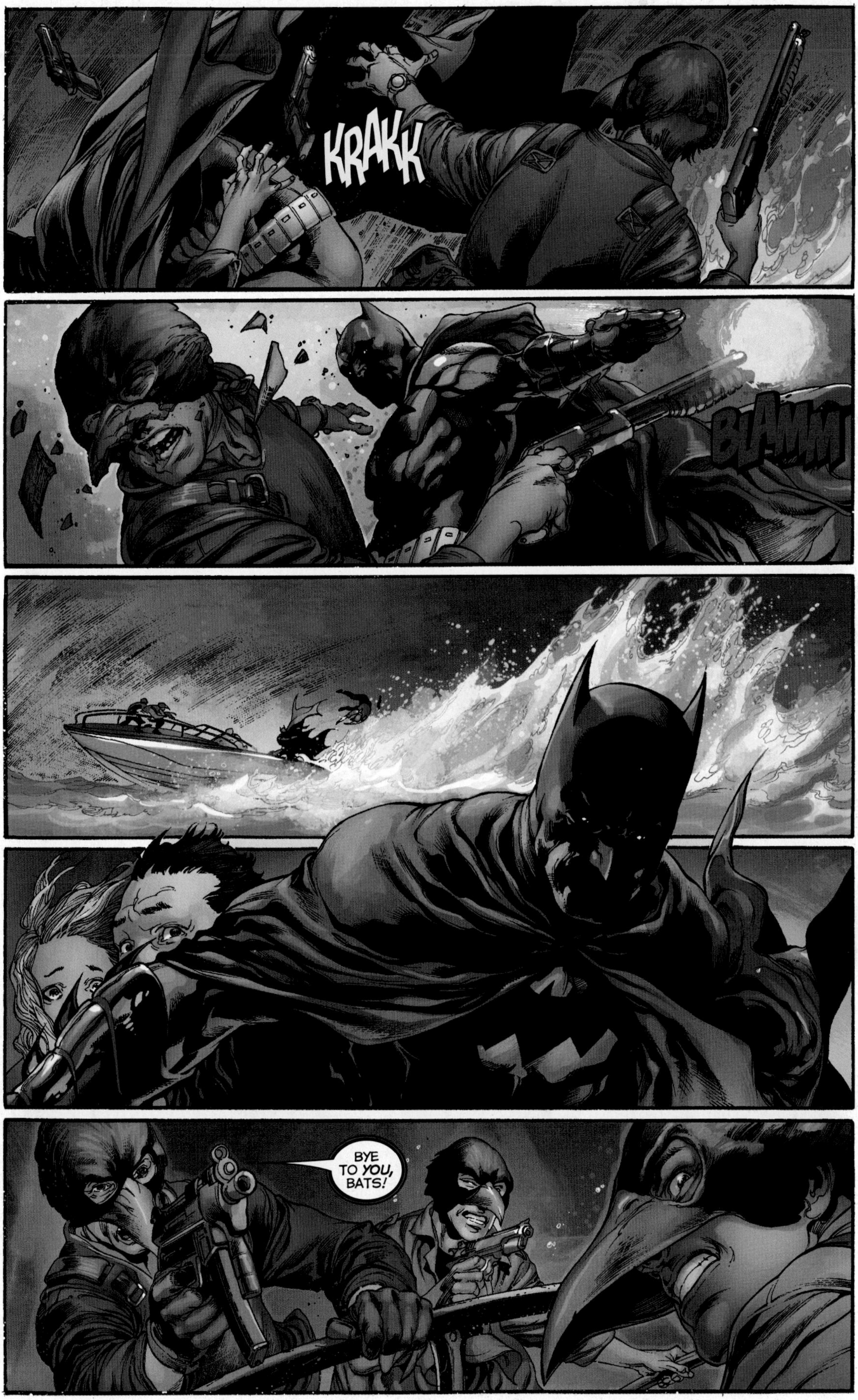
KRAKK
BLAMM!
BYE TO YOU, BATS!

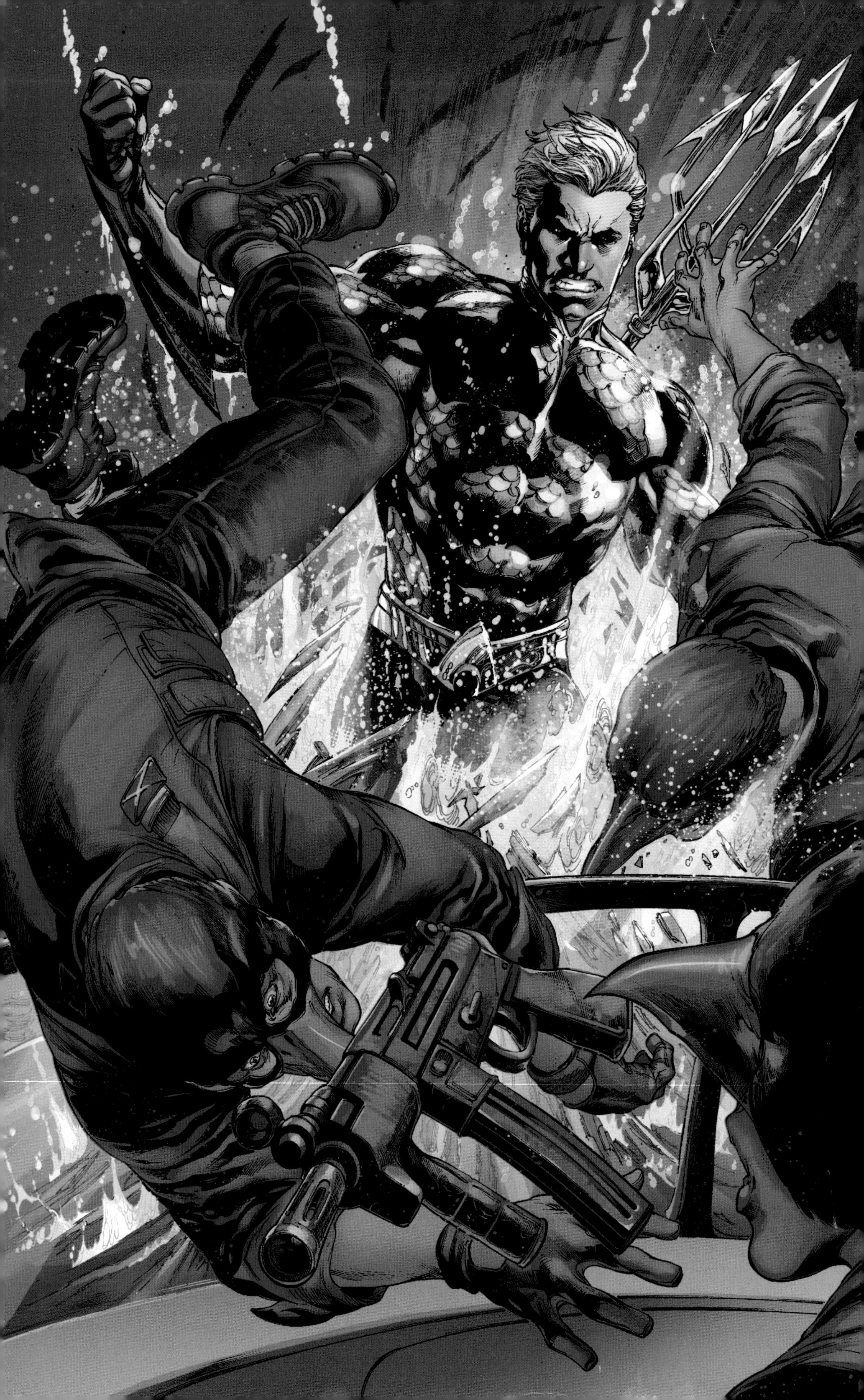

MY KID SAYS AQUAMAN'S *REALLY* FROM ATLANTIS.

THAT'S THE *TABLOIDS.* AQUAMAN LIVES IN A LIGHTHOUSE OUTSIDE OF BOSTON WITH HIS MERMAID.

YOUR COUSIN WORK WITH HIM LIKE GORDON WORKS WITH BATMAN?

HOW DO YOU KNOW *THAT?*

MY COUSIN'S ON THE FORCE UP THERE.

OH, YEAH, *SURE.* HE'S GOT AN *AQUA-SIGNAL* THAT THROWS *FIFTY POUNDS* OF FISH FOOD INTO THE BAY WHENEVER A SAILBOAT CAPSIZES.

HAHAHAHAHA

WHAT ARE YOU DOING IN GOTHAM?

DON'T TELL ME YOU'RE UPSET THAT I HELPED STOP THESE KIDNAPPERS?

I APPRECIATE THE ASSISTANCE TAKING DOWN SCARECROW'S MEN, EVEN IF I DON'T *NEED* IT.

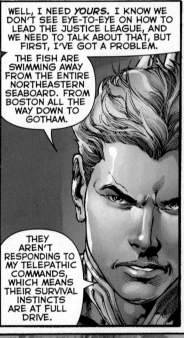

WELL, I NEED *YOURS.* I KNOW WE DON'T SEE EYE-TO-EYE ON HOW TO LEAD THE JUSTICE LEAGUE, AND WE NEED TO TALK ABOUT THAT, BUT FIRST, I'VE GOT A PROBLEM.

THE FISH ARE SWIMMING AWAY FROM THE ENTIRE NORTHEASTERN SEABOARD. FROM BOSTON ALL THE WAY DOWN TO GOTHAM.

THEY AREN'T RESPONDING TO MY TELEPATHIC COMMANDS, WHICH MEANS THEIR SURVIVAL INSTINCTS ARE AT FULL DRIVE.

THE LAST TIME THIS HAPPENED, IT WAS ON AN ISOLATED BEACH WHERE A GROUP OF FLESH-EATING CREATURES ROSE FROM THE OCEANS AND ATTACKED A TOWN.

I THOUGHT THEY'D BEEN...TAKEN CARE OF, BUT IF THESE THINGS ARE BACK AND IN NUMBERS GREATER THAN BEFORE, IT'S A JUSTICE LEAGUE-LEVEL PROBLEM, NOT JUST--

I'M NOT GOING TO JAIL AGAIN!

WATCH OUT! HE'S GOT MY GUN!

SBLOOOSHH!

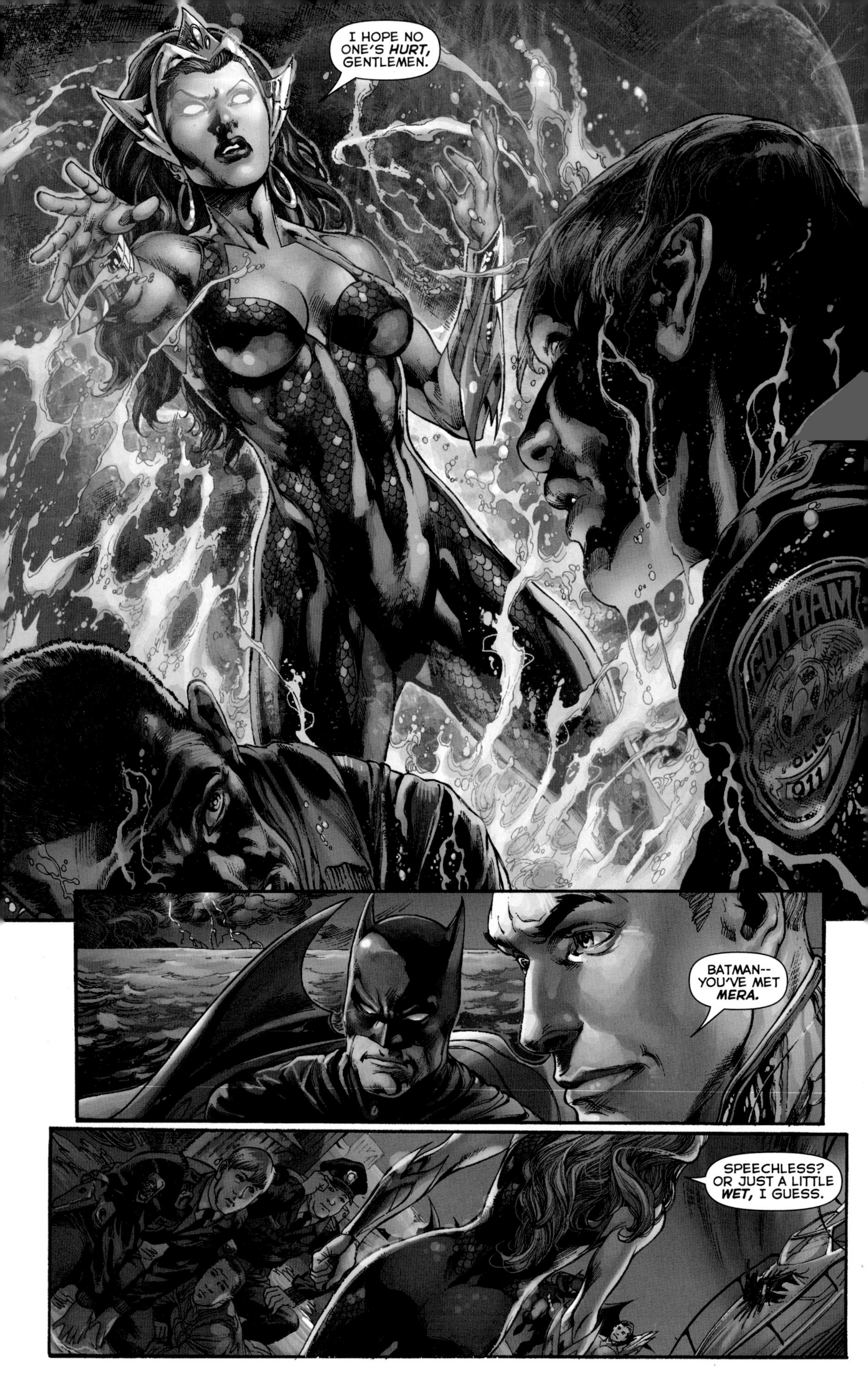
I HOPE NO ONE'S *HURT*, GENTLEMEN.
GOTHAM
POLICE
911
BATMAN-- YOU'VE MET *MERA*.
SPEECHLESS? OR JUST A LITTLE *WET*, I GUESS.

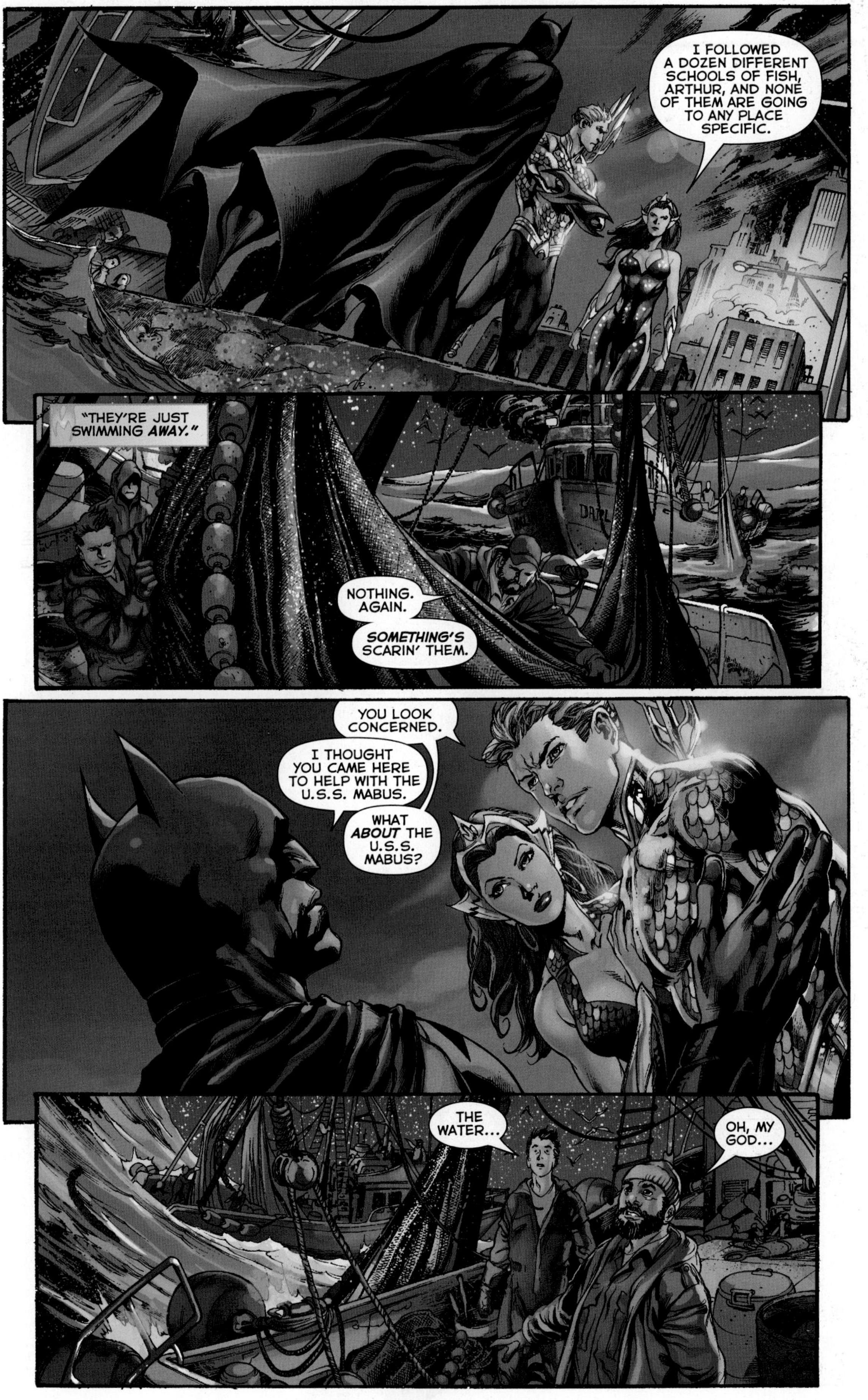
I FOLLOWED A DOZEN DIFFERENT SCHOOLS OF FISH, ARTHUR, AND NONE OF THEM ARE GOING TO ANY PLACE SPECIFIC.
"THEY'RE JUST SWIMMING AWAY."
NOTHING. AGAIN.
SOMETHING'S SCARIN' THEM.
YOU LOOK CONCERNED.
I THOUGHT YOU CAME HERE TO HELP WITH THE U.S.S. MABUS.
WHAT ABOUT THE U.S.S. MABUS?
THE WATER...
OH, MY GOD...

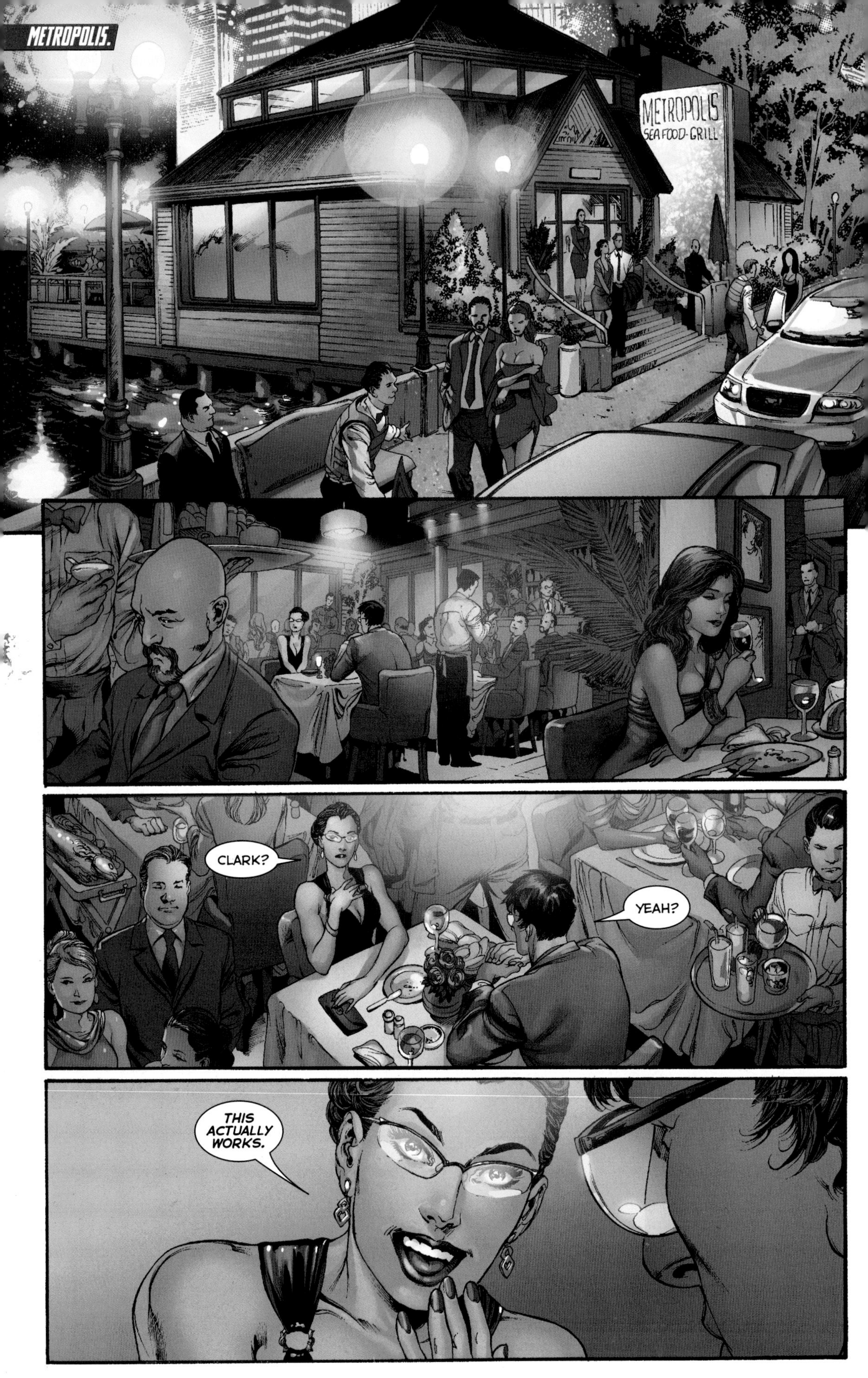
METROPOLIS.
METROPOLIS SEA FOOD-GRILL
CLARK?
YEAH?
THIS ACTUALLY WORKS.

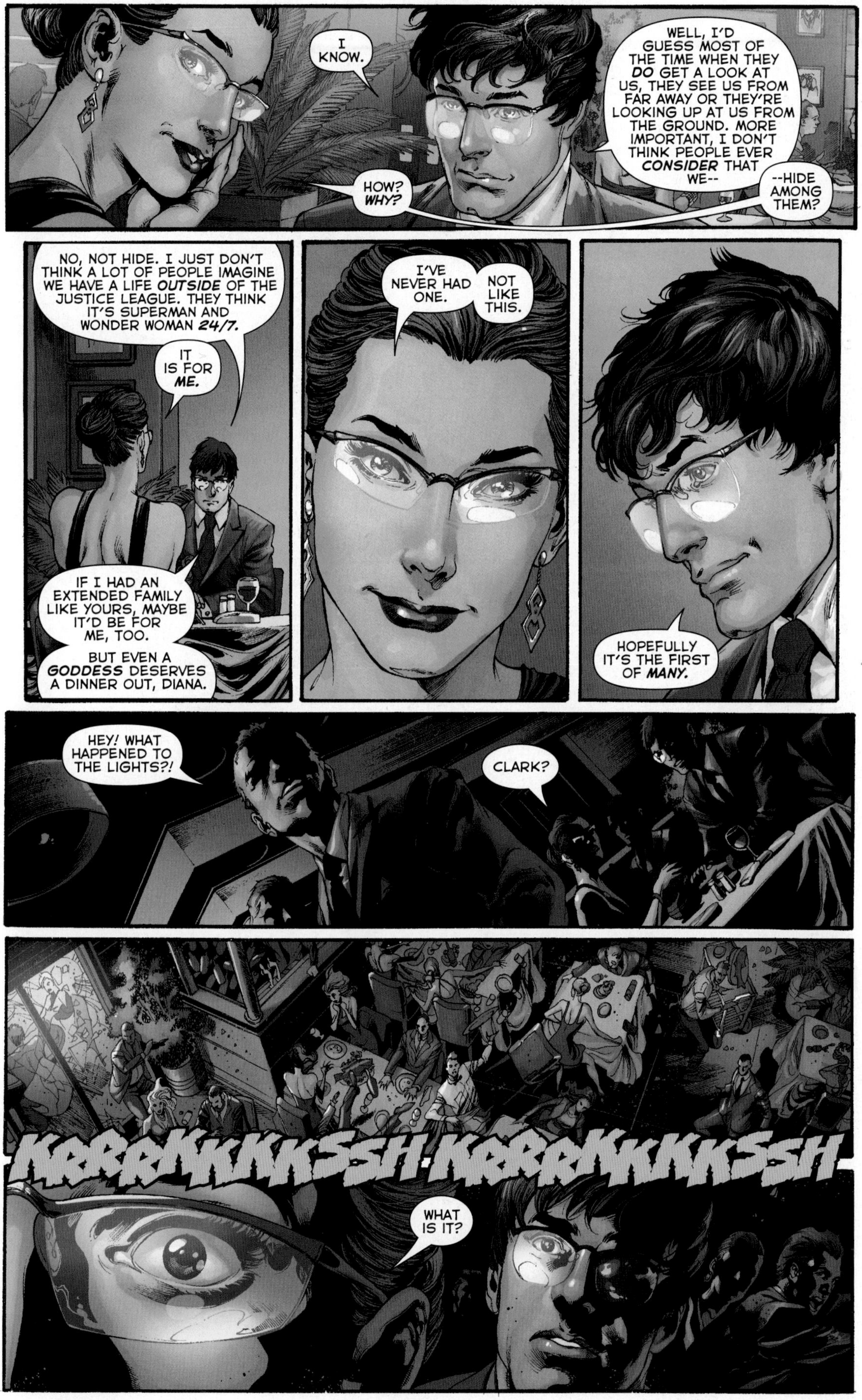
I KNOW.
WELL, I'D GUESS MOST OF THE TIME WHEN THEY DO GET A LOOK AT US, THEY SEE US FROM FAR AWAY OR THEY'RE LOOKING UP AT US FROM THE GROUND. MORE IMPORTANT, I DON'T THINK PEOPLE EVER CONSIDER THAT WE--
HOW? WHY?
--HIDE AMONG THEM?
NO, NOT HIDE. I JUST DON'T THINK A LOT OF PEOPLE IMAGINE WE HAVE A LIFE OUTSIDE OF THE JUSTICE LEAGUE. THEY THINK IT'S SUPERMAN AND WONDER WOMAN 24/7.
IT IS FOR ME.
IF I HAD AN EXTENDED FAMILY LIKE YOURS, MAYBE IT'D BE FOR ME, TOO.
BUT EVEN A GODDESS DESERVES A DINNER OUT, DIANA.
I'VE NEVER HAD ONE.
NOT LIKE THIS.
HOPEFULLY IT'S THE FIRST OF MANY.
HEY! WHAT HAPPENED TO THE LIGHTS?!
CLARK?
KRRRKKKKSSH-KRRRKKKKSSH
WHAT IS IT?

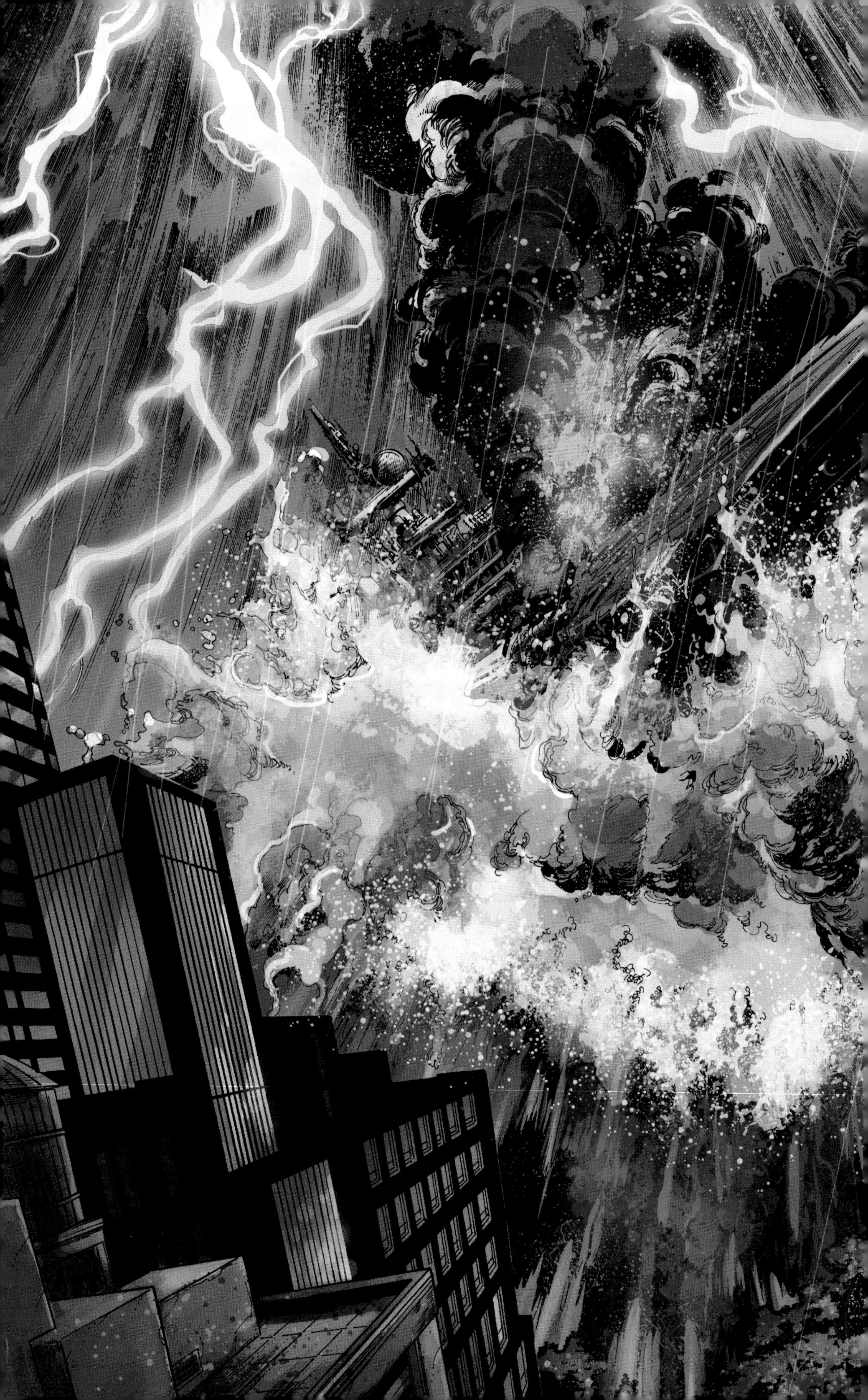

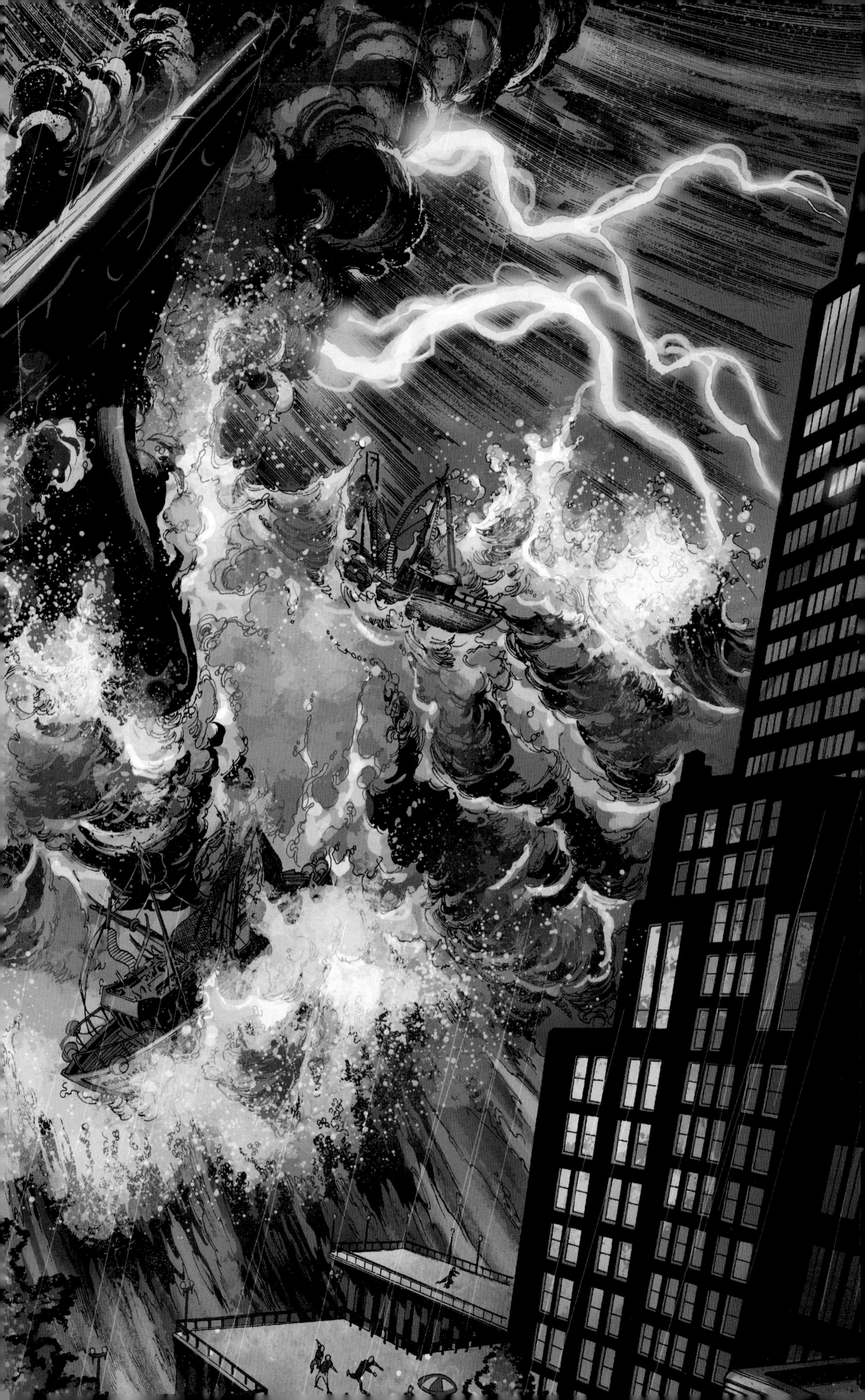

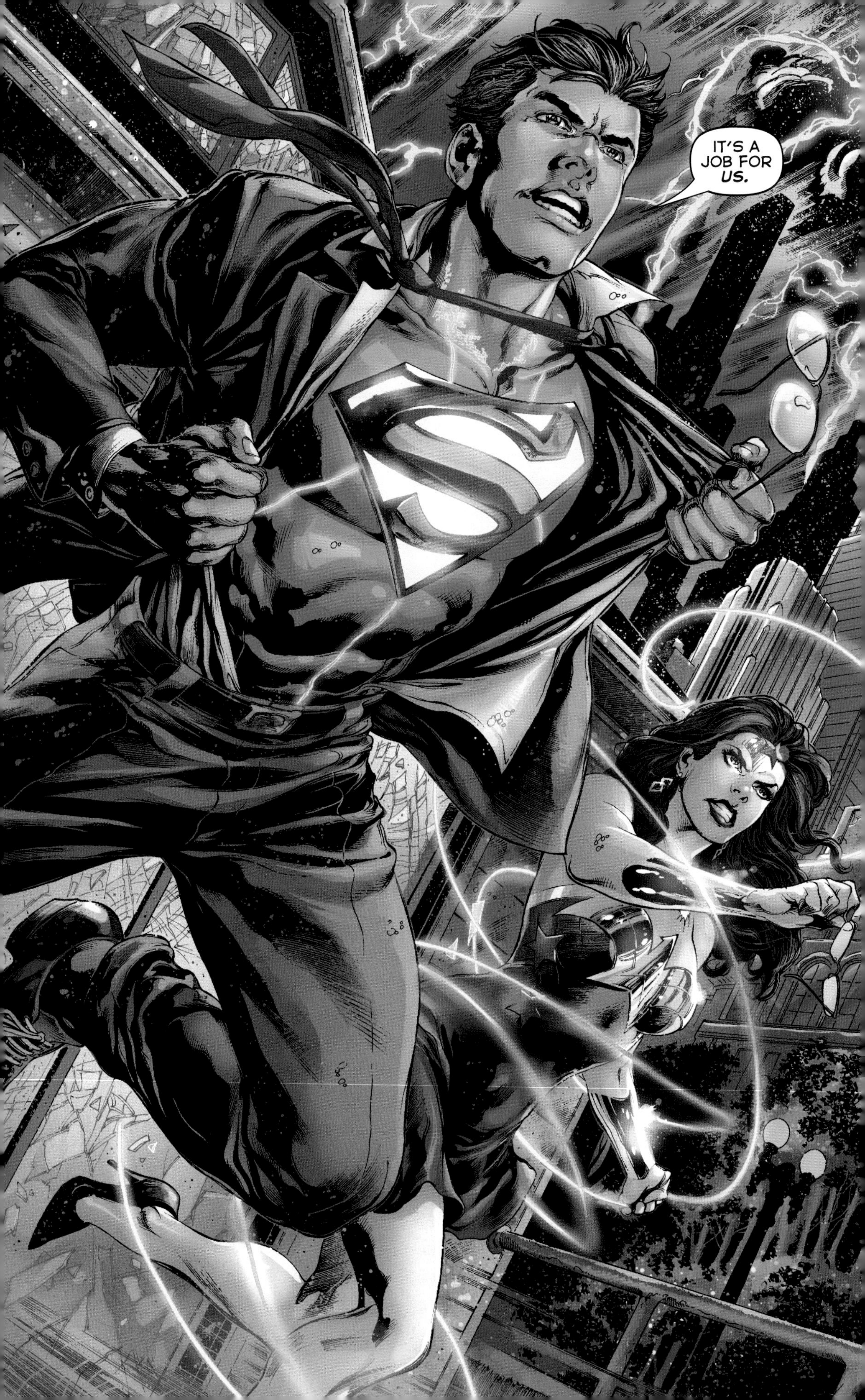
IT'S A JOB FOR US.

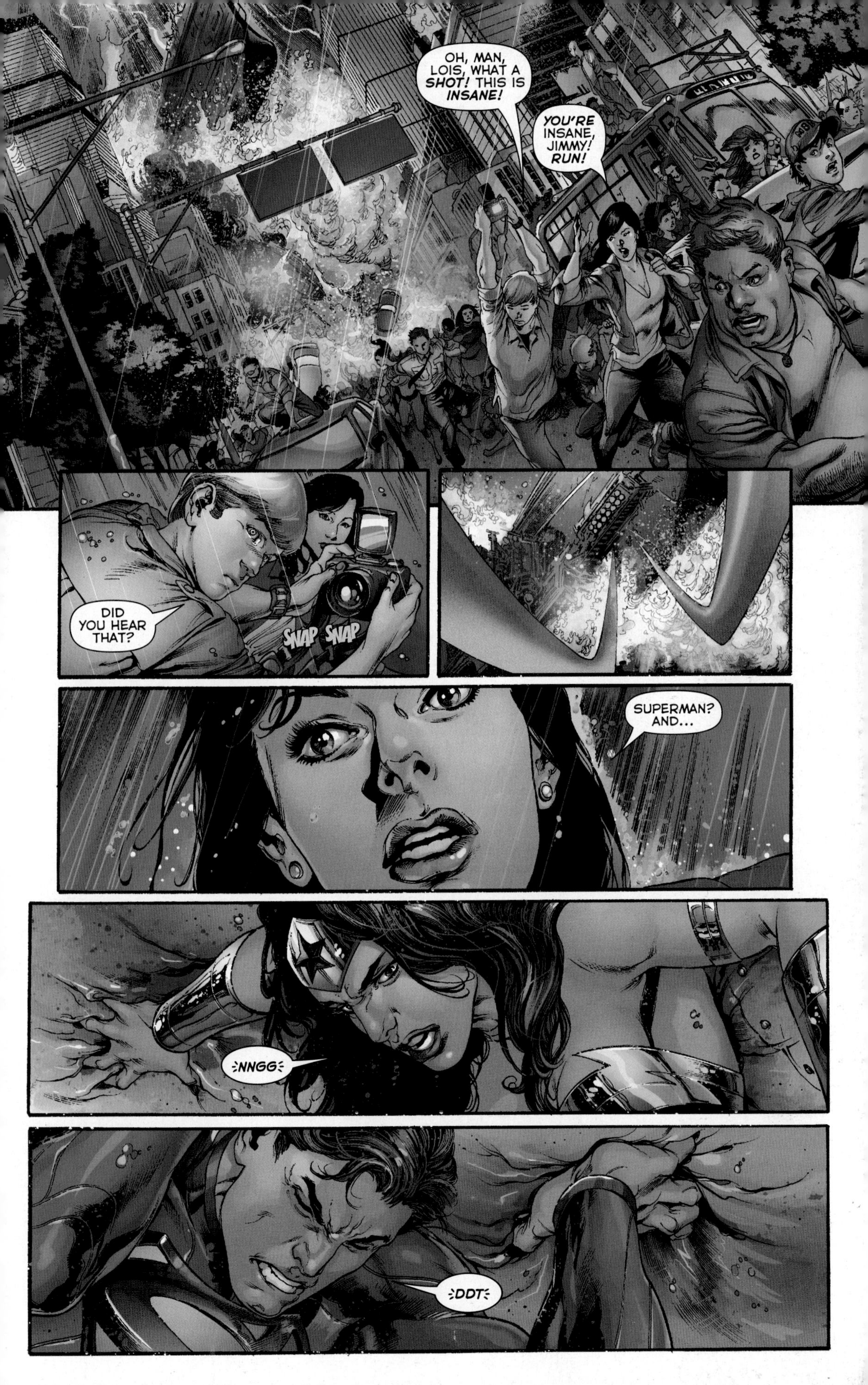

OH, MAN, LOIS, WHAT A SHOT! THIS IS INSANE!
YOU'RE INSANE, JIMMY! RUN!
DID YOU HEAR THAT?
SNAP SNAP
SUPERMAN? AND...
NNGG
DDT

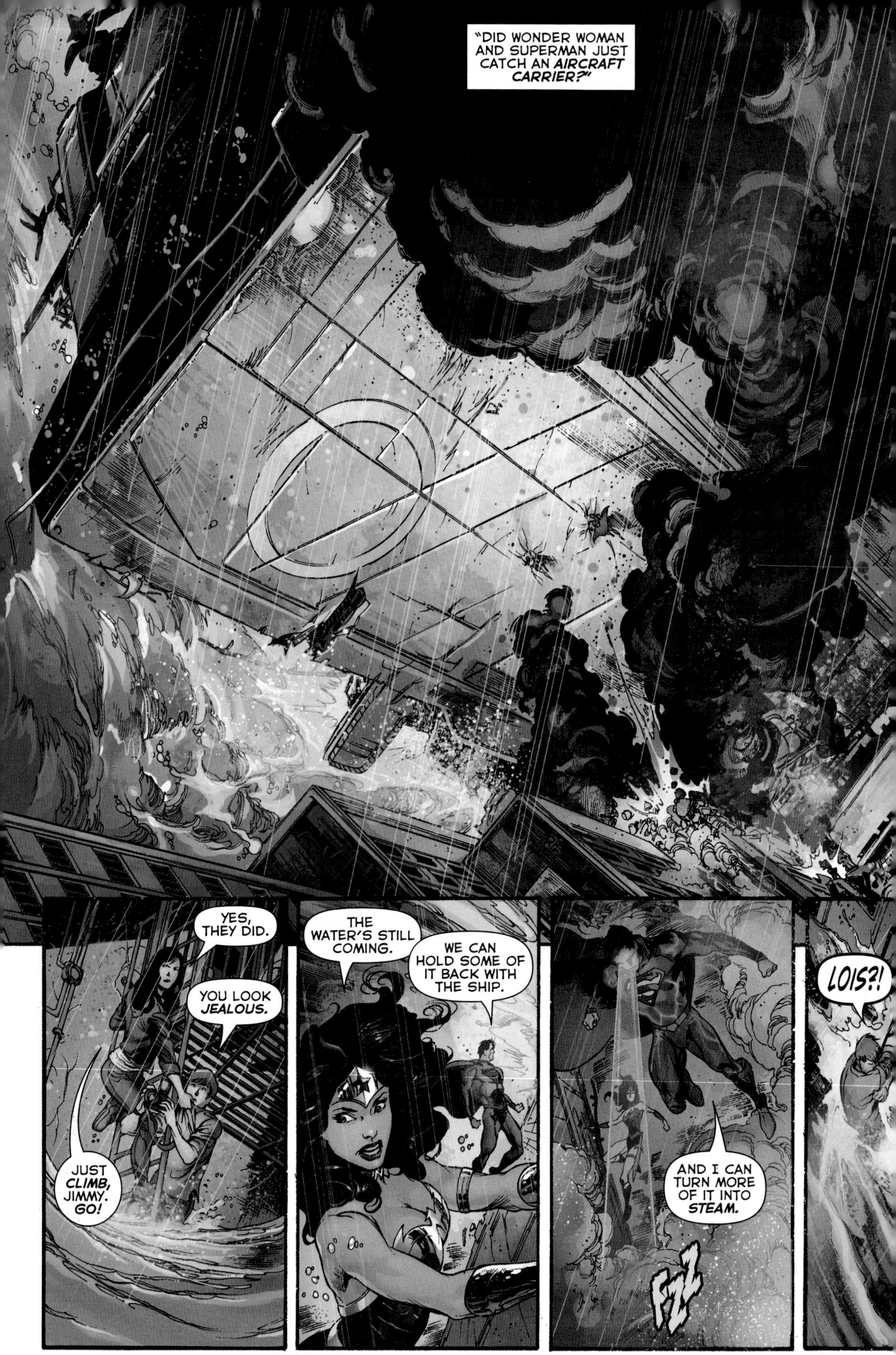
"DID WONDER WOMAN AND SUPERMAN JUST CATCH AN AIRCRAFT CARRIER?"
YES, THEY DID.
YOU LOOK JEALOUS.
JUST CLIMB, JIMMY. GO!
THE WATER'S STILL COMING.
WE CAN HOLD SOME OF IT BACK WITH THE SHIP.
AND I CAN TURN MORE OF IT INTO STEAM.
FZZ
LOIS?!

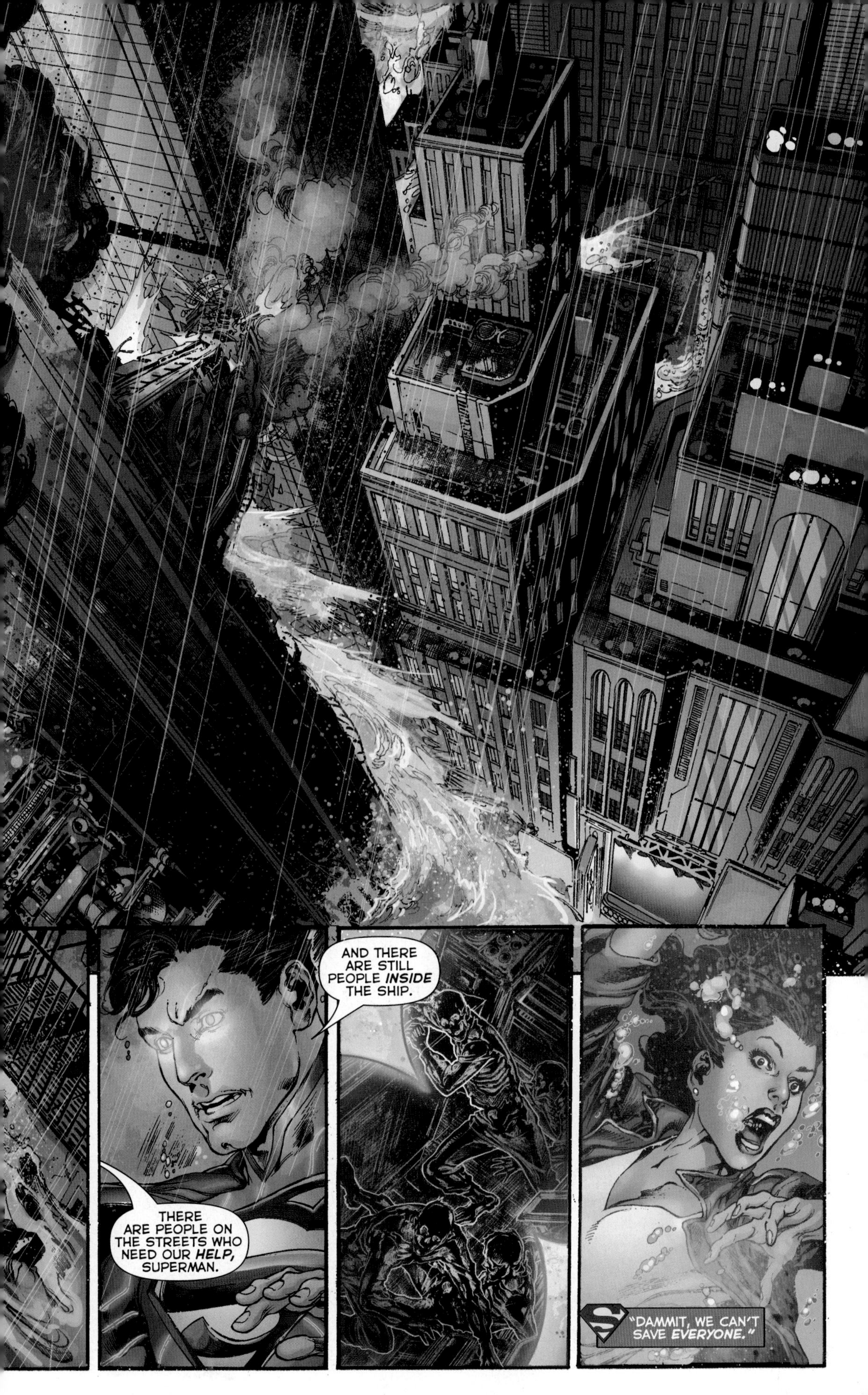
THERE ARE PEOPLE ON THE STREETS WHO NEED OUR HELP, SUPERMAN.
AND THERE ARE STILL PEOPLE INSIDE THE SHIP.
"DAMMIT, WE CAN'T SAVE EVERYONE."

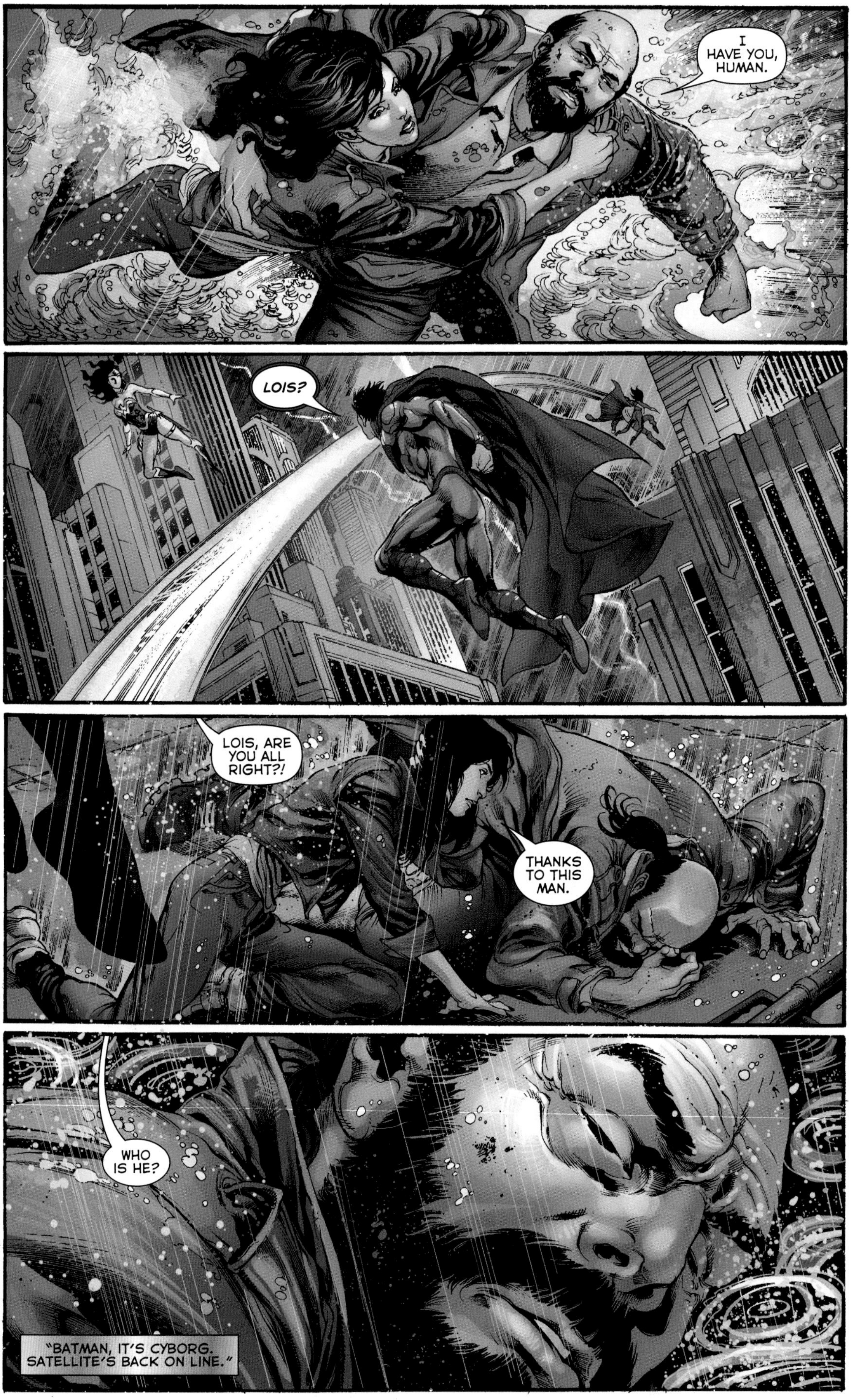
I HAVE YOU, HUMAN.
LOIS?
LOIS, ARE YOU ALL RIGHT?!
THANKS TO THIS MAN.
WHO IS HE?
"BATMAN, IT'S CYBORG. SATELLITE'S BACK ON LINE."

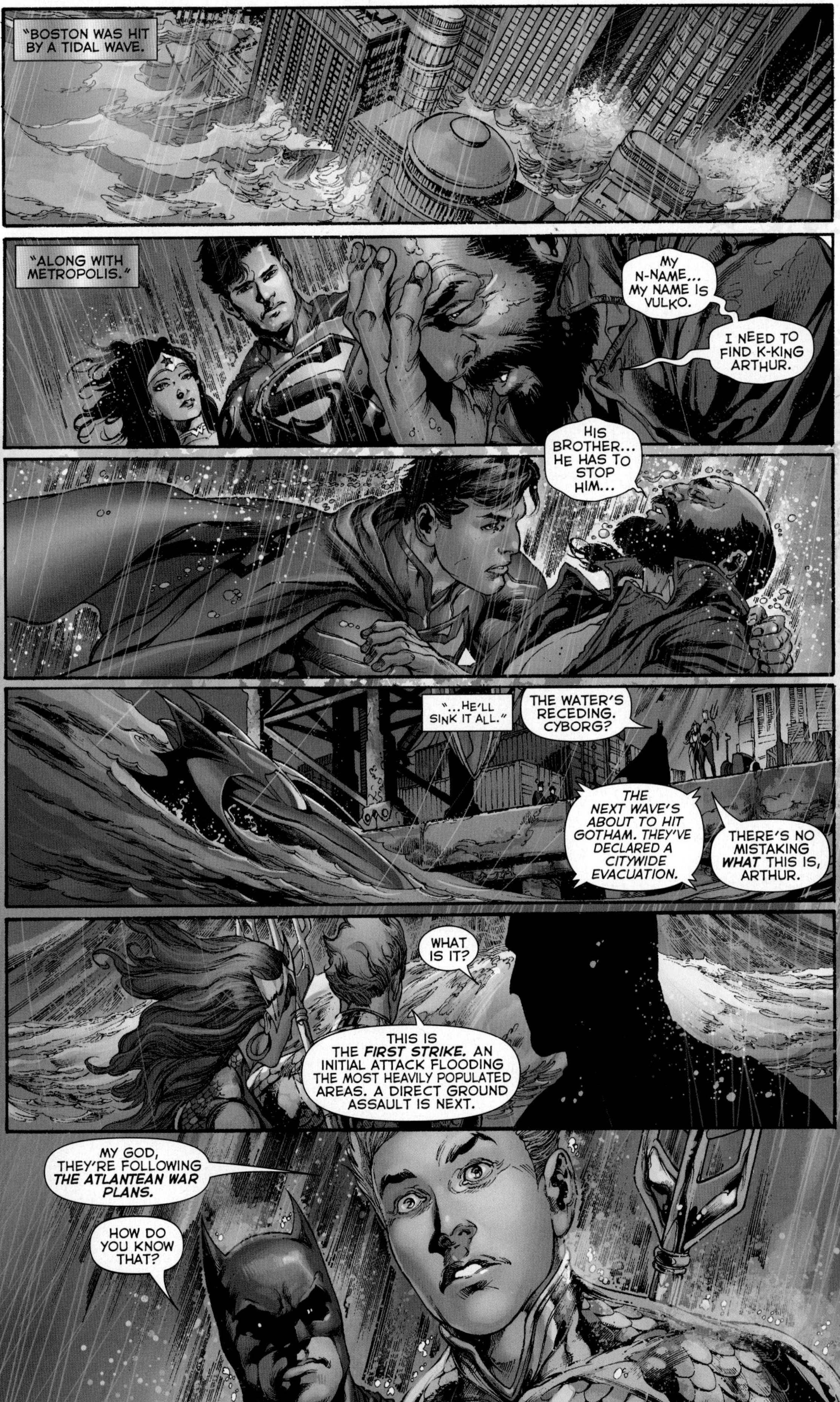
"BOSTON WAS HIT BY A TIDAL WAVE.
"ALONG WITH METROPOLIS."
MY N-NAME... MY NAME IS VULKO.
I NEED TO FIND K-KING ARTHUR.
HIS BROTHER... HE HAS TO STOP HIM...
"...HE'LL SINK IT ALL."
THE WATER'S RECEDING. CYBORG?
THE NEXT WAVE'S ABOUT TO HIT GOTHAM. THEY'VE DECLARED A CITYWIDE EVACUATION.
THERE'S NO MISTAKING WHAT THIS IS, ARTHUR.
WHAT IS IT?
THIS IS THE FIRST STRIKE. AN INITIAL ATTACK FLOODING THE MOST HEAVILY POPULATED AREAS. A DIRECT GROUND ASSAULT IS NEXT.
MY GOD, THEY'RE FOLLOWING THE ATLANTEAN WAR PLANS.
HOW DO YOU KNOW THAT?

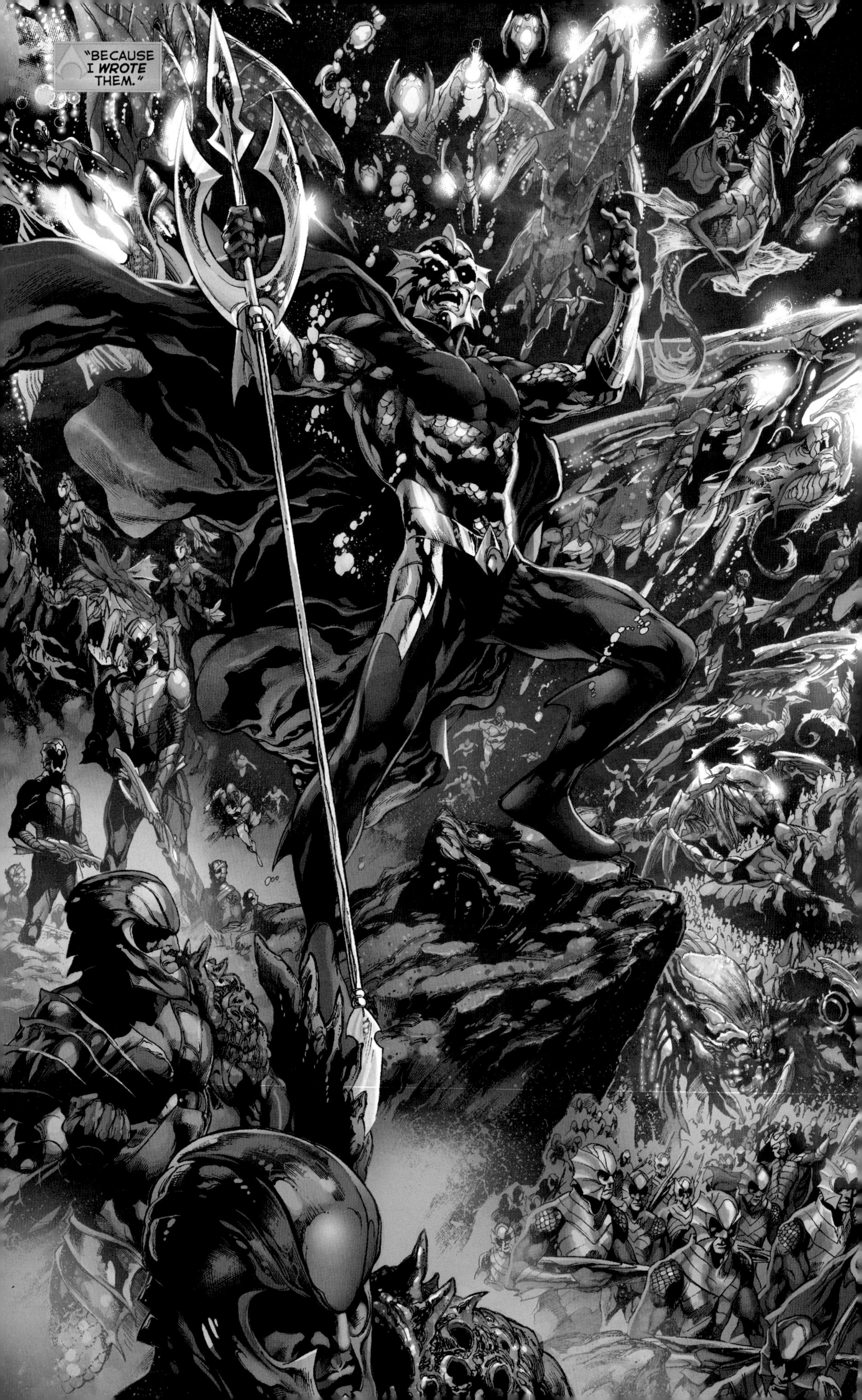
"BECAUSE I *WROTE* THEM."

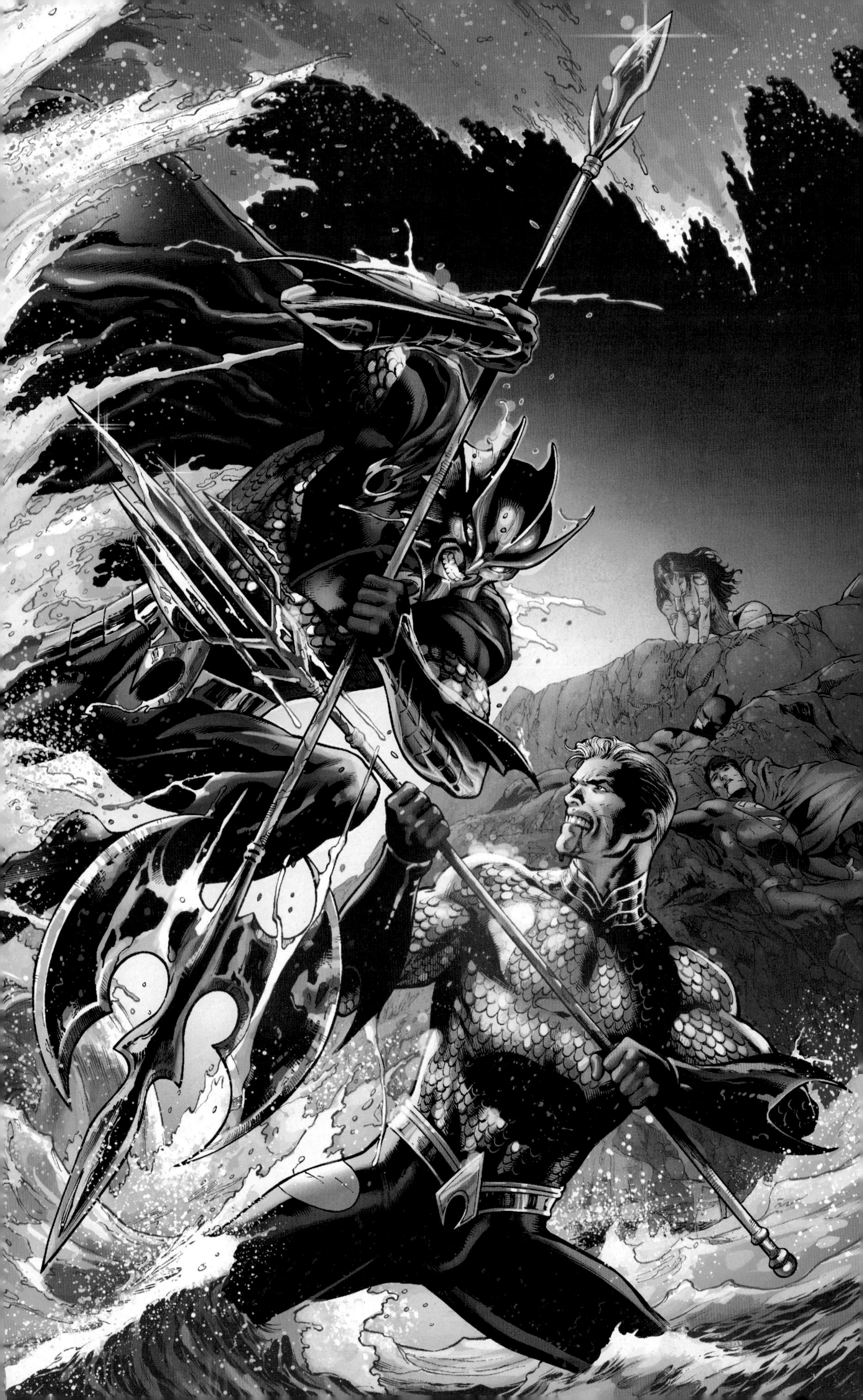

GEOFF JOHNS writer PAUL PELLETIER penciller ART THIBERT with KARL KESEL inkers cover by EDDY BARROWS, EBER FERREIRA & ROD REIS

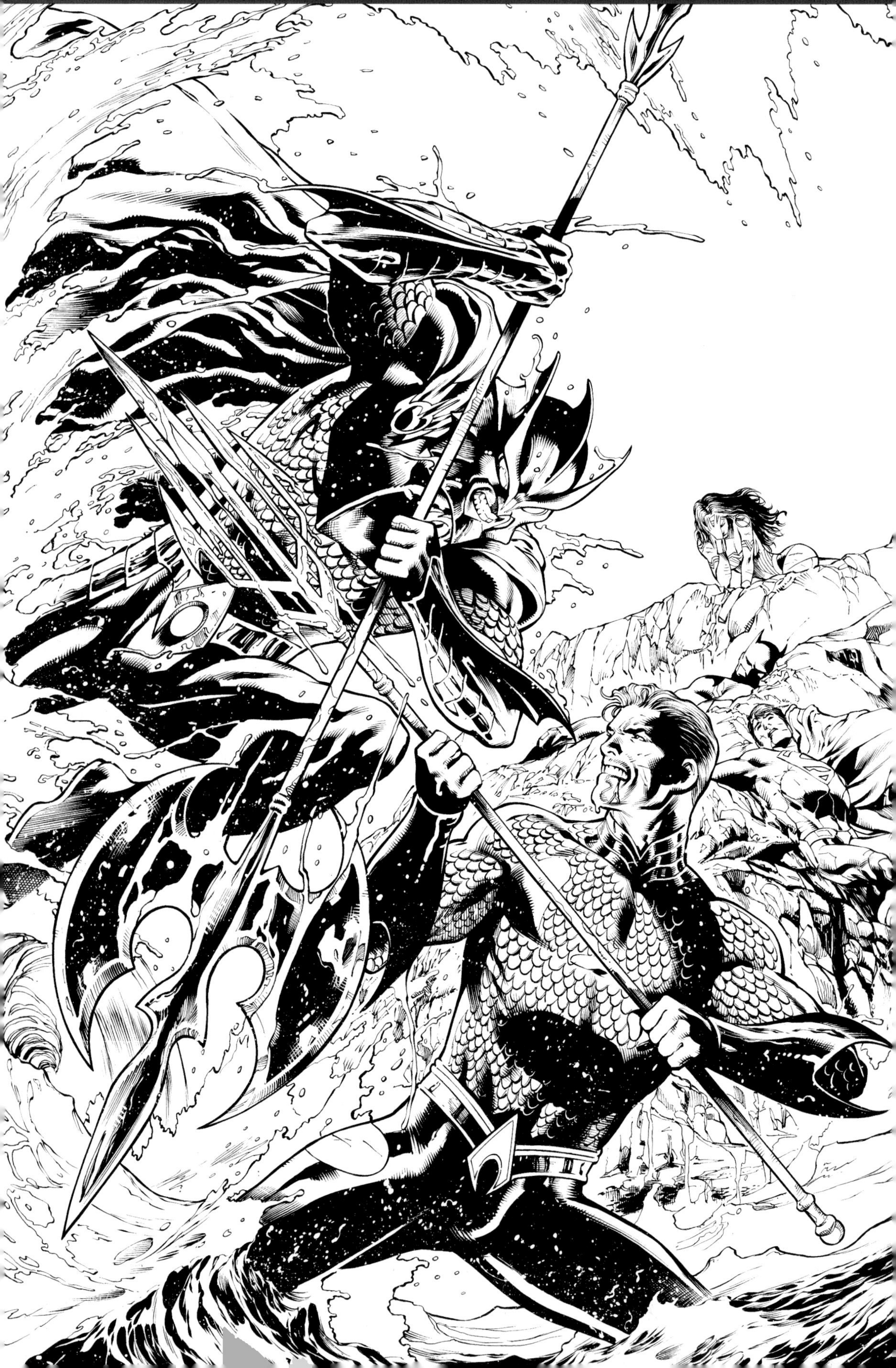

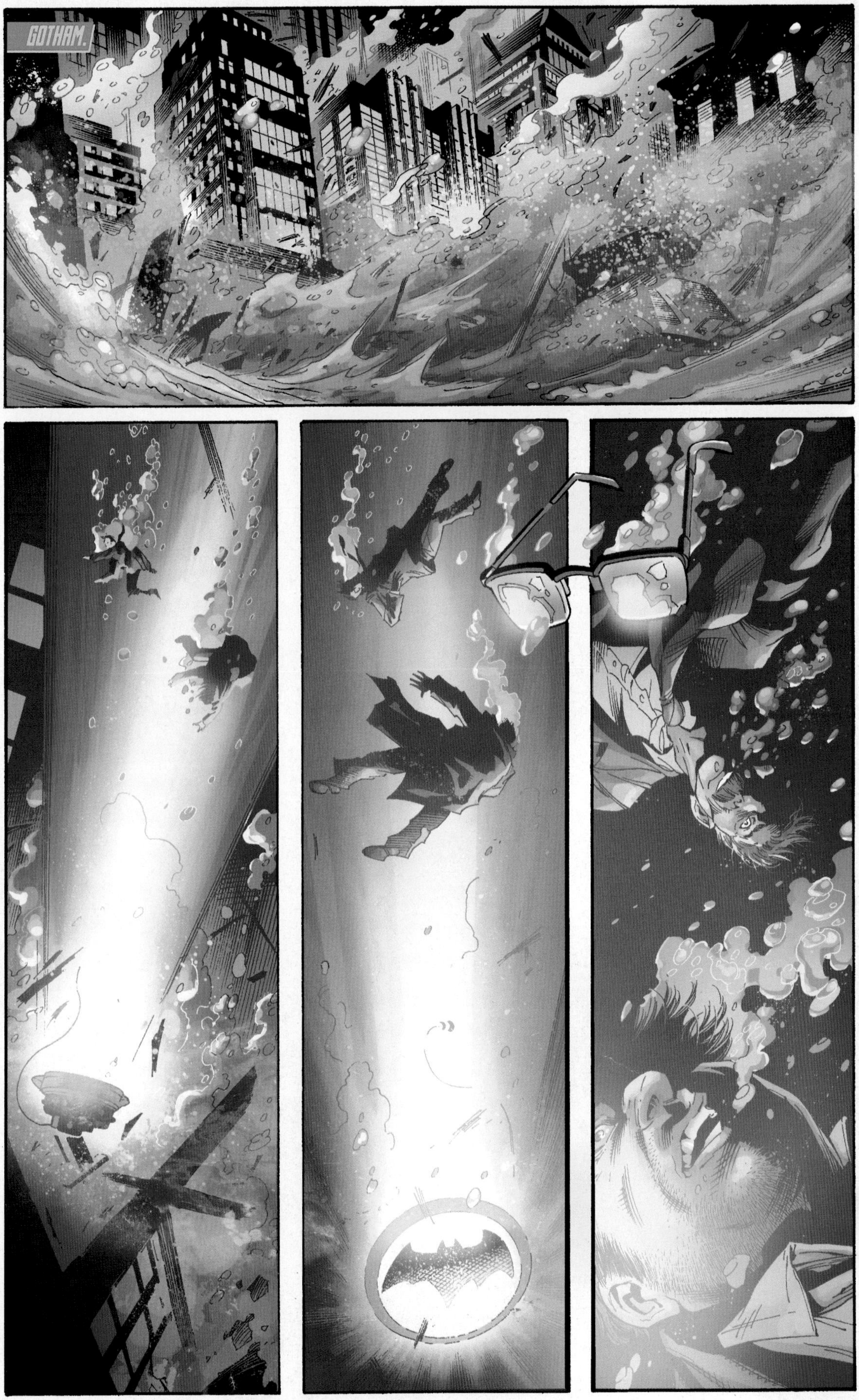
GOTHAM.

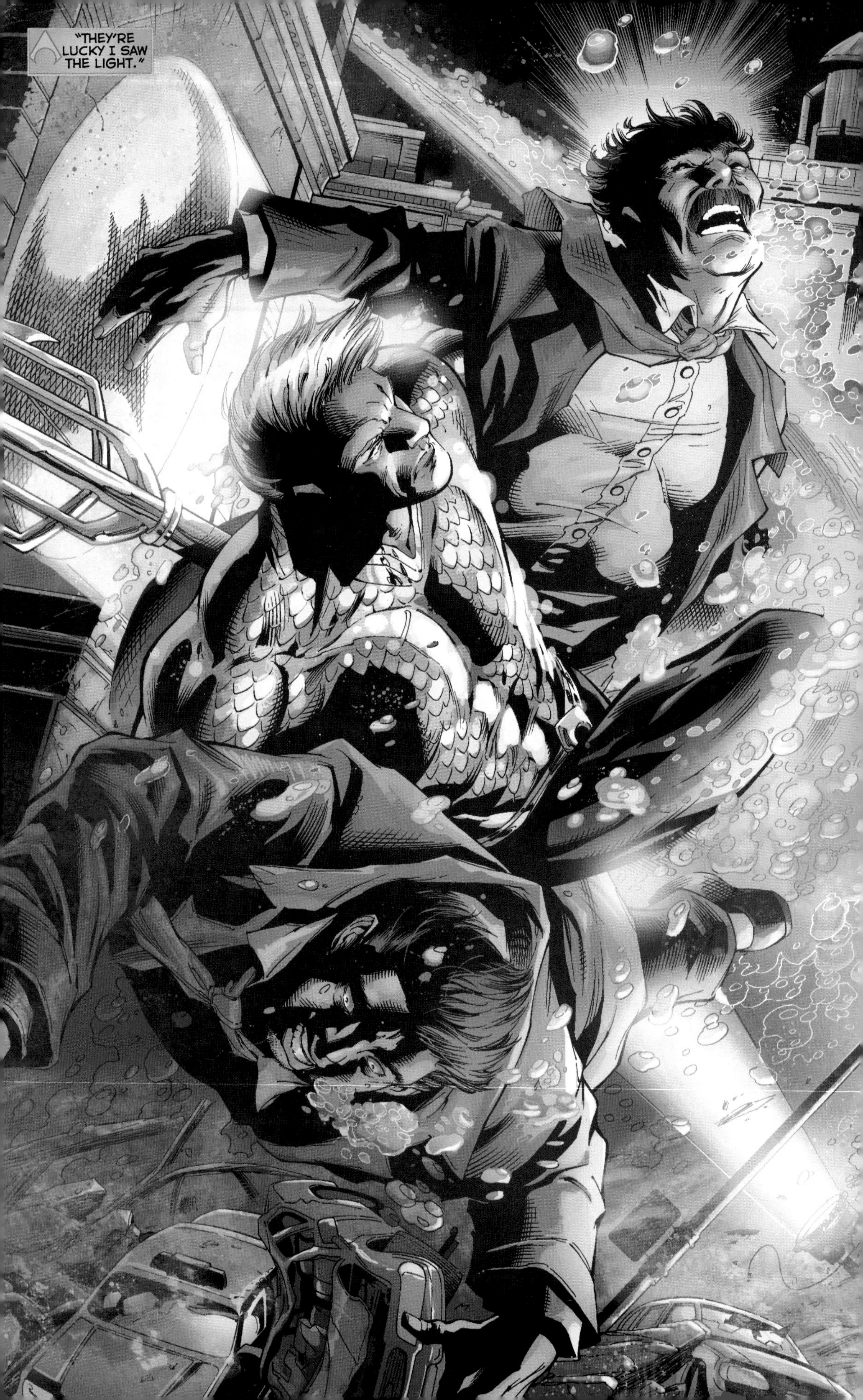
"THEY'RE LUCKY I SAW THE LIGHT."

"AND HEARD ONE OF THEM SHOUTING UNDERWATER."

"'BARBARA!'"

WHAT THE HELL JUST *HAPPENED?*

KAFFF

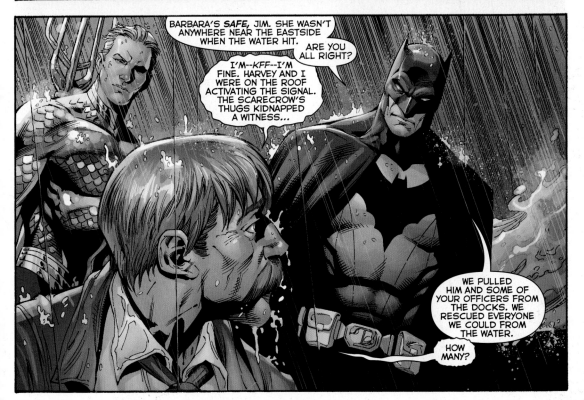

BARBARA'S *SAFE*, JIM. SHE WASN'T ANYWHERE NEAR THE EASTSIDE WHEN THE WATER HIT. ARE YOU ALL RIGHT?

I'M--KFF--I'M FINE. HARVEY AND I WERE ON THE ROOF ACTIVATING THE SIGNAL. THE SCARECROW'S THUGS KIDNAPPED A WITNESS...

WE PULLED HIM AND SOME OF YOUR OFFICERS FROM THE DOCKS. WE RESCUED EVERYONE WE COULD FROM THE WATER.

HOW MANY?

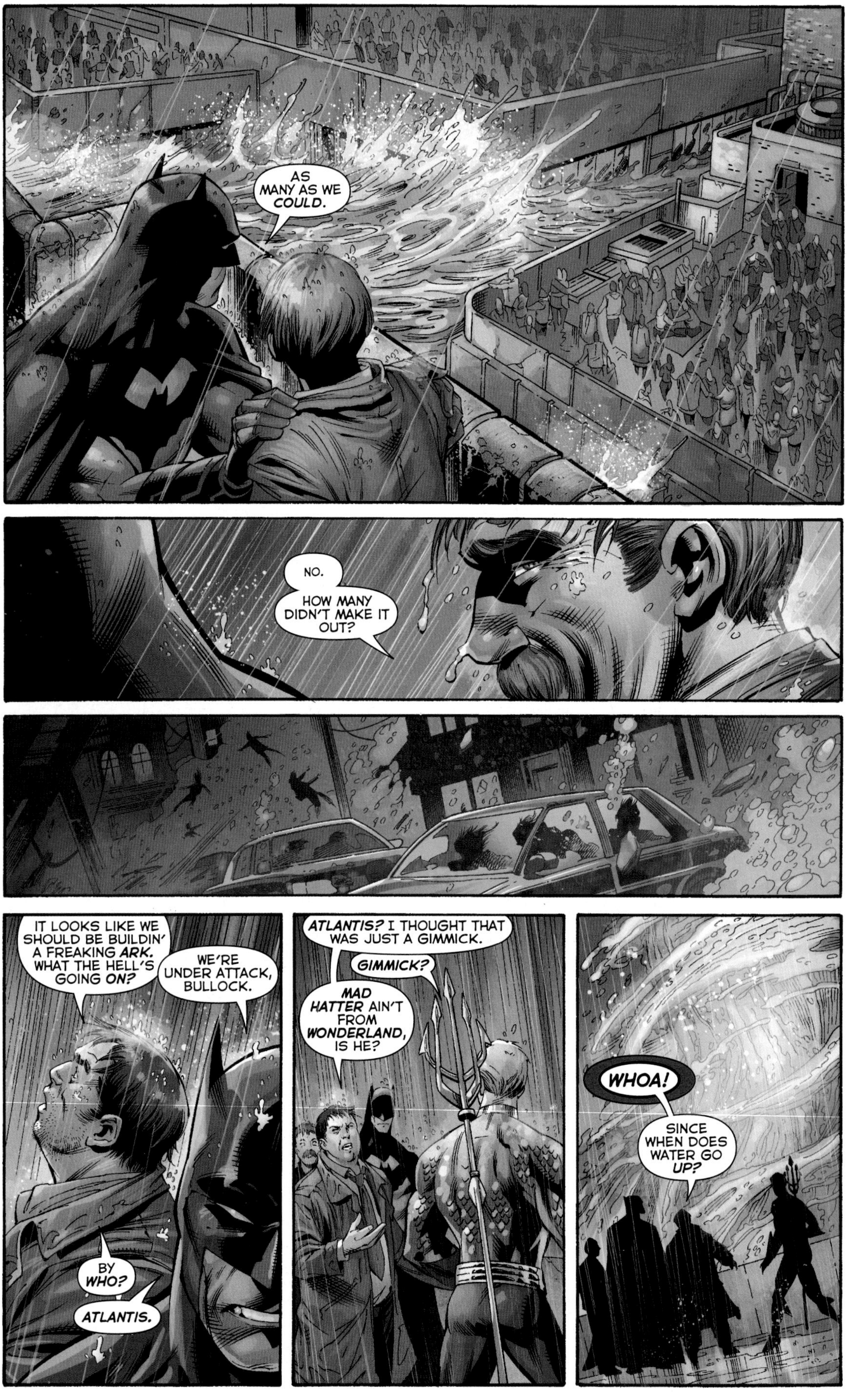
AS MANY AS WE COULD.
NO.
HOW MANY DIDN'T MAKE IT OUT?
IT LOOKS LIKE WE SHOULD BE BUILDIN' A FREAKING ARK. WHAT THE HELL'S GOING ON?
WE'RE UNDER ATTACK, BULLOCK.
BY WHO?
ATLANTIS.
ATLANTIS? I THOUGHT THAT WAS JUST A GIMMICK.
GIMMICK?
MAD HATTER AIN'T FROM WONDERLAND, IS HE?
WHOA!
SINCE WHEN DOES WATER GO UP?

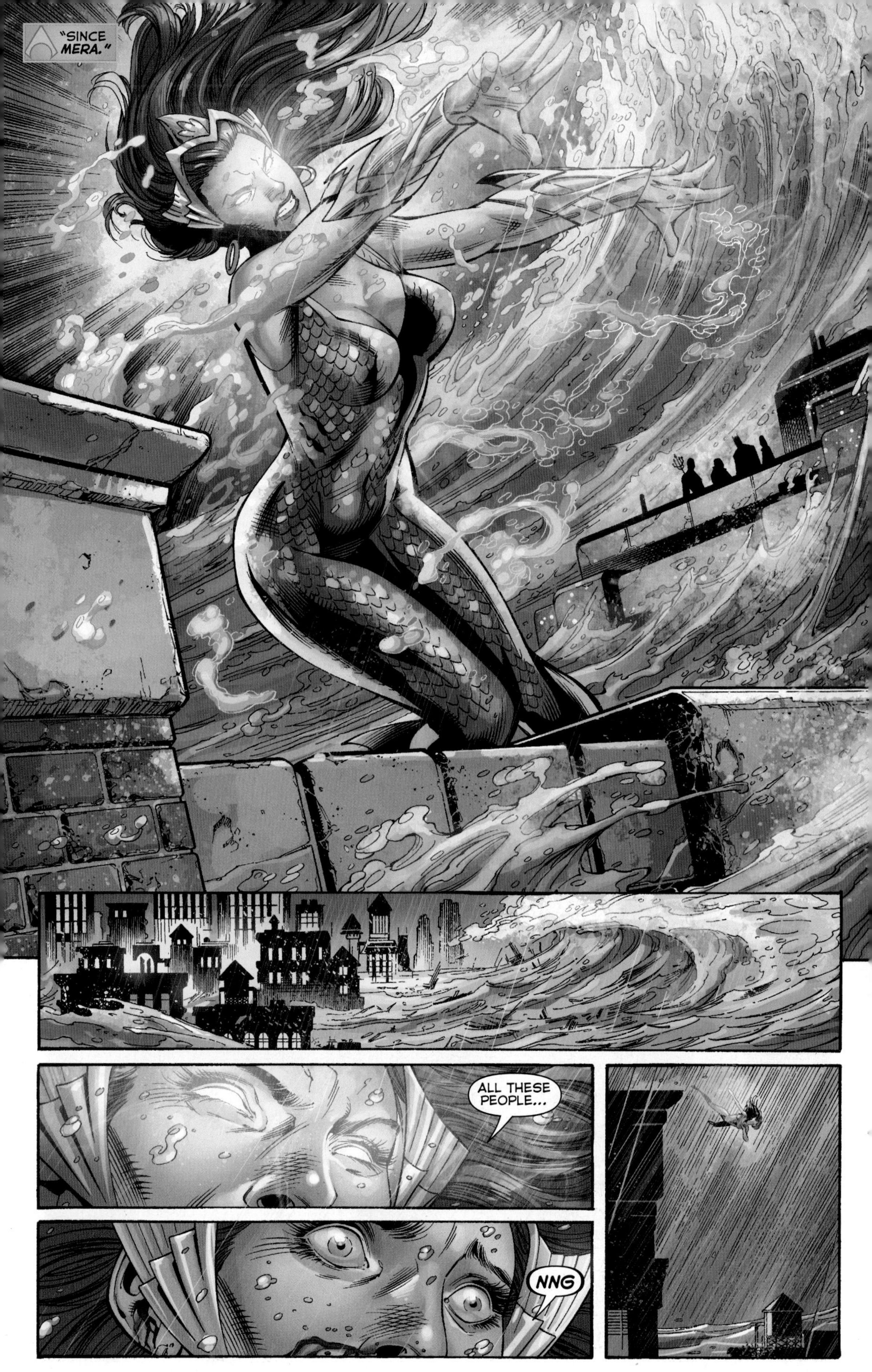
"SINCE MERA."
ALL THESE PEOPLE...
NNG

MERA!

GOT YOU.

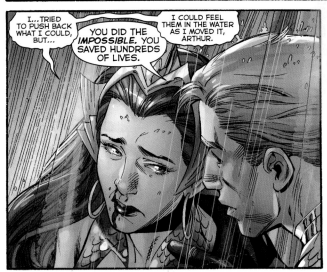

I...TRIED TO PUSH BACK WHAT I COULD, BUT...

YOU DID THE *IMPOSSIBLE.* YOU SAVED HUNDREDS OF LIVES.

I COULD FEEL THEM IN THE WATER AS I MOVED IT, ARTHUR.

BODIES.

THERE ARE SO MANY BODIES DOWN THERE.

IF CYBORG HADN'T ALERTED THE CITY BEFOREHAND, AND IF WE HADN'T BEEN HERE, IT COULD'VE BEEN A LOT WORSE.

IT *WILL* BE A LOT WORSE, ARTHUR.

IF YOUR BROTHER IS FOLLOWING THE *ATLANTEAN WAR PLANS...*FIRST THE FLOODS, THEN GROUND ASSAULT, AND THEN--

I KNOW, BUT WE HAVE TO KEEP THEIR END GOAL BETWEEN US RIGHT NOW.

I DON'T WANT TO PANIC THE LEAGUE.

YOU HAVE TO *TELL* THEM, ARTHUR. YOU HAVE TO WARN THE JUSTICE LEAGUE THAT IF THIS PROGRESSES, IF ATLANTIS CONTINUES THEIR ATTACK, THEY'RE GOING TO *SINK* WHATEVER CITY THEY TARGET.

AND IF IT'S NOT GOTHAM--

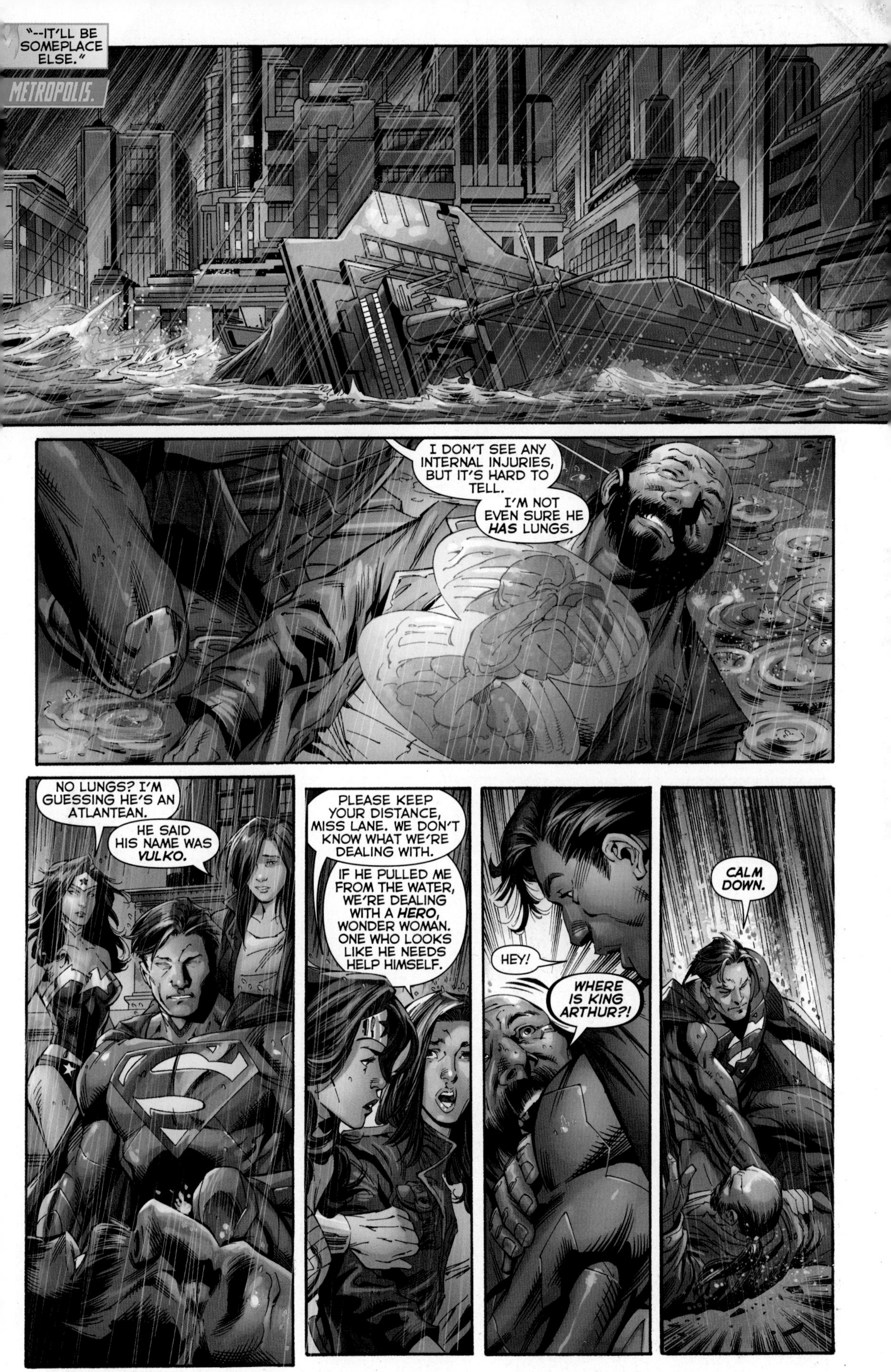
"--IT'LL BE SOMEPLACE ELSE."
METROPOLIS.
I DON'T SEE ANY INTERNAL INJURIES, BUT IT'S HARD TO TELL.
I'M NOT EVEN SURE HE *HAS* LUNGS.
NO LUNGS? I'M GUESSING HE'S AN ATLANTEAN.
HE SAID HIS NAME WAS *VULKO.*
PLEASE KEEP YOUR DISTANCE, MISS LANE. WE DON'T KNOW WHAT WE'RE DEALING WITH.
IF HE PULLED ME FROM THE WATER, WE'RE DEALING WITH A *HERO,* WONDER WOMAN. ONE WHO LOOKS LIKE HE NEEDS HELP HIMSELF.
HEY!
WHERE IS KING ARTHUR?!
CALM DOWN.

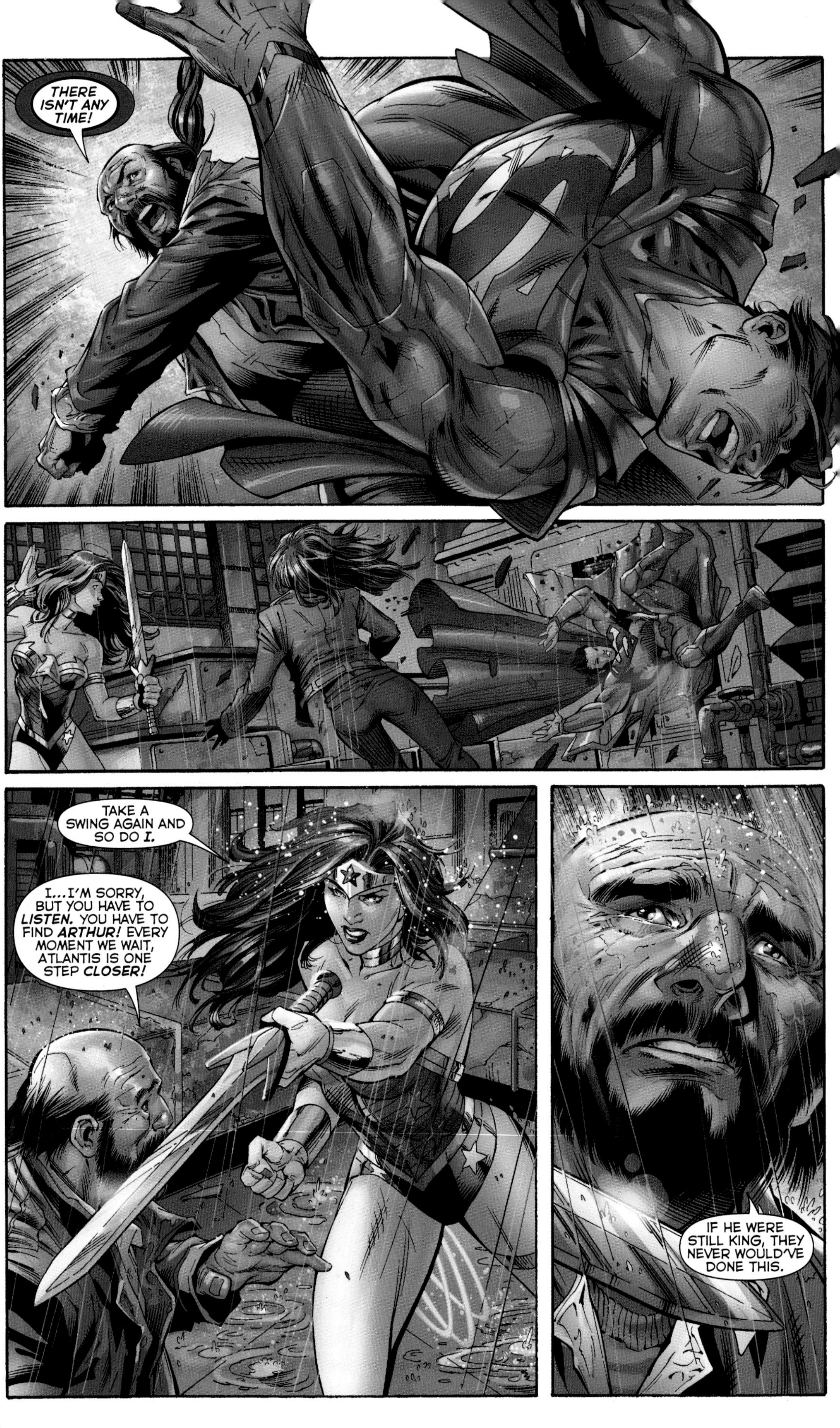
THERE ISN'T ANY TIME!
TAKE A SWING AGAIN AND SO DO I.
I...I'M SORRY, BUT YOU HAVE TO LISTEN. YOU HAVE TO FIND ARTHUR! EVERY MOMENT WE WAIT, ATLANTIS IS ONE STEP CLOSER!
IF HE WERE STILL KING, THEY NEVER WOULD'VE DONE THIS.

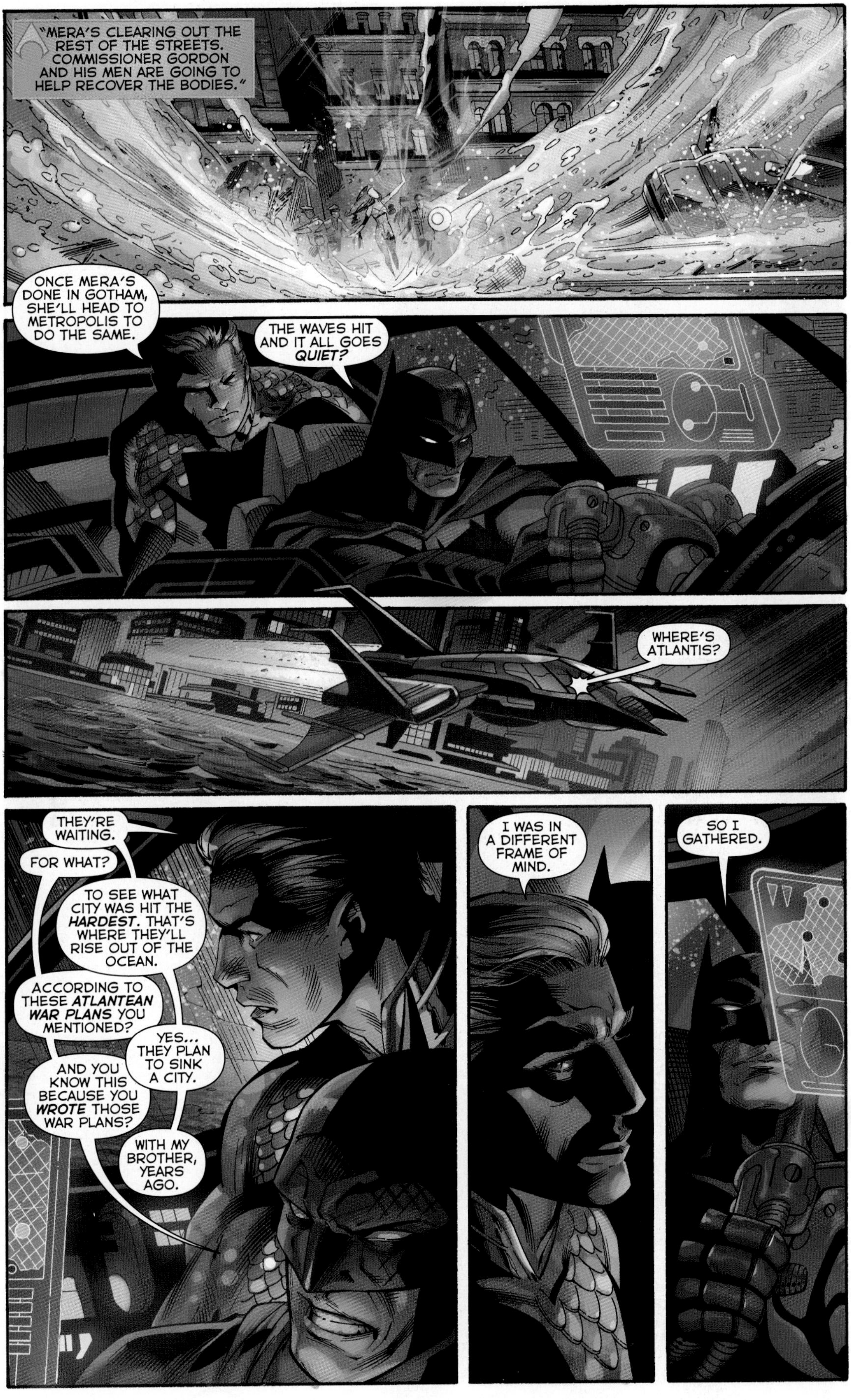
"MERA'S CLEARING OUT THE REST OF THE STREETS. COMMISSIONER GORDON AND HIS MEN ARE GOING TO HELP RECOVER THE BODIES."
ONCE MERA'S DONE IN GOTHAM, SHE'LL HEAD TO METROPOLIS TO DO THE SAME.
THE WAVES HIT AND IT ALL GOES *QUIET?*
WHERE'S ATLANTIS?
THEY'RE WAITING.
FOR WHAT?
TO SEE WHAT CITY WAS HIT THE *HARDEST*. THAT'S WHERE THEY'LL RISE OUT OF THE OCEAN.
ACCORDING TO THESE *ATLANTEAN WAR PLANS* YOU MENTIONED?
YES... THEY PLAN TO SINK A CITY.
AND YOU KNOW THIS BECAUSE YOU *WROTE* THOSE WAR PLANS?
WITH MY BROTHER, YEARS AGO.
I WAS IN A DIFFERENT FRAME OF MIND.
SO I GATHERED.

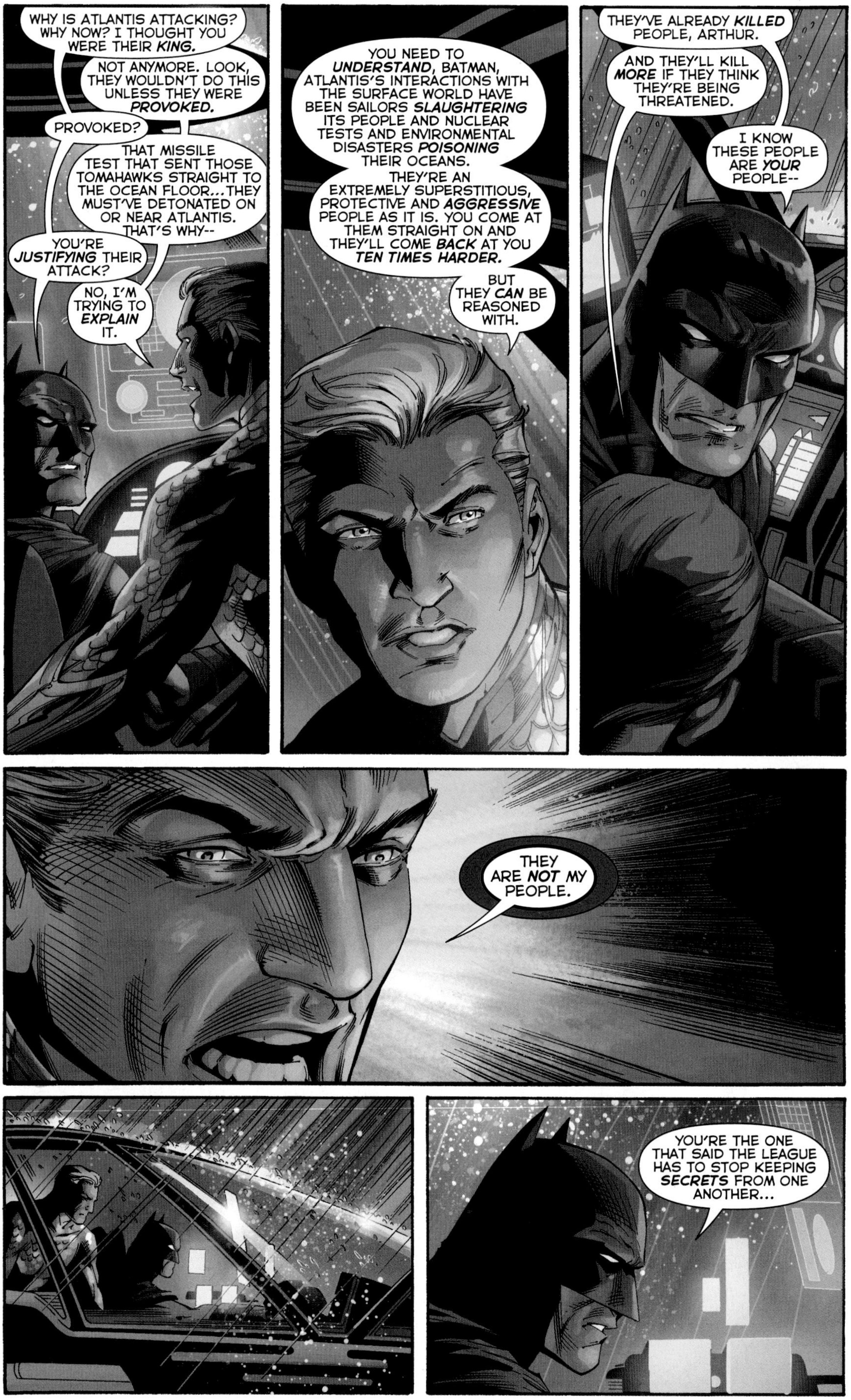
WHY IS ATLANTIS ATTACKING? WHY NOW? I THOUGHT YOU WERE THEIR KING.
NOT ANYMORE. LOOK, THEY WOULDN'T DO THIS UNLESS THEY WERE PROVOKED.
PROVOKED?
THAT MISSILE TEST THAT SENT THOSE TOMAHAWKS STRAIGHT TO THE OCEAN FLOOR...THEY MUST'VE DETONATED ON OR NEAR ATLANTIS. THAT'S WHY--
YOU'RE JUSTIFYING THEIR ATTACK?
NO, I'M TRYING TO EXPLAIN IT.
YOU NEED TO UNDERSTAND, BATMAN, ATLANTIS'S INTERACTIONS WITH THE SURFACE WORLD HAVE BEEN SAILORS SLAUGHTERING ITS PEOPLE AND NUCLEAR TESTS AND ENVIRONMENTAL DISASTERS POISONING THEIR OCEANS.
THEY'RE AN EXTREMELY SUPERSTITIOUS, PROTECTIVE AND AGGRESSIVE PEOPLE AS IT IS. YOU COME AT THEM STRAIGHT ON AND THEY'LL COME BACK AT YOU TEN TIMES HARDER.
BUT THEY CAN BE REASONED WITH.
THEY'VE ALREADY KILLED PEOPLE, ARTHUR.
AND THEY'LL KILL MORE IF THEY THINK THEY'RE BEING THREATENED.
I KNOW THESE PEOPLE ARE YOUR PEOPLE--
THEY ARE NOT MY PEOPLE.
YOU'RE THE ONE THAT SAID THE LEAGUE HAS TO STOP KEEPING SECRETS FROM ONE ANOTHER...

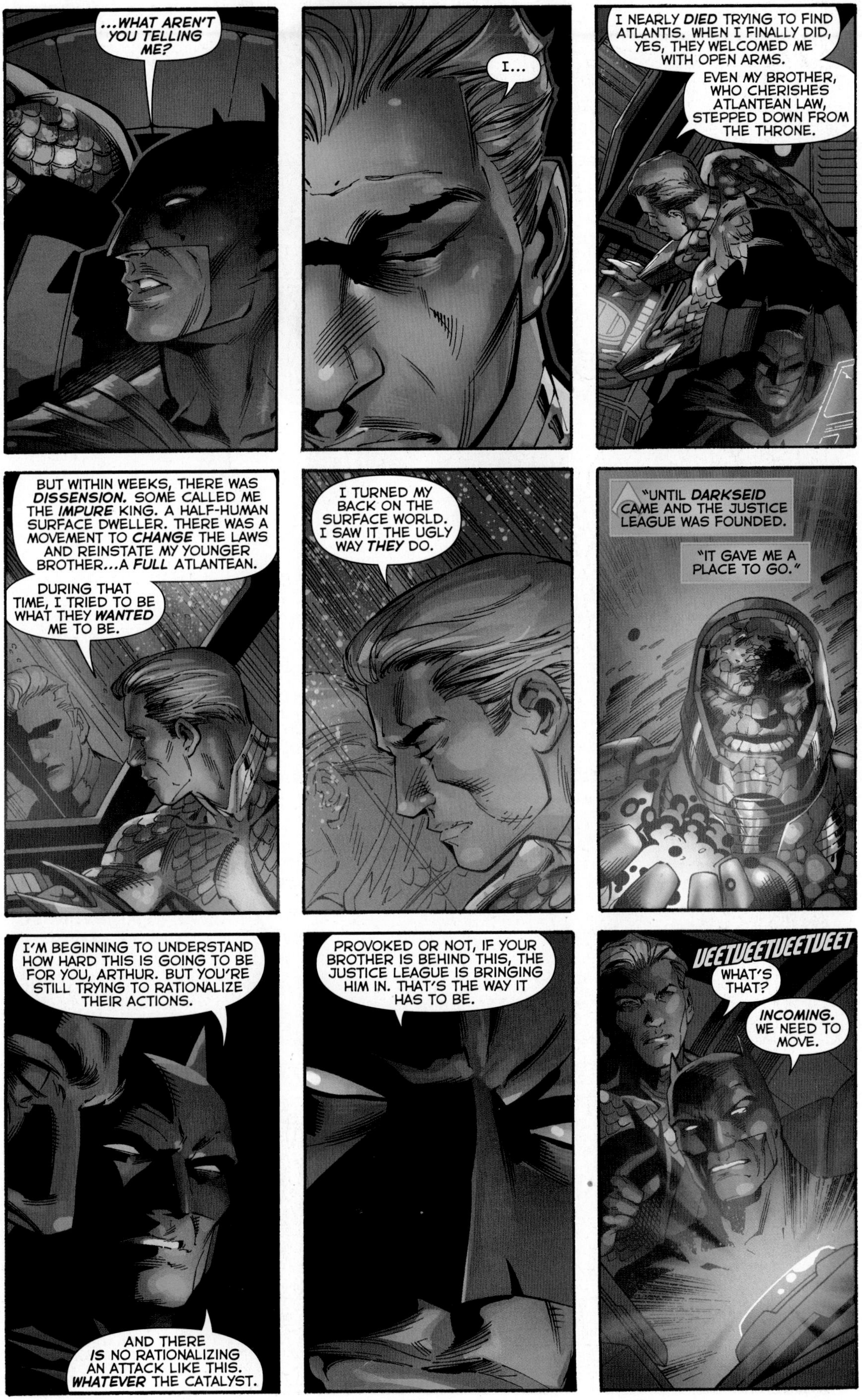
...WHAT AREN'T YOU TELLING ME?
I...
I NEARLY DIED TRYING TO FIND ATLANTIS. WHEN I FINALLY DID, YES, THEY WELCOMED ME WITH OPEN ARMS.
EVEN MY BROTHER, WHO CHERISHES ATLANTEAN LAW, STEPPED DOWN FROM THE THRONE.
BUT WITHIN WEEKS, THERE WAS DISSENSION. SOME CALLED ME THE IMPURE KING. A HALF-HUMAN SURFACE DWELLER. THERE WAS A MOVEMENT TO CHANGE THE LAWS AND REINSTATE MY YOUNGER BROTHER...A FULL ATLANTEAN.
DURING THAT TIME, I TRIED TO BE WHAT THEY WANTED ME TO BE.
I TURNED MY BACK ON THE SURFACE WORLD. I SAW IT THE UGLY WAY THEY DO.
"UNTIL DARKSEID CAME AND THE JUSTICE LEAGUE WAS FOUNDED.
"IT GAVE ME A PLACE TO GO."
I'M BEGINNING TO UNDERSTAND HOW HARD THIS IS GOING TO BE FOR YOU, ARTHUR. BUT YOU'RE STILL TRYING TO RATIONALIZE THEIR ACTIONS.
AND THERE IS NO RATIONALIZING AN ATTACK LIKE THIS. WHATEVER THE CATALYST.
PROVOKED OR NOT, IF YOUR BROTHER IS BEHIND THIS, THE JUSTICE LEAGUE IS BRINGING HIM IN. THAT'S THE WAY IT HAS TO BE.
VEETVEETVEETVEET
WHAT'S THAT?
INCOMING. WE NEED TO MOVE.

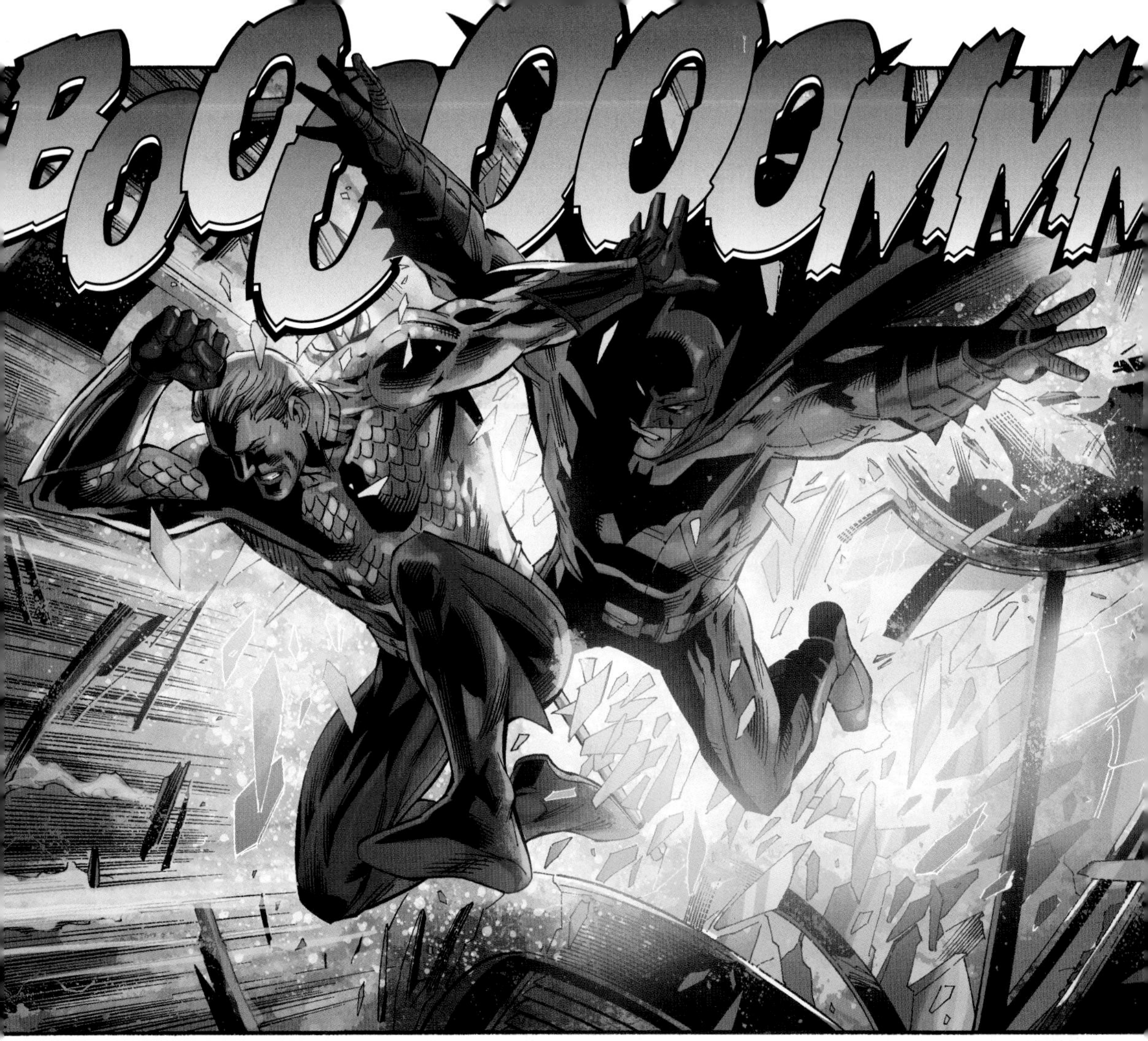
BOOOOOOMM

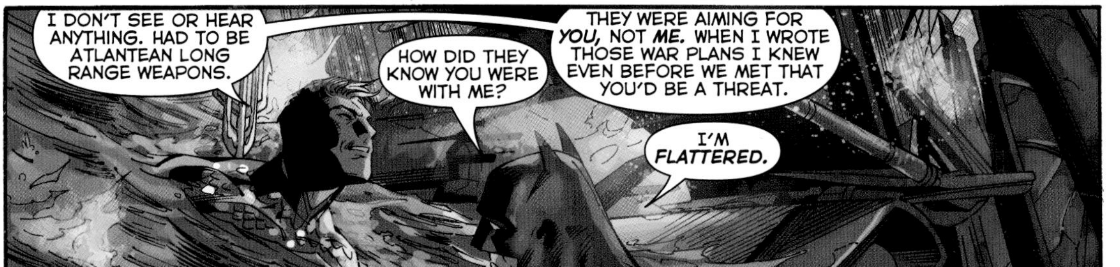
I DON'T SEE OR HEAR ANYTHING. HAD TO BE ATLANTEAN LONG RANGE WEAPONS.
HOW DID THEY KNOW YOU WERE WITH ME?
THEY WERE AIMING FOR *YOU,* NOT *ME.* WHEN I WROTE THOSE WAR PLANS I KNEW EVEN BEFORE WE MET THAT YOU'D BE A THREAT.
I'M *FLATTERED.*

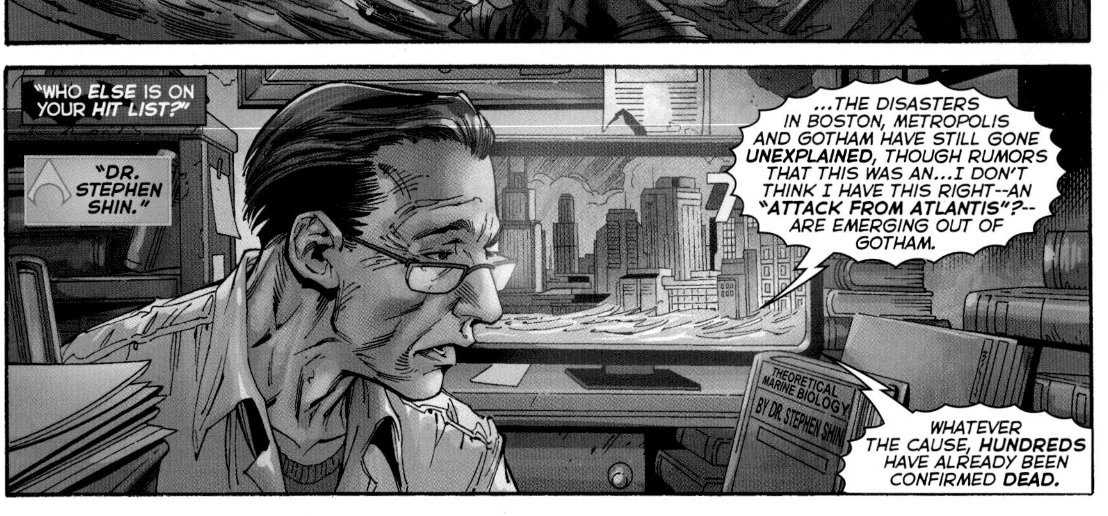
"WHO *ELSE* IS ON YOUR *HIT LIST?"*
"DR. STEPHEN SHIN."
...THE DISASTERS IN BOSTON, METROPOLIS AND GOTHAM HAVE STILL GONE *UNEXPLAINED,* THOUGH RUMORS THAT THIS WAS AN...I DON'T THINK I HAVE THIS RIGHT--AN *"ATTACK FROM ATLANTIS"?*-- ARE EMERGING OUT OF GOTHAM.
THEORETICAL MARINE BIOLOGY BY DR. STEPHEN SHIN
WHATEVER THE CAUSE, *HUNDREDS* HAVE ALREADY BEEN CONFIRMED *DEAD.*

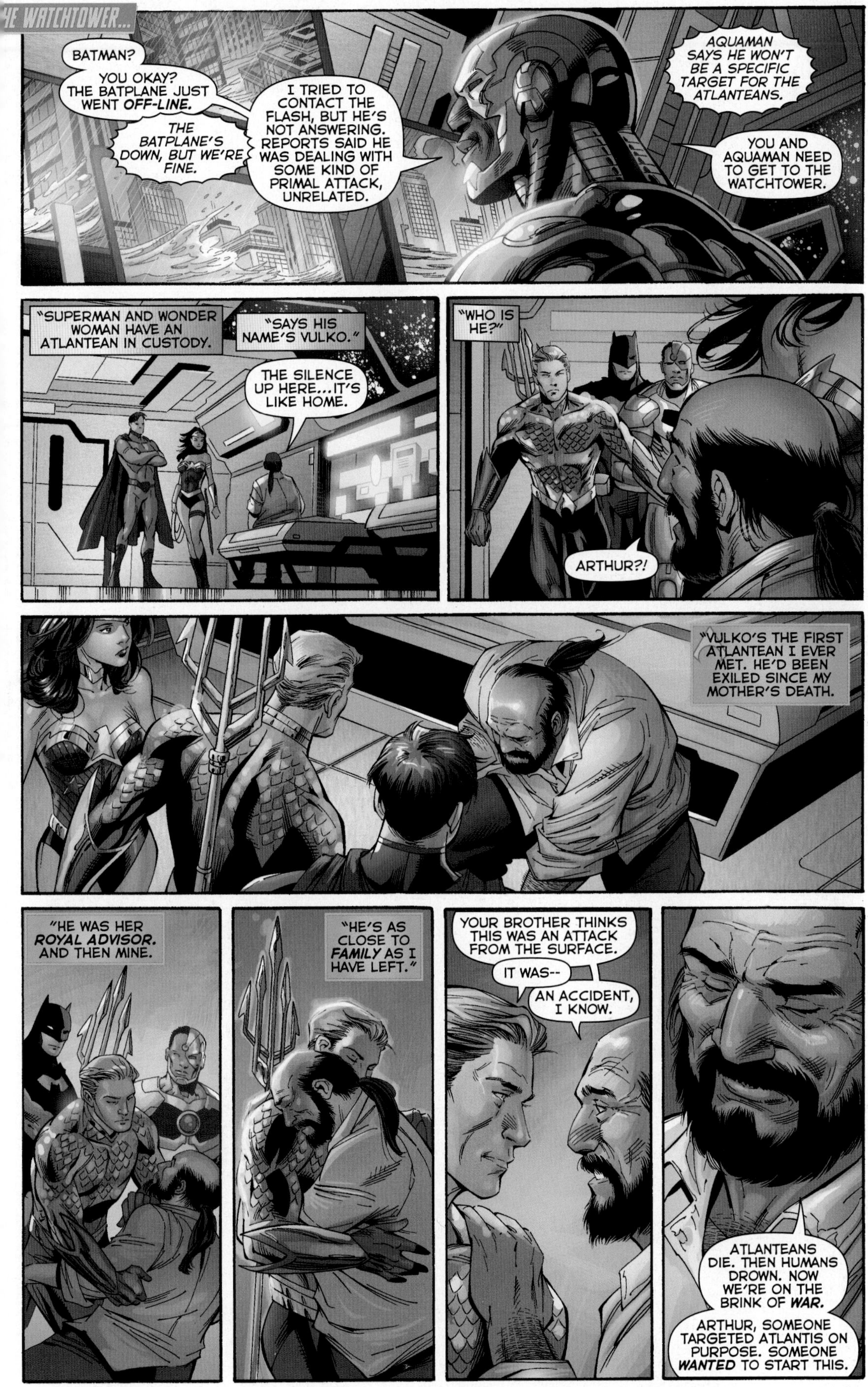

HE WATCHTOWER...
BATMAN?
YOU OKAY? THE BATPLANE JUST WENT OFF-LINE.
THE BATPLANE'S DOWN, BUT WE'RE FINE.
I TRIED TO CONTACT THE FLASH, BUT HE'S NOT ANSWERING. REPORTS SAID HE WAS DEALING WITH SOME KIND OF PRIMAL ATTACK, UNRELATED.
AQUAMAN SAYS HE WON'T BE A SPECIFIC TARGET FOR THE ATLANTEANS.
YOU AND AQUAMAN NEED TO GET TO THE WATCHTOWER.
"SUPERMAN AND WONDER WOMAN HAVE AN ATLANTEAN IN CUSTODY.
"SAYS HIS NAME'S VULKO."
THE SILENCE UP HERE...IT'S LIKE HOME.
"WHO IS HE?"
ARTHUR?!
"VULKO'S THE FIRST ATLANTEAN I EVER MET. HE'D BEEN EXILED SINCE MY MOTHER'S DEATH.
"HE WAS HER ROYAL ADVISOR. AND THEN MINE.
"HE'S AS CLOSE TO FAMILY AS I HAVE LEFT."
YOUR BROTHER THINKS THIS WAS AN ATTACK FROM THE SURFACE.
IT WAS--
AN ACCIDENT, I KNOW.
ATLANTEANS DIE. THEN HUMANS DROWN. NOW WE'RE ON THE BRINK OF WAR.
ARTHUR, SOMEONE TARGETED ATLANTIS ON PURPOSE. SOMEONE WANTED TO START THIS.

"I JUST DON'T KNOW *WHO.*"

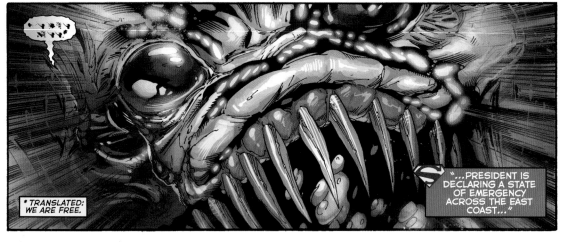

".'.'.'.'."

* TRANSLATED: WE ARE FREE.

"...PRESIDENT IS DECLARING A STATE OF EMERGENCY ACROSS THE EAST COAST..."

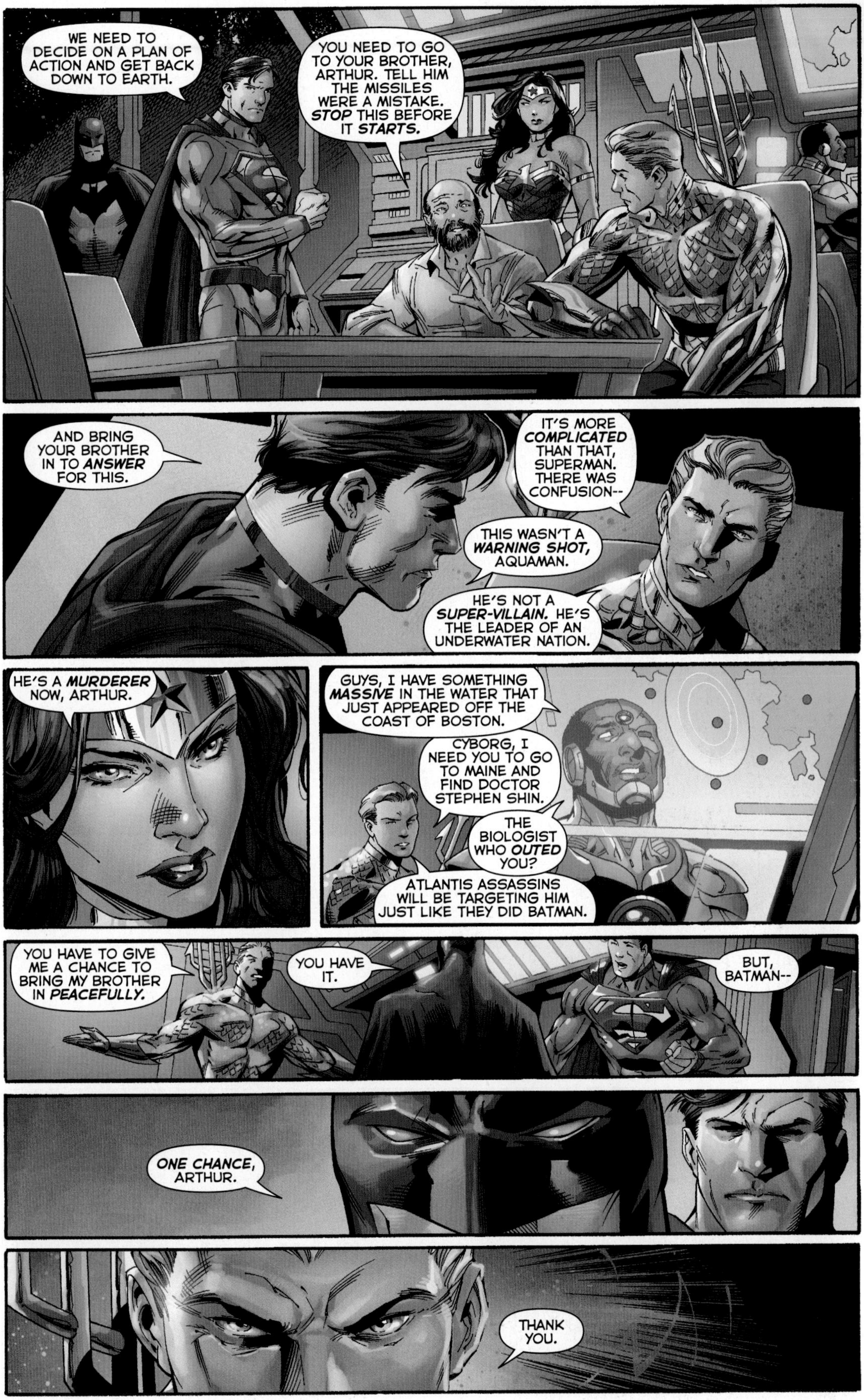
WE NEED TO DECIDE ON A PLAN OF ACTION AND GET BACK DOWN TO EARTH.
YOU NEED TO GO TO YOUR BROTHER, ARTHUR. TELL HIM THE MISSILES WERE A MISTAKE. *STOP* THIS BEFORE IT *STARTS.*
AND BRING YOUR BROTHER IN TO *ANSWER* FOR THIS.
IT'S MORE *COMPLICATED* THAN THAT, SUPERMAN. THERE WAS CONFUSION--
THIS WASN'T A *WARNING SHOT,* AQUAMAN.
HE'S NOT A *SUPER-VILLAIN.* HE'S THE LEADER OF AN UNDERWATER NATION.
HE'S A *MURDERER* NOW, ARTHUR.
GUYS, I HAVE SOMETHING *MASSIVE* IN THE WATER THAT JUST APPEARED OFF THE COAST OF BOSTON.
CYBORG, I NEED YOU TO GO TO MAINE AND FIND DOCTOR STEPHEN SHIN.
THE BIOLOGIST WHO *OUTED* YOU?
ATLANTIS ASSASSINS WILL BE TARGETING HIM JUST LIKE THEY DID BATMAN.
YOU HAVE TO GIVE ME A CHANCE TO BRING MY BROTHER IN *PEACEFULLY.*
YOU HAVE IT.
BUT, BATMAN--
ONE CHANCE, ARTHUR.
THANK YOU.

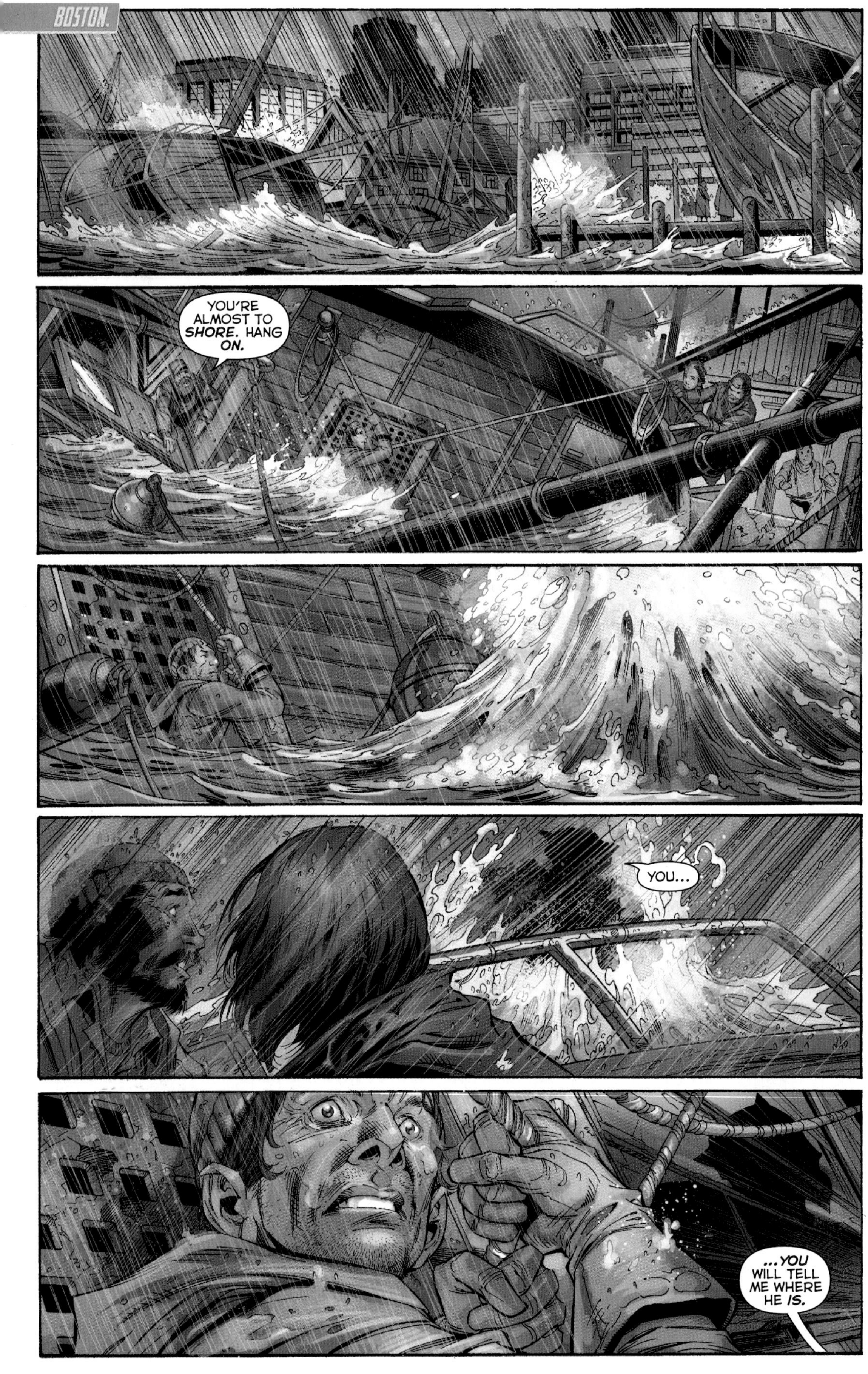
BOSTON.
YOU'RE ALMOST TO SHORE. HANG ON.
YOU...
...YOU WILL TELL ME WHERE HE IS.

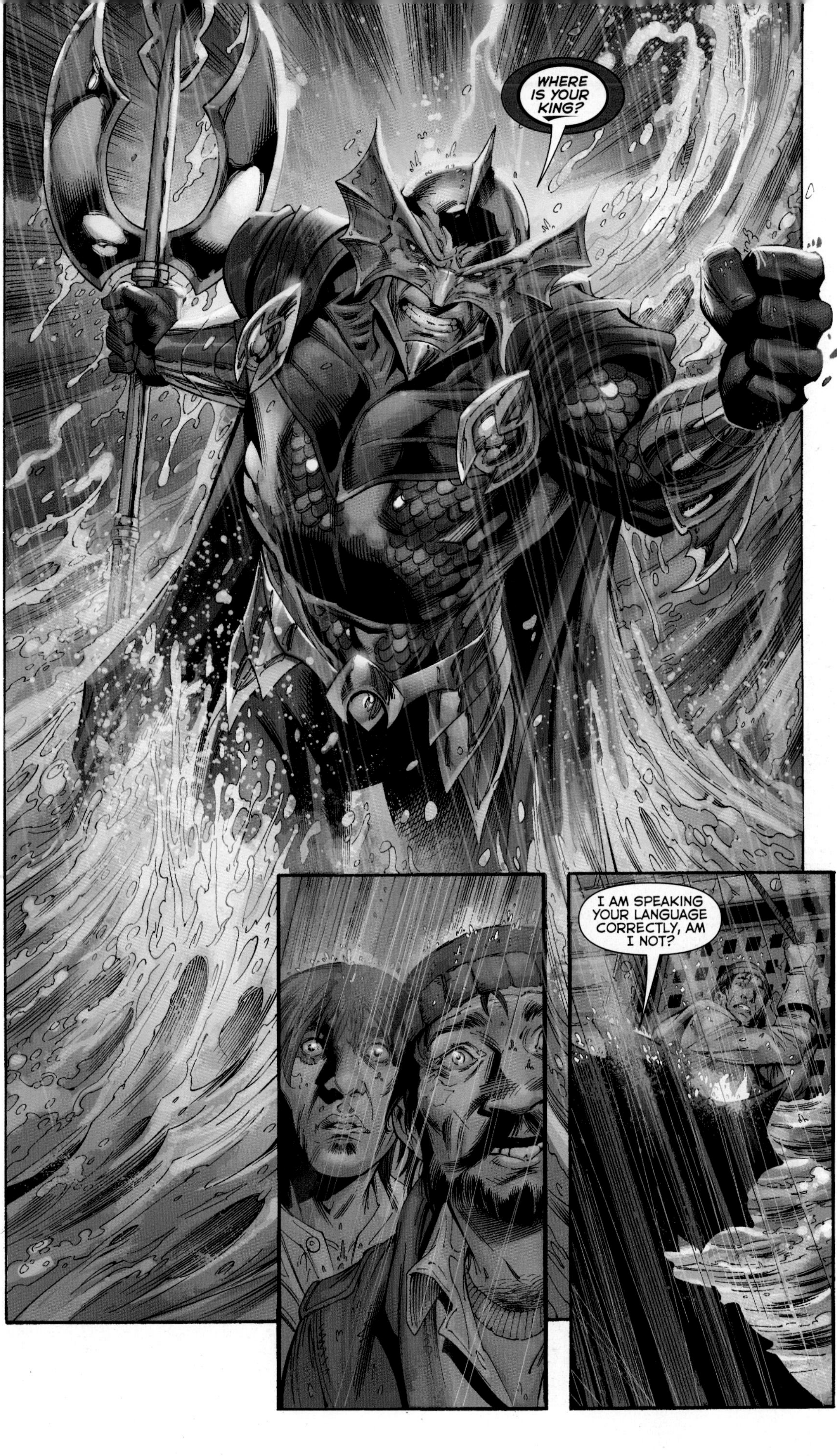
WHERE IS YOUR KING?
I AM SPEAKING YOUR LANGUAGE CORRECTLY, AM I NOT?

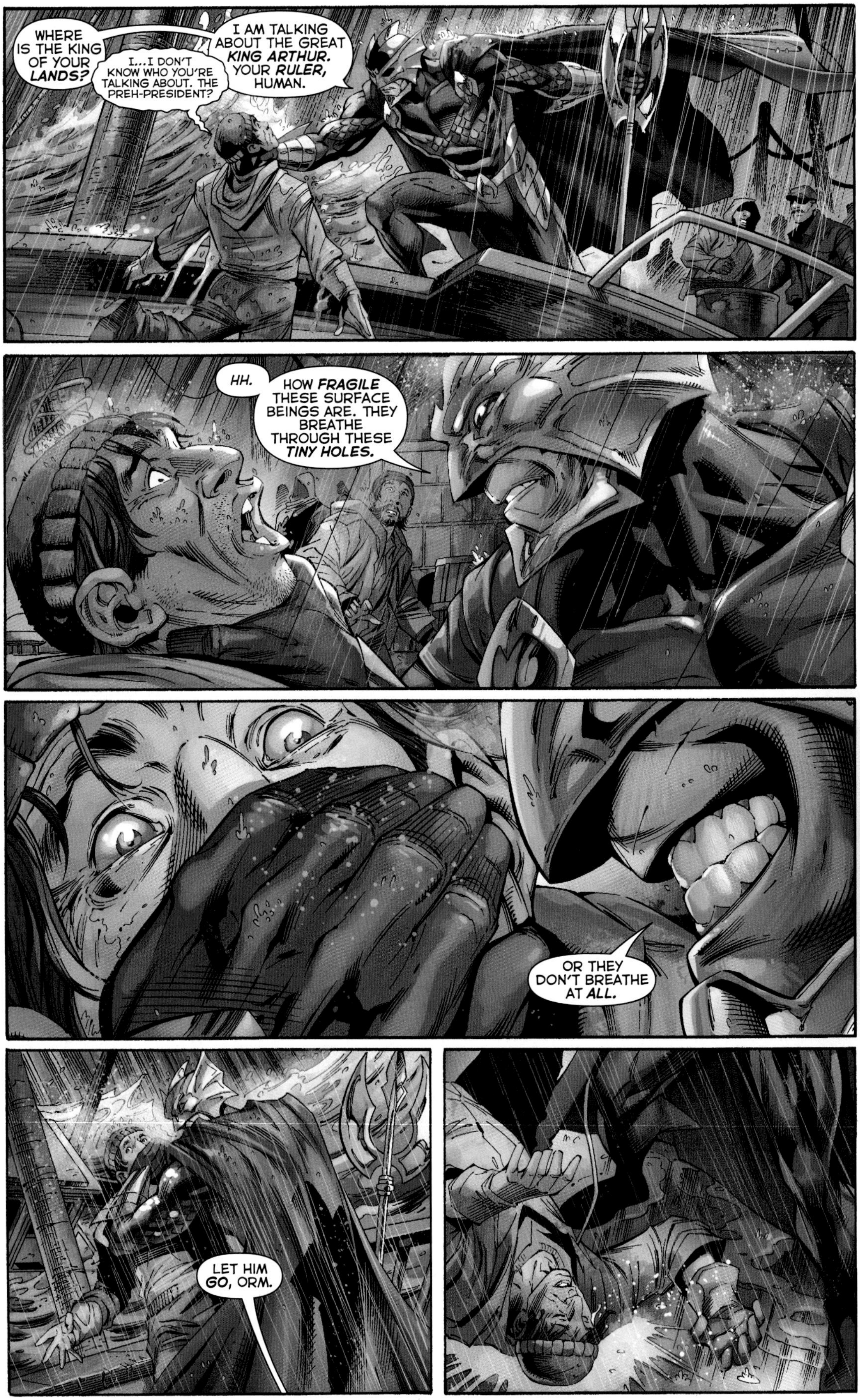
WHERE IS THE KING OF YOUR LANDS?
I AM TALKING ABOUT THE GREAT KING ARTHUR. YOUR RULER, HUMAN.
I...I DON'T KNOW WHO YOU'RE TALKING ABOUT. THE PREH-PRESIDENT?
HH.
HOW FRAGILE THESE SURFACE BEINGS ARE. THEY BREATHE THROUGH THESE TINY HOLES.
OR THEY DON'T BREATHE AT ALL.
LET HIM GO, ORM.

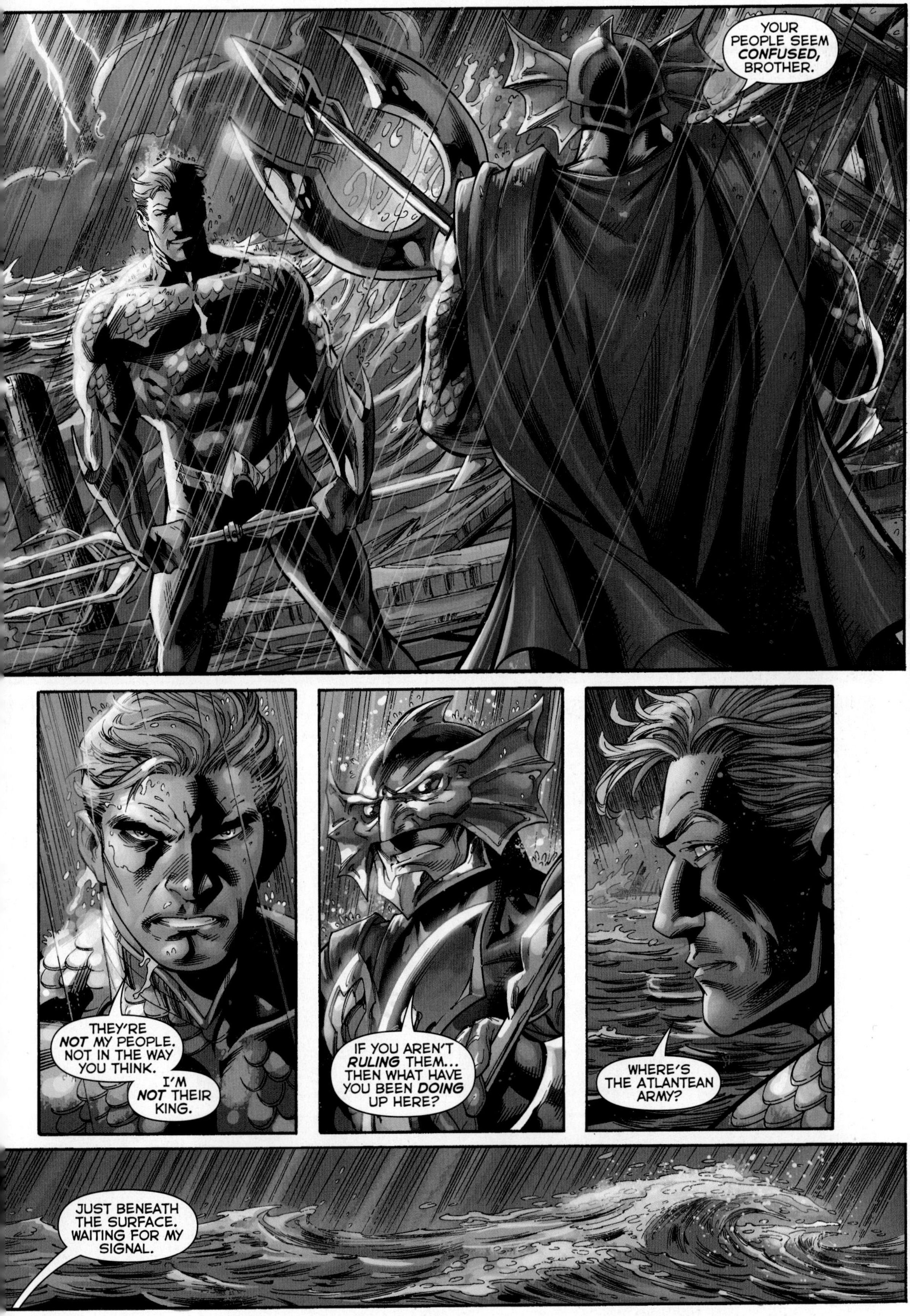
YOUR PEOPLE SEEM CONFUSED, BROTHER.
THEY'RE NOT MY PEOPLE. NOT IN THE WAY YOU THINK.
I'M NOT THEIR KING.
IF YOU AREN'T RULING THEM... THEN WHAT HAVE YOU BEEN DOING UP HERE?
WHERE'S THE ATLANTEAN ARMY?
JUST BENEATH THE SURFACE. WAITING FOR MY SIGNAL.

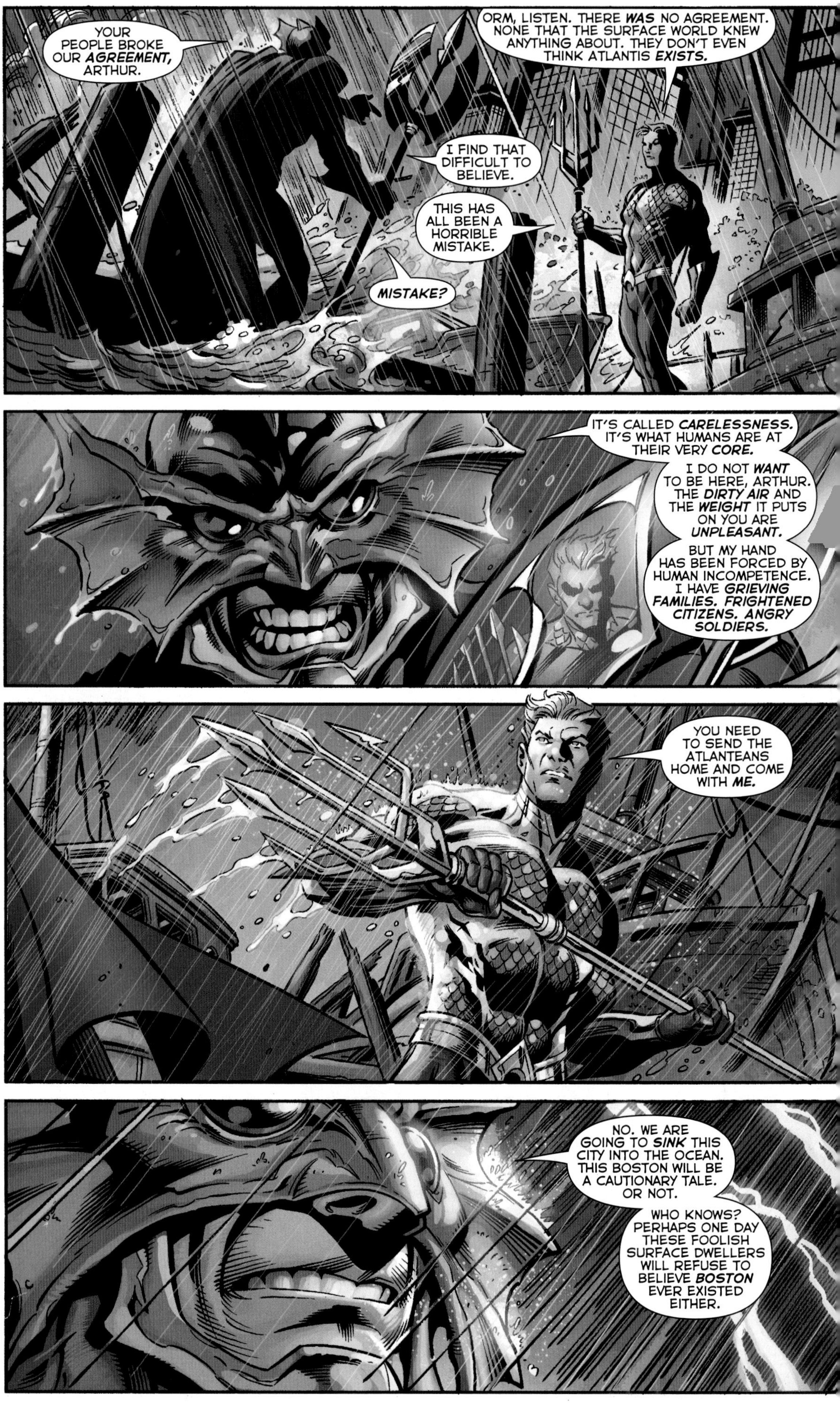
YOUR PEOPLE BROKE OUR AGREEMENT, ARTHUR.
ORM, LISTEN. THERE WAS NO AGREEMENT. NONE THAT THE SURFACE WORLD KNEW ANYTHING ABOUT. THEY DON'T EVEN THINK ATLANTIS EXISTS.
I FIND THAT DIFFICULT TO BELIEVE.
THIS HAS ALL BEEN A HORRIBLE MISTAKE.
MISTAKE?
IT'S CALLED CARELESSNESS. IT'S WHAT HUMANS ARE AT THEIR VERY CORE.
I DO NOT WANT TO BE HERE, ARTHUR. THE DIRTY AIR AND THE WEIGHT IT PUTS ON YOU ARE UNPLEASANT.
BUT MY HAND HAS BEEN FORCED BY HUMAN INCOMPETENCE. I HAVE GRIEVING FAMILIES. FRIGHTENED CITIZENS. ANGRY SOLDIERS.
YOU NEED TO SEND THE ATLANTEANS HOME AND COME WITH ME.
NO. WE ARE GOING TO SINK THIS CITY INTO THE OCEAN. THIS BOSTON WILL BE A CAUTIONARY TALE. OR NOT.
WHO KNOWS? PERHAPS ONE DAY THESE FOOLISH SURFACE DWELLERS WILL REFUSE TO BELIEVE BOSTON EVER EXISTED EITHER.

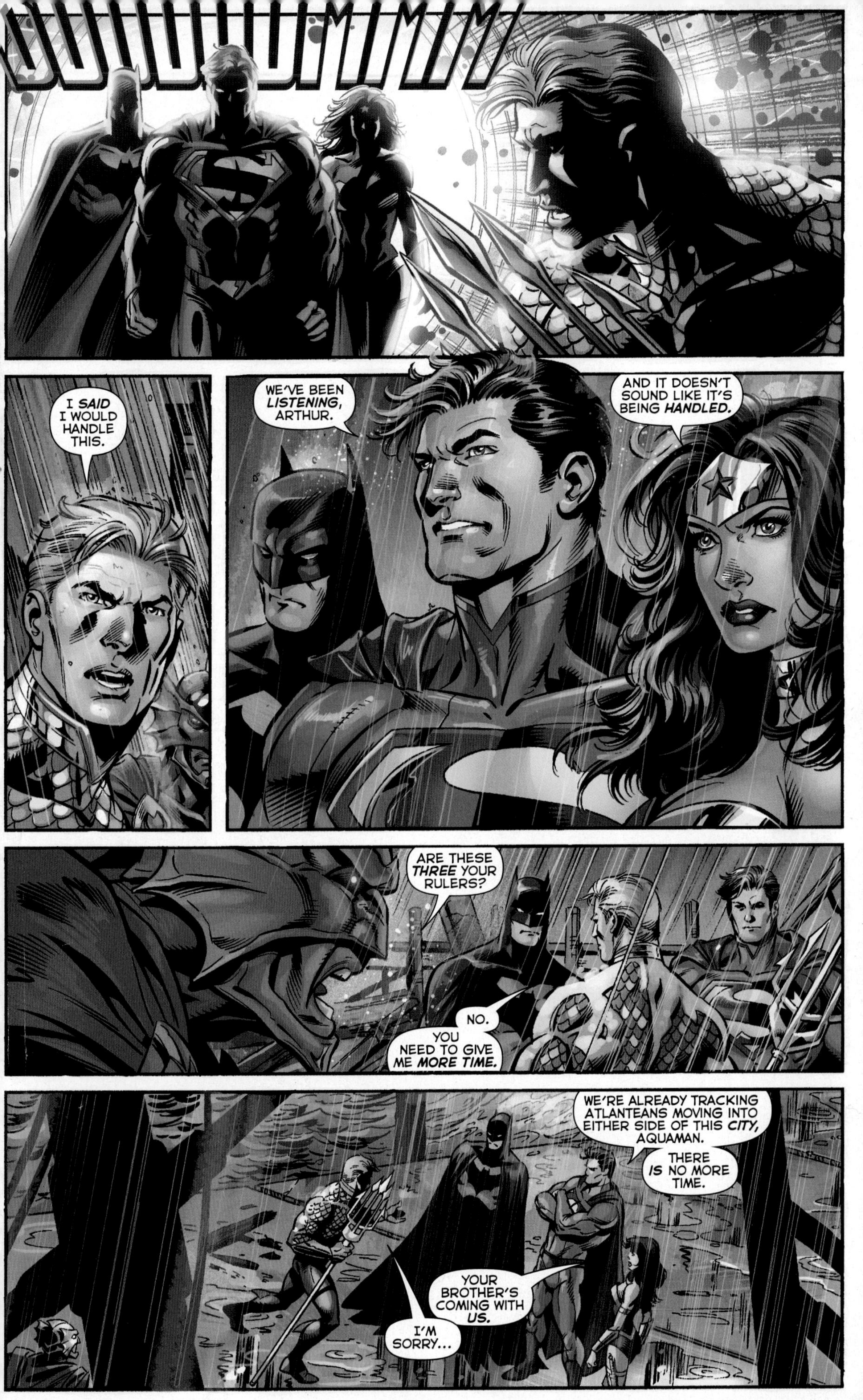

I SAID I WOULD HANDLE THIS.
WE'VE BEEN LISTENING, ARTHUR.
AND IT DOESN'T SOUND LIKE IT'S BEING HANDLED.
ARE THESE THREE YOUR RULERS?
NO.
YOU NEED TO GIVE ME MORE TIME.
WE'RE ALREADY TRACKING ATLANTEANS MOVING INTO EITHER SIDE OF THIS CITY, AQUAMAN.
THERE IS NO MORE TIME.
YOUR BROTHER'S COMING WITH US.
I'M SORRY...

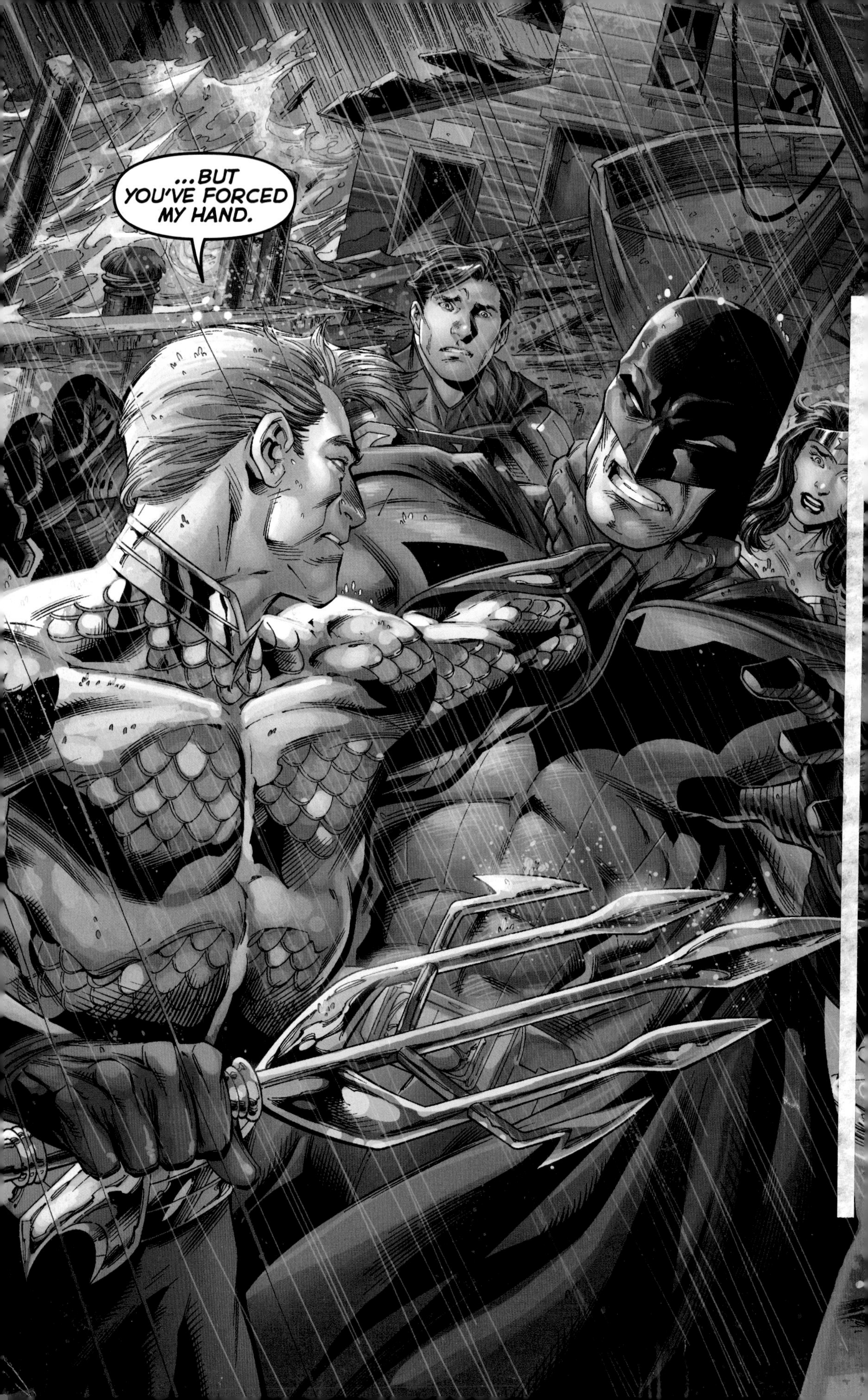
...BUT YOU'VE FORCED MY HAND.

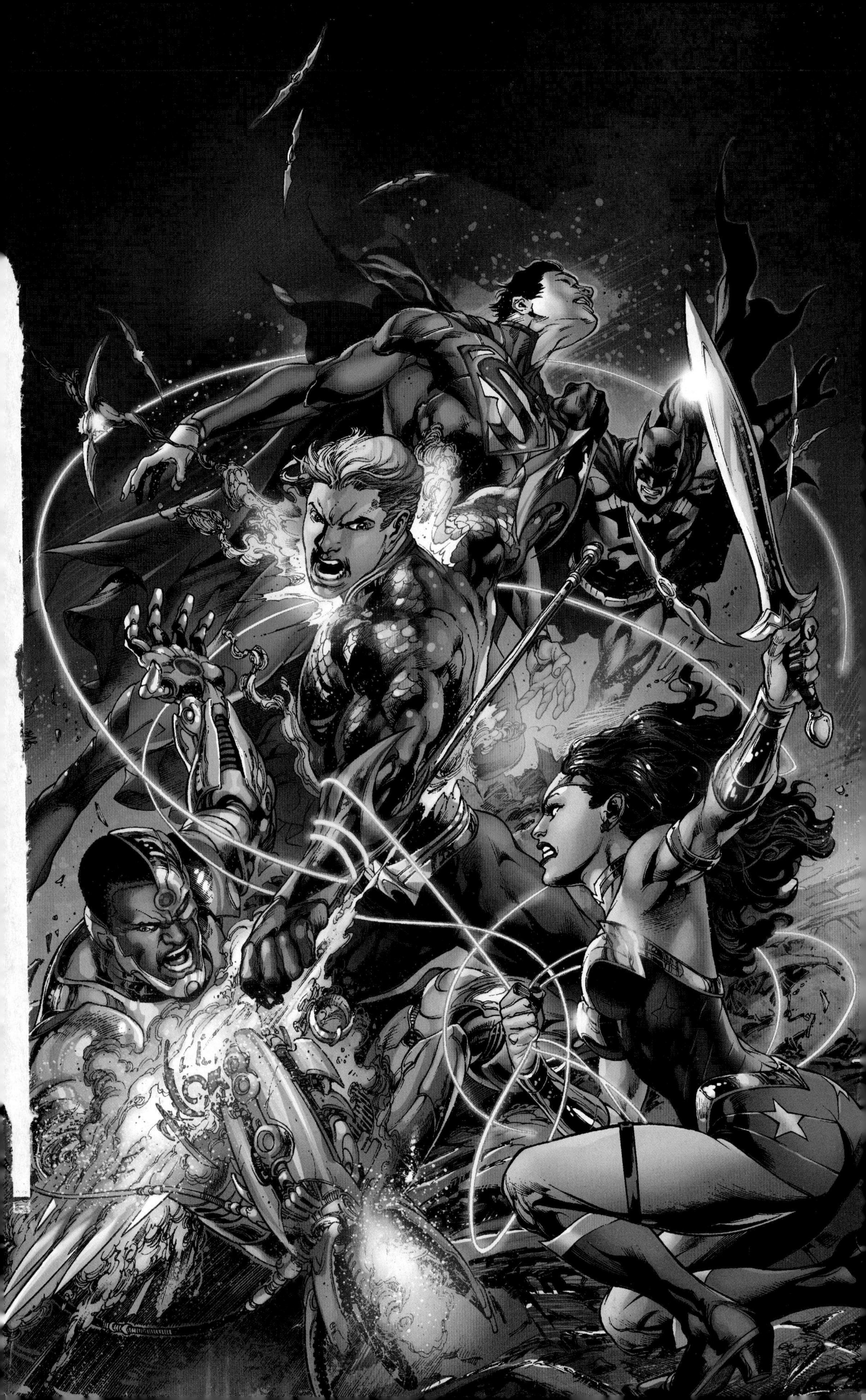

GEOFF JOHNS writer **IVAN REIS** penciller **JOE PRADO & IVAN REIS** inkers cover by **IVAN REIS, JOE PRADO & ROD REIS**

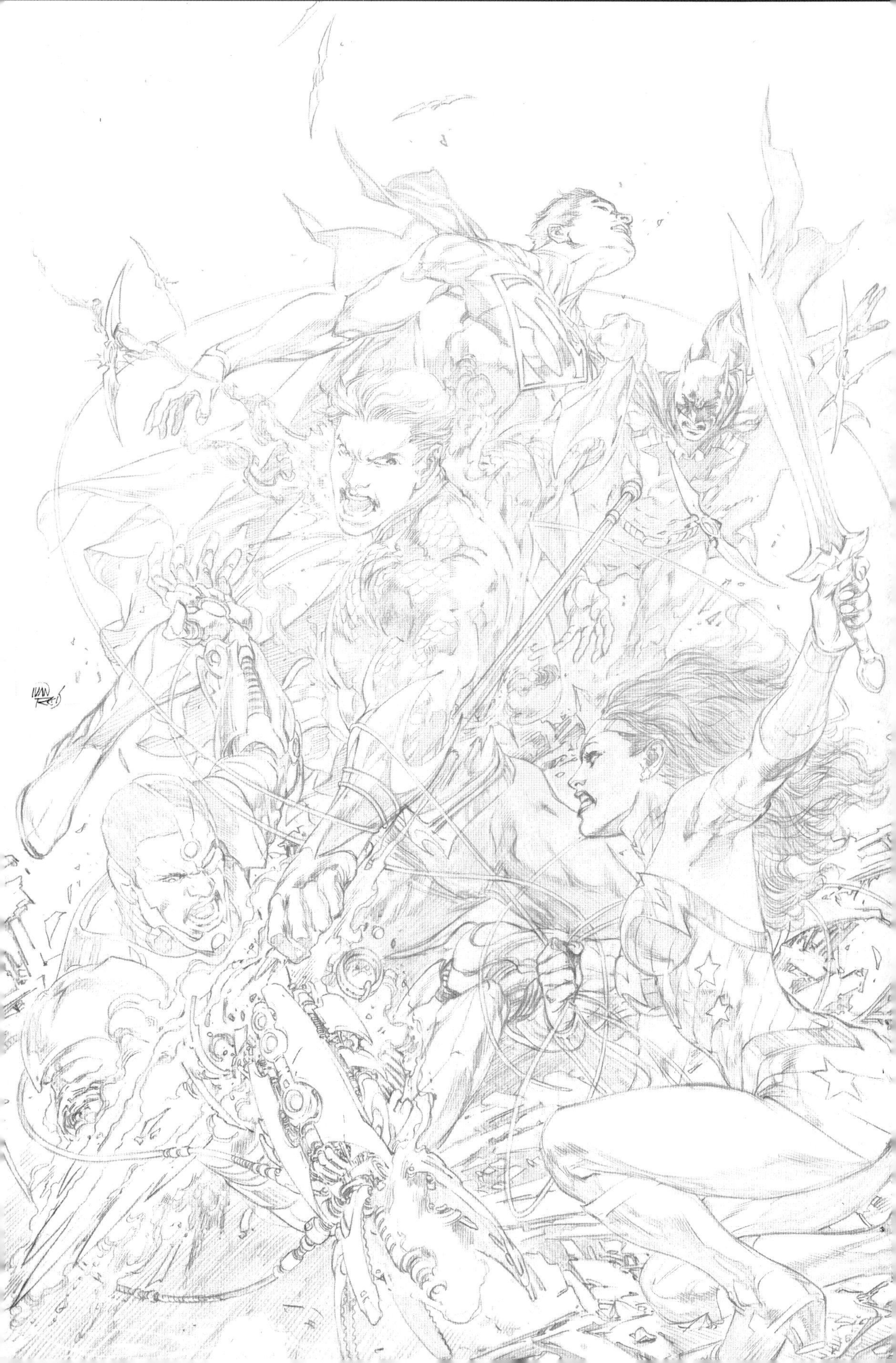

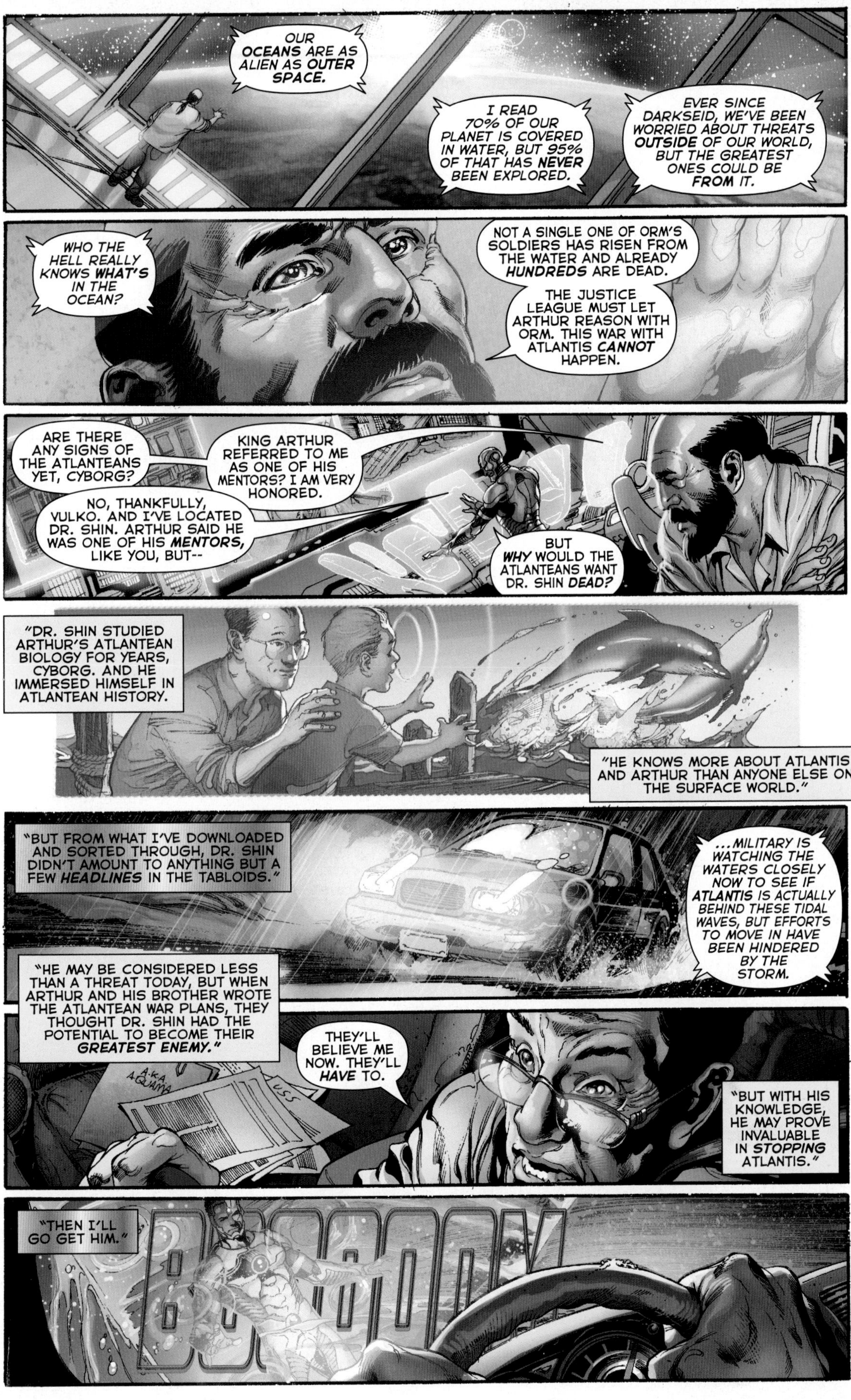

OUR OCEANS ARE AS ALIEN AS OUTER SPACE.
I READ 70% OF OUR PLANET IS COVERED IN WATER, BUT 95% OF THAT HAS NEVER BEEN EXPLORED.
EVER SINCE DARKSEID, WE'VE BEEN WORRIED ABOUT THREATS OUTSIDE OF OUR WORLD, BUT THE GREATEST ONES COULD BE FROM IT.
WHO THE HELL REALLY KNOWS WHAT'S IN THE OCEAN?
NOT A SINGLE ONE OF ORM'S SOLDIERS HAS RISEN FROM THE WATER AND ALREADY HUNDREDS ARE DEAD.
THE JUSTICE LEAGUE MUST LET ARTHUR REASON WITH ORM. THIS WAR WITH ATLANTIS CANNOT HAPPEN.
ARE THERE ANY SIGNS OF THE ATLANTEANS YET, CYBORG?
NO, THANKFULLY, VULKO. AND I'VE LOCATED DR. SHIN. ARTHUR SAID HE WAS ONE OF HIS MENTORS, LIKE YOU, BUT--
KING ARTHUR REFERRED TO ME AS ONE OF HIS MENTORS? I AM VERY HONORED.
BUT WHY WOULD THE ATLANTEANS WANT DR. SHIN DEAD?
"DR. SHIN STUDIED ARTHUR'S ATLANTEAN BIOLOGY FOR YEARS, CYBORG. AND HE IMMERSED HIMSELF IN ATLANTEAN HISTORY.
"HE KNOWS MORE ABOUT ATLANTIS AND ARTHUR THAN ANYONE ELSE ON THE SURFACE WORLD."
"BUT FROM WHAT I'VE DOWNLOADED AND SORTED THROUGH, DR. SHIN DIDN'T AMOUNT TO ANYTHING BUT A FEW HEADLINES IN THE TABLOIDS."
...MILITARY IS WATCHING THE WATERS CLOSELY NOW TO SEE IF ATLANTIS IS ACTUALLY BEHIND THESE TIDAL WAVES, BUT EFFORTS TO MOVE IN HAVE BEEN HINDERED BY THE STORM.
"HE MAY BE CONSIDERED LESS THAN A THREAT TODAY, BUT WHEN ARTHUR AND HIS BROTHER WROTE THE ATLANTEAN WAR PLANS, THEY THOUGHT DR. SHIN HAD THE POTENTIAL TO BECOME THEIR GREATEST ENEMY."
THEY'LL BELIEVE ME NOW. THEY'LL HAVE TO.
"BUT WITH HIS KNOWLEDGE, HE MAY PROVE INVALUABLE IN STOPPING ATLANTIS."
"THEN I'LL GO GET HIM."

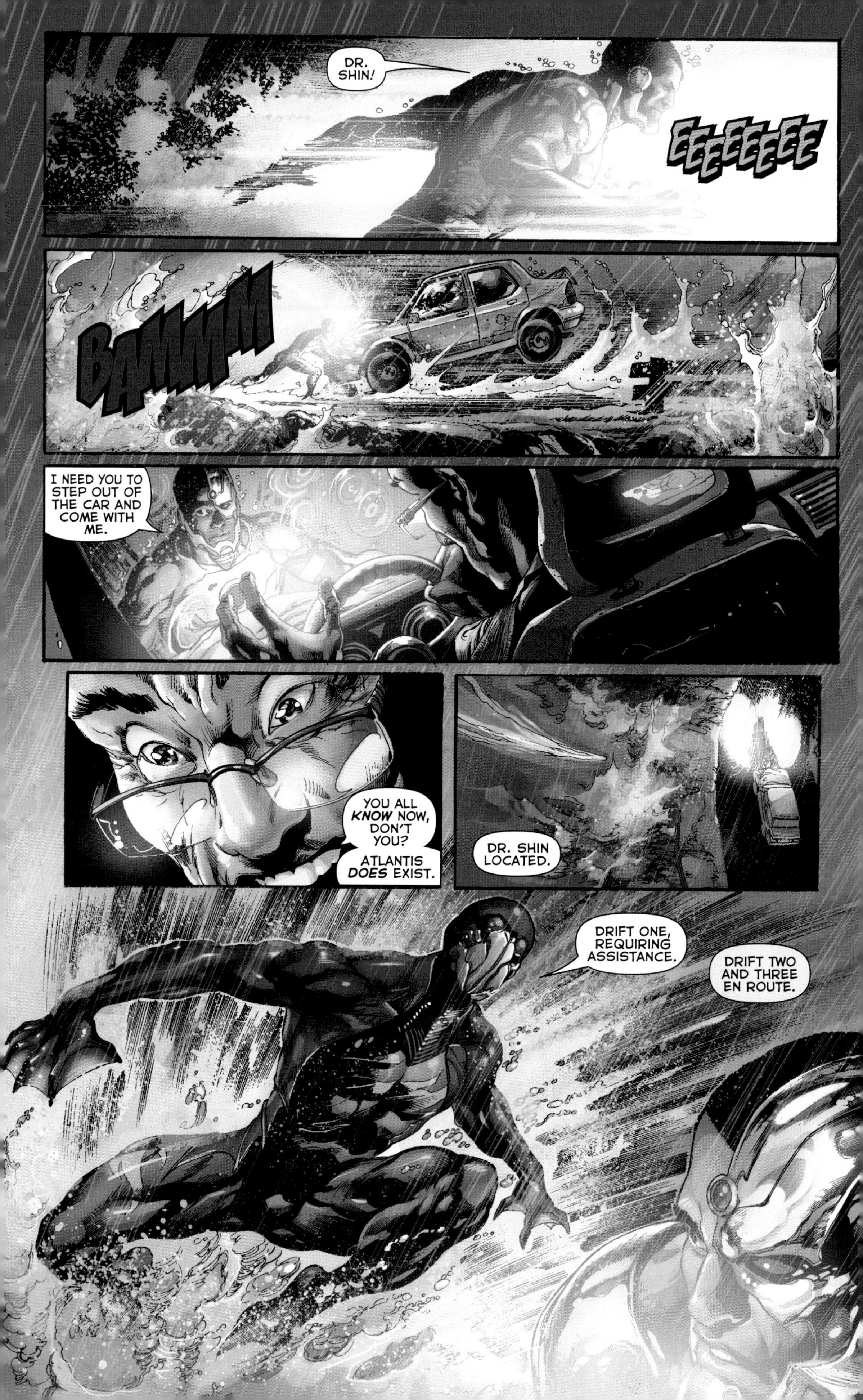
DR. SHIN!
EEEEEEEE
BAMMM
I NEED YOU TO STEP OUT OF THE CAR AND COME WITH ME.
YOU ALL KNOW NOW, DON'T YOU?
ATLANTIS DOES EXIST.
DR. SHIN LOCATED.
DRIFT ONE, REQUIRING ASSISTANCE.
DRIFT TWO AND THREE EN ROUTE.

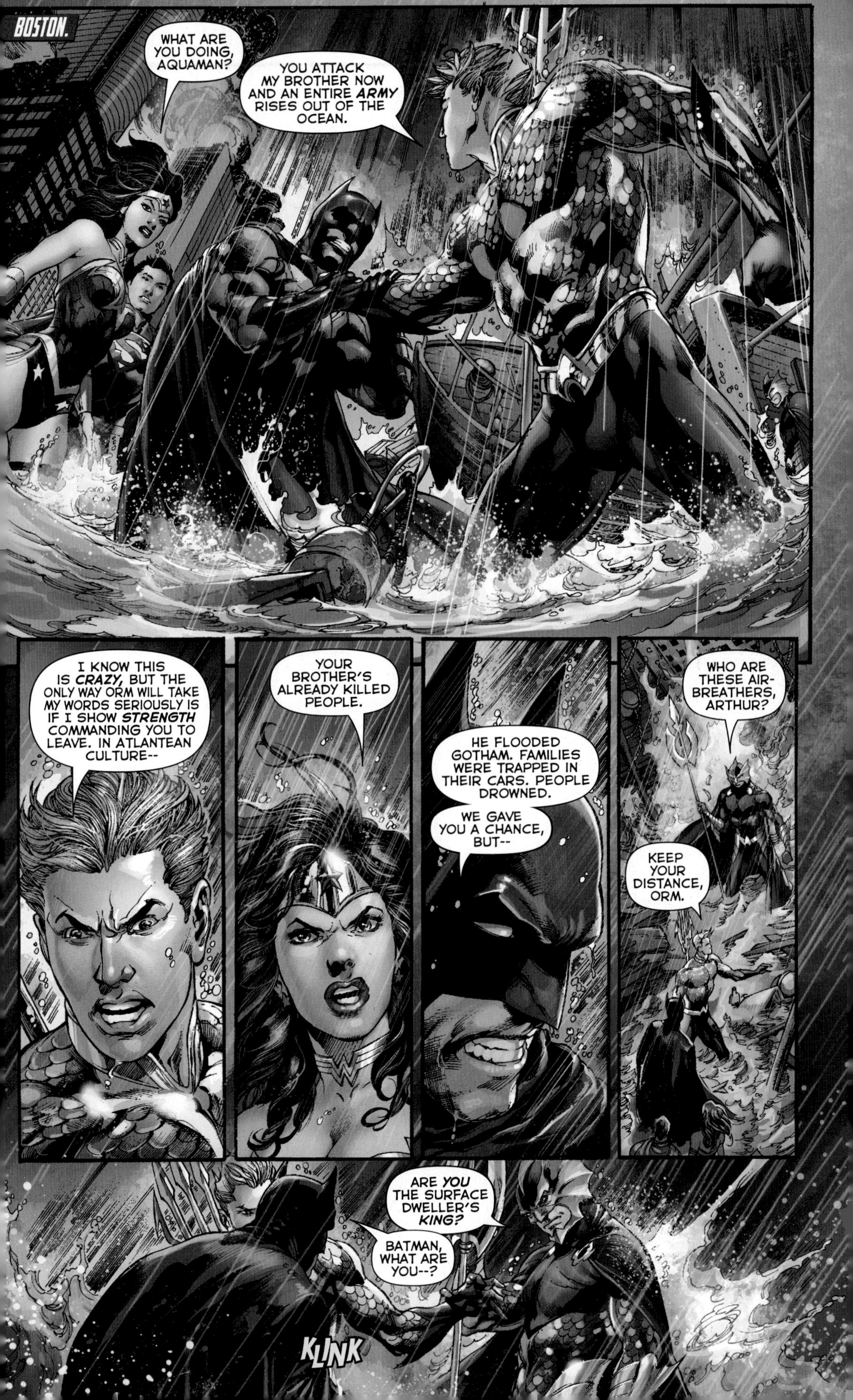
BOSTON.
WHAT ARE YOU DOING, AQUAMAN?
YOU ATTACK MY BROTHER NOW AND AN ENTIRE ARMY RISES OUT OF THE OCEAN.
I KNOW THIS IS CRAZY, BUT THE ONLY WAY ORM WILL TAKE MY WORDS SERIOUSLY IS IF I SHOW STRENGTH COMMANDING YOU TO LEAVE. IN ATLANTEAN CULTURE--
YOUR BROTHER'S ALREADY KILLED PEOPLE.
HE FLOODED GOTHAM. FAMILIES WERE TRAPPED IN THEIR CARS. PEOPLE DROWNED.
WE GAVE YOU A CHANCE, BUT--
WHO ARE THESE AIR-BREATHERS, ARTHUR?
KEEP YOUR DISTANCE, ORM.
ARE YOU THE SURFACE DWELLER'S KING?
BATMAN, WHAT ARE YOU--?
KLINK

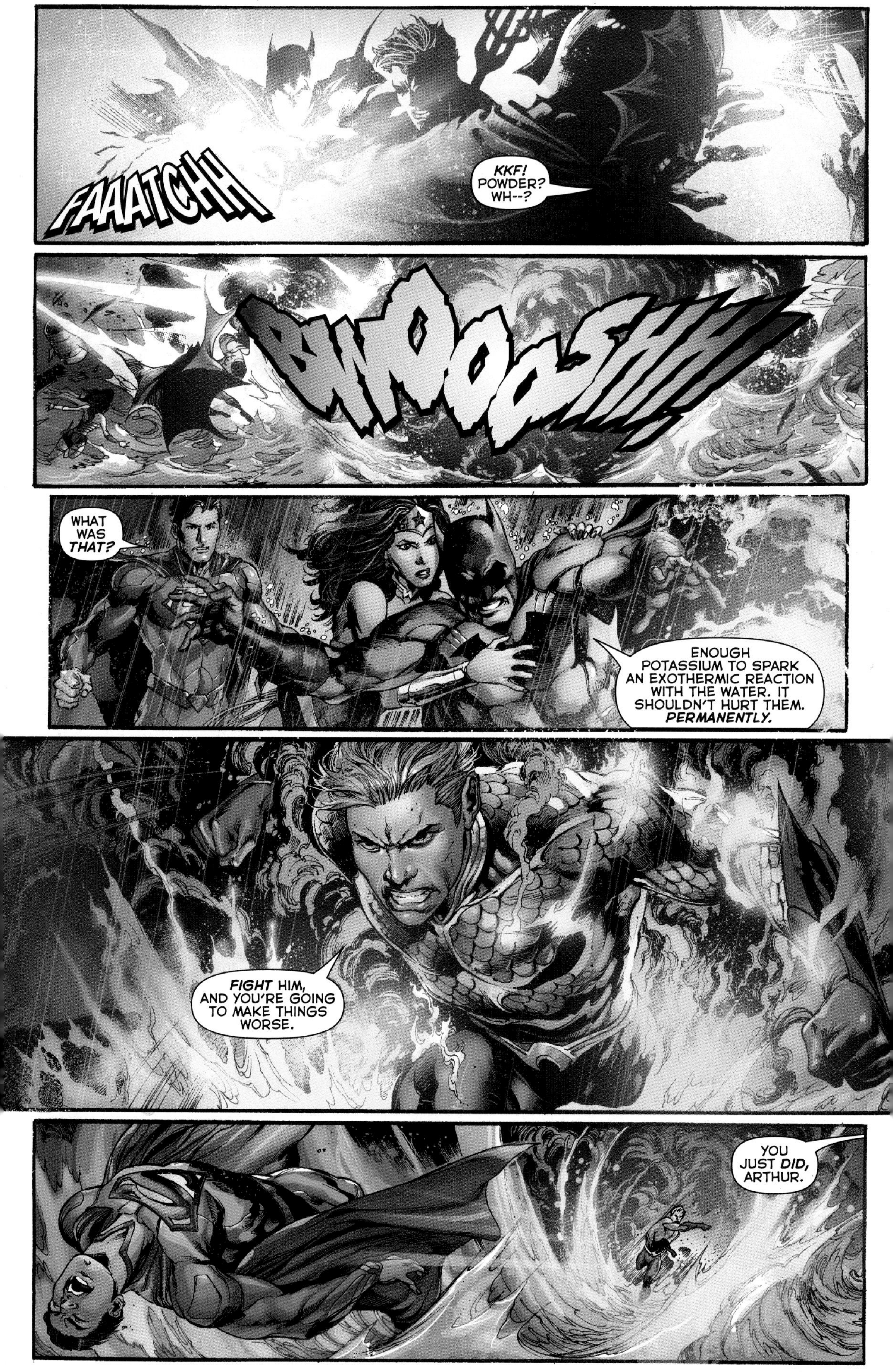
KKF! POWDER? WH--?
FAAATCHH
BWOOASHH
WHAT WAS THAT?
ENOUGH POTASSIUM TO SPARK AN EXOTHERMIC REACTION WITH THE WATER. IT SHOULDN'T HURT THEM. PERMANENTLY.
FIGHT HIM, AND YOU'RE GOING TO MAKE THINGS WORSE.
YOU JUST DID, ARTHUR.

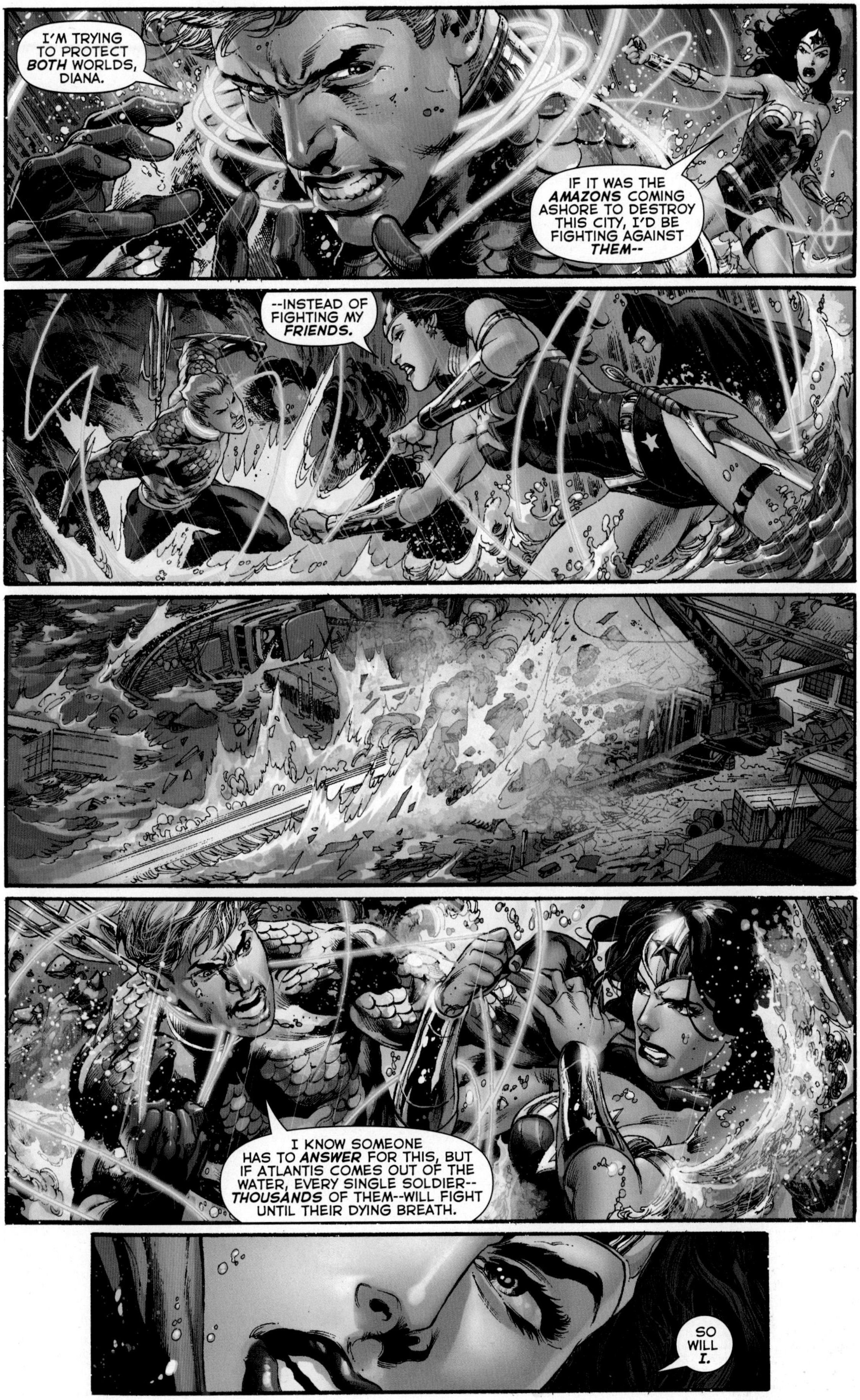
I'M TRYING TO PROTECT BOTH WORLDS, DIANA.
IF IT WAS THE AMAZONS COMING ASHORE TO DESTROY THIS CITY, I'D BE FIGHTING AGAINST THEM--
--INSTEAD OF FIGHTING MY FRIENDS.
I KNOW SOMEONE HAS TO ANSWER FOR THIS, BUT IF ATLANTIS COMES OUT OF THE WATER, EVERY SINGLE SOLDIER--THOUSANDS OF THEM--WILL FIGHT UNTIL THEIR DYING BREATH.
SO WILL I.

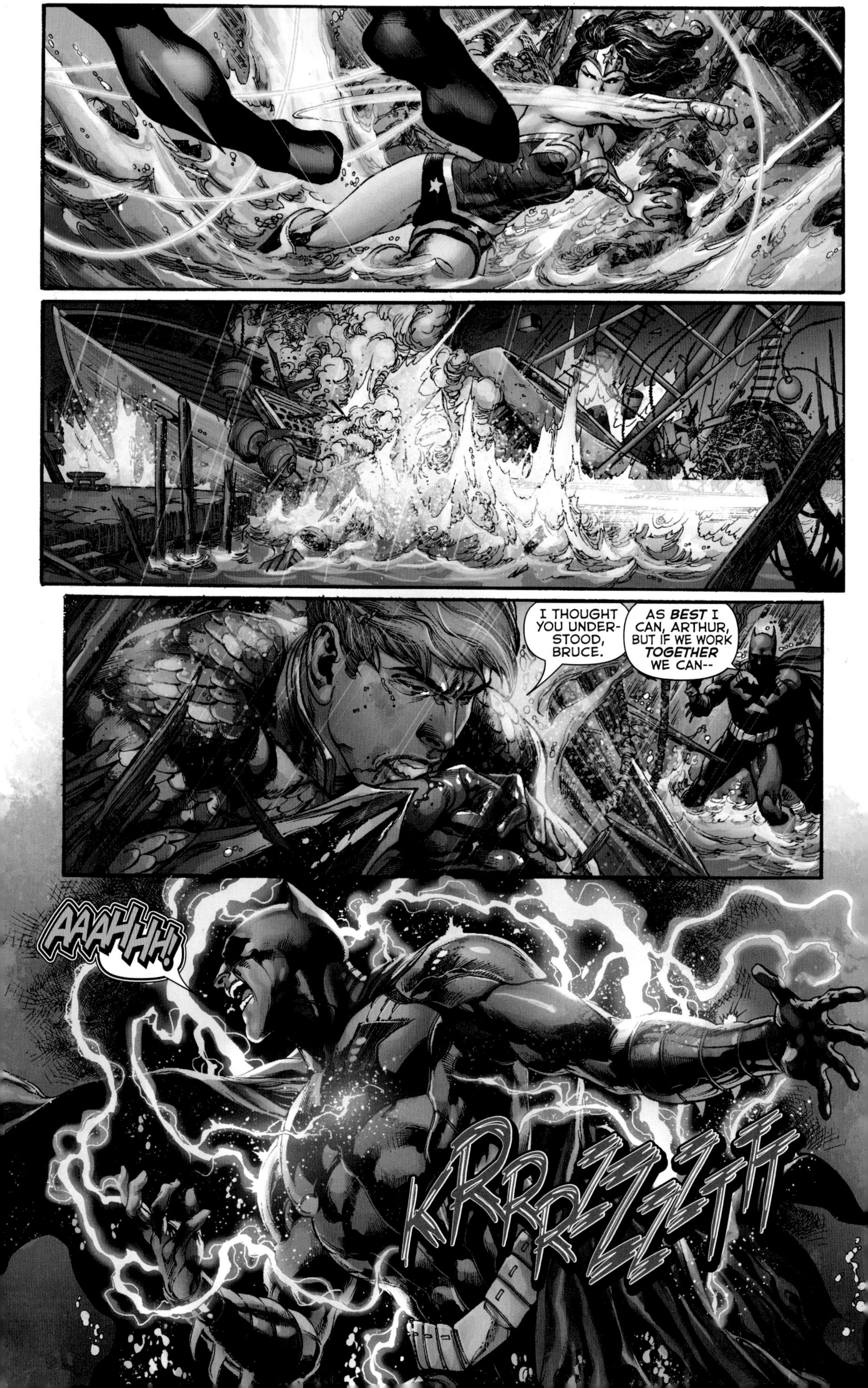
I THOUGHT YOU UNDER-STOOD, BRUCE.
AS BEST I CAN, ARTHUR, BUT IF WE WORK TOGETHER WE CAN--
AAAHHH!
KRRRZZZZTT

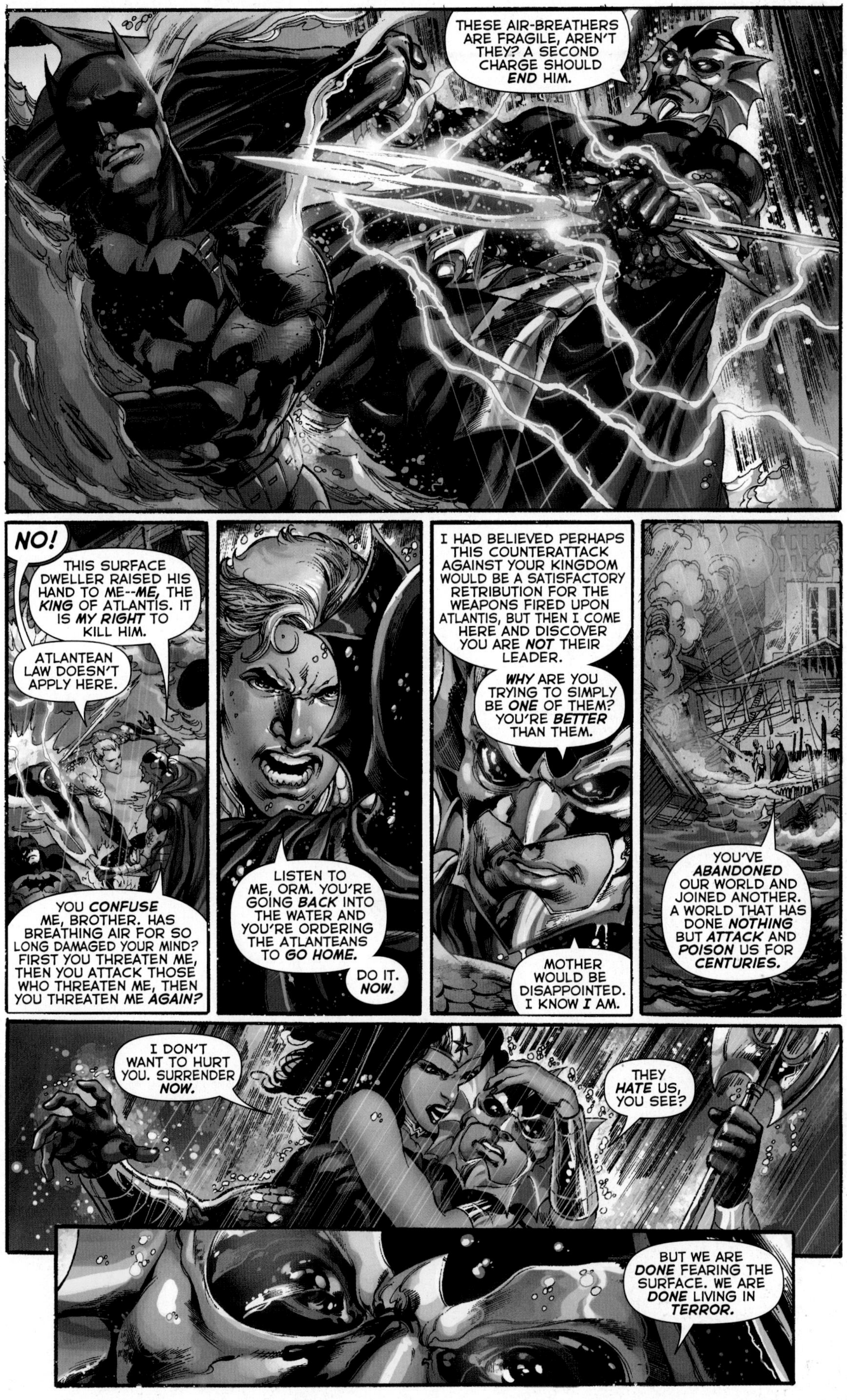
THESE AIR-BREATHERS ARE FRAGILE, AREN'T THEY? A SECOND CHARGE SHOULD END HIM.
NO!
THIS SURFACE DWELLER RAISED HIS HAND TO ME--ME, THE KING OF ATLANTIS. IT IS MY RIGHT TO KILL HIM.
ATLANTEAN LAW DOESN'T APPLY HERE.
YOU CONFUSE ME, BROTHER. HAS BREATHING AIR FOR SO LONG DAMAGED YOUR MIND? FIRST YOU THREATEN ME, THEN YOU ATTACK THOSE WHO THREATEN ME, THEN YOU THREATEN ME AGAIN?
LISTEN TO ME, ORM. YOU'RE GOING BACK INTO THE WATER AND YOU'RE ORDERING THE ATLANTEANS TO GO HOME.
DO IT. NOW.
I HAD BELIEVED PERHAPS THIS COUNTERATTACK AGAINST YOUR KINGDOM WOULD BE A SATISFACTORY RETRIBUTION FOR THE WEAPONS FIRED UPON ATLANTIS, BUT THEN I COME HERE AND DISCOVER YOU ARE NOT THEIR LEADER.
WHY ARE YOU TRYING TO SIMPLY BE ONE OF THEM? YOU'RE BETTER THAN THEM.
MOTHER WOULD BE DISAPPOINTED. I KNOW I AM.
YOU'VE ABANDONED OUR WORLD AND JOINED ANOTHER. A WORLD THAT HAS DONE NOTHING BUT ATTACK AND POISON US FOR CENTURIES.
I DON'T WANT TO HURT YOU. SURRENDER NOW.
THEY HATE US, YOU SEE?
BUT WE ARE DONE FEARING THE SURFACE. WE ARE DONE LIVING IN TERROR.

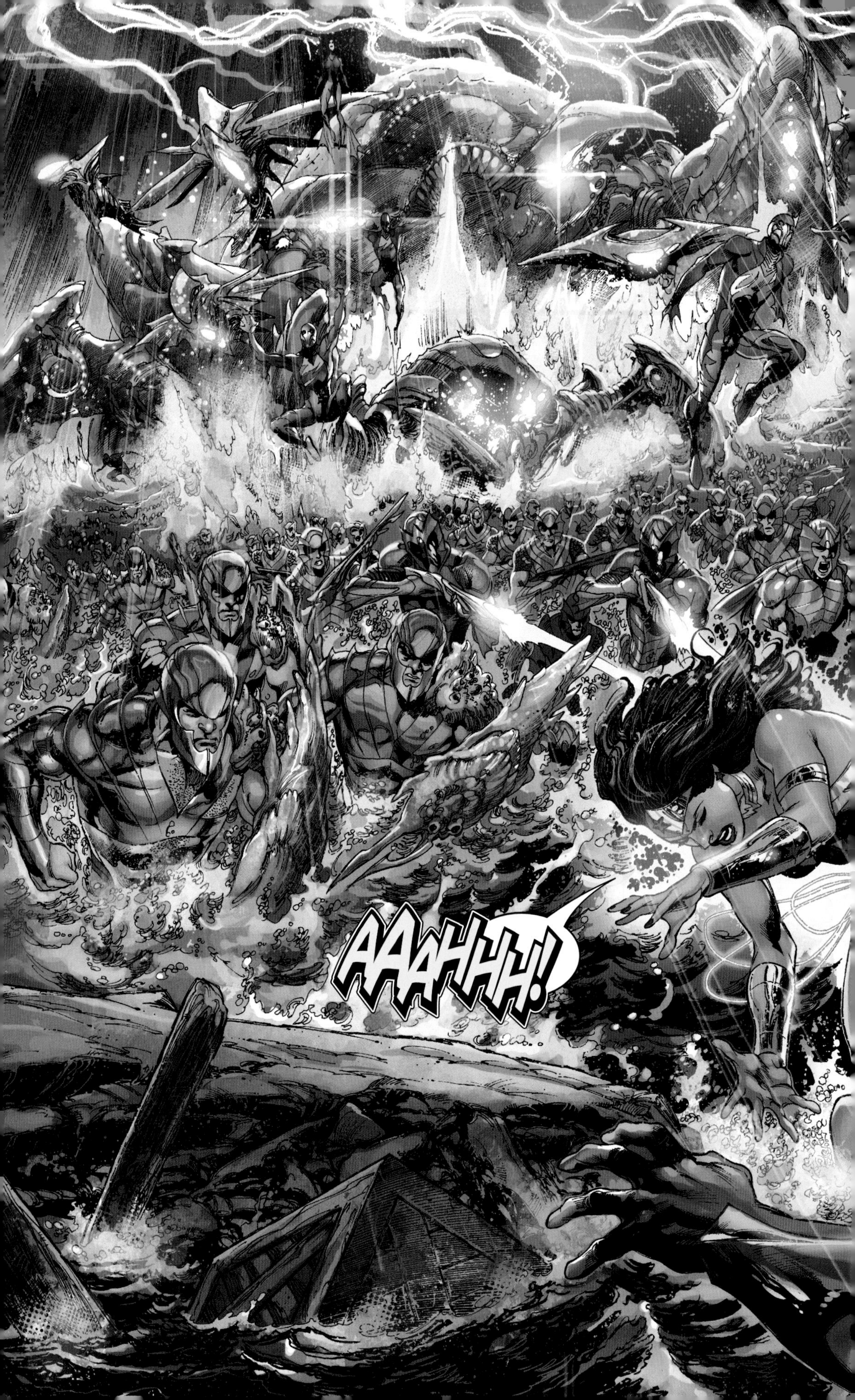
AAAHHH!

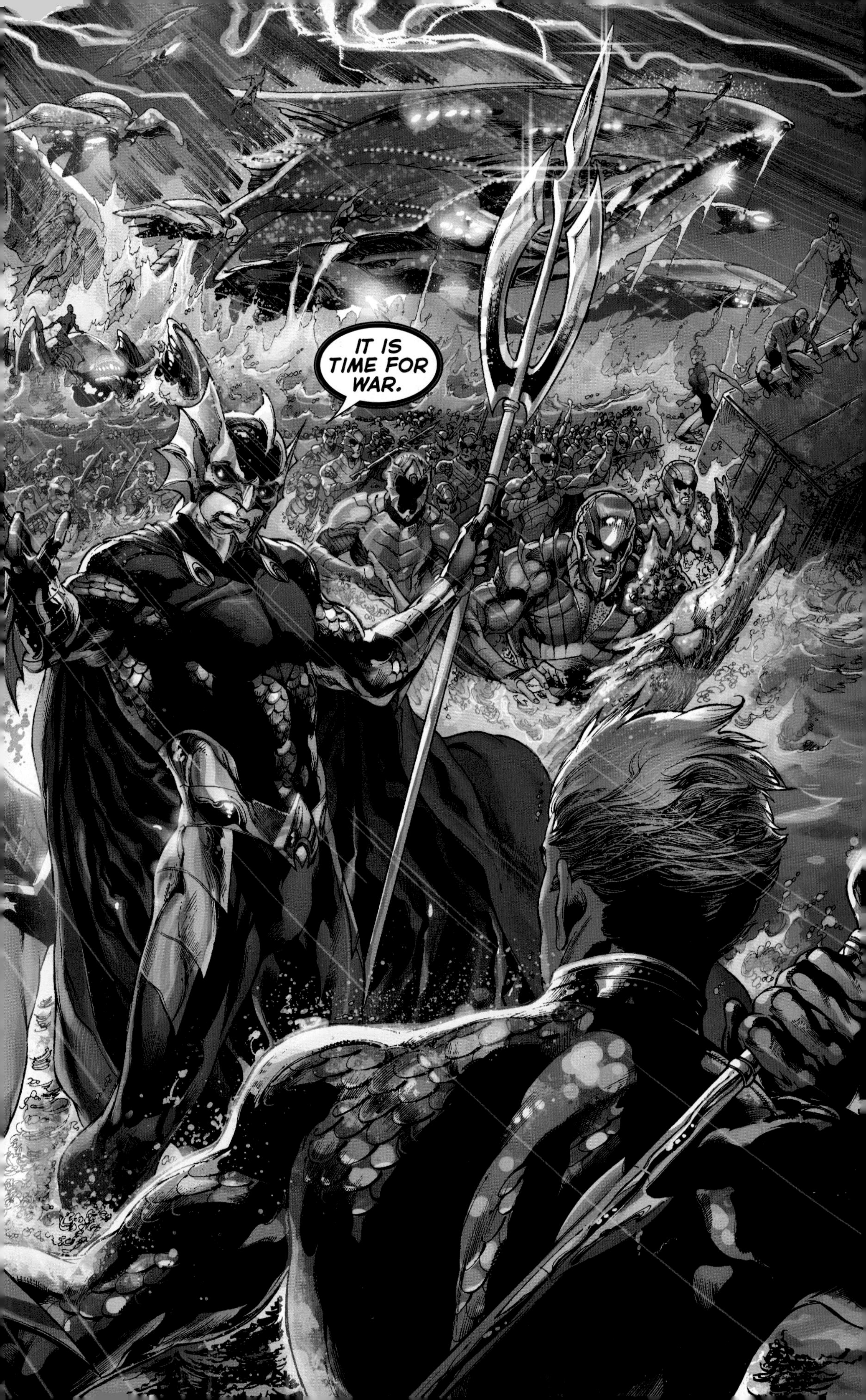
IT IS TIME FOR WAR.

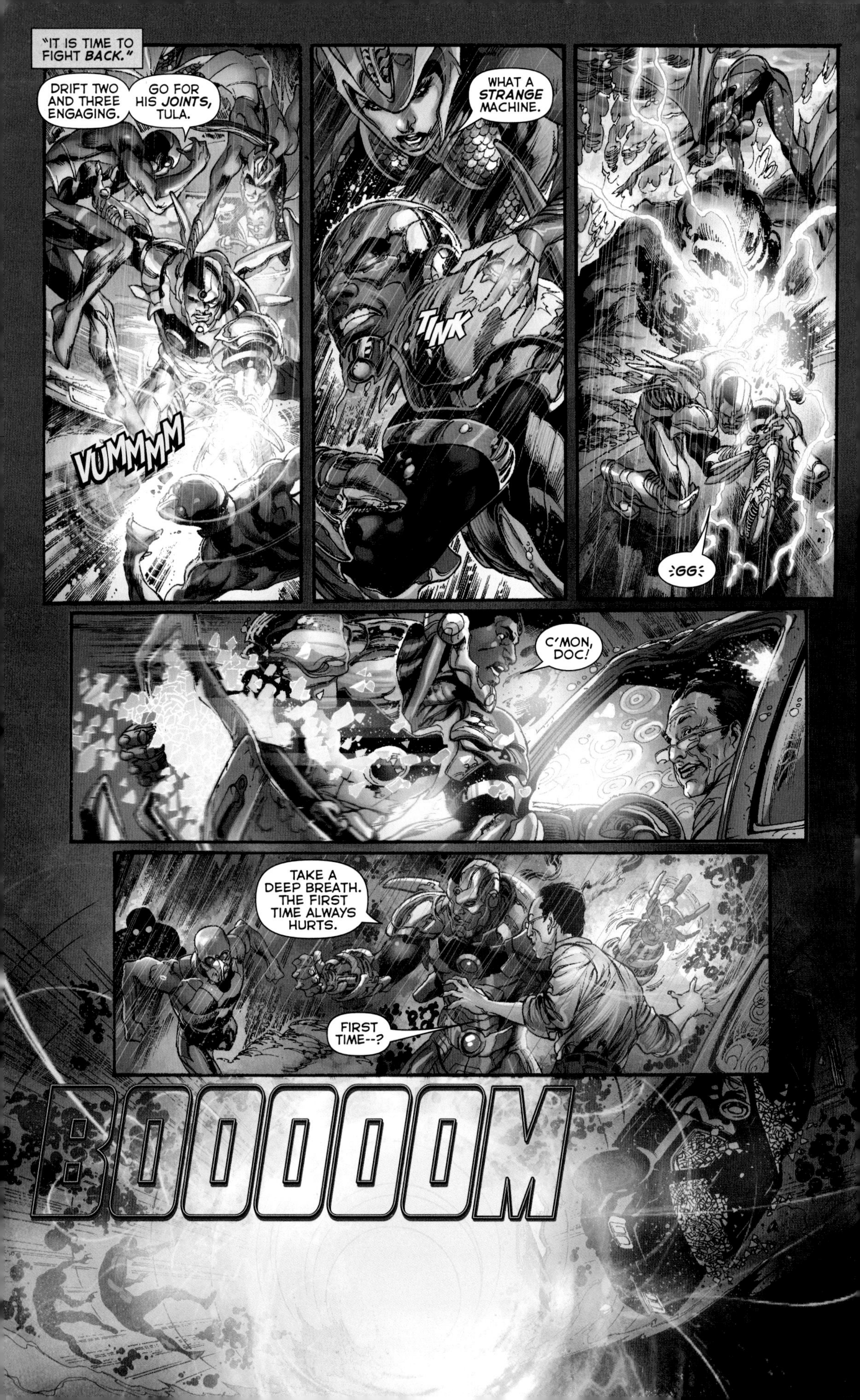
"IT IS TIME TO FIGHT BACK."
DRIFT TWO AND THREE ENGAGING.
GO FOR HIS JOINTS, TULA.
VUMMMM
WHAT A STRANGE MACHINE.
TINK
GG
C'MON, DOC!
TAKE A DEEP BREATH. THE FIRST TIME ALWAYS HURTS.
FIRST TIME--?
BOOOOOM

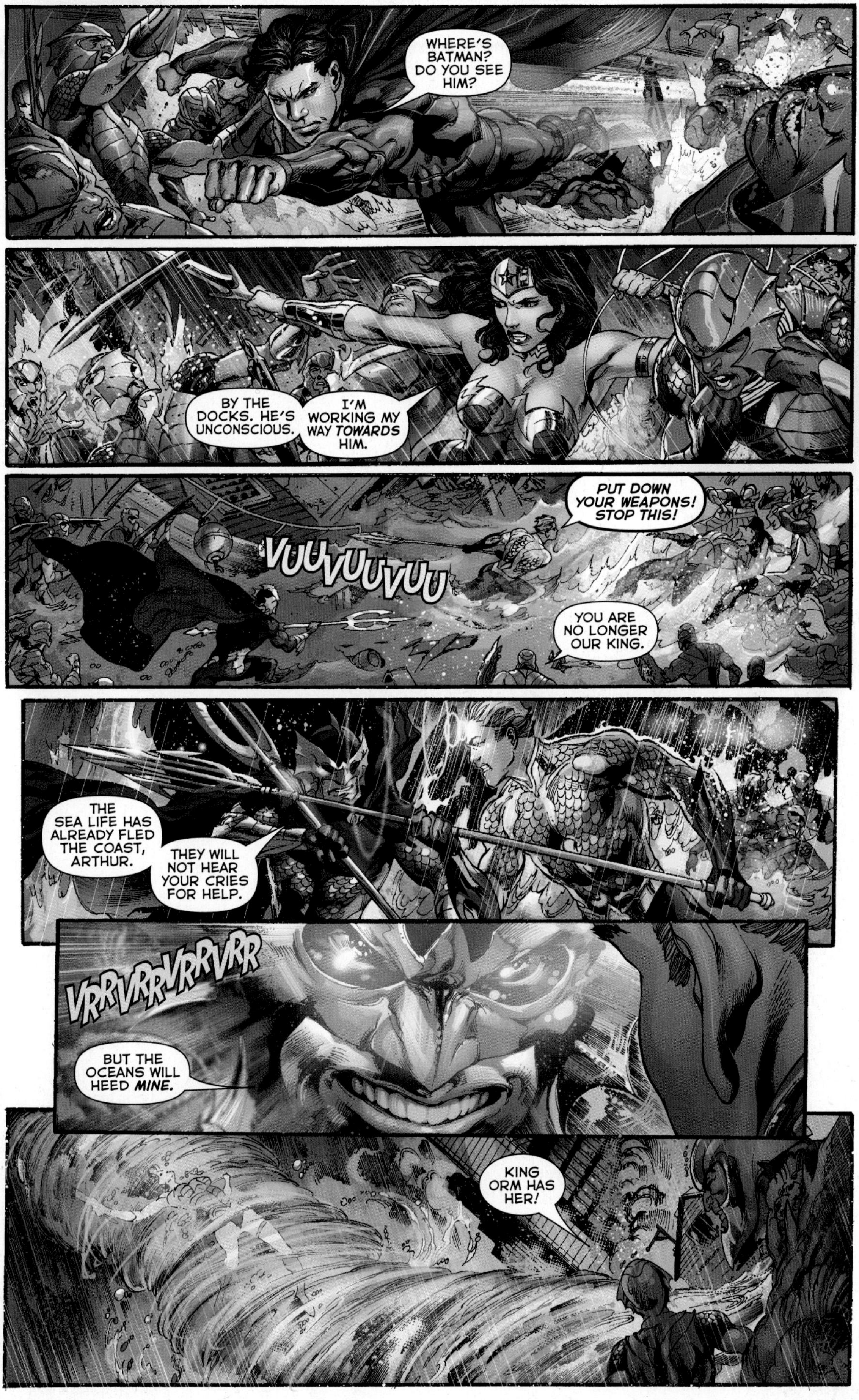
WHERE'S BATMAN? DO YOU SEE HIM?
BY THE DOCKS. HE'S UNCONSCIOUS.
I'M WORKING MY WAY TOWARDS HIM.
PUT DOWN YOUR WEAPONS! STOP THIS!
VUUVUUVUU
YOU ARE NO LONGER OUR KING.
THE SEA LIFE HAS ALREADY FLED THE COAST, ARTHUR.
THEY WILL NOT HEAR YOUR CRIES FOR HELP.
VRRVRRVRRVRR
BUT THE OCEANS WILL HEED MINE.
KING ORM HAS HER!

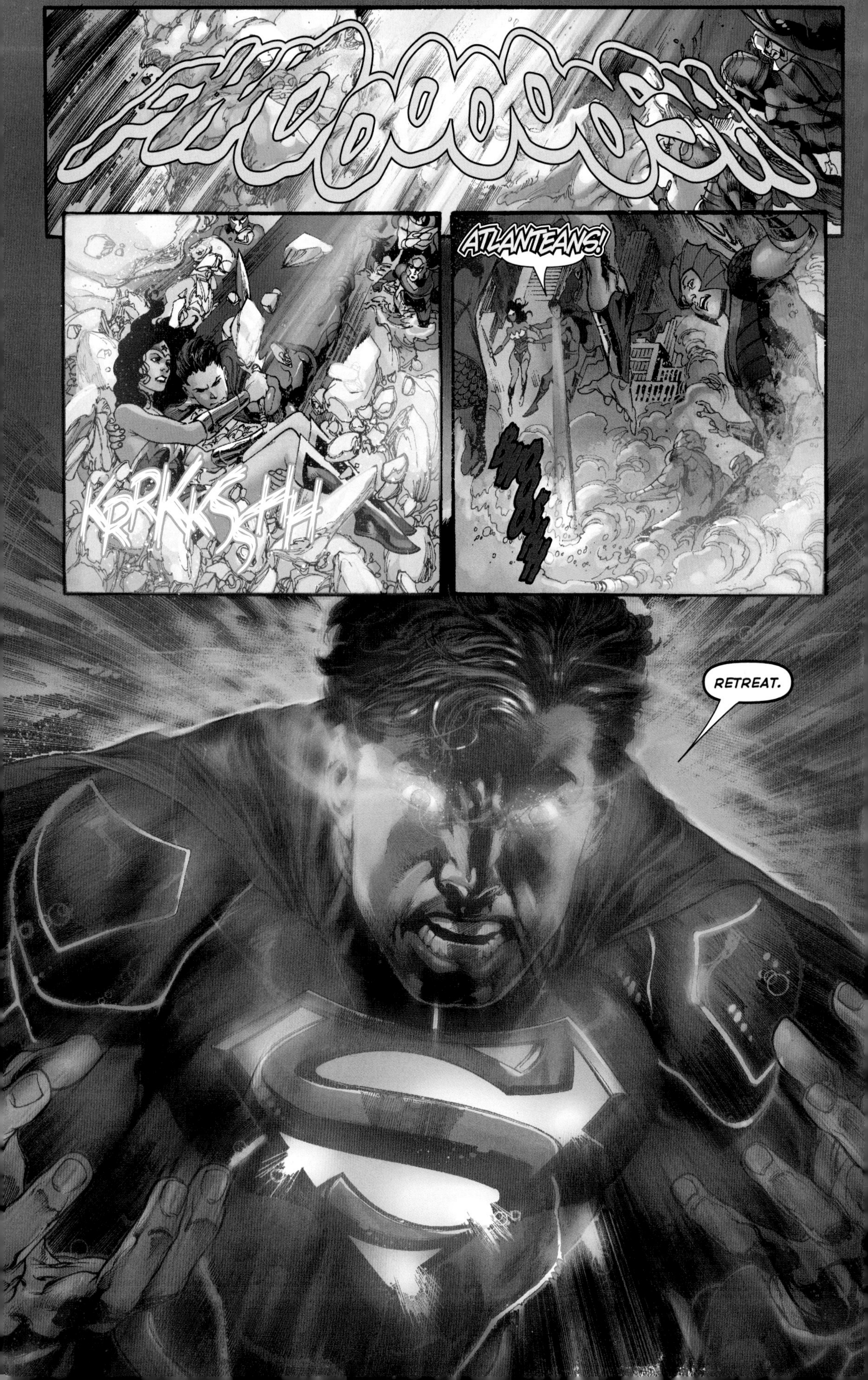
KRRKKSHH
ATLANTEANS!
RETREAT.

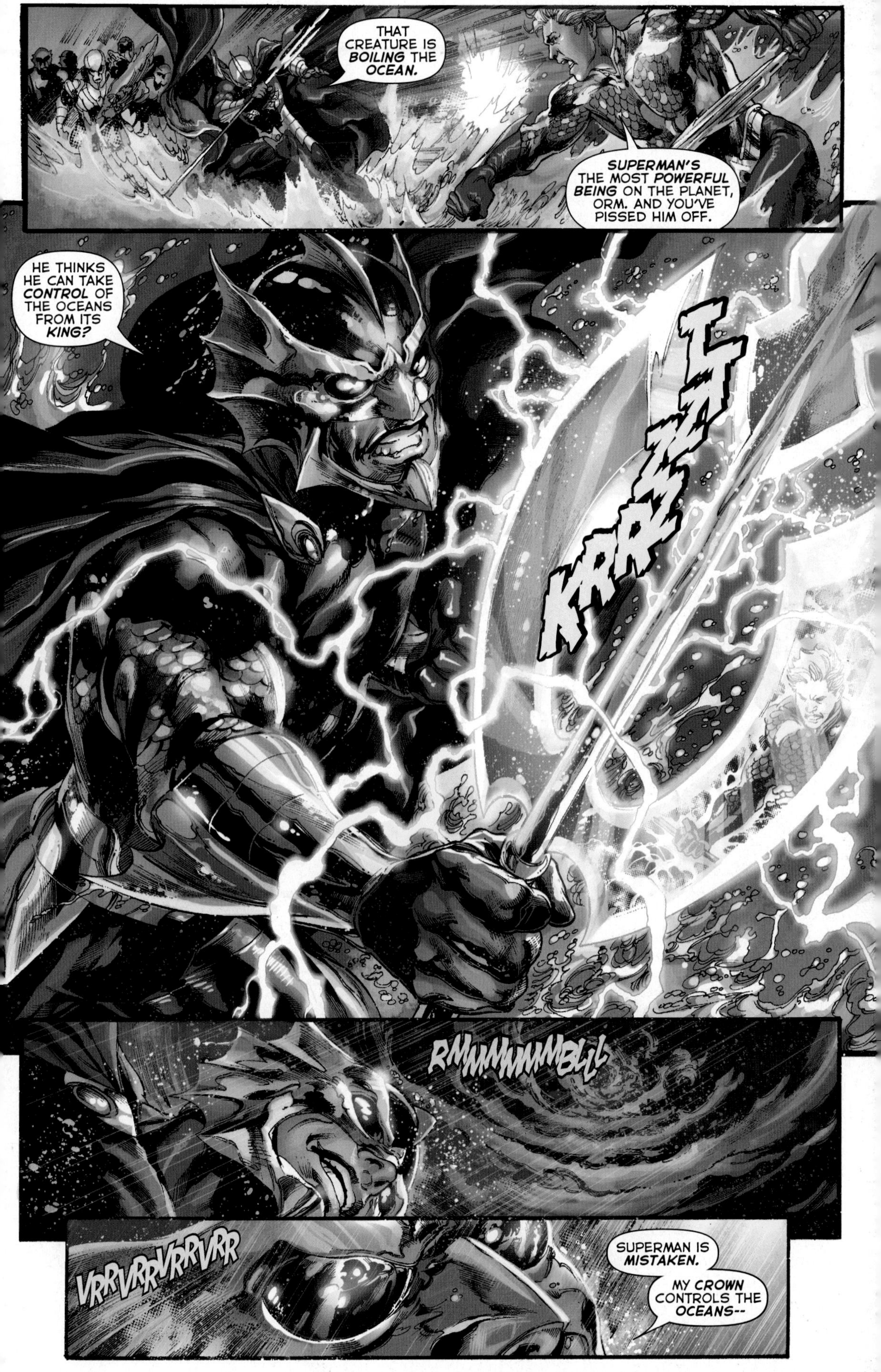
THAT CREATURE IS BOILING THE OCEAN.
SUPERMAN'S THE MOST POWERFUL BEING ON THE PLANET, ORM. AND YOU'VE PISSED HIM OFF.
HE THINKS HE CAN TAKE CONTROL OF THE OCEANS FROM ITS KING?
KRRZZZZT
RMMMMMMBLLL
VRRVRRVRRVRR
SUPERMAN IS MISTAKEN.
MY CROWN CONTROLS THE OCEANS--

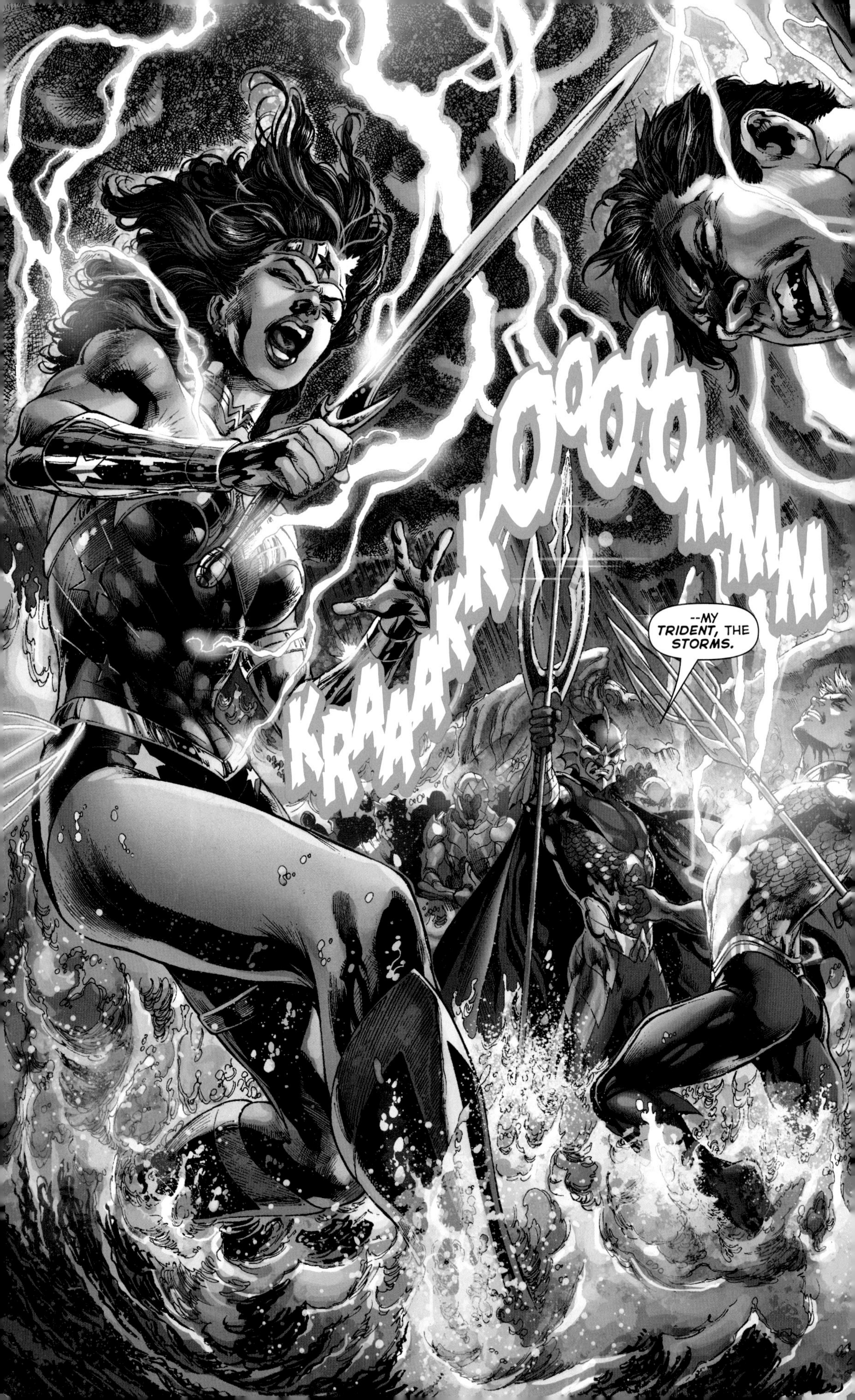
KRAAAKKOOOOOMMM
--MY TRIDENT, THE STORMS.

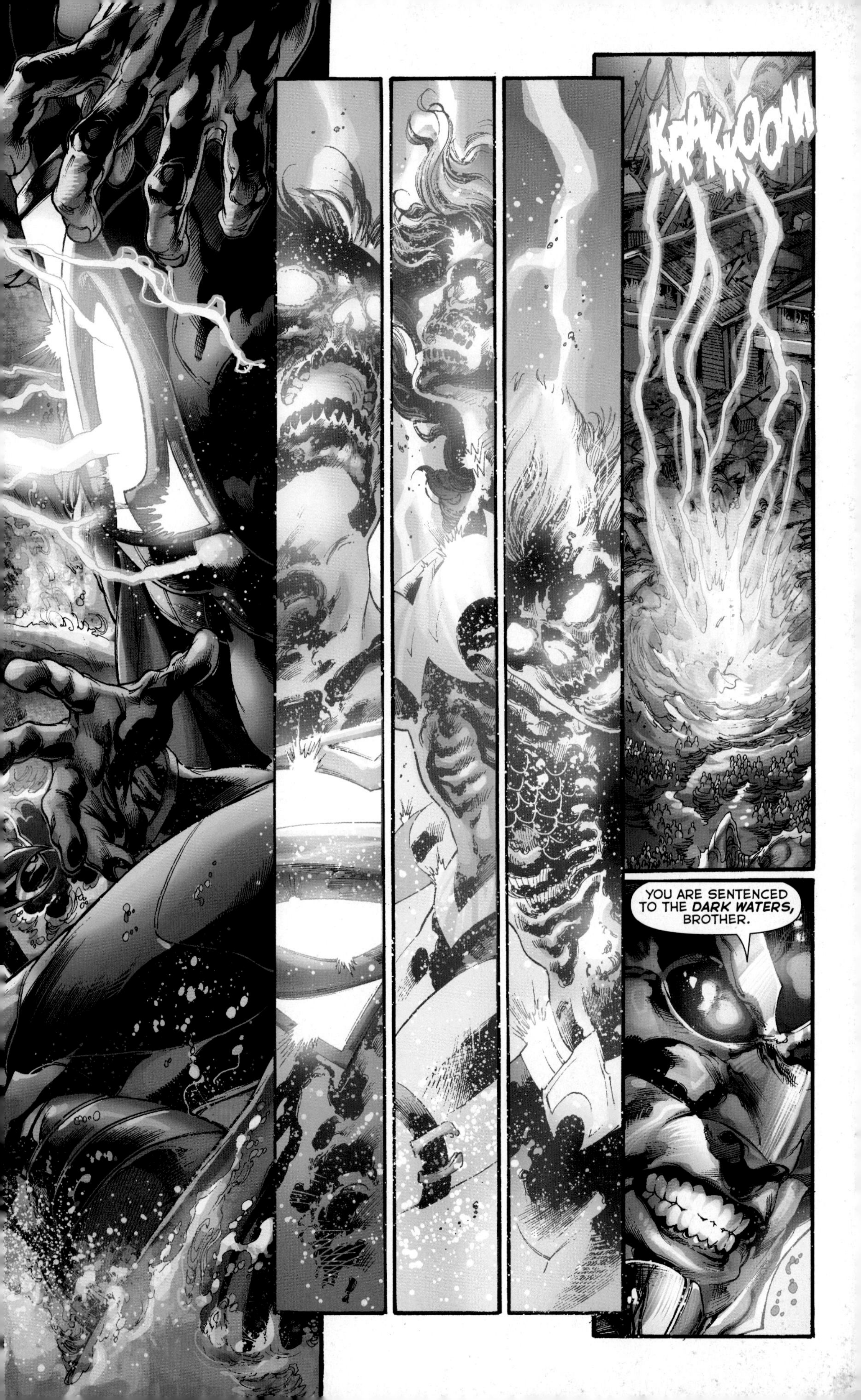
KRAKOOM
YOU ARE SENTENCED TO THE DARK WATERS, BROTHER.

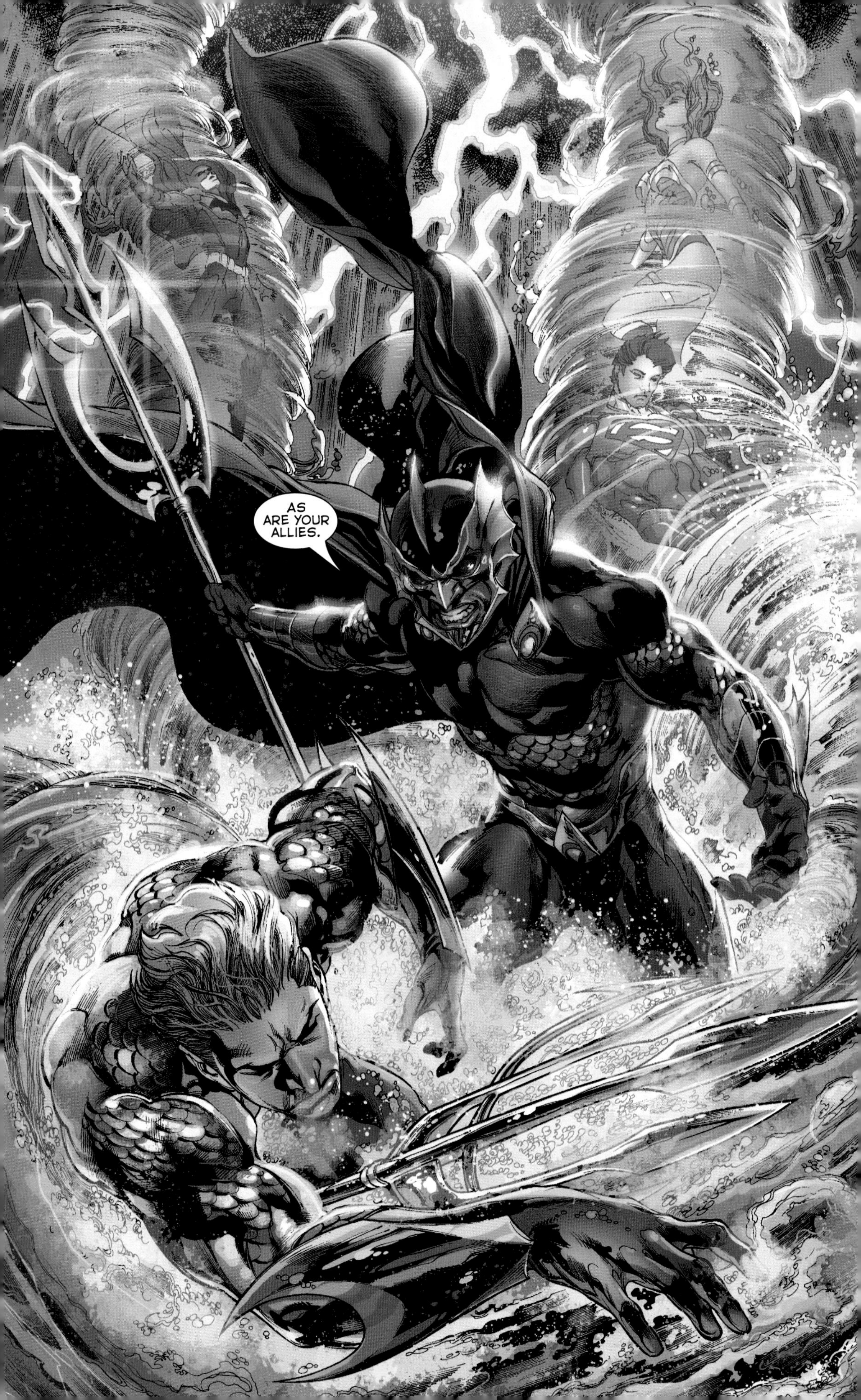
AS ARE YOUR ALLIES.

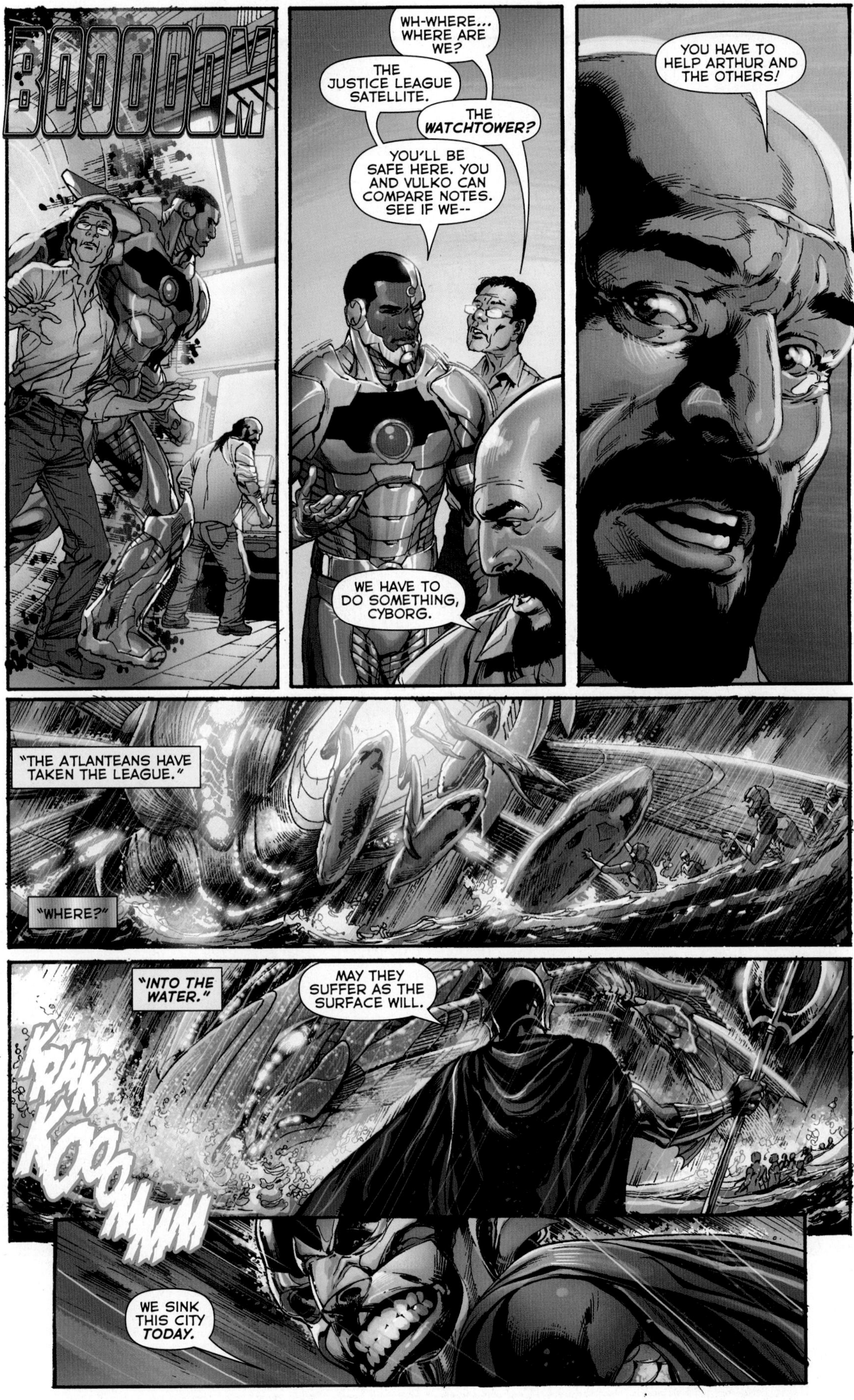
BOOOOOM
WH-WHERE... WHERE ARE WE?
THE JUSTICE LEAGUE SATELLITE.
THE *WATCHTOWER?*
YOU'LL BE SAFE HERE. YOU AND VULKO CAN COMPARE NOTES. SEE IF WE--
WE HAVE TO DO SOMETHING, CYBORG.
YOU HAVE TO HELP ARTHUR AND THE OTHERS!
"THE ATLANTEANS HAVE TAKEN THE LEAGUE."
"WHERE?"
"INTO THE WATER."
MAY THEY SUFFER AS THE SURFACE WILL.
KRAK KOOOMMM
WE SINK THIS CITY *TODAY.*

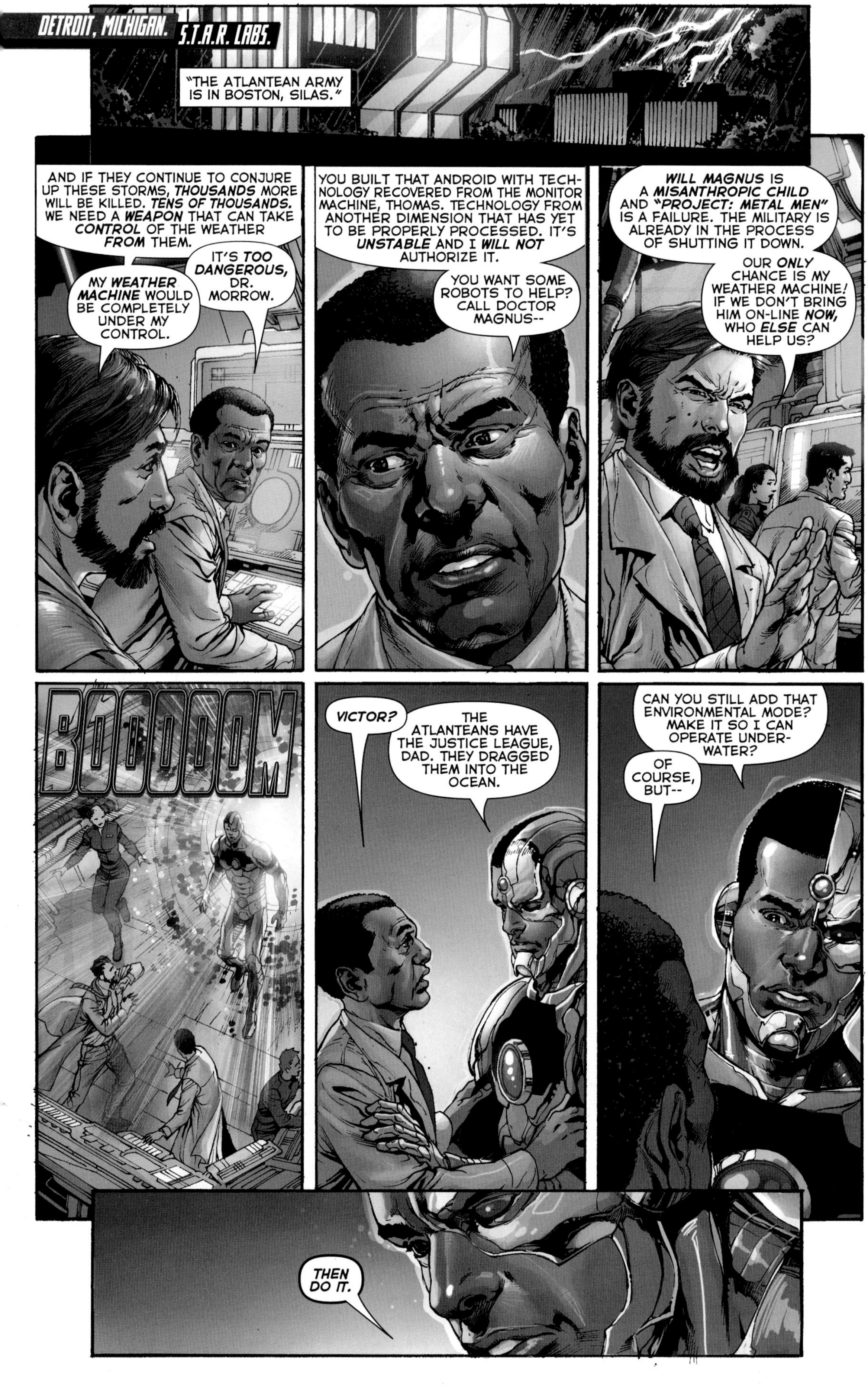
DETROIT, MICHIGAN.
S.T.A.R. LABS.
"THE ATLANTEAN ARMY IS IN BOSTON, SILAS."
AND IF THEY CONTINUE TO CONJURE UP THESE STORMS, THOUSANDS MORE WILL BE KILLED. TENS OF THOUSANDS. WE NEED A WEAPON THAT CAN TAKE CONTROL OF THE WEATHER FROM THEM.
MY WEATHER MACHINE WOULD BE COMPLETELY UNDER MY CONTROL.
IT'S TOO DANGEROUS, DR. MORROW.
YOU BUILT THAT ANDROID WITH TECHNOLOGY RECOVERED FROM THE MONITOR MACHINE, THOMAS. TECHNOLOGY FROM ANOTHER DIMENSION THAT HAS YET TO BE PROPERLY PROCESSED. IT'S UNSTABLE AND I WILL NOT AUTHORIZE IT.
YOU WANT SOME ROBOTS TO HELP? CALL DOCTOR MAGNUS--
WILL MAGNUS IS A MISANTHROPIC CHILD AND "PROJECT: METAL MEN" IS A FAILURE. THE MILITARY IS ALREADY IN THE PROCESS OF SHUTTING IT DOWN.
OUR ONLY CHANCE IS MY WEATHER MACHINE! IF WE DON'T BRING HIM ON-LINE NOW, WHO ELSE CAN HELP US?
BOOOOOM
VICTOR?
THE ATLANTEANS HAVE THE JUSTICE LEAGUE, DAD. THEY DRAGGED THEM INTO THE OCEAN.
CAN YOU STILL ADD THAT ENVIRONMENTAL MODE? MAKE IT SO I CAN OPERATE UNDERWATER?
OF COURSE, BUT--
THEN DO IT.

VICTOR, YOU KNOW WHAT WE'D HAVE TO DO. YOUR REMAINING *LUNG*--

GOES IN THE TRASH. JUST KEEP MY BRAIN AND MY HEART INTACT, DAD.

YOU TOLD ME THAT'S ALL I *NEED* TO STILL BE *ME*, RIGHT?

"HOW LONG WILL THIS TAKE?"

WE'LL PERFORM THE OPERATION AS QUICKLY AS POSSIBLE.

HOW LONG, DAD?

WE'LL NEED AT LEAST A FEW *HOURS*.

THEN I'VE GOT NO CHOICE BUT TO ASK FOR HELP.

WE WANTED TO *VET* THESE GUYS BEFORE BRINGING THEM ON BOARD, BUT THERE'S NO TIME.

CONNECT ME TO THE GRID.

VEET

CONNECTED.

THIS IS *CYBORG* OF THE *JUSTICE LEAGUE.*

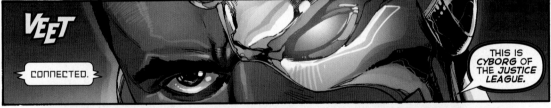

"WE NEED YOUR HELP."

THE *WORLD* NEEDS YOUR HELP.

WHAT'S CYBORG DOING? WHO'S HE TALKING TO?

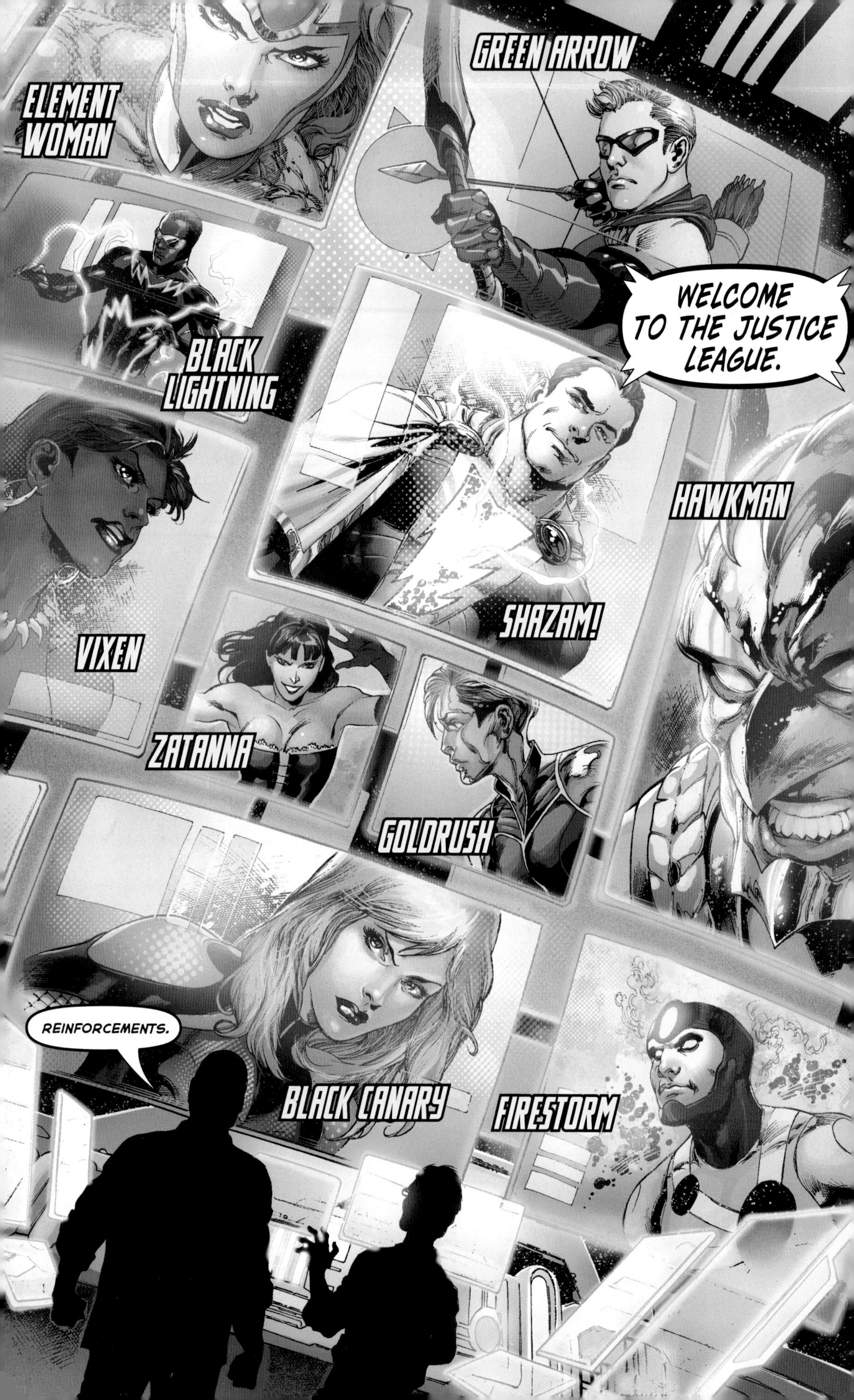
ELEMENT WOMAN
GREEN ARROW
BLACK LIGHTNING
WELCOME TO THE JUSTICE LEAGUE.
HAWKMAN
VIXEN
SHAZAM!
ZATANNA
GOLDRUSH
REINFORCEMENTS.
BLACK CANARY
FIRESTORM

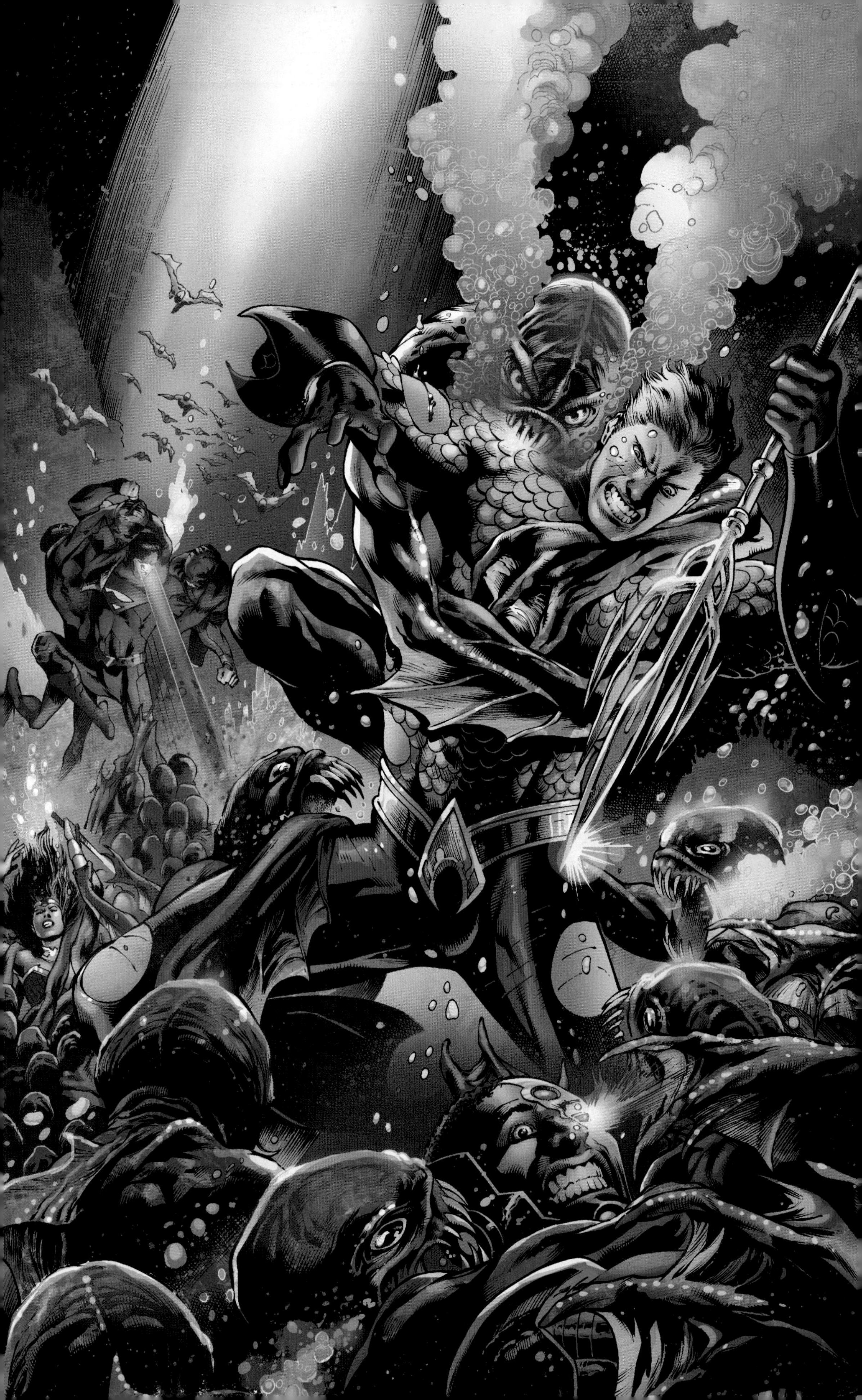

GEOFF JOHNS writer PAUL PELLETIER penciller SEAN PARSONS inker cover by EDDY BARROWS, EBER FERREIRA & ROD REIS

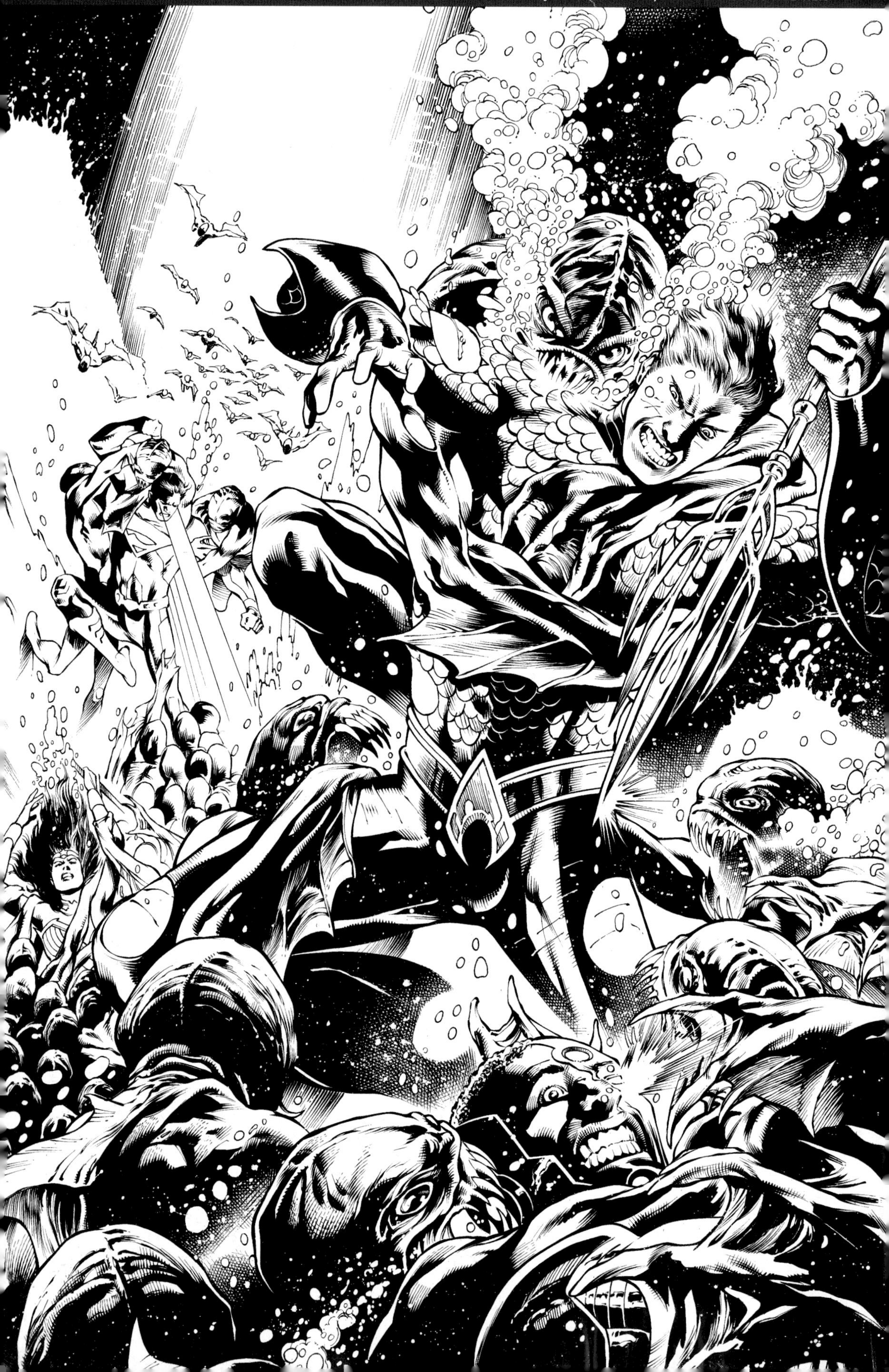

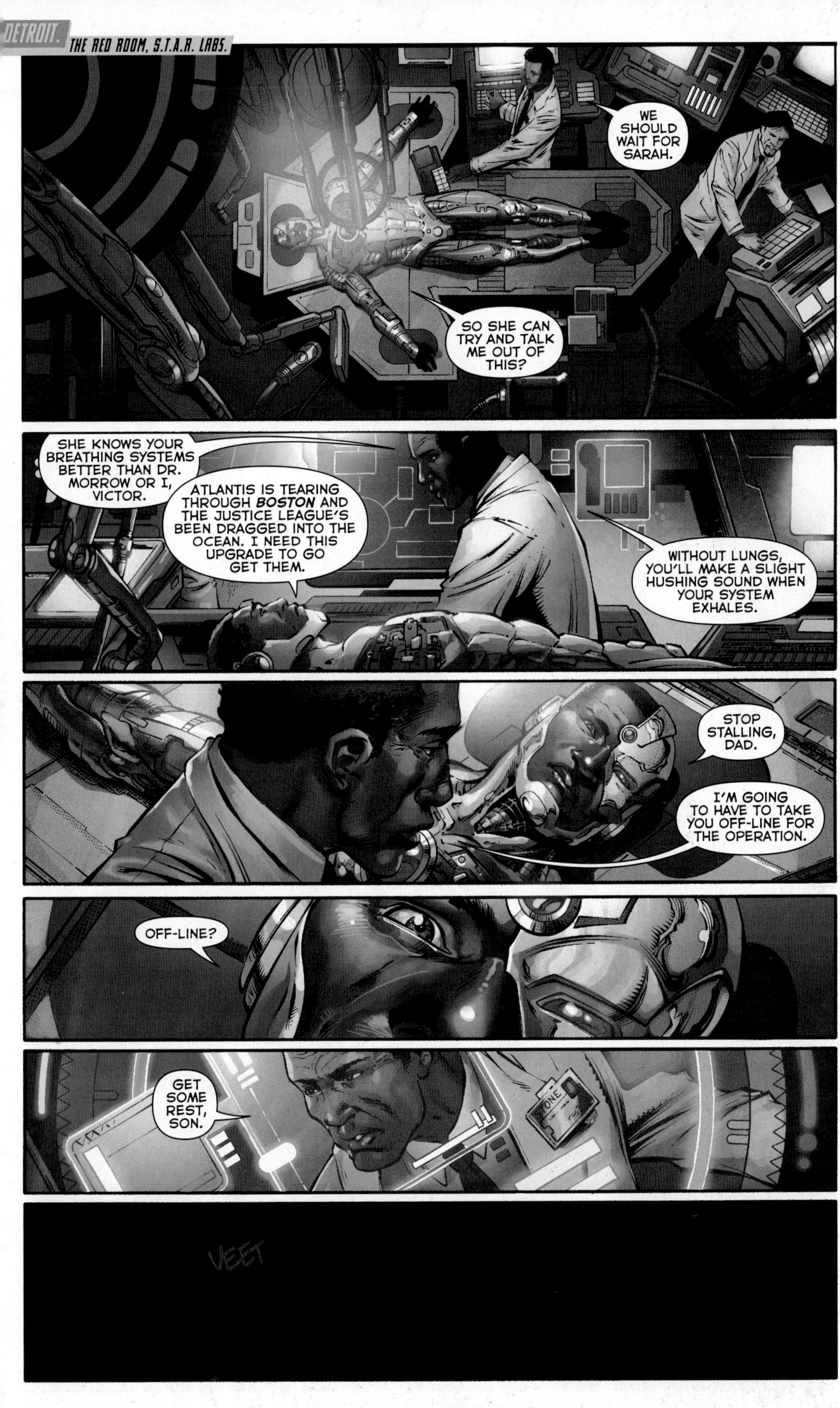
DETROIT.
THE RED ROOM, S.T.A.R. LABS.
WE SHOULD WAIT FOR SARAH.
SO SHE CAN TRY AND TALK ME OUT OF THIS?
SHE KNOWS YOUR BREATHING SYSTEMS BETTER THAN DR. MORROW OR I, VICTOR.
ATLANTIS IS TEARING THROUGH BOSTON AND THE JUSTICE LEAGUE'S BEEN DRAGGED INTO THE OCEAN. I NEED THIS UPGRADE TO GO GET THEM.
WITHOUT LUNGS, YOU'LL MAKE A SLIGHT HUSHING SOUND WHEN YOUR SYSTEM EXHALES.
STOP STALLING, DAD.
I'M GOING TO HAVE TO TAKE YOU OFF-LINE FOR THE OPERATION.
OFF-LINE?
GET SOME REST, SON.
VEET

WE NEED TO MOVE QUICKLY, THOMAS.

WE WOULDN'T HAVE TO SUBJECT YOUR SON TO THIS *HORRIFIC* OPERATION IF YOU'D JUST AGREED TO LETTING ME *ACTIVATE* THE *ANDROID*.

I'M NOT HAVING THIS DISCUSSION *AGAIN*, THOMAS.

BUT THE TORNADO COULD--

WHAT IS THAT?

FILE PROCESSING.

VICTOR UPLOADED A *VIDEO SIGNAL* OF SOME KIND.

HIS MIND'S GONE DORMANT, BUT HE'S STILL RUNNING A PROGRAM.

IT'S THE SECURITY FEED FROM THE U.S.S. MABUS. THE FILE'S BEEN BADLY CORRUPTED, BUT HE'S TRYING TO *REBUILD* IT.

...GMENTATION 13%

WHY?

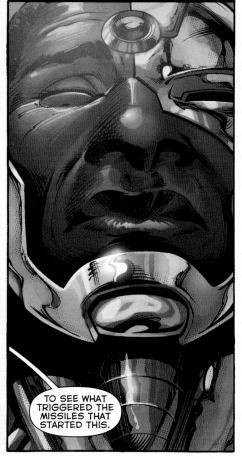

TO SEE WHAT TRIGGERED THE MISSILES THAT STARTED THIS.

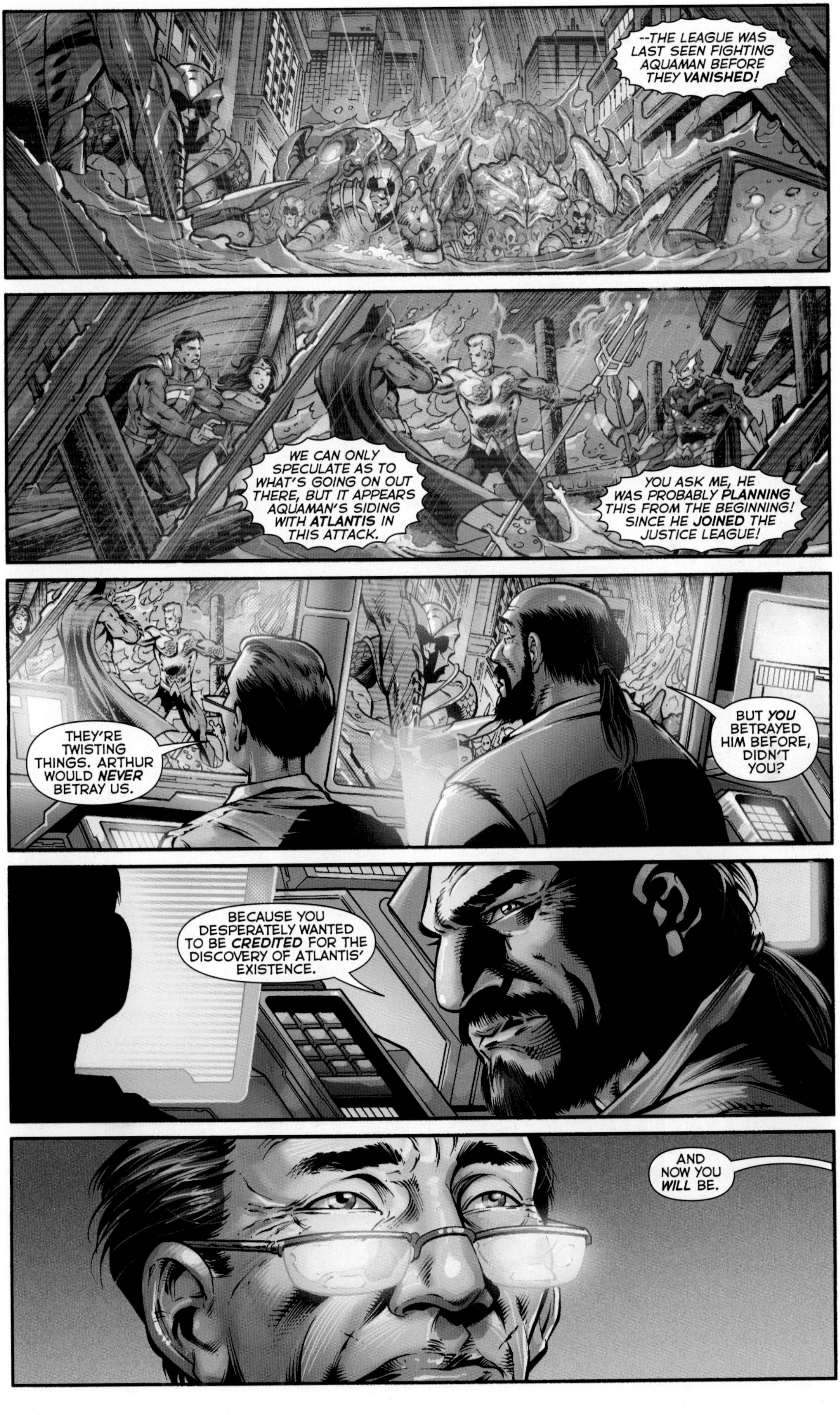
--THE LEAGUE WAS LAST SEEN FIGHTING AQUAMAN BEFORE THEY VANISHED!
WE CAN ONLY SPECULATE AS TO WHAT'S GOING ON OUT THERE, BUT IT APPEARS AQUAMAN'S SIDING WITH ATLANTIS IN THIS ATTACK.
YOU ASK ME, HE WAS PROBABLY PLANNING THIS FROM THE BEGINNING! SINCE HE JOINED THE JUSTICE LEAGUE!
THEY'RE TWISTING THINGS. ARTHUR WOULD NEVER BETRAY US.
BUT YOU BETRAYED HIM BEFORE, DIDN'T YOU?
BECAUSE YOU DESPERATELY WANTED TO BE CREDITED FOR THE DISCOVERY OF ATLANTIS' EXISTENCE.
AND NOW YOU WILL BE.

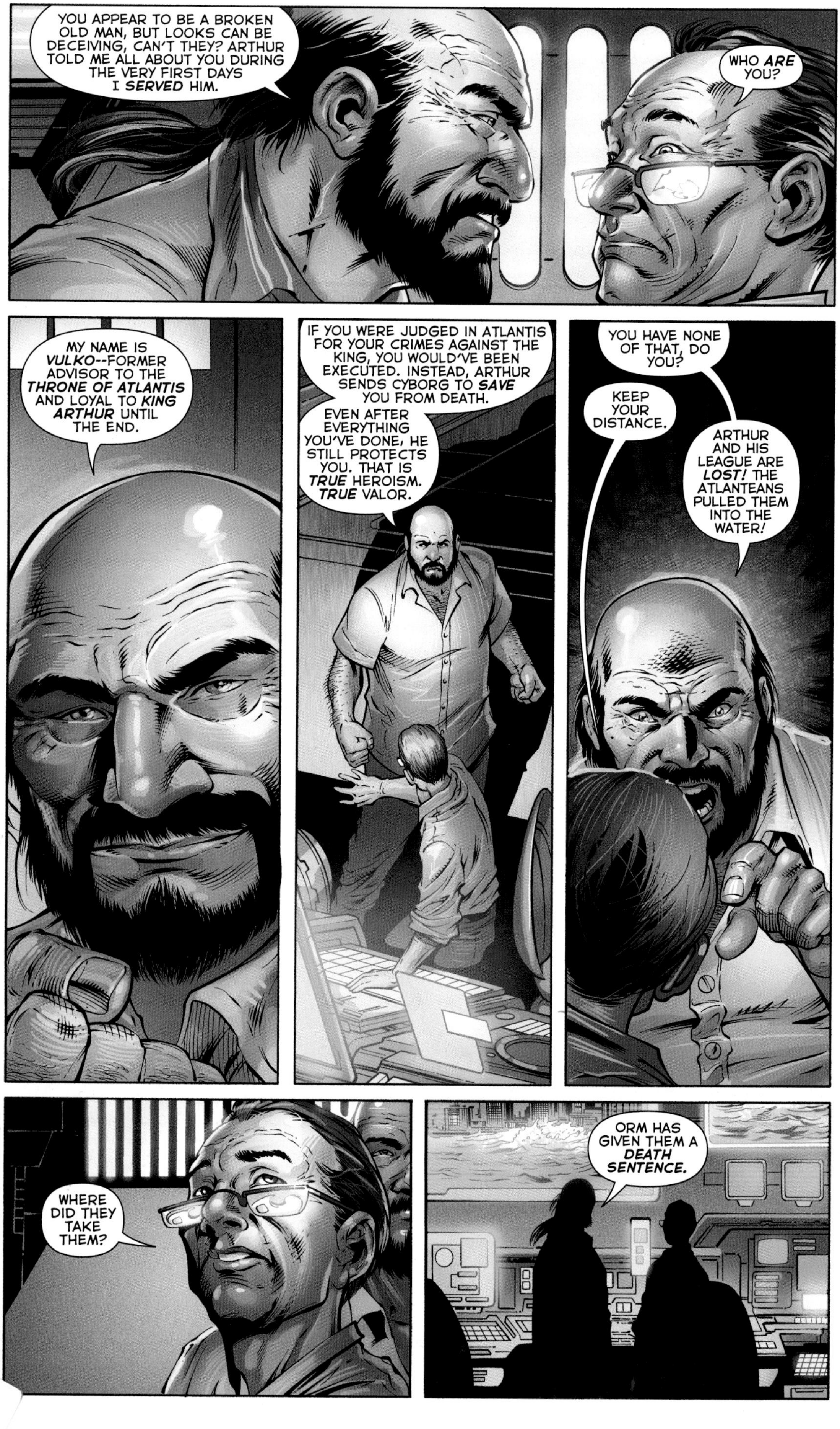
YOU APPEAR TO BE A BROKEN OLD MAN, BUT LOOKS CAN BE DECEIVING, CAN'T THEY? ARTHUR TOLD ME ALL ABOUT YOU DURING THE VERY FIRST DAYS I SERVED HIM.
WHO ARE YOU?
MY NAME IS VULKO--FORMER ADVISOR TO THE THRONE OF ATLANTIS AND LOYAL TO KING ARTHUR UNTIL THE END.
IF YOU WERE JUDGED IN ATLANTIS FOR YOUR CRIMES AGAINST THE KING, YOU WOULD'VE BEEN EXECUTED. INSTEAD, ARTHUR SENDS CYBORG TO SAVE YOU FROM DEATH.
EVEN AFTER EVERYTHING YOU'VE DONE, HE STILL PROTECTS YOU. THAT IS TRUE HEROISM. TRUE VALOR.
YOU HAVE NONE OF THAT, DO YOU?
KEEP YOUR DISTANCE.
ARTHUR AND HIS LEAGUE ARE LOST! THE ATLANTEANS PULLED THEM INTO THE WATER!
WHERE DID THEY TAKE THEM?
ORM HAS GIVEN THEM A DEATH SENTENCE.

"HE'S BANISHED THEM TO THE DARK WATERS."

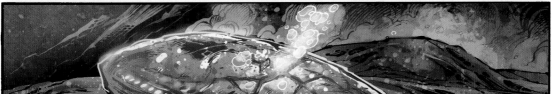

AQUAMAN?

BATMAN?

YOU OKAY?

MY REGULATOR IS ADJUSTING THE OXYGEN LEVELS TO *AVOID* TOXICITY, AND I'VE ACTIVATED A *BEACON* TO ALERT CYBORG, THOUGH *VOICE COMMUNICATION* ISN'T GETTING THROUGH. WE MUST BE ON THE OTHER SIDE OF THE THERMOCLINE.

MY SUIT CAN HANDLE EXTREME PRESSURES.

NOT THIS EXTREME, BRUCE.

HOW DEEP ARE WE?

LASER CUTTER SHOULD GET ME OUT--

I'D RECOMMEND SITTING TIGHT. THE PODS ARE DESIGNED TO KEEP THE IMPRISONED *ALIVE* SO THEY'RE MAINTAINING PRESSURE.

BOTTOM OF THE OCEAN. MAYBE FURTHER. I'M GOING TO GATHER WHAT BIOLUMINESCENT FISH I CAN TO LIGHT UP THE AREA.

WE DON'T NEED LIGHT TO SEE WHERE WE ARE.

VUU VUUVUU VUU VUU

YOU HAVE A *POWER* I DON'T KNOW ABOUT?

THIS ISN'T THE FIRST TIME I'VE BEEN TRAPPED IN A CONFINED SPACE.

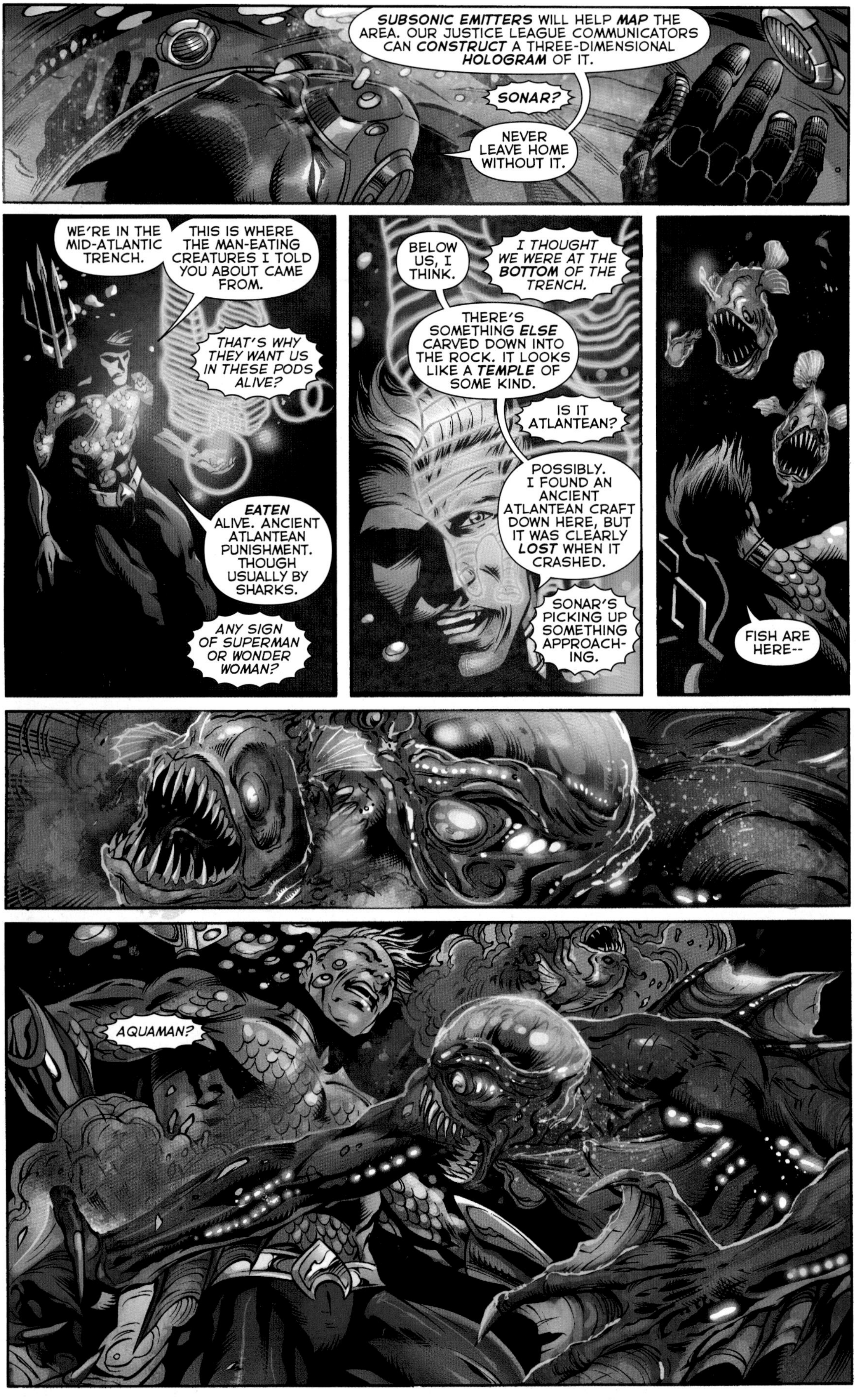

SUBSONIC EMITTERS WILL HELP MAP THE AREA. OUR JUSTICE LEAGUE COMMUNICATORS CAN CONSTRUCT A THREE-DIMENSIONAL HOLOGRAM OF IT.
SONAR?
NEVER LEAVE HOME WITHOUT IT.
WE'RE IN THE MID-ATLANTIC TRENCH.
THIS IS WHERE THE MAN-EATING CREATURES I TOLD YOU ABOUT CAME FROM.
THAT'S WHY THEY WANT US IN THESE PODS ALIVE?
EATEN ALIVE. ANCIENT ATLANTEAN PUNISHMENT. THOUGH USUALLY BY SHARKS.
ANY SIGN OF SUPERMAN OR WONDER WOMAN?
BELOW US, I THINK.
I THOUGHT WE WERE AT THE BOTTOM OF THE TRENCH.
THERE'S SOMETHING ELSE CARVED DOWN INTO THE ROCK. IT LOOKS LIKE A TEMPLE OF SOME KIND.
IS IT ATLANTEAN?
POSSIBLY. I FOUND AN ANCIENT ATLANTEAN CRAFT DOWN HERE, BUT IT WAS CLEARLY LOST WHEN IT CRASHED.
SONAR'S PICKING UP SOMETHING APPROACH-ING.
FISH ARE HERE--
AQUAMAN?

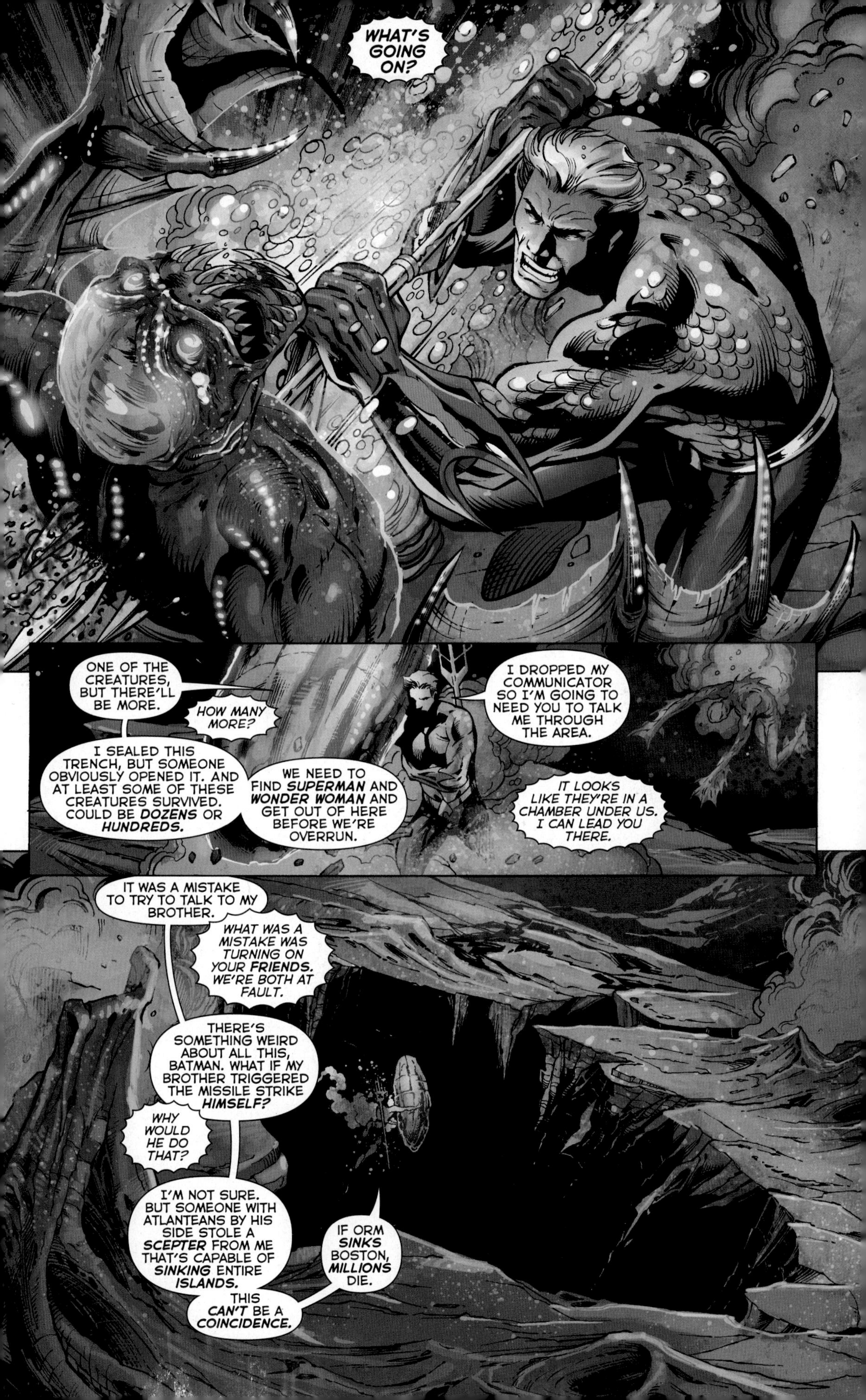
WHAT'S GOING ON?
ONE OF THE CREATURES, BUT THERE'LL BE MORE.
HOW MANY MORE?
I SEALED THIS TRENCH, BUT SOMEONE OBVIOUSLY OPENED IT. AND AT LEAST SOME OF THESE CREATURES SURVIVED. COULD BE DOZENS OR HUNDREDS.
WE NEED TO FIND SUPERMAN AND WONDER WOMAN AND GET OUT OF HERE BEFORE WE'RE OVERRUN.
I DROPPED MY COMMUNICATOR SO I'M GOING TO NEED YOU TO TALK ME THROUGH THE AREA.
IT LOOKS LIKE THEY'RE IN A CHAMBER UNDER US. I CAN LEAD YOU THERE.
IT WAS A MISTAKE TO TRY TO TALK TO MY BROTHER.
WHAT WAS A MISTAKE WAS TURNING ON YOUR FRIENDS. WE'RE BOTH AT FAULT.
THERE'S SOMETHING WEIRD ABOUT ALL THIS, BATMAN. WHAT IF MY BROTHER TRIGGERED THE MISSILE STRIKE HIMSELF?
WHY WOULD HE DO THAT?
I'M NOT SURE. BUT SOMEONE WITH ATLANTEANS BY HIS SIDE STOLE A SCEPTER FROM ME THAT'S CAPABLE OF SINKING ENTIRE ISLANDS.
THIS CAN'T BE A COINCIDENCE.
IF ORM SINKS BOSTON, MILLIONS DIE.

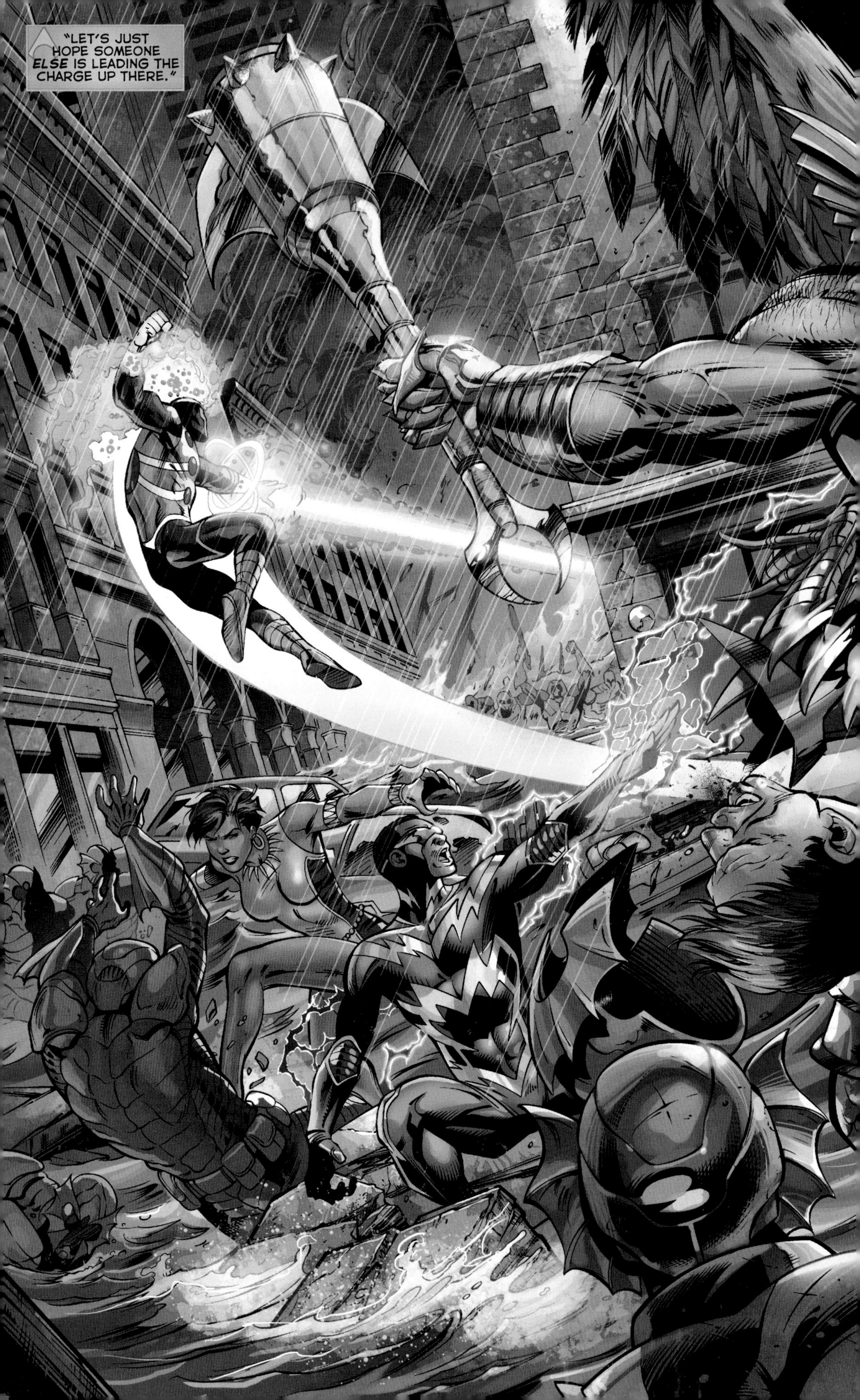
"LET'S JUST HOPE SOMEONE ELSE IS LEADING THE CHARGE UP THERE."

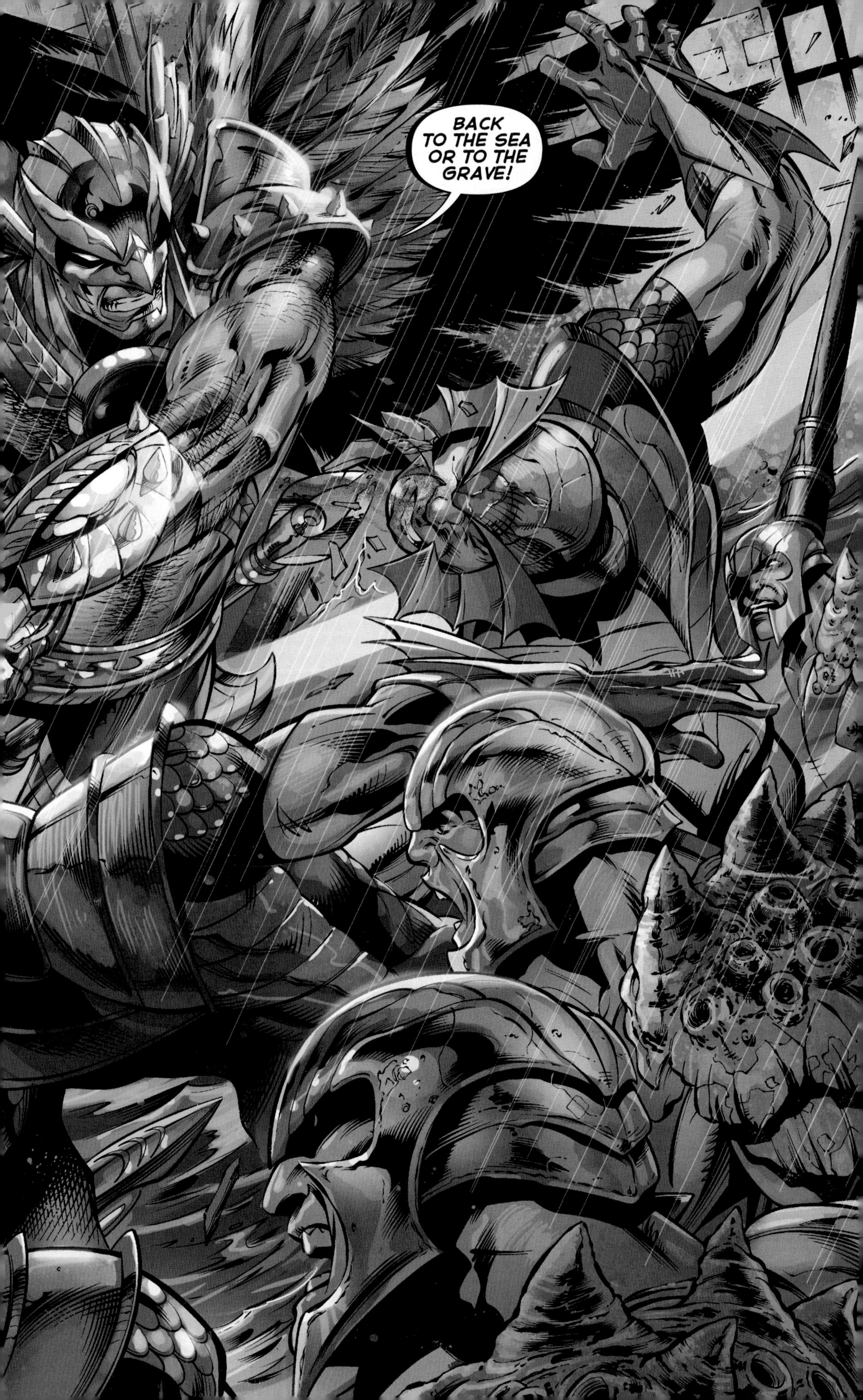
BACK TO THE SEA OR TO THE GRAVE!

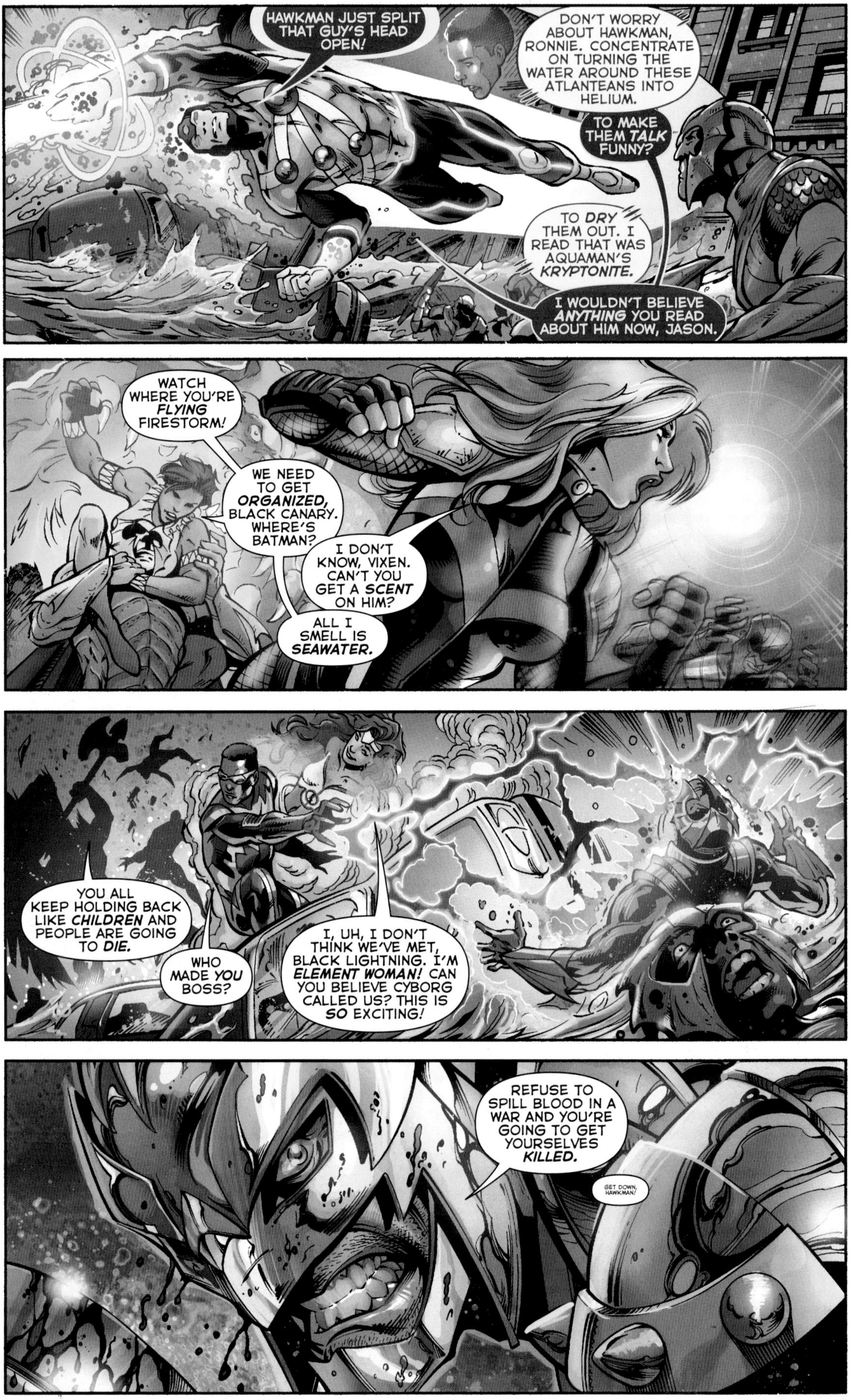
HAWKMAN JUST SPLIT THAT GUY'S HEAD OPEN!
DON'T WORRY ABOUT HAWKMAN, RONNIE. CONCENTRATE ON TURNING THE WATER AROUND THESE ATLANTEANS INTO HELIUM.
TO MAKE THEM TALK FUNNY?
TO DRY THEM OUT. I READ THAT WAS AQUAMAN'S KRYPTONITE.
I WOULDN'T BELIEVE ANYTHING YOU READ ABOUT HIM NOW, JASON.
WATCH WHERE YOU'RE FLYING FIRESTORM!
WE NEED TO GET ORGANIZED, BLACK CANARY. WHERE'S BATMAN?
I DON'T KNOW, VIXEN. CAN'T YOU GET A SCENT ON HIM?
ALL I SMELL IS SEAWATER.
YOU ALL KEEP HOLDING BACK LIKE CHILDREN AND PEOPLE ARE GOING TO DIE.
WHO MADE YOU BOSS?
I, UH, I DON'T THINK WE'VE MET, BLACK LIGHTNING. I'M ELEMENT WOMAN! CAN YOU BELIEVE CYBORG CALLED US? THIS IS SO EXCITING!
REFUSE TO SPILL BLOOD IN A WAR AND YOU'RE GOING TO GET YOURSELVES KILLED.
GET DOWN, HAWKMAN!

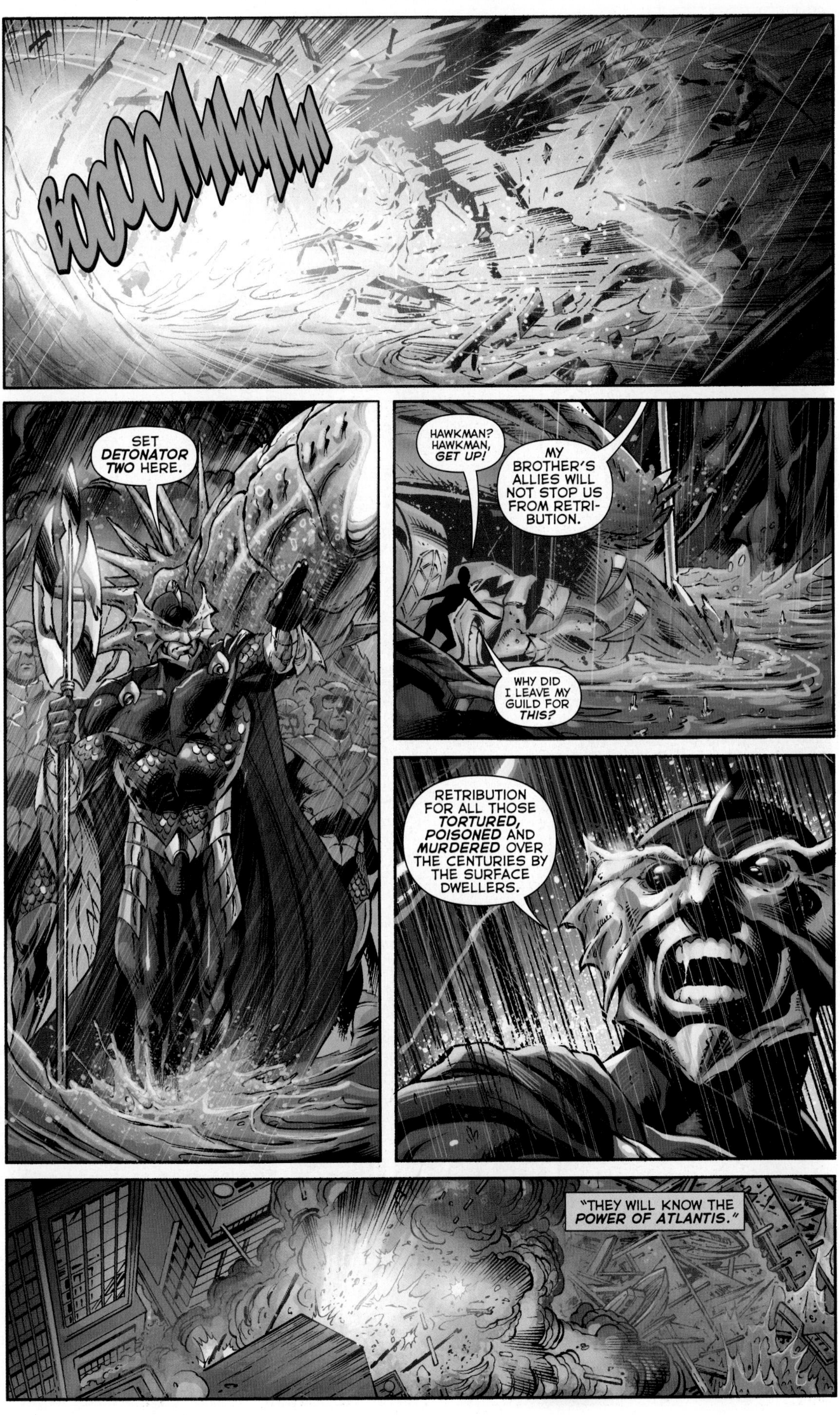
BOOOOMMMMMM
SET DETONATOR TWO HERE.
HAWKMAN? HAWKMAN, GET UP!
MY BROTHER'S ALLIES WILL NOT STOP US FROM RETRI-BUTION.
WHY DID I LEAVE MY GUILD FOR THIS?
RETRIBUTION FOR ALL THOSE TORTURED, POISONED AND MURDERED OVER THE CENTURIES BY THE SURFACE DWELLERS.
"THEY WILL KNOW THE POWER OF ATLANTIS."

"AND THEY WILL FEAR *US* AS WE ONCE DID THEM."

I'M SORRY ABOUT MY PARENTS.

THEY WANT TO KNOW MORE ABOUT WHO THEIR DAUGHTER'S SPENDING TIME WITH. I *EXPECTED* THE THIRD DEGREE, SARAH.

BUT NOT *ADVICE* ON HOW TO TAKE THE LIONS TO THE PLAY-OFFS.

HE'S A FAN. AND AT LEAST *ONE* OF OUR FATHERS HAS *SOME* INTEREST IN WHAT I DO.

VICTOR?

IT'S TIME TO WAKE UP.

NO. PLEASE. JUST A LITTLE LONG--

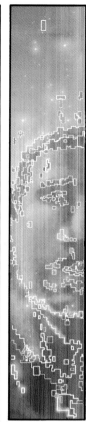

VICTOR?

I'M BACK ONLINE.

YOUR SYSTEM WILL SUPPLY THE OXYGEN YOUR BRAIN NEEDS NOW. YOU CAN SURVIVE IN WATER OR IN SPACE. NOTHING CAN HURT YOU.

YEAH.

THE RESERVES YOU CALLED IN TO HELP ARE SLOWING ATLANTIS DOWN.

THAT'S ALL I NEED THEM TO DO. GRID, KEEP ME UPDATED ON THEIR PROGRESS.

AFFIRMITIVE.

VICTOR? THE FILE YOU'RE WORKING ON--

THANKS FOR THE HELP, DAD. TELL SARAH HELLO FOR ME.

71% COMPLE

I'VE GOT A LOCK ON BATMAN'S BEACON.

THEN LET'S GO GET THEM.

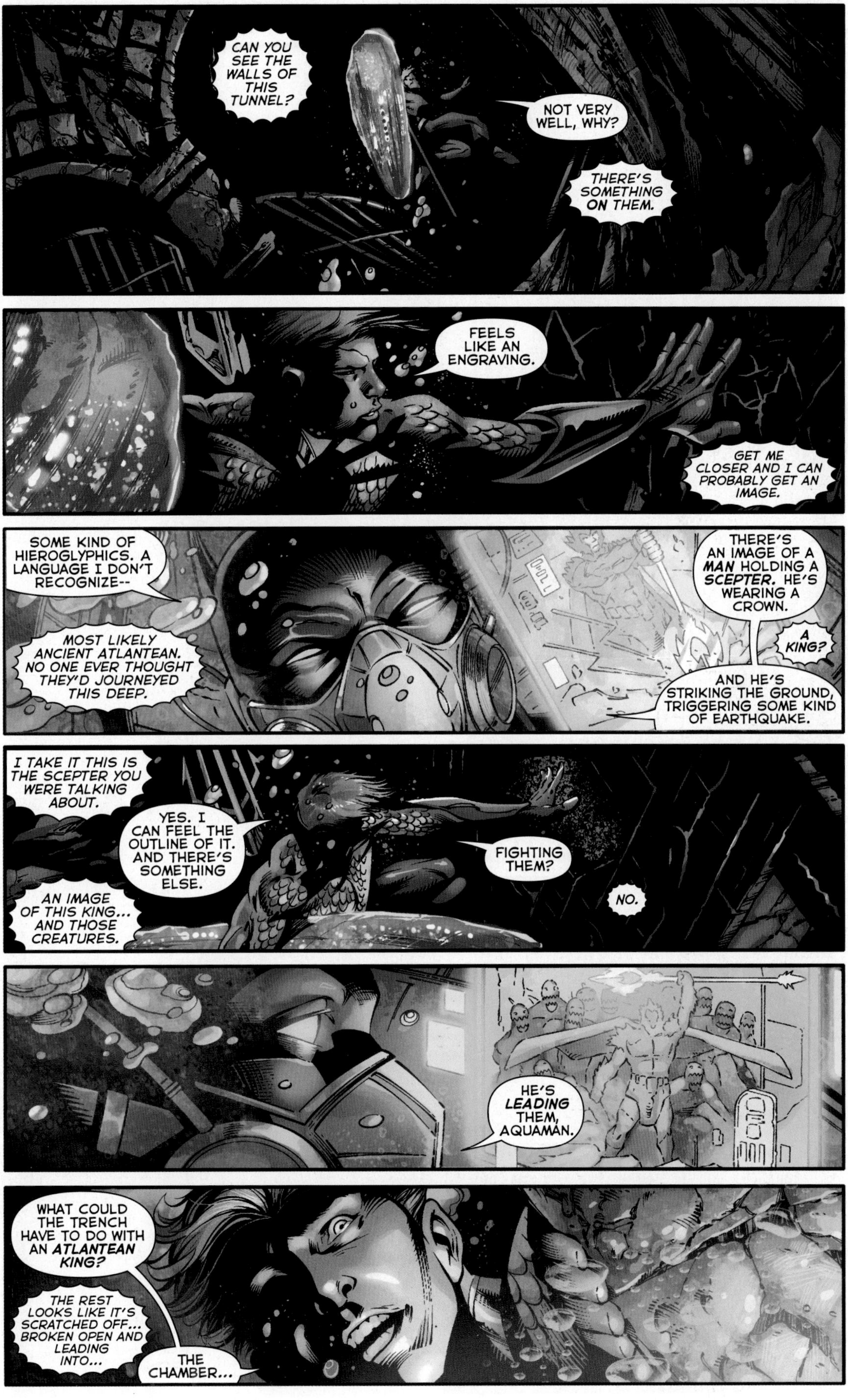
CAN YOU SEE THE WALLS OF THIS TUNNEL?
NOT VERY WELL, WHY?
THERE'S SOMETHING ON THEM.
FEELS LIKE AN ENGRAVING.
GET ME CLOSER AND I CAN PROBABLY GET AN IMAGE.
SOME KIND OF HIEROGLYPHICS. A LANGUAGE I DON'T RECOGNIZE--
MOST LIKELY ANCIENT ATLANTEAN. NO ONE EVER THOUGHT THEY'D JOURNEYED THIS DEEP.
THERE'S AN IMAGE OF A MAN HOLDING A SCEPTER. HE'S WEARING A CROWN.
A KING?
AND HE'S STRIKING THE GROUND, TRIGGERING SOME KIND OF EARTHQUAKE.
I TAKE IT THIS IS THE SCEPTER YOU WERE TALKING ABOUT.
YES. I CAN FEEL THE OUTLINE OF IT. AND THERE'S SOMETHING ELSE.
AN IMAGE OF THIS KING... AND THOSE CREATURES.
FIGHTING THEM?
NO.
HE'S LEADING THEM, AQUAMAN.
WHAT COULD THE TRENCH HAVE TO DO WITH AN ATLANTEAN KING?
THE REST LOOKS LIKE IT'S SCRATCHED OFF... BROKEN OPEN AND LEADING INTO...
THE CHAMBER...

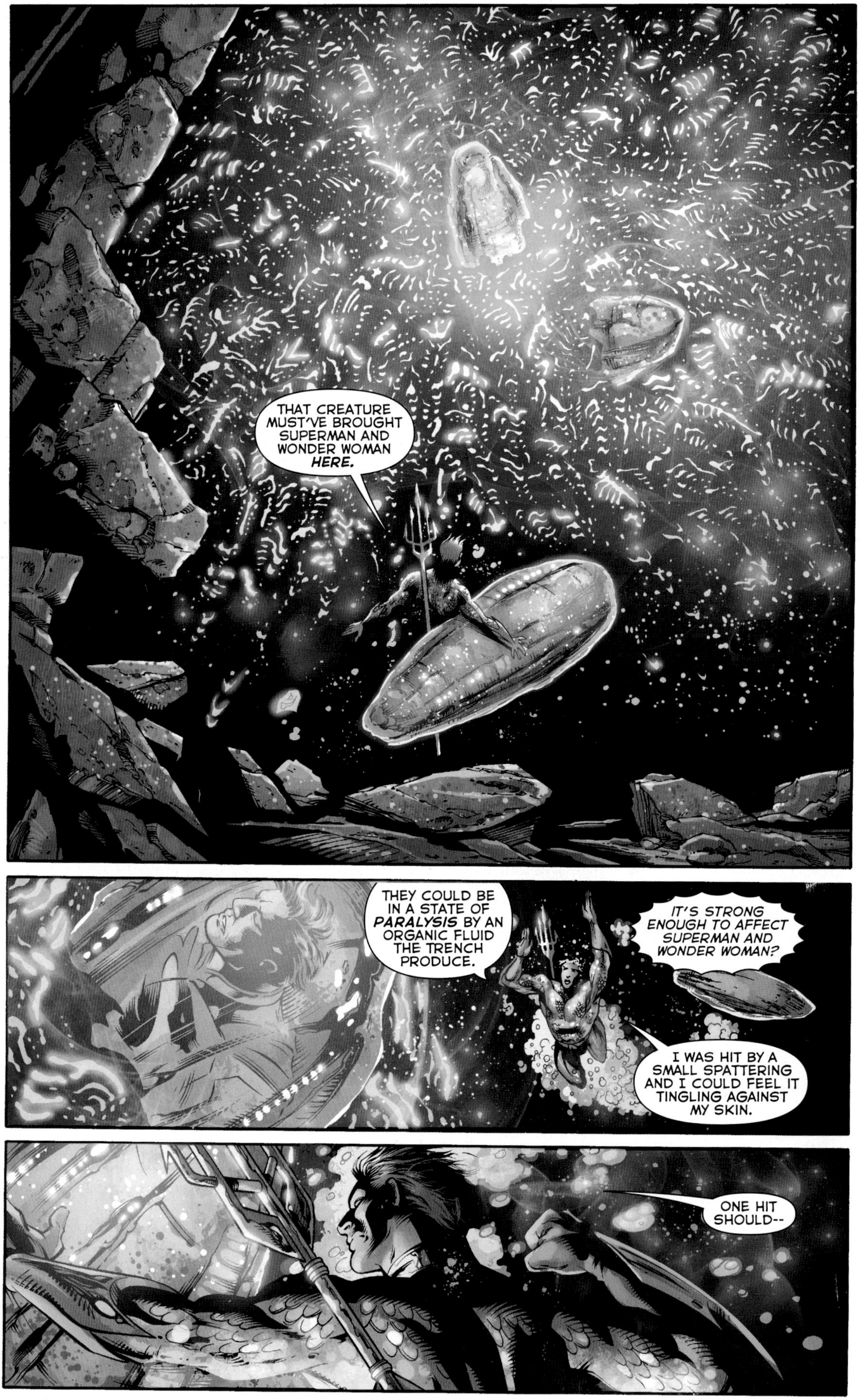
THAT CREATURE MUST'VE BROUGHT SUPERMAN AND WONDER WOMAN *HERE.*
THEY COULD BE IN A STATE OF *PARALYSIS* BY AN ORGANIC FLUID THE TRENCH PRODUCE.
IT'S STRONG ENOUGH TO AFFECT SUPERMAN AND WONDER WOMAN?
I WAS HIT BY A SMALL SPATTERING AND I COULD FEEL IT TINGLING AGAINST MY SKIN.
ONE HIT SHOULD--

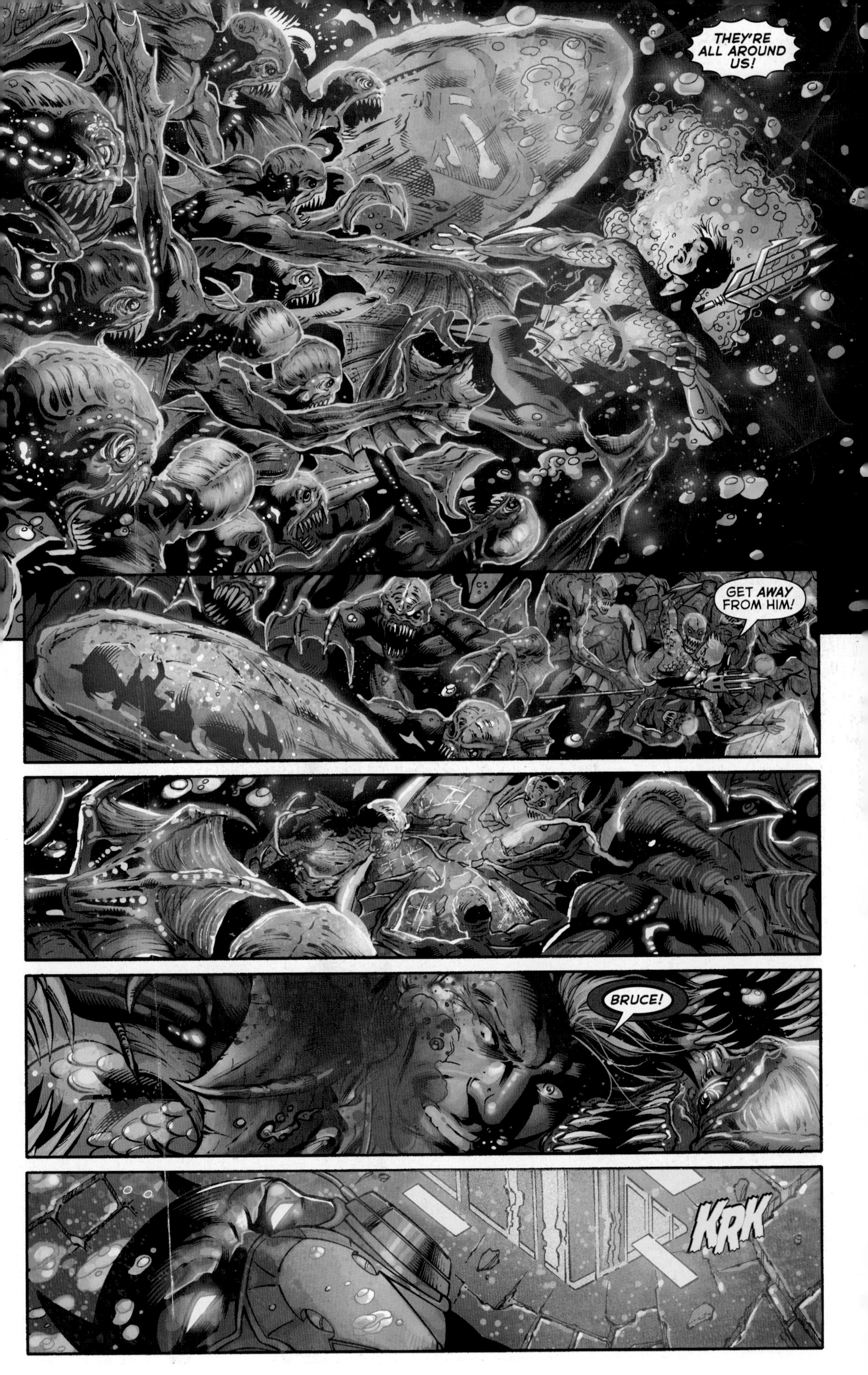
THEY'RE ALL AROUND US!
GET AWAY FROM HIM!
BRUCE!
KRK

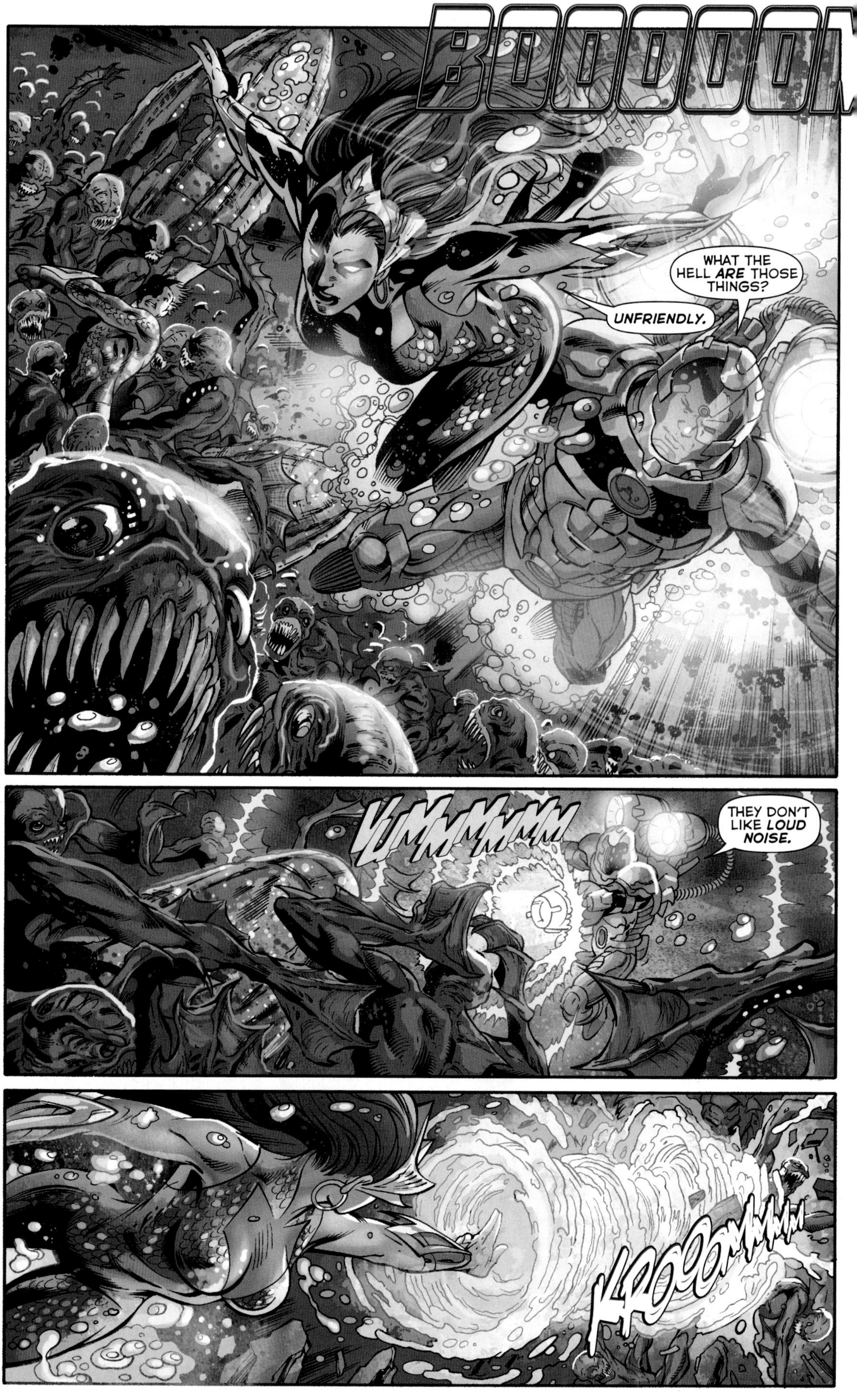
WHAT THE HELL ARE THOSE THINGS?
UNFRIENDLY.
THEY DON'T LIKE LOUD NOISE.

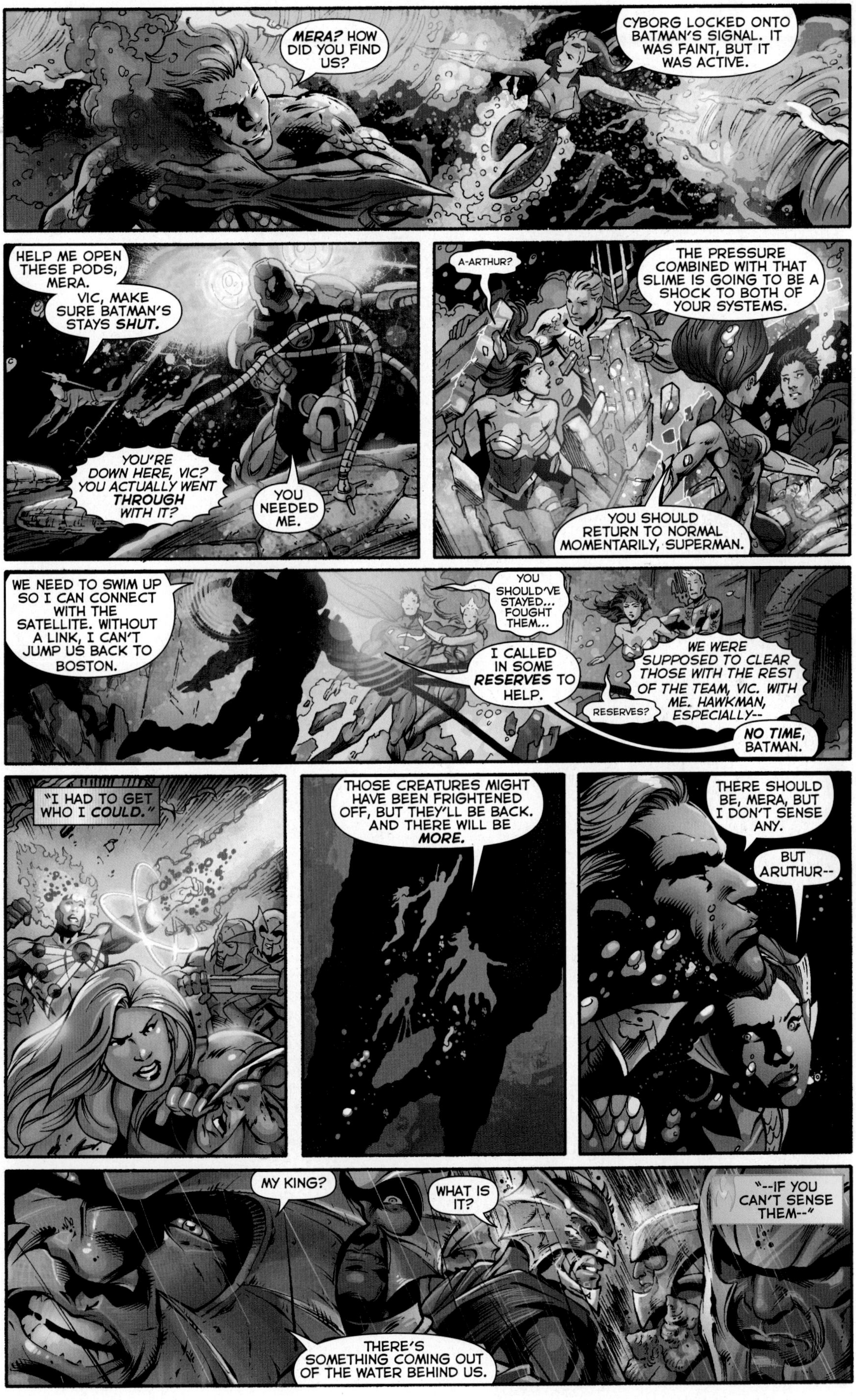
MERA? HOW DID YOU FIND US?
CYBORG LOCKED ONTO BATMAN'S SIGNAL. IT WAS FAINT, BUT IT WAS ACTIVE.
HELP ME OPEN THESE PODS, MERA.
VIC, MAKE SURE BATMAN'S STAYS SHUT.
YOU'RE DOWN HERE, VIC? YOU ACTUALLY WENT THROUGH WITH IT?
YOU NEEDED ME.
A-ARTHUR?
THE PRESSURE COMBINED WITH THAT SLIME IS GOING TO BE A SHOCK TO BOTH OF YOUR SYSTEMS.
YOU SHOULD RETURN TO NORMAL MOMENTARILY, SUPERMAN.
WE NEED TO SWIM UP SO I CAN CONNECT WITH THE SATELLITE. WITHOUT A LINK, I CAN'T JUMP US BACK TO BOSTON.
YOU SHOULD'VE STAYED... FOUGHT THEM...
I CALLED IN SOME RESERVES TO HELP.
RESERVES?
WE WERE SUPPOSED TO CLEAR THOSE WITH THE REST OF THE TEAM, VIC. WITH ME. HAWKMAN, ESPECIALLY--
NO TIME, BATMAN.
"I HAD TO GET WHO I COULD."
THOSE CREATURES MIGHT HAVE BEEN FRIGHTENED OFF, BUT THEY'LL BE BACK. AND THERE WILL BE MORE.
THERE SHOULD BE, MERA, BUT I DON'T SENSE ANY.
BUT ARUTHUR--
MY KING?
WHAT IS IT?
"--IF YOU CAN'T SENSE THEM--"
THERE'S SOMETHING COMING OUT OF THE WATER BEHIND US.

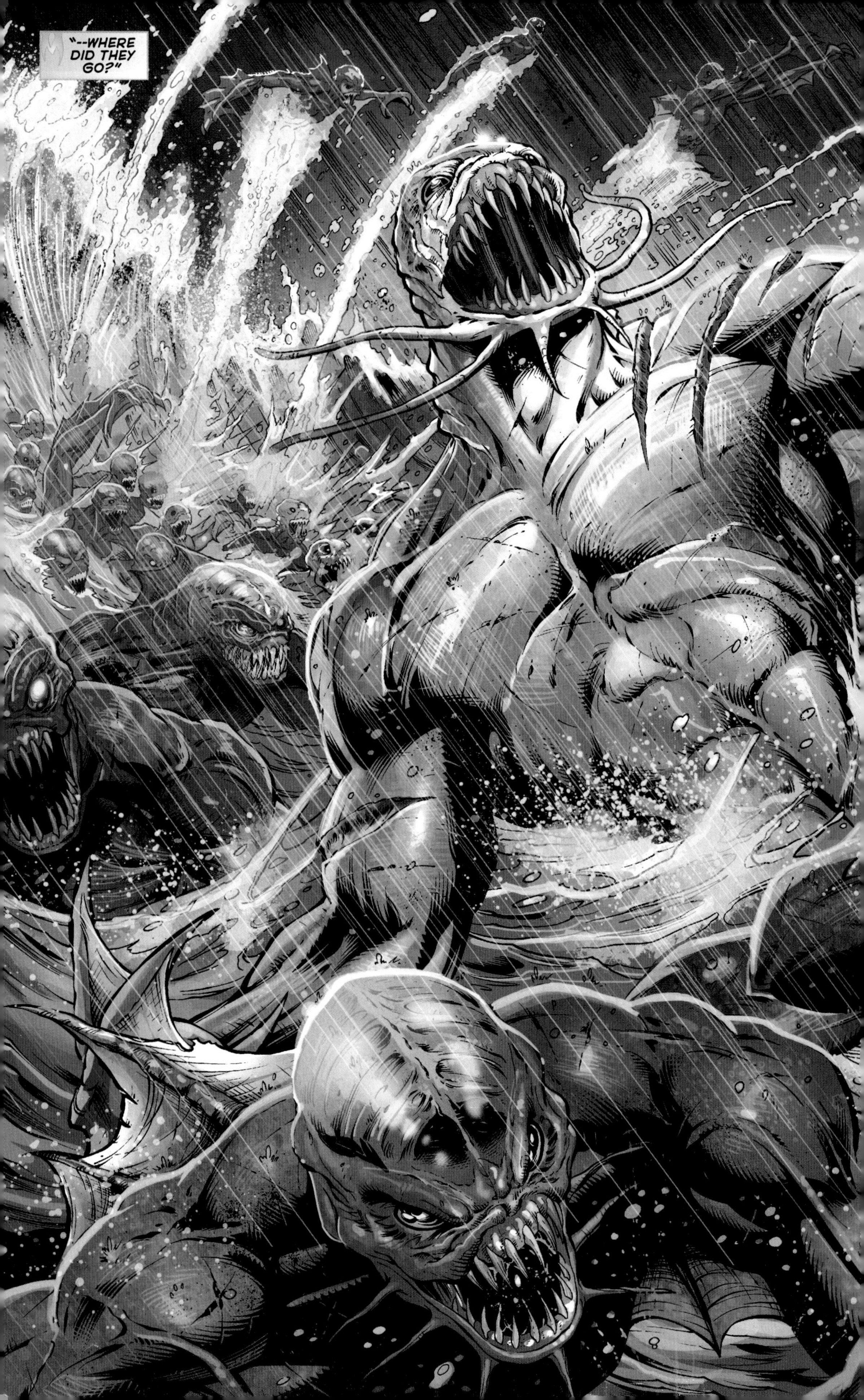
"--WHERE DID THEY GO?"

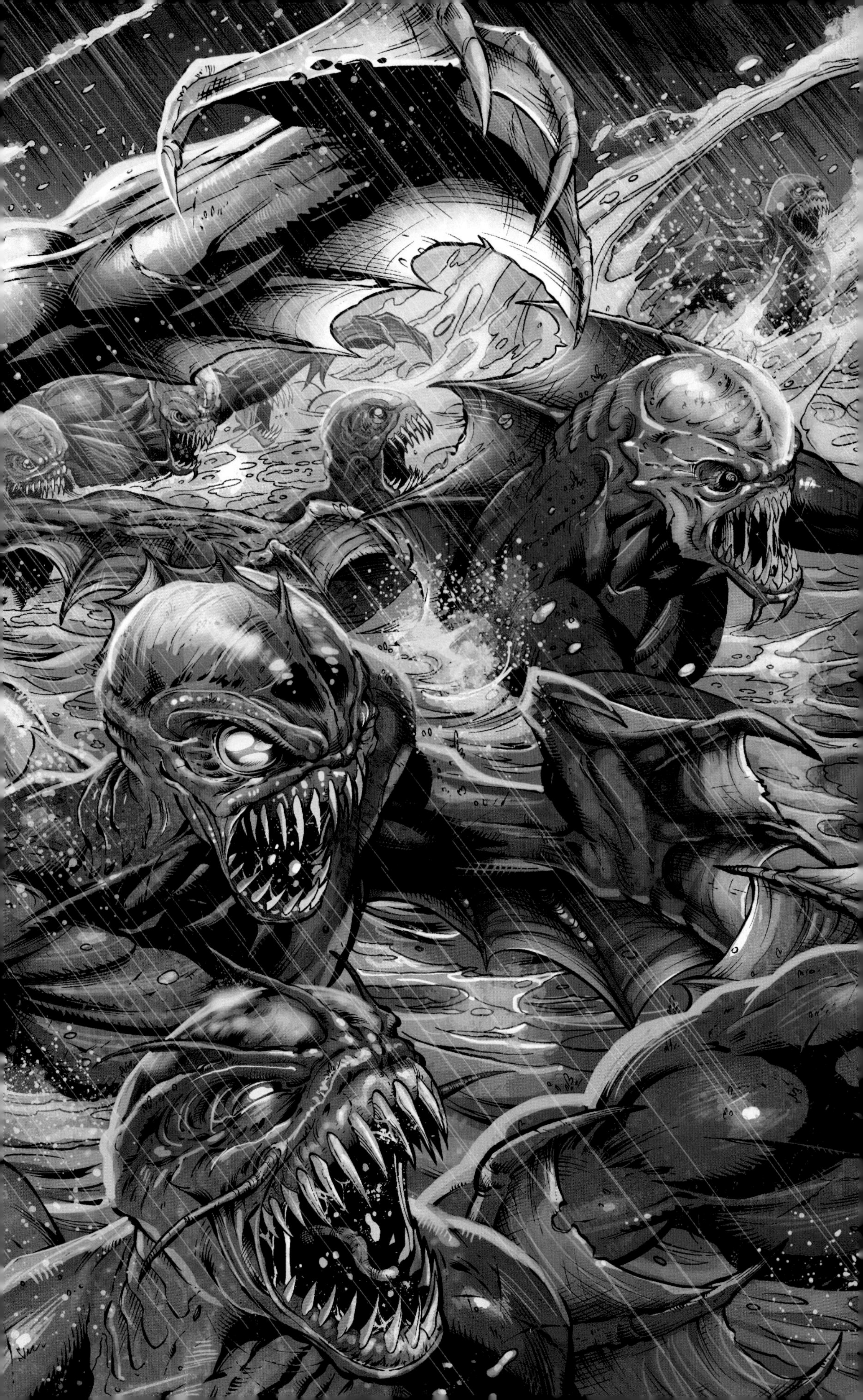

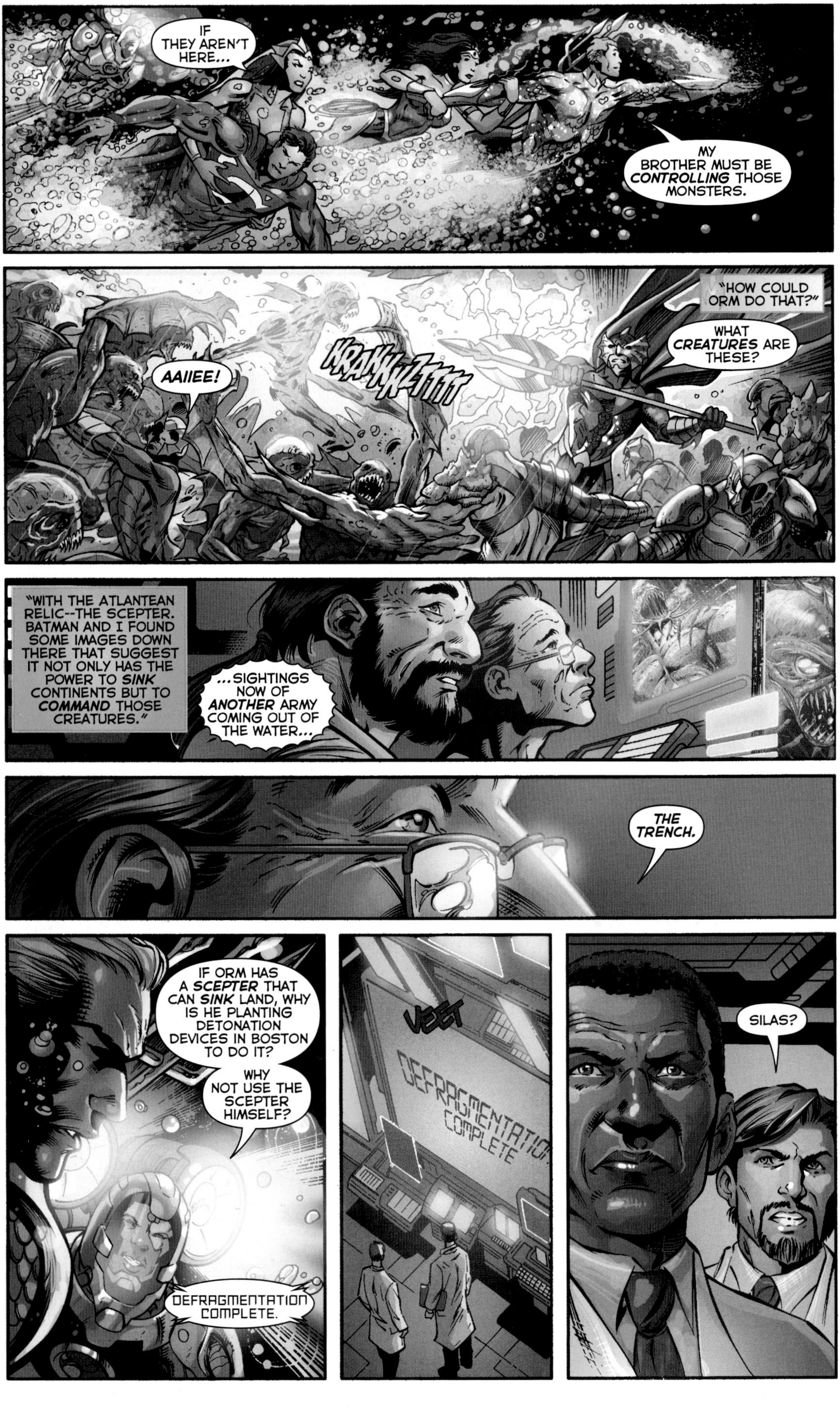
IF THEY AREN'T HERE...
MY BROTHER MUST BE CONTROLLING THOSE MONSTERS.
"HOW COULD ORM DO THAT?"
WHAT CREATURES ARE THESE?
AAIIEE!
KRAKKKLZTTTT
"WITH THE ATLANTEAN RELIC--THE SCEPTER. BATMAN AND I FOUND SOME IMAGES DOWN THERE THAT SUGGEST IT NOT ONLY HAS THE POWER TO SINK CONTINENTS BUT TO COMMAND THOSE CREATURES."
...SIGHTINGS NOW OF ANOTHER ARMY COMING OUT OF THE WATER...
THE TRENCH.
IF ORM HAS A SCEPTER THAT CAN SINK LAND, WHY IS HE PLANTING DETONATION DEVICES IN BOSTON TO DO IT?
WHY NOT USE THE SCEPTER HIMSELF?
DEFRAGMENTATION COMPLETE.
VEET
DEFRAGMENTATION COMPLETE
SILAS?

"WHO *IS* THAT?"

DR. SHIN.

ARTHUR, THE SECURITY VIDEO FROM THE U.S.S. MABUS...I'VE GOT IT.

I BLAME *YOU* FOR THIS.

WHAT ARE YOU DOING?

YOU *ENTANGLED* ARTHUR IN A GAME OF *REVENGE* AGAINST BLACK MANTA. YOU TURNED THE WORLD *AGAINST* HIM.

ORM ISN'T USING THE SCEPTER, BECAUSE HE DOESN'T HAVE IT.

AND WHEN HE LEFT ATLANTIS, THEY TURNED AGAINST *ME.*

SOMEONE ELSE STARTED THIS WAR.

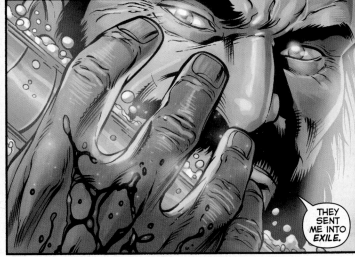

THEY SENT ME INTO *EXILE.*

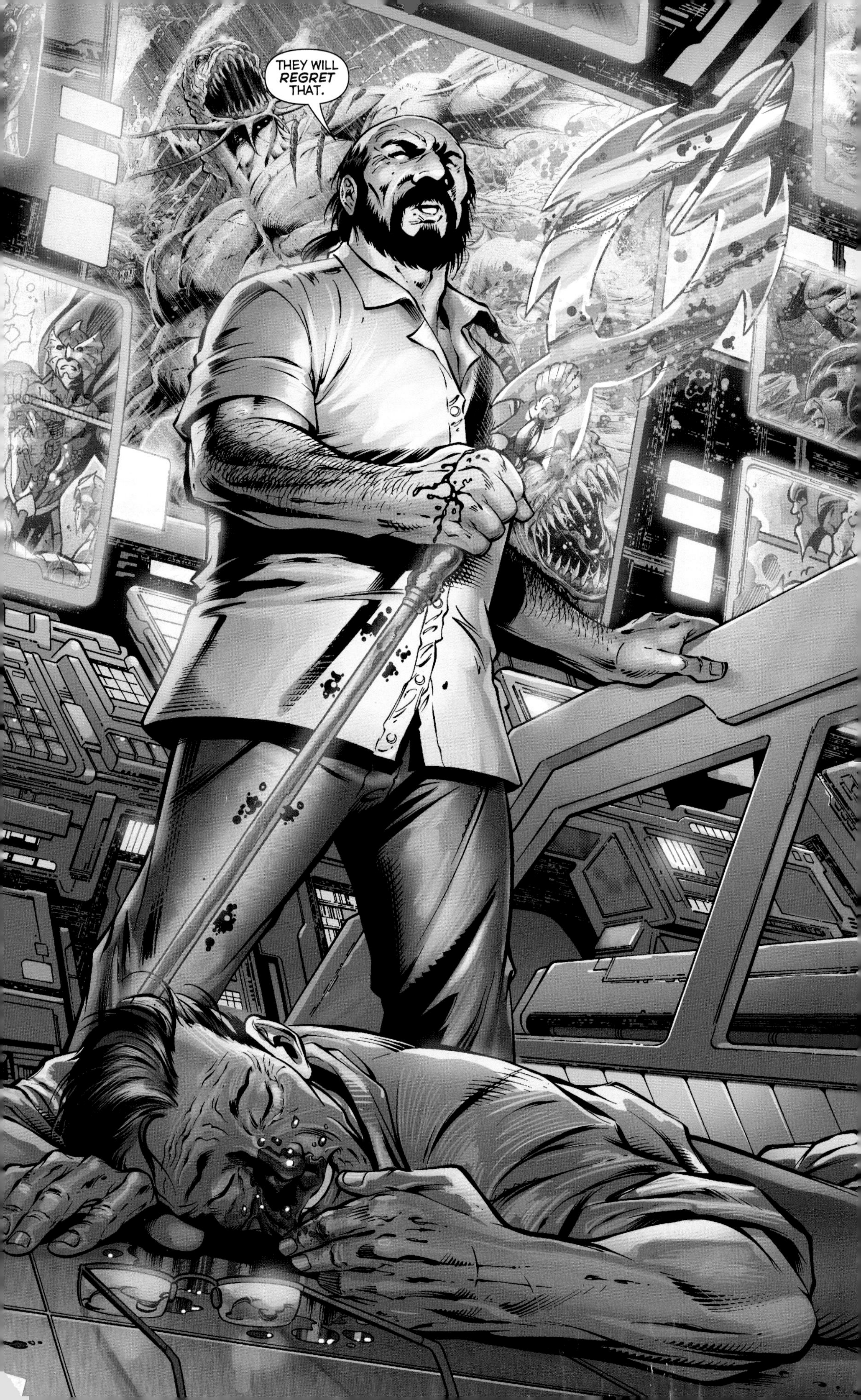
THEY WILL REGRET THAT.

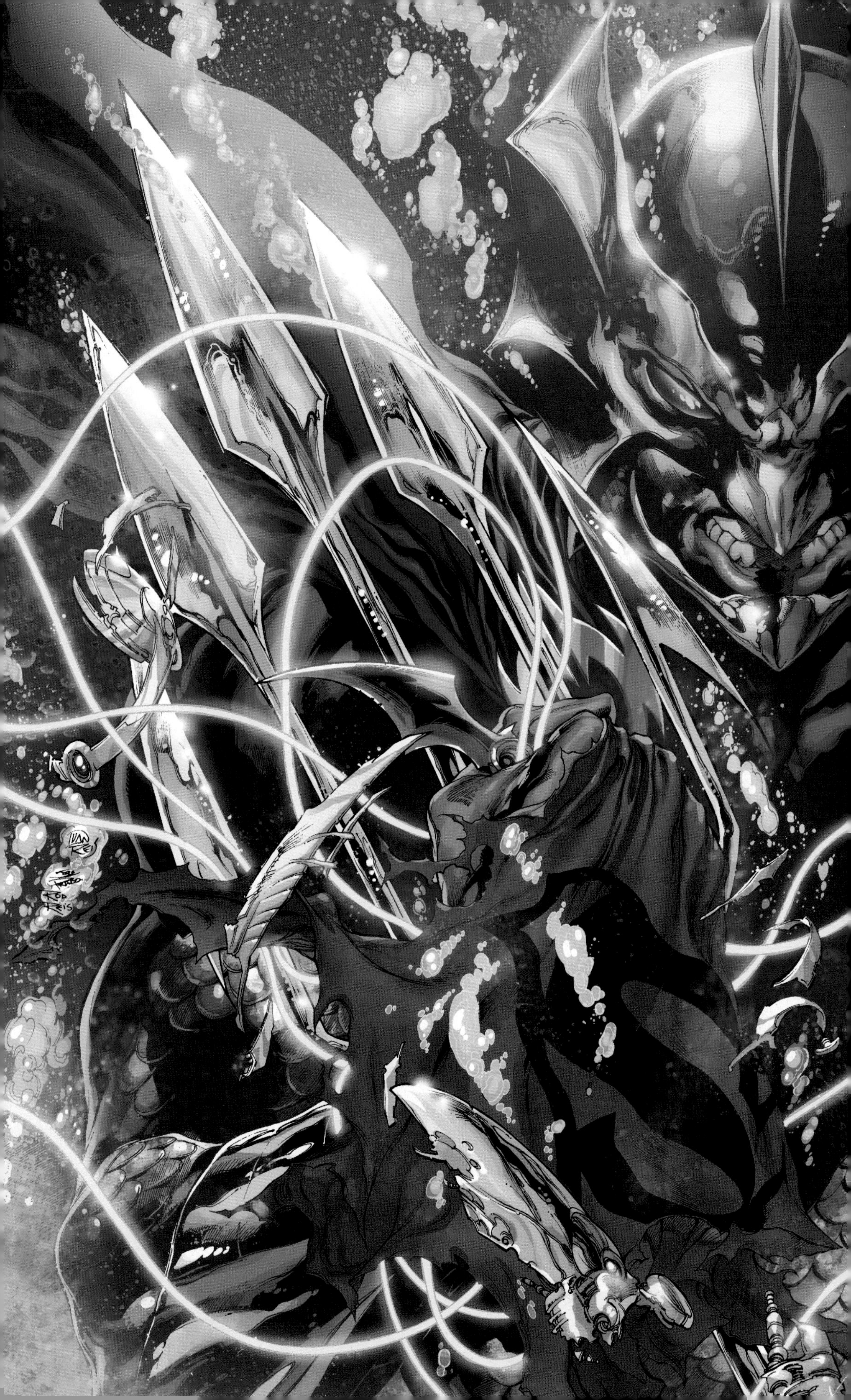

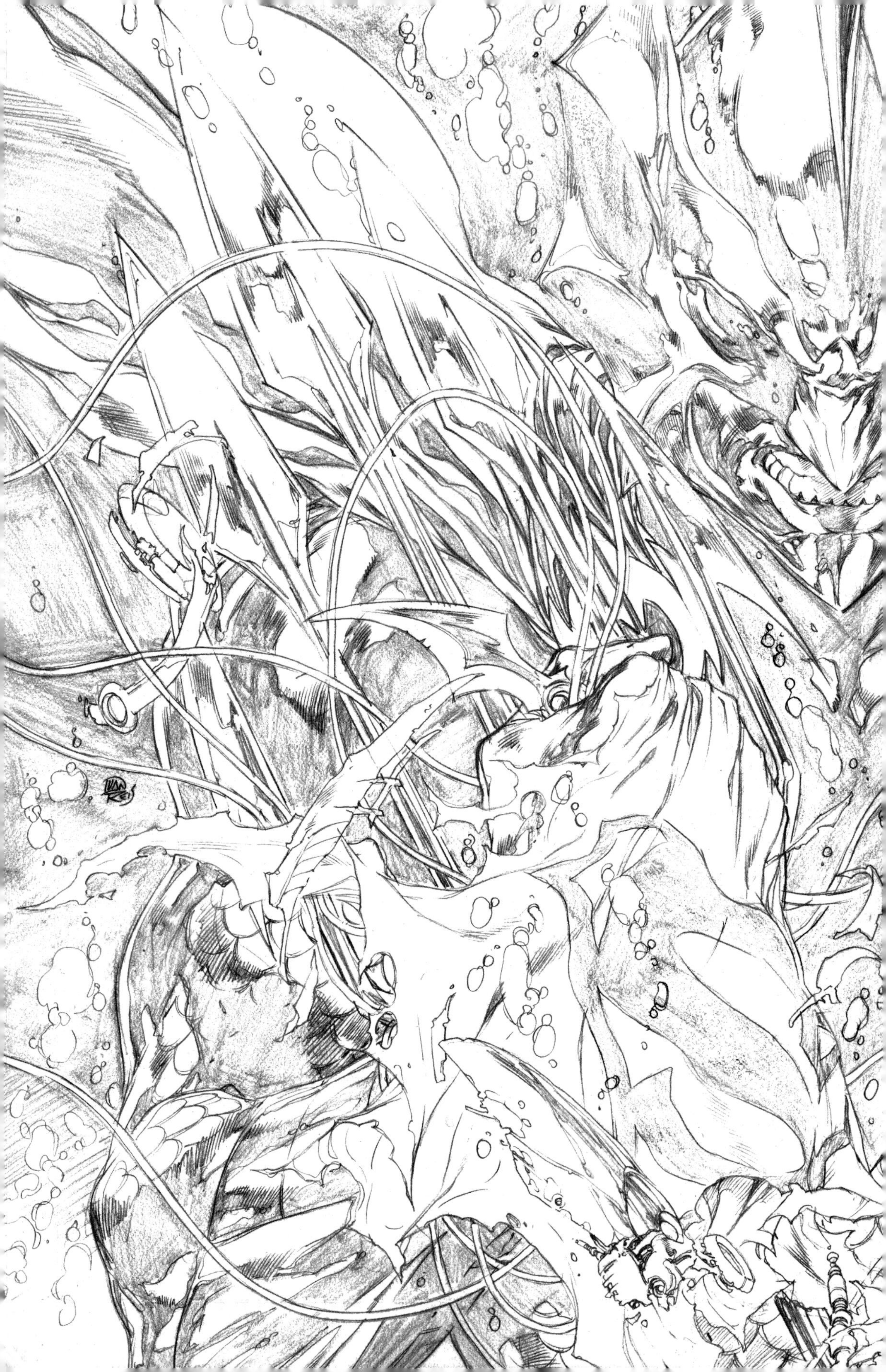

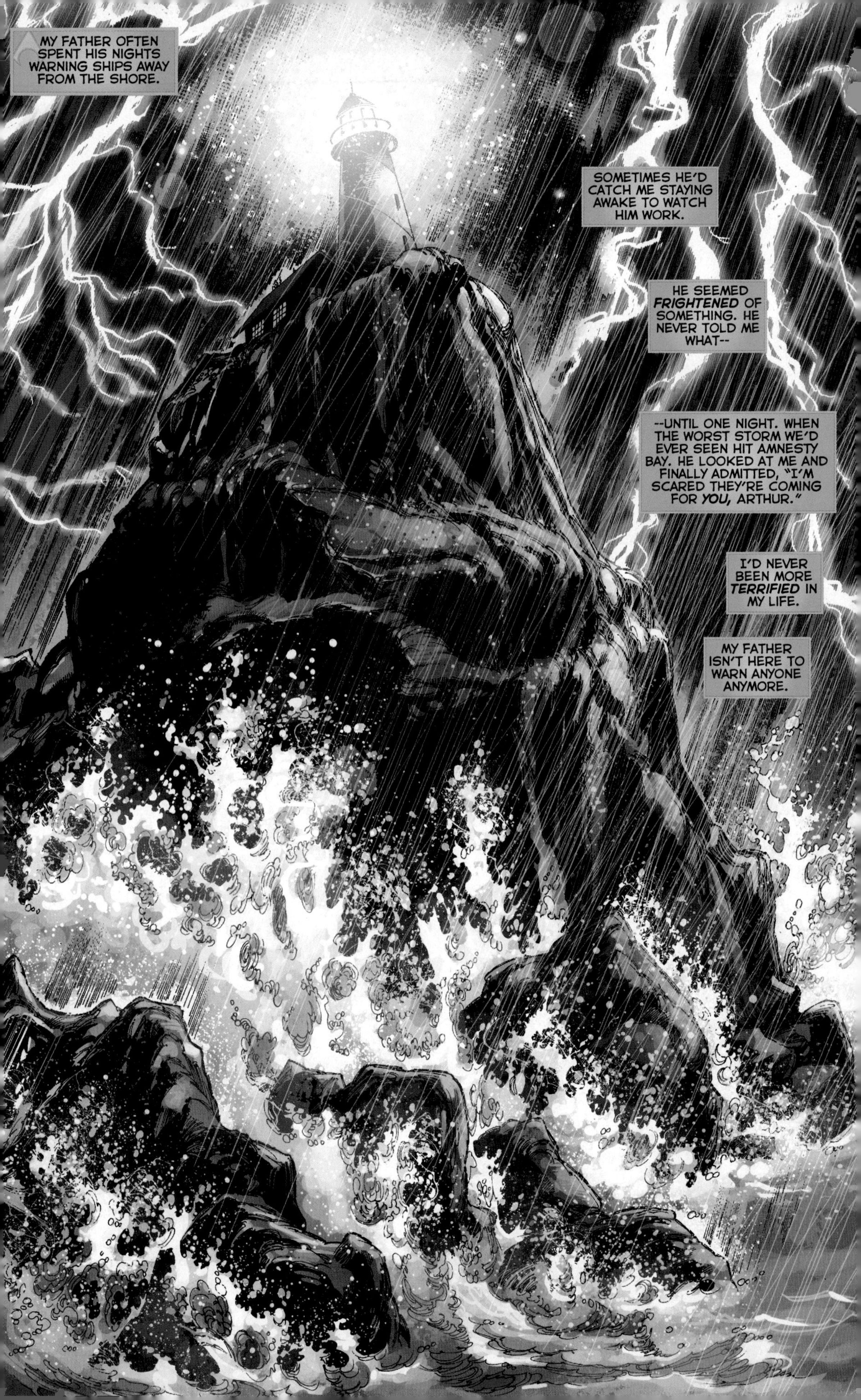
MY FATHER OFTEN SPENT HIS NIGHTS WARNING SHIPS AWAY FROM THE SHORE.
SOMETIMES HE'D CATCH ME STAYING AWAKE TO WATCH HIM WORK.
HE SEEMED *FRIGHTENED* OF SOMETHING. HE NEVER TOLD ME WHAT--
--UNTIL ONE NIGHT. WHEN THE WORST STORM WE'D EVER SEEN HIT AMNESTY BAY. HE LOOKED AT ME AND FINALLY ADMITTED, "I'M SCARED THEY'RE COMING FOR *YOU*, ARTHUR."
I'D NEVER BEEN MORE *TERRIFIED* IN MY LIFE.
MY FATHER ISN'T HERE TO WARN ANYONE ANYMORE.

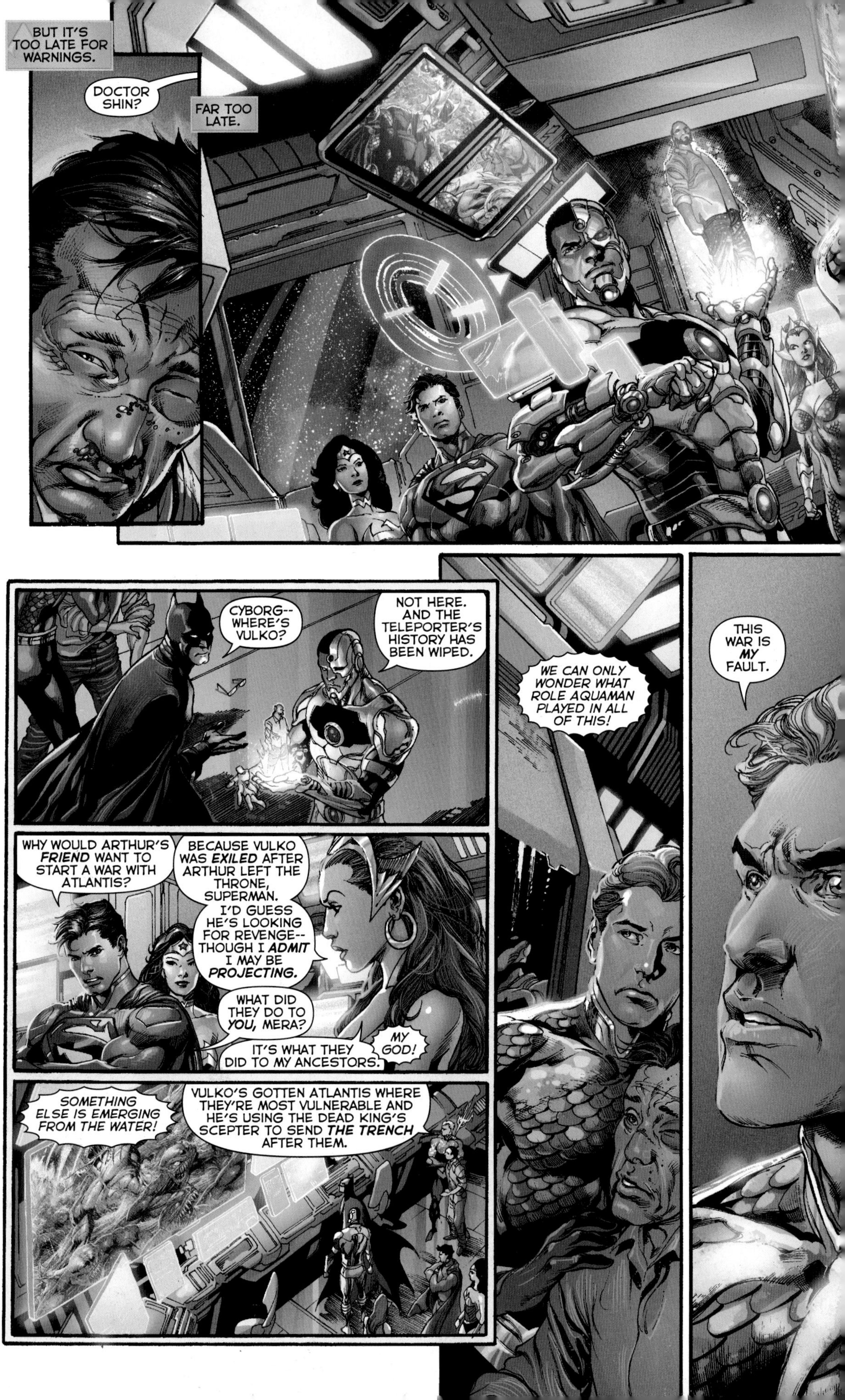
BUT IT'S TOO LATE FOR WARNINGS.
DOCTOR SHIN?
FAR TOO LATE.
CYBORG-- WHERE'S VULKO?
NOT HERE. AND THE TELEPORTER'S HISTORY HAS BEEN WIPED.
WE CAN ONLY WONDER WHAT ROLE AQUAMAN PLAYED IN ALL OF THIS!
THIS WAR IS MY FAULT.
WHY WOULD ARTHUR'S FRIEND WANT TO START A WAR WITH ATLANTIS?
BECAUSE VULKO WAS EXILED AFTER ARTHUR LEFT THE THRONE, SUPERMAN.
I'D GUESS HE'S LOOKING FOR REVENGE-- THOUGH I ADMIT I MAY BE PROJECTING.
WHAT DID THEY DO TO YOU, MERA?
IT'S WHAT THEY DID TO MY ANCESTORS.
MY GOD!
SOMETHING ELSE IS EMERGING FROM THE WATER!
VULKO'S GOTTEN ATLANTIS WHERE THEY'RE MOST VULNERABLE AND HE'S USING THE DEAD KING'S SCEPTER TO SEND THE TRENCH AFTER THEM.

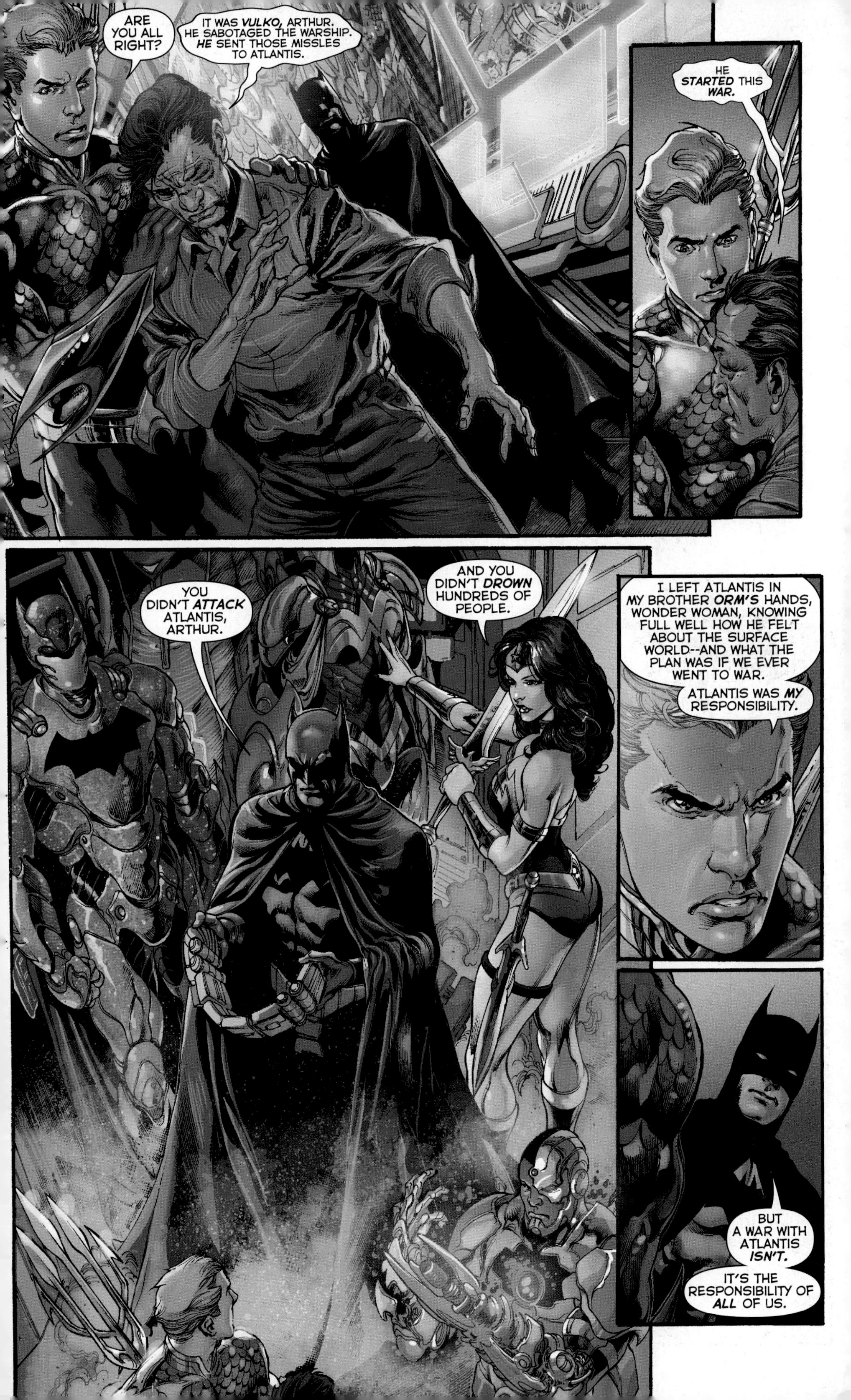
ARE YOU ALL RIGHT?
IT WAS VULKO, ARTHUR. HE SABOTAGED THE WARSHIP. HE SENT THOSE MISSLES TO ATLANTIS.
HE STARTED THIS WAR.
YOU DIDN'T ATTACK ATLANTIS, ARTHUR.
AND YOU DIDN'T DROWN HUNDREDS OF PEOPLE.
I LEFT ATLANTIS IN MY BROTHER ORM'S HANDS, WONDER WOMAN, KNOWING FULL WELL HOW HE FELT ABOUT THE SURFACE WORLD--AND WHAT THE PLAN WAS IF WE EVER WENT TO WAR.
ATLANTIS WAS MY RESPONSIBILITY.
BUT A WAR WITH ATLANTIS ISN'T.
IT'S THE RESPONSIBILITY OF ALL OF US.

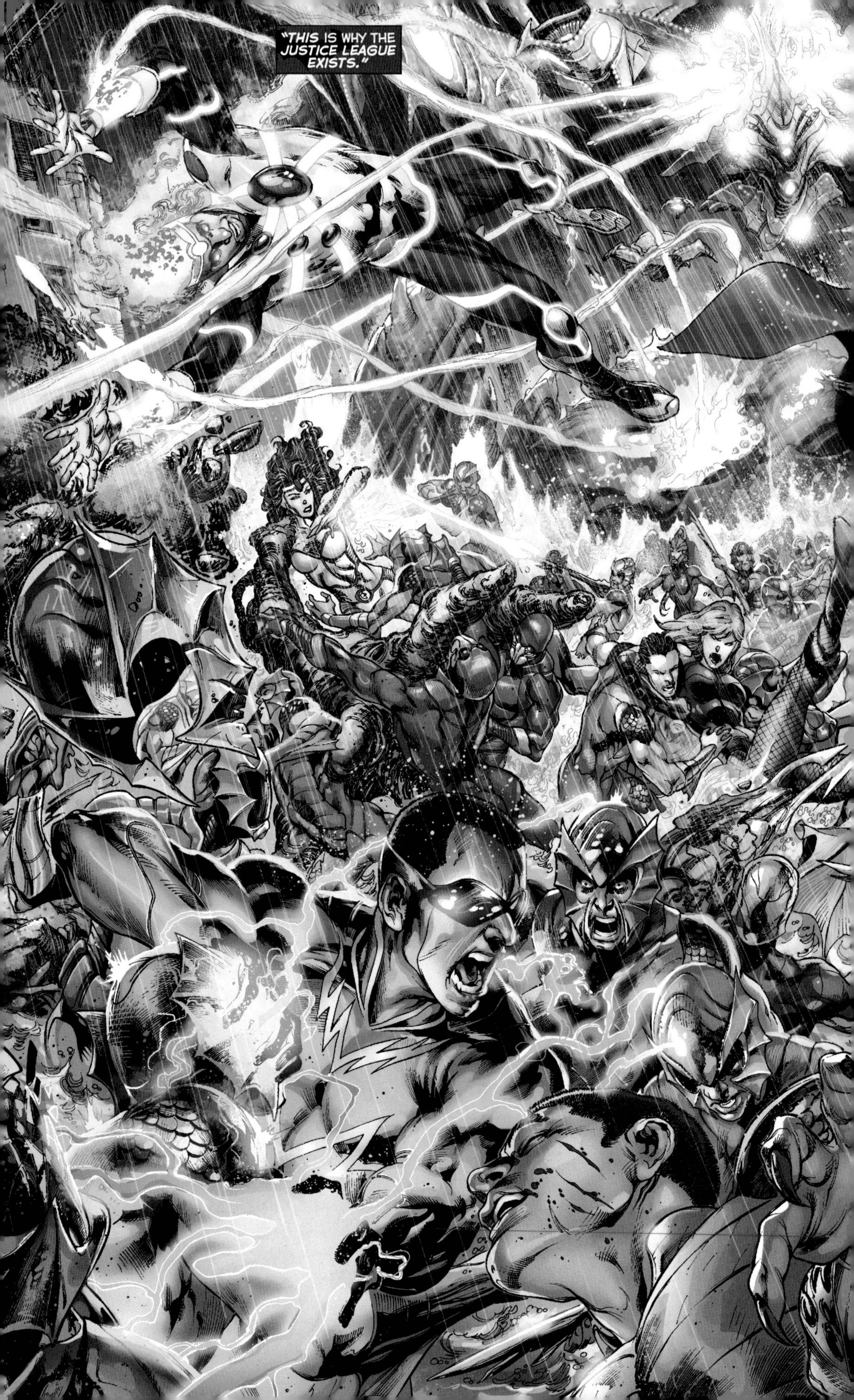
"THIS IS WHY THE JUSTICE LEAGUE EXISTS."

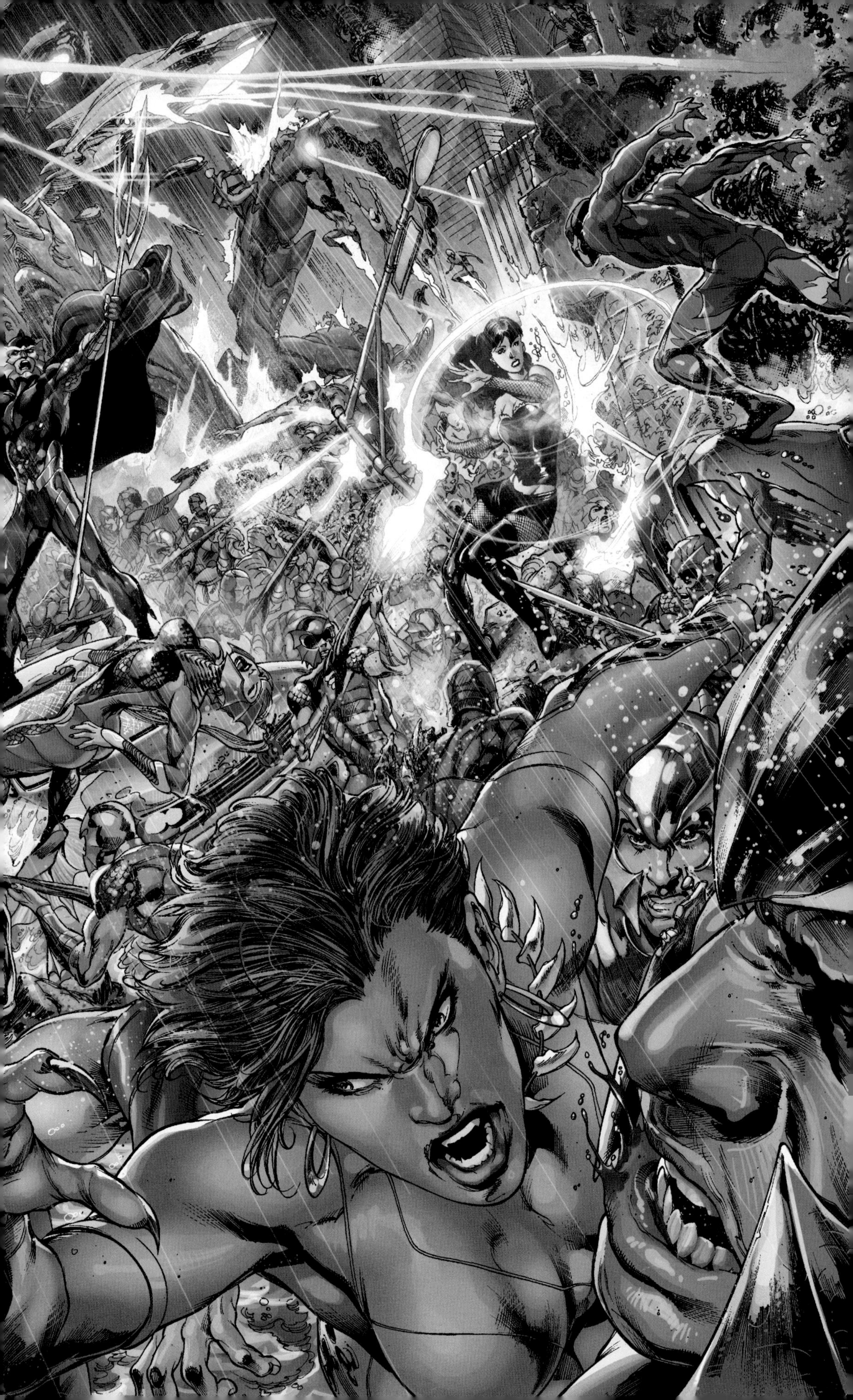

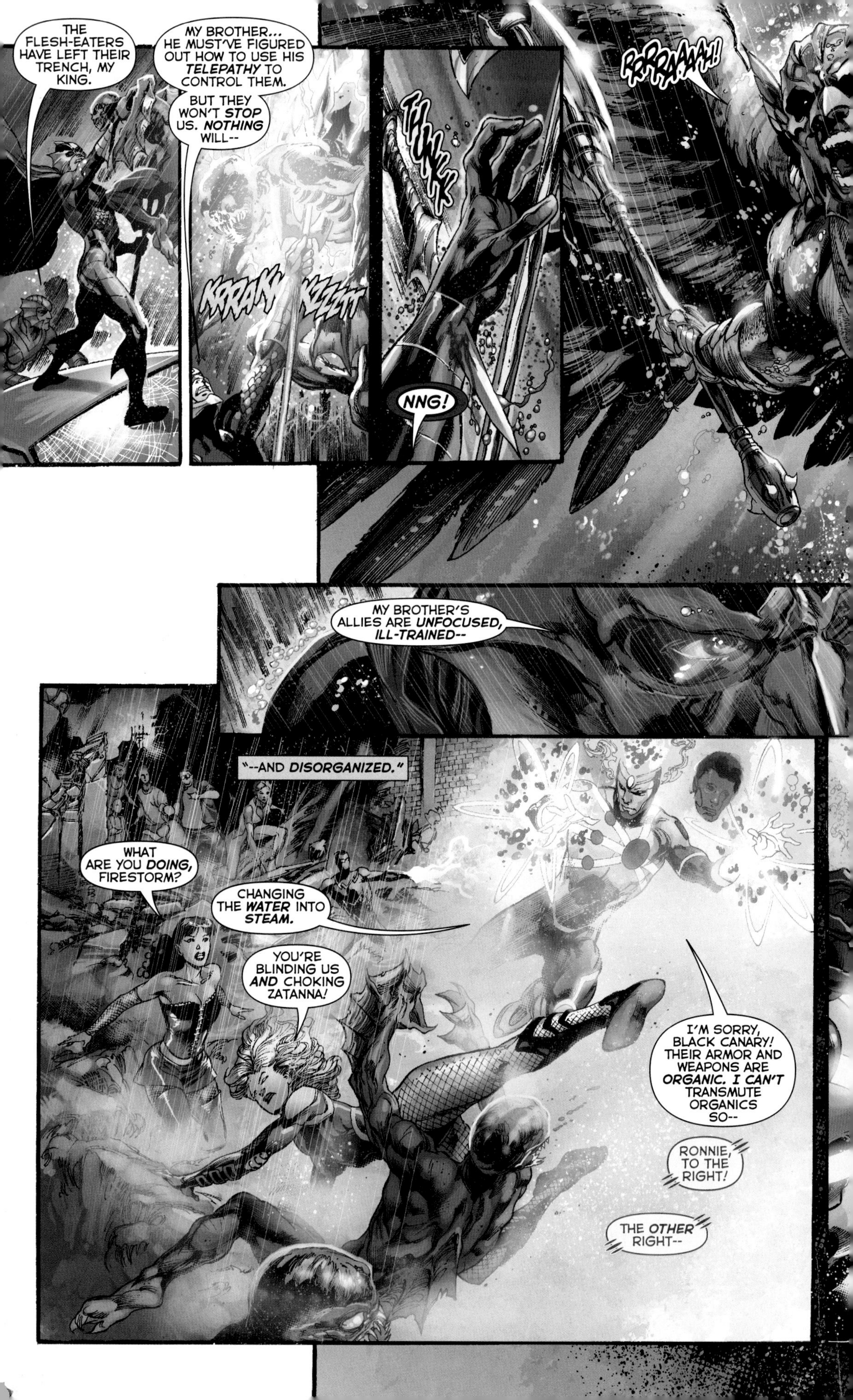

THE FLESH-EATERS HAVE LEFT THEIR TRENCH, MY KING.
MY BROTHER... HE MUST'VE FIGURED OUT HOW TO USE HIS TELEPATHY TO CONTROL THEM.
BUT THEY WON'T STOP US. NOTHING WILL--
KRRAKK
KZZZTT
THUNKK
NNG!
RRRRAAAAH!
MY BROTHER'S ALLIES ARE UNFOCUSED, ILL-TRAINED--
"--AND DISORGANIZED."
WHAT ARE YOU DOING, FIRESTORM?
CHANGING THE WATER INTO STEAM.
YOU'RE BLINDING US AND CHOKING ZATANNA!
I'M SORRY, BLACK CANARY! THEIR ARMOR AND WEAPONS ARE ORGANIC. I CAN'T TRANSMUTE ORGANICS SO--
RONNIE, TO THE RIGHT!
THE OTHER RIGHT--

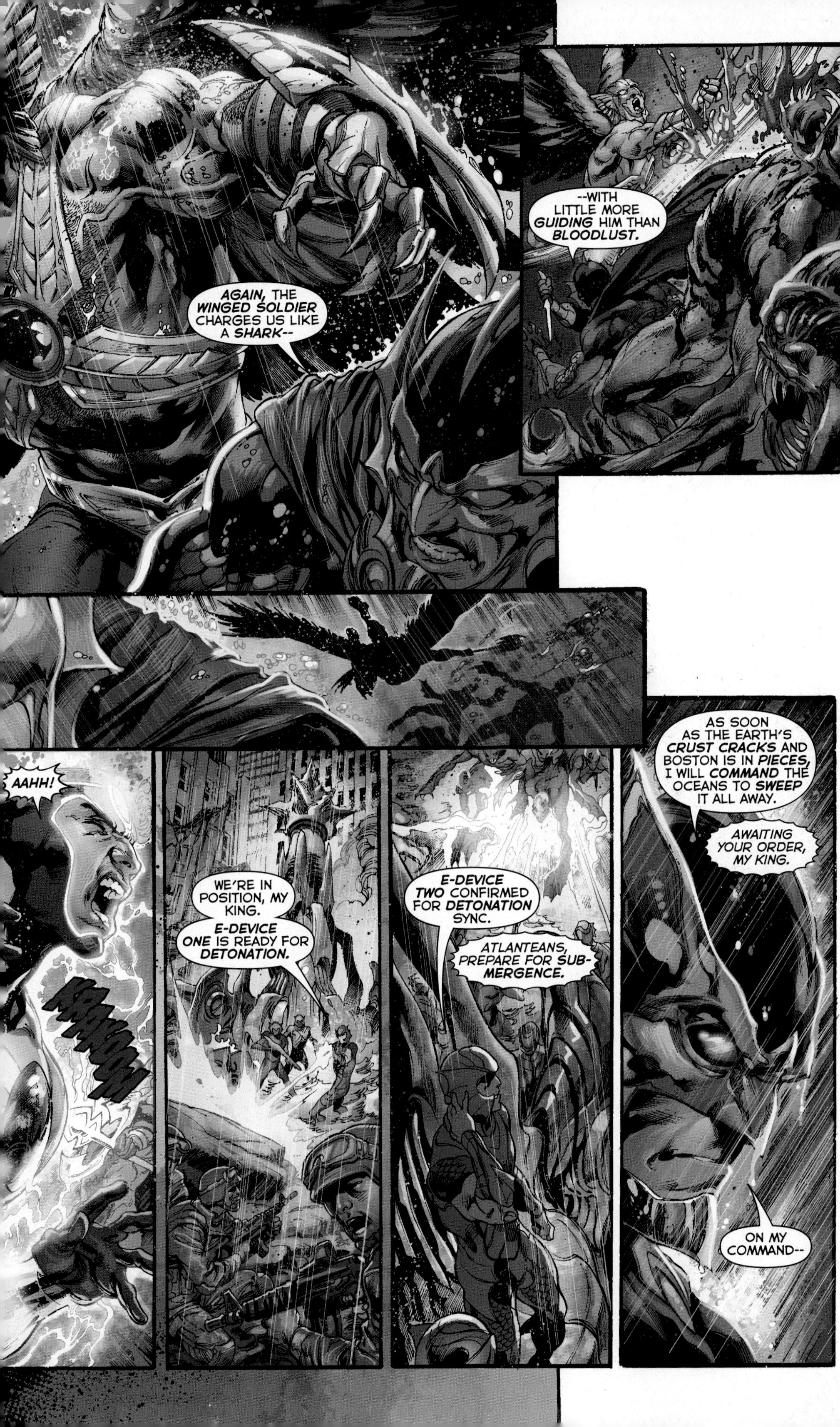
AGAIN, THE WINGED SOLDIER CHARGES US LIKE A SHARK--
--WITH LITTLE MORE GUIDING HIM THAN BLOODLUST.
AAHH!
KRAKOOM
WE'RE IN POSITION, MY KING.
E-DEVICE ONE IS READY FOR DETONATION.
E-DEVICE TWO CONFIRMED FOR DETONATION SYNC.
ATLANTEANS, PREPARE FOR SUB-MERGENCE.
AS SOON AS THE EARTH'S CRUST CRACKS AND BOSTON IS IN PIECES, I WILL COMMAND THE OCEANS TO SWEEP IT ALL AWAY.
AWAITING YOUR ORDER, MY KING.
ON MY COMMAND--

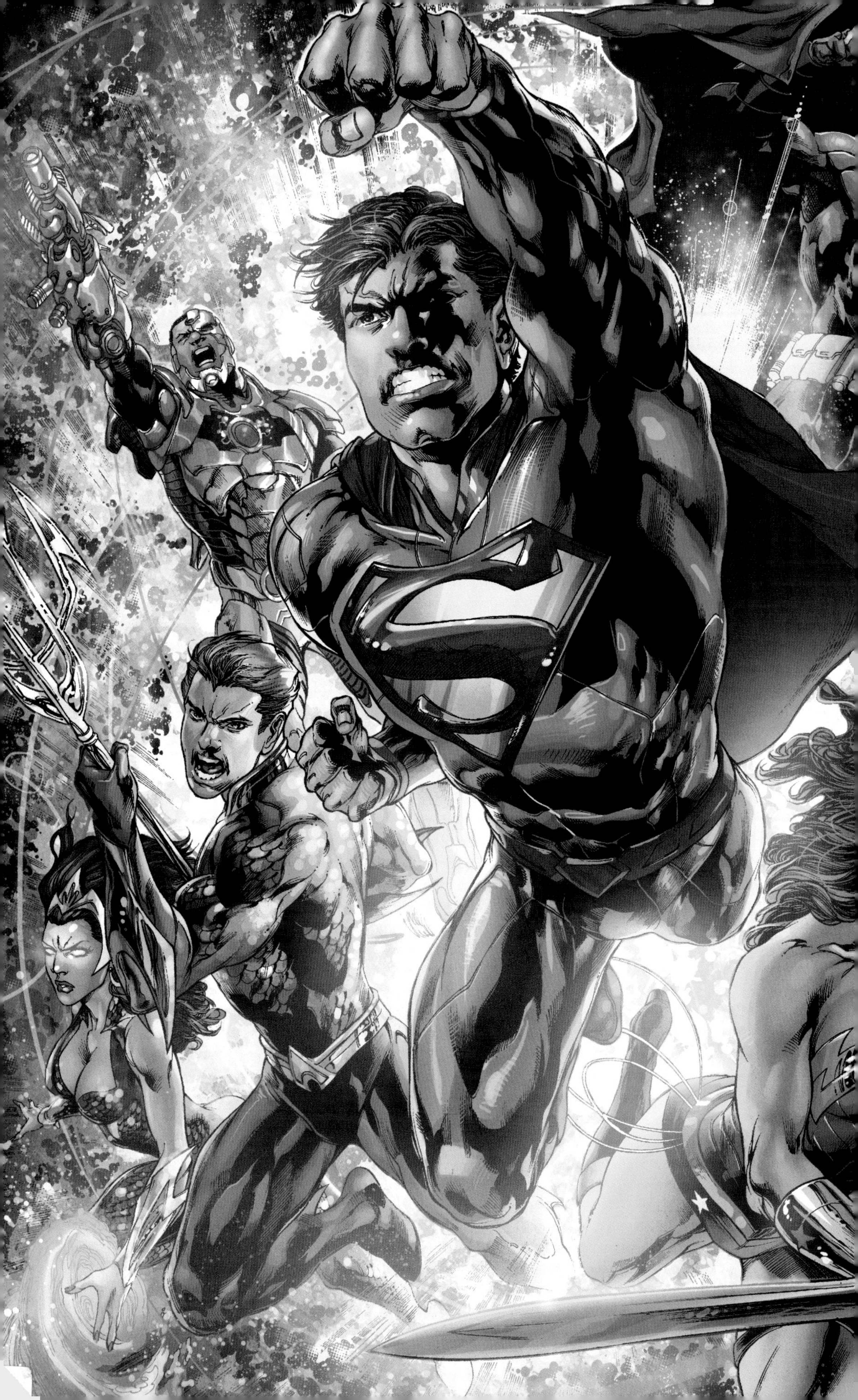

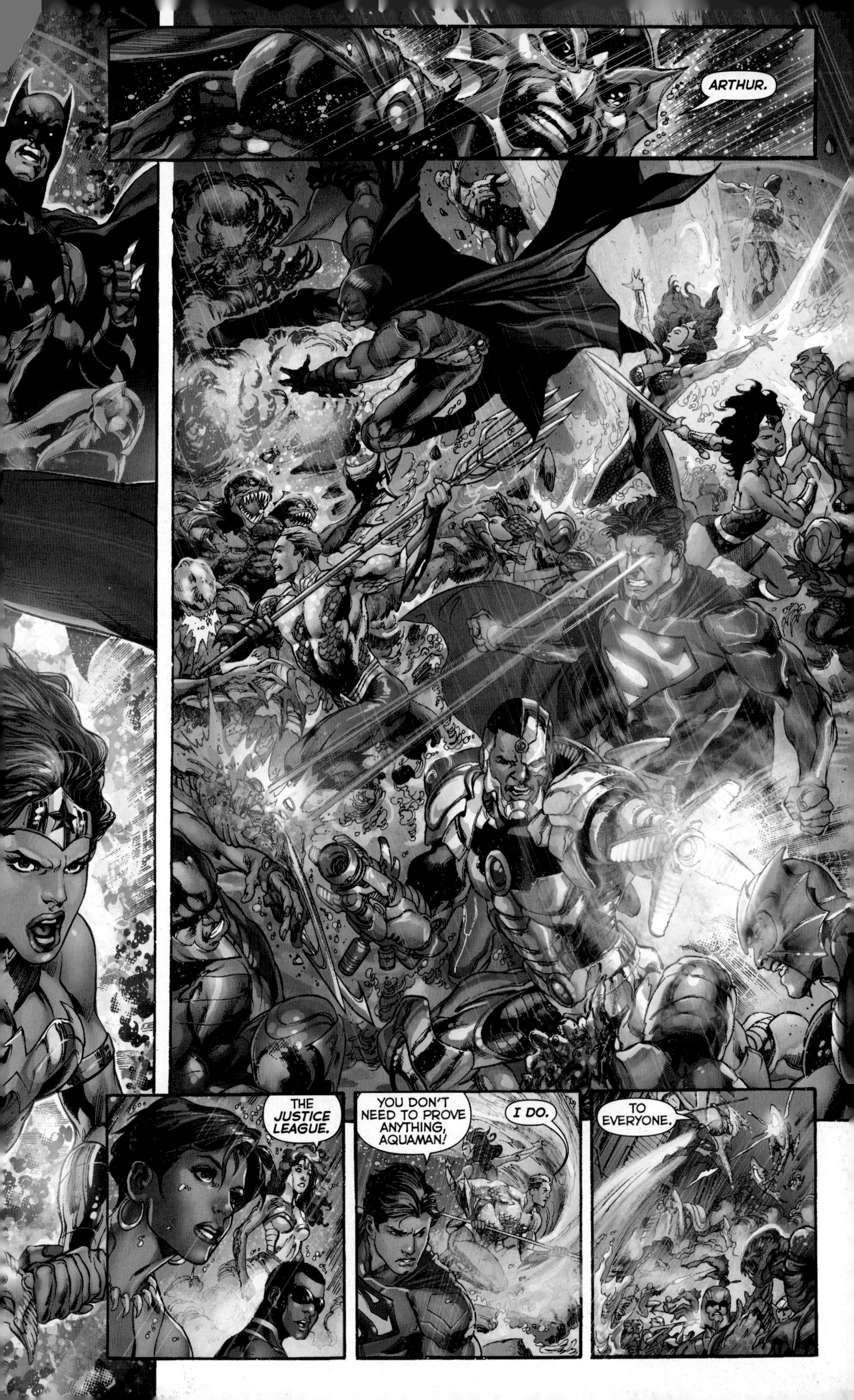
ARTHUR.
THE JUSTICE LEAGUE.
YOU DON'T NEED TO PROVE ANYTHING, AQUAMAN!
I DO.
TO EVERYONE.

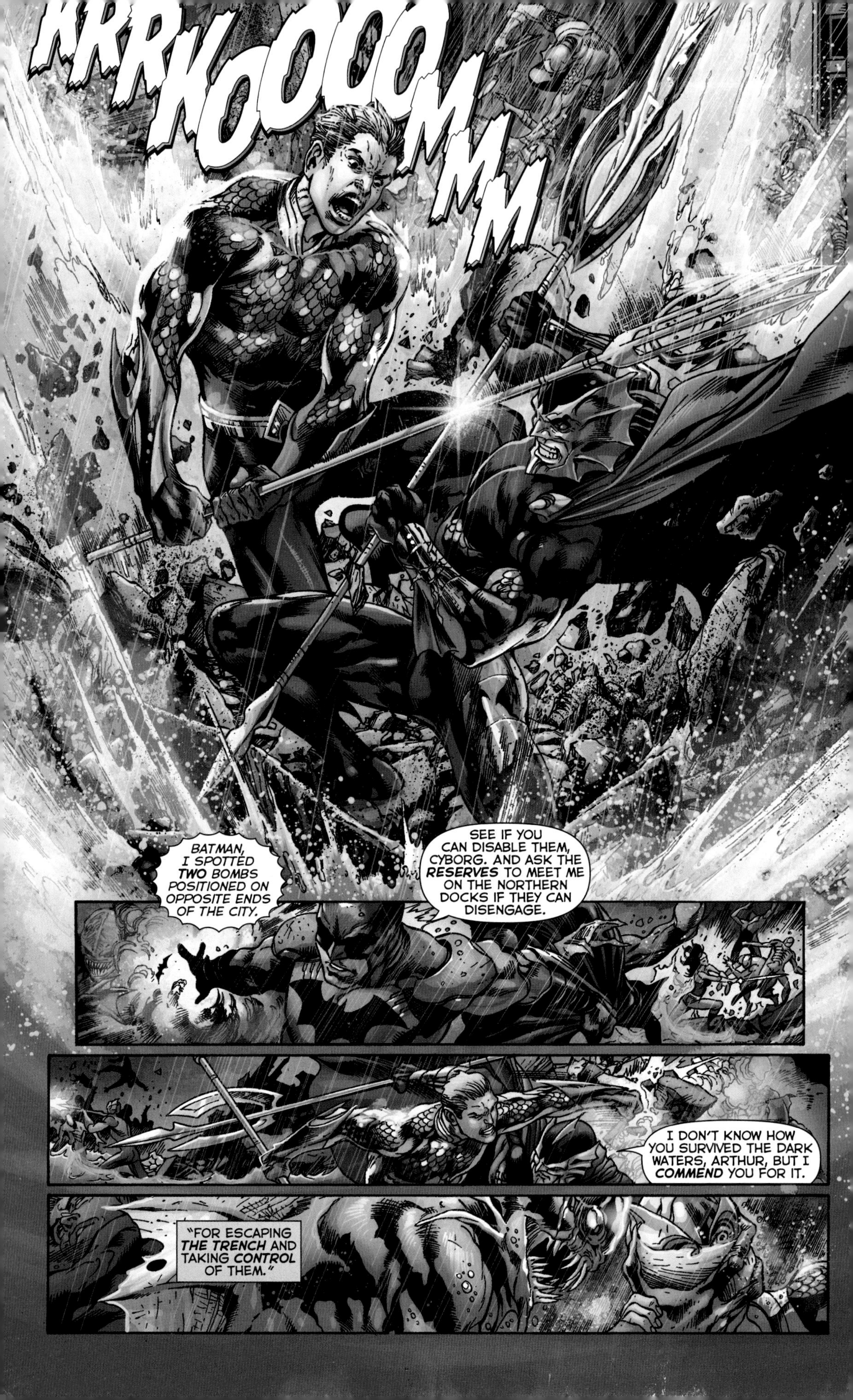
KRRKOOOOMMM
BATMAN, I SPOTTED **TWO** BOMBS POSITIONED ON OPPOSITE ENDS OF THE CITY.
SEE IF YOU CAN DISABLE THEM, CYBORG. AND ASK THE ***RESERVES*** TO MEET ME ON THE NORTHERN DOCKS IF THEY CAN DISENGAGE.
I DON'T KNOW HOW YOU SURVIVED THE DARK WATERS, ARTHUR, BUT I ***COMMEND*** YOU FOR IT.
"FOR ESCAPING ***THE TRENCH*** AND TAKING ***CONTROL*** OF THEM."

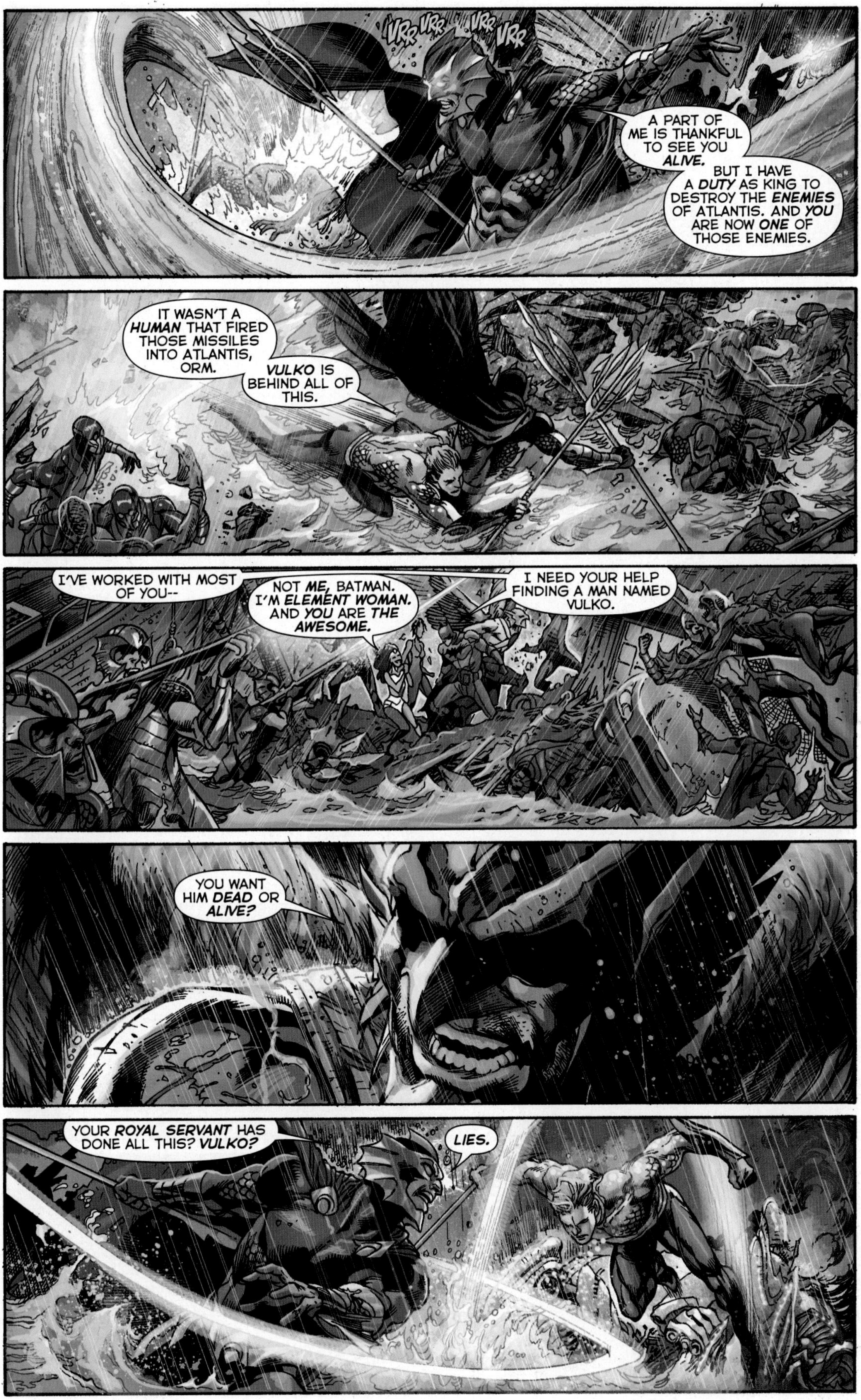
VRR VRR VRR VRR
A PART OF ME IS THANKFUL TO SEE YOU ALIVE.
BUT I HAVE A DUTY AS KING TO DESTROY THE ENEMIES OF ATLANTIS. AND YOU ARE NOW ONE OF THOSE ENEMIES.
IT WASN'T A HUMAN THAT FIRED THOSE MISSILES INTO ATLANTIS, ORM.
VULKO IS BEHIND ALL OF THIS.
I'VE WORKED WITH MOST OF YOU--
NOT ME, BATMAN. I'M ELEMENT WOMAN. AND YOU ARE THE AWESOME.
I NEED YOUR HELP FINDING A MAN NAMED VULKO.
YOU WANT HIM DEAD OR ALIVE?
YOUR ROYAL SERVANT HAS DONE ALL THIS? VULKO?
LIES.

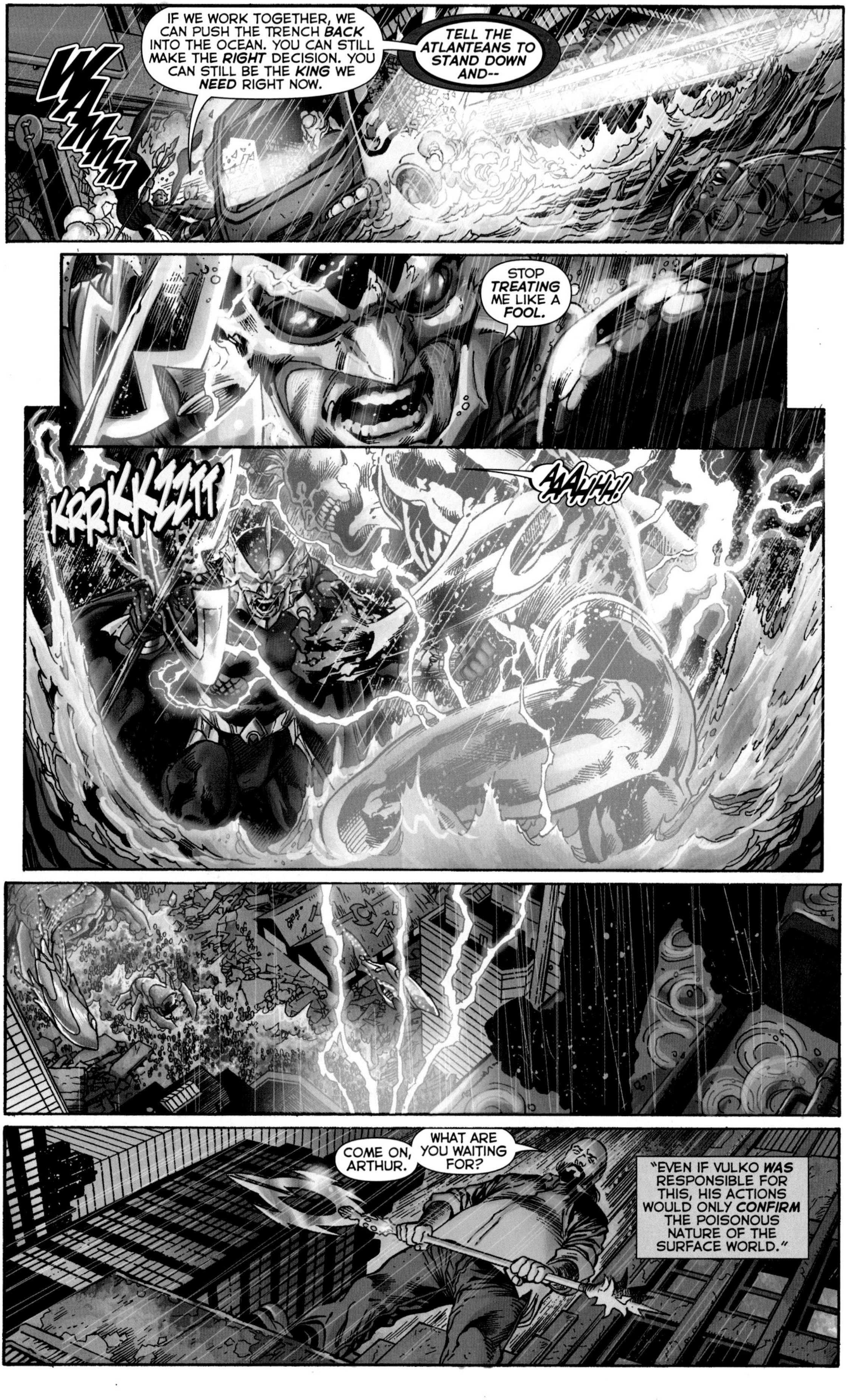
WHAM
IF WE WORK TOGETHER, WE CAN PUSH THE TRENCH BACK INTO THE OCEAN. YOU CAN STILL MAKE THE RIGHT DECISION. YOU CAN STILL BE THE KING WE NEED RIGHT NOW.
TELL THE ATLANTEANS TO STAND DOWN AND--
STOP TREATING ME LIKE A FOOL.
KRRKKZZTT
AAAHHH!
COME ON, ARTHUR.
WHAT ARE YOU WAITING FOR?
"EVEN IF VULKO WAS RESPONSIBLE FOR THIS, HIS ACTIONS WOULD ONLY CONFIRM THE POISONOUS NATURE OF THE SURFACE WORLD."

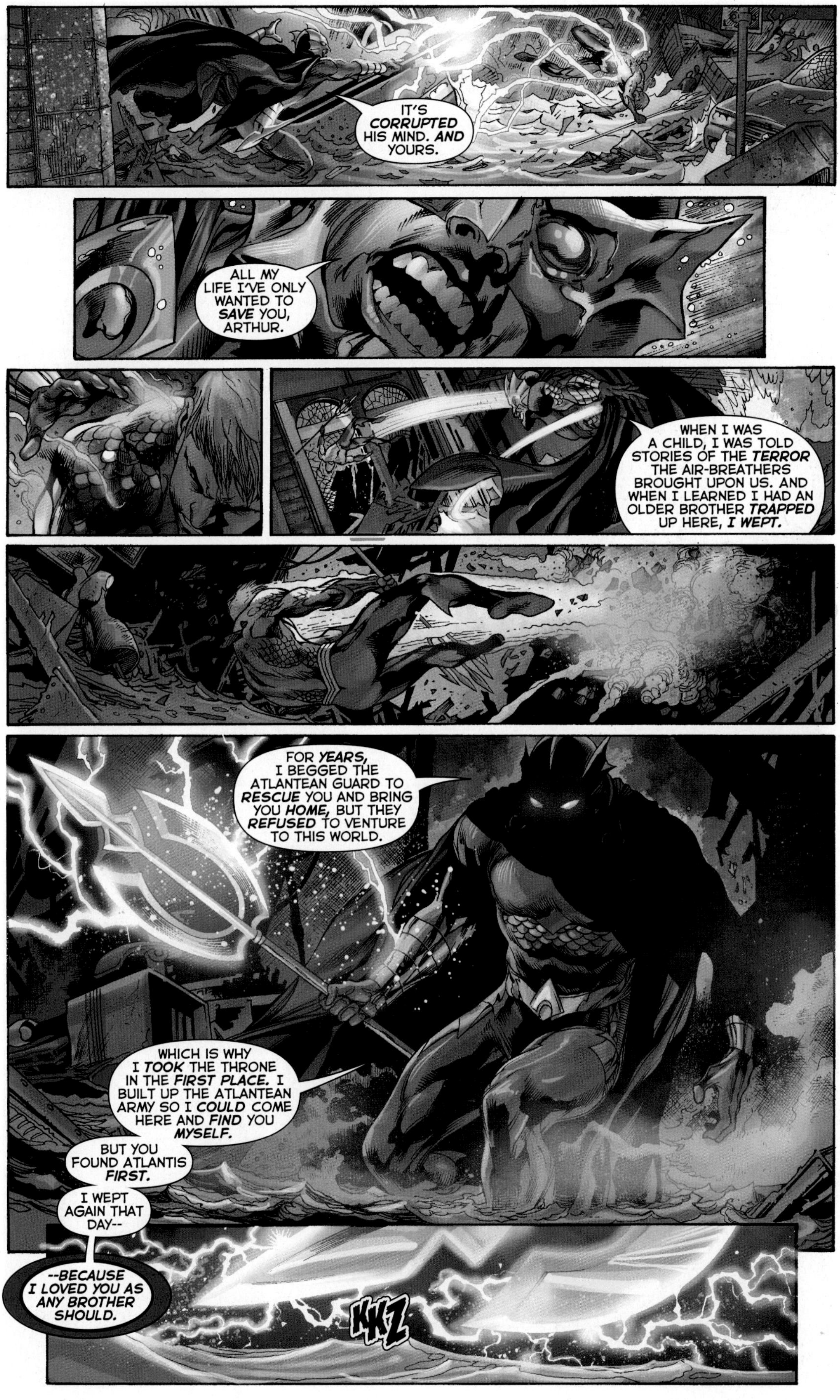
IT'S CORRUPTED HIS MIND. AND YOURS.
ALL MY LIFE I'VE ONLY WANTED TO SAVE YOU, ARTHUR.
WHEN I WAS A CHILD, I WAS TOLD STORIES OF THE TERROR THE AIR-BREATHERS BROUGHT UPON US. AND WHEN I LEARNED I HAD AN OLDER BROTHER TRAPPED UP HERE, I WEPT.
FOR YEARS, I BEGGED THE ATLANTEAN GUARD TO RESCUE YOU AND BRING YOU HOME, BUT THEY REFUSED TO VENTURE TO THIS WORLD.
WHICH IS WHY I TOOK THE THRONE IN THE FIRST PLACE. I BUILT UP THE ATLANTEAN ARMY SO I COULD COME HERE AND FIND YOU MYSELF.
BUT YOU FOUND ATLANTIS FIRST.
I WEPT AGAIN THAT DAY--
--BECAUSE I LOVED YOU AS ANY BROTHER SHOULD.
KKZ

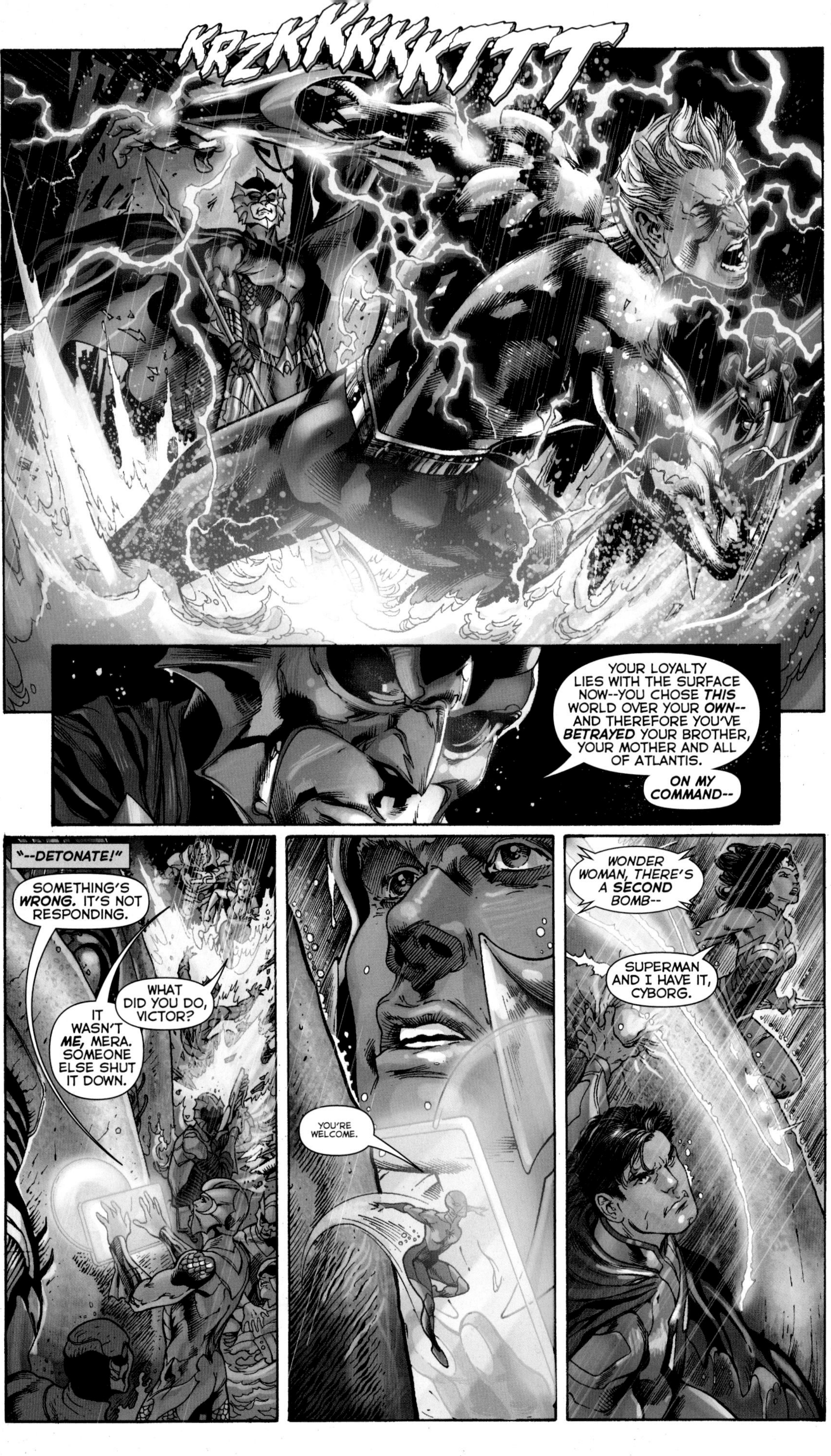
KRZKKKKKKTTTT
YOUR LOYALTY LIES WITH THE SURFACE NOW--YOU CHOSE THIS WORLD OVER YOUR OWN-- AND THEREFORE YOU'VE BETRAYED YOUR BROTHER, YOUR MOTHER AND ALL OF ATLANTIS.
ON MY COMMAND--
"--DETONATE!"
SOMETHING'S WRONG. IT'S NOT RESPONDING.
WHAT DID YOU DO, VICTOR?
IT WASN'T ME, MERA. SOMEONE ELSE SHUT IT DOWN.
YOU'RE WELCOME.
WONDER WOMAN, THERE'S A SECOND BOMB--
SUPERMAN AND I HAVE IT, CYBORG.

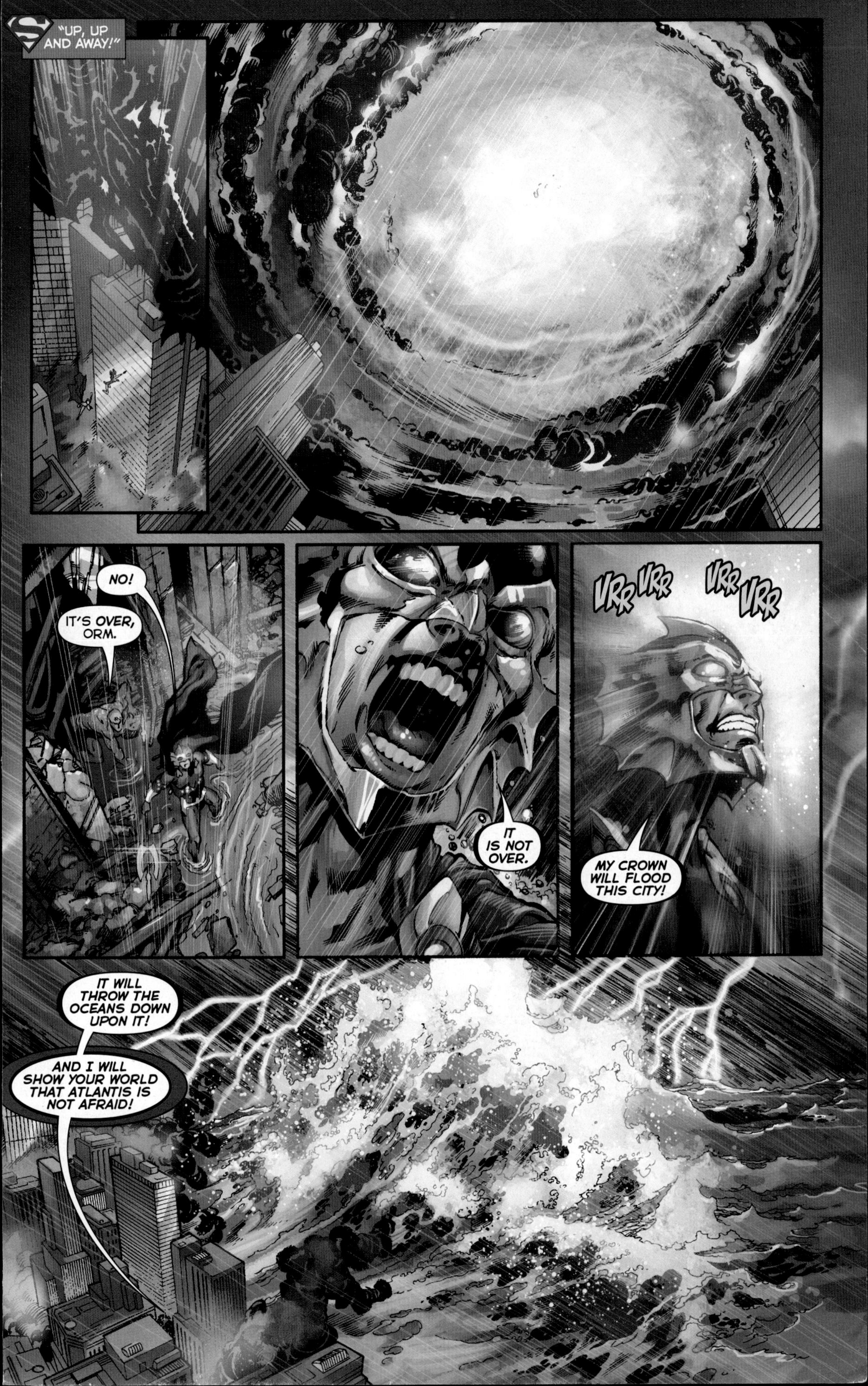
"UP, UP AND AWAY!"
NO!
IT'S OVER, ORM.
IT IS NOT OVER.
VRR VRR VRR VRR
MY CROWN WILL FLOOD THIS CITY!
IT WILL THROW THE OCEANS DOWN UPON IT!
AND I WILL SHOW YOUR WORLD THAT ATLANTIS IS NOT AFRAID!

KKRAKKOBOOMM

VRR VRR VRR VRR

THAT *CONVICT* CAN'T HOLD THE *WATER* UP FOREVER.

RETAW OT ECI.

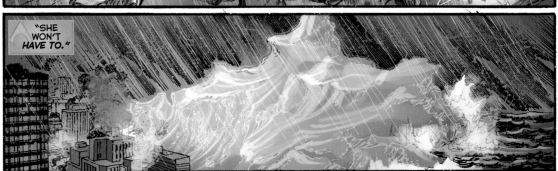

"SHE WON'T HAVE TO."

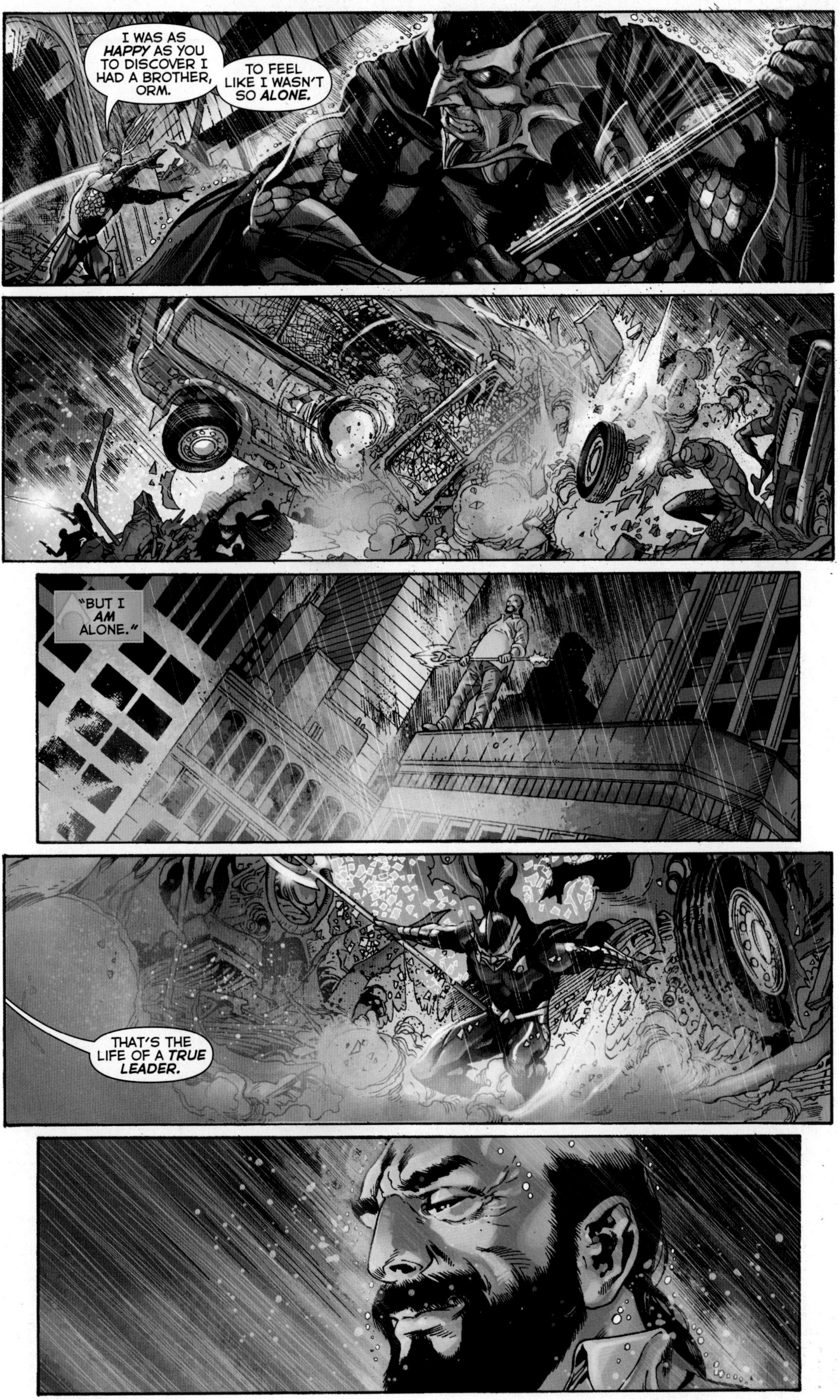
I WAS AS HAPPY AS YOU TO DISCOVER I HAD A BROTHER, ORM.
TO FEEL LIKE I WASN'T SO ALONE.
"BUT I AM ALONE."
THAT'S THE LIFE OF A TRUE LEADER.

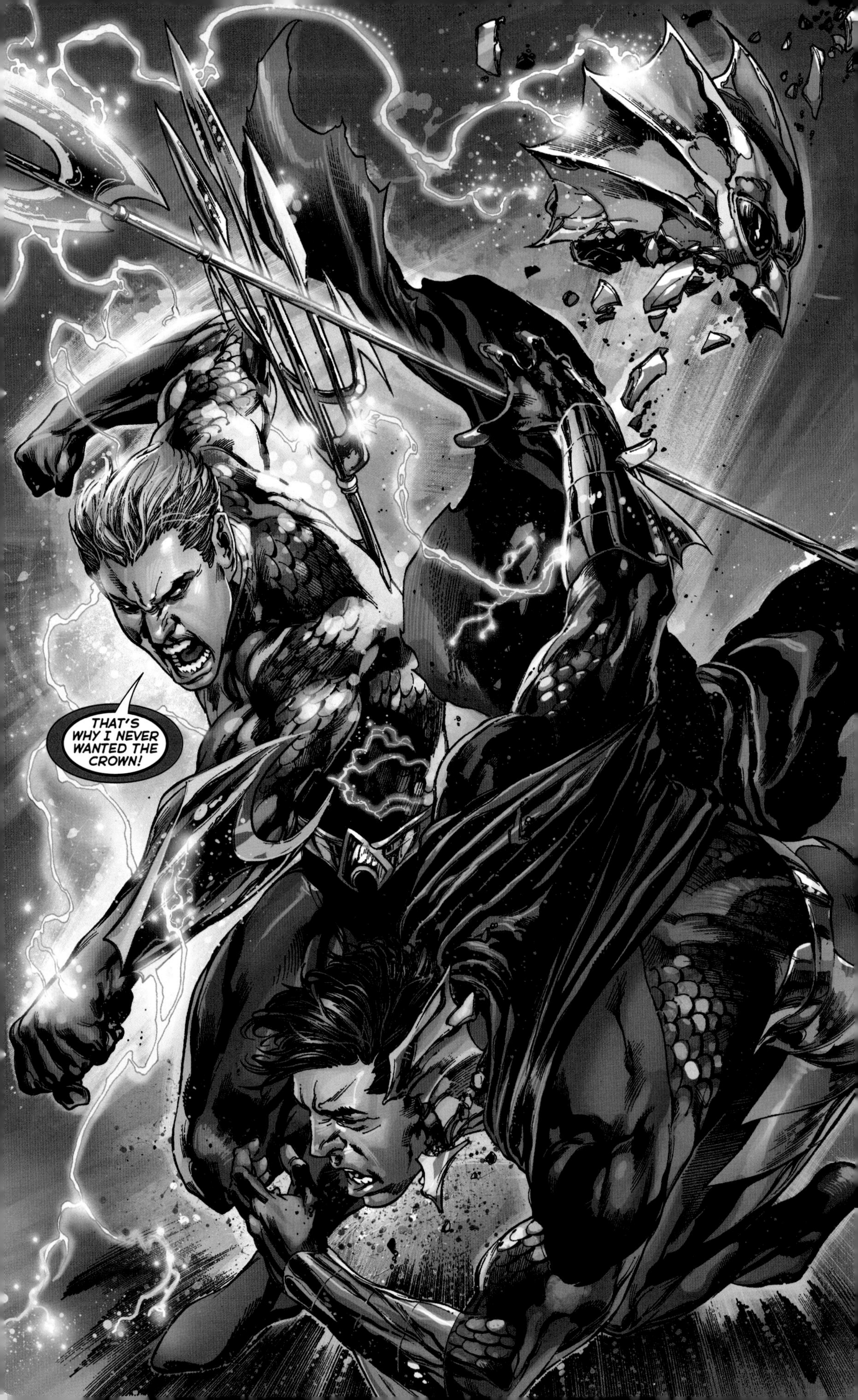
THAT'S WHY I NEVER WANTED THE CROWN!

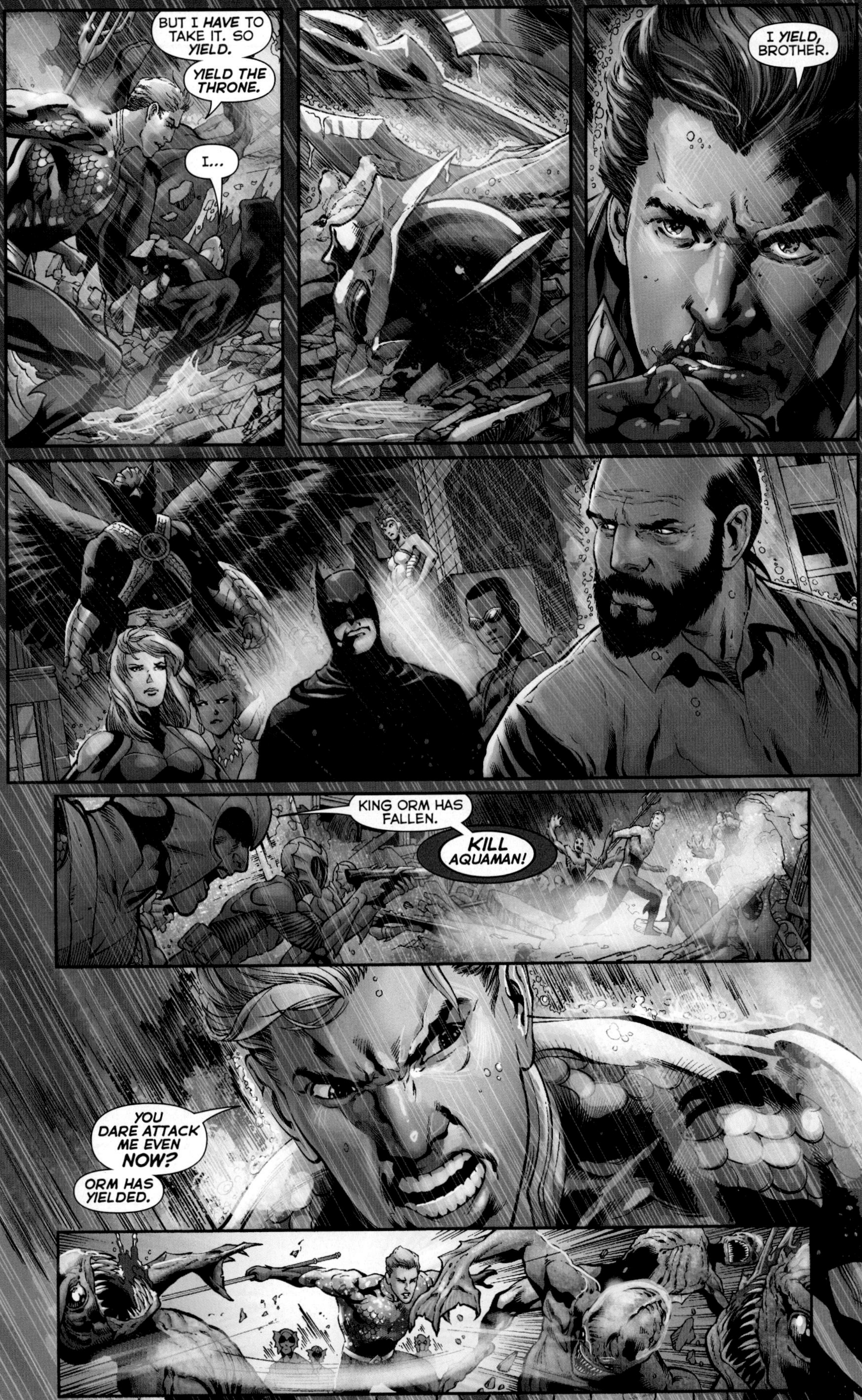
BUT I HAVE TO TAKE IT. SO YIELD.
YIELD THE THRONE.
I...
I YIELD, BROTHER.
KING ORM HAS FALLEN.
KILL AQUAMAN!
YOU DARE ATTACK ME EVEN NOW?
ORM HAS YIELDED.

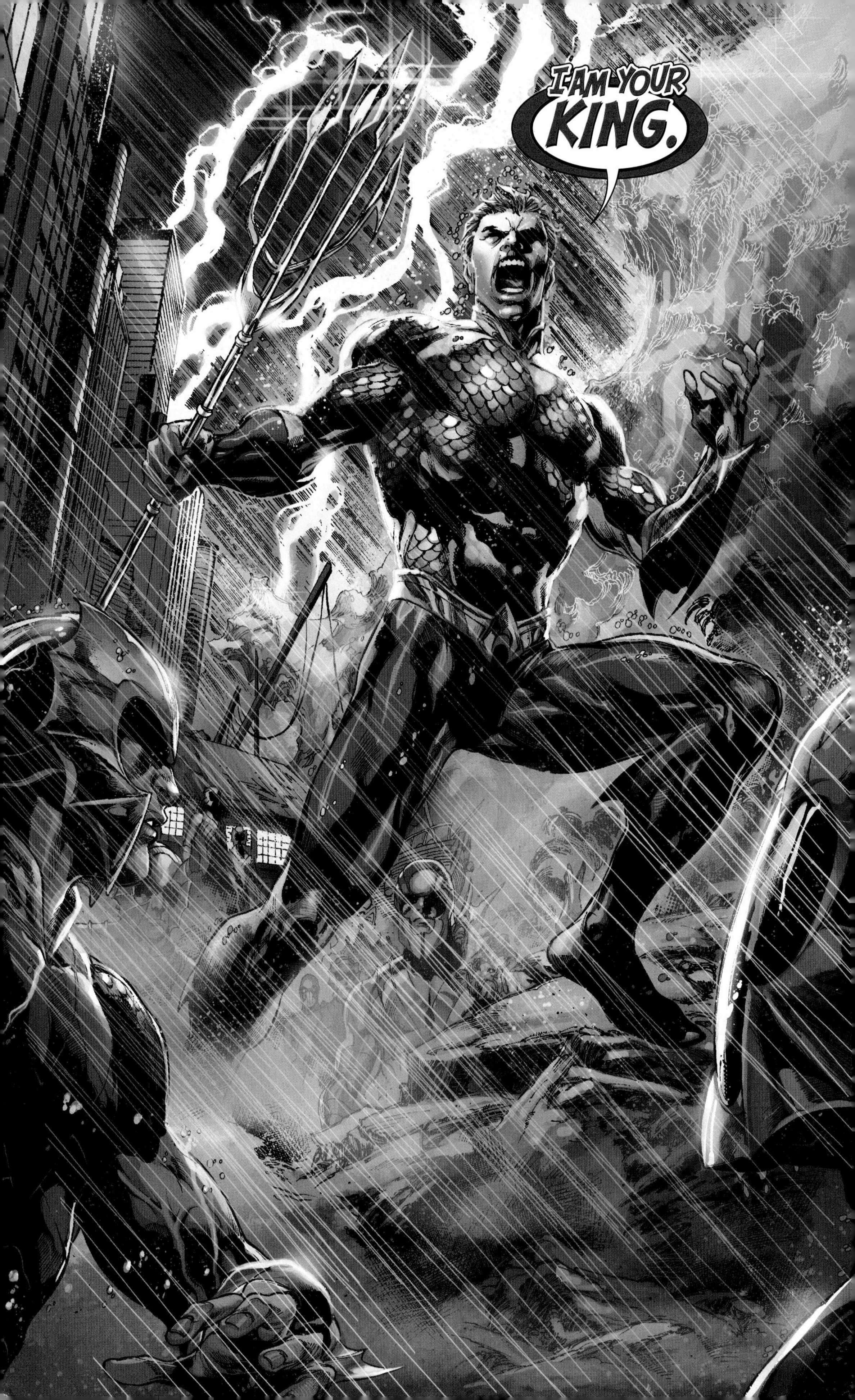
I AM YOUR KING.

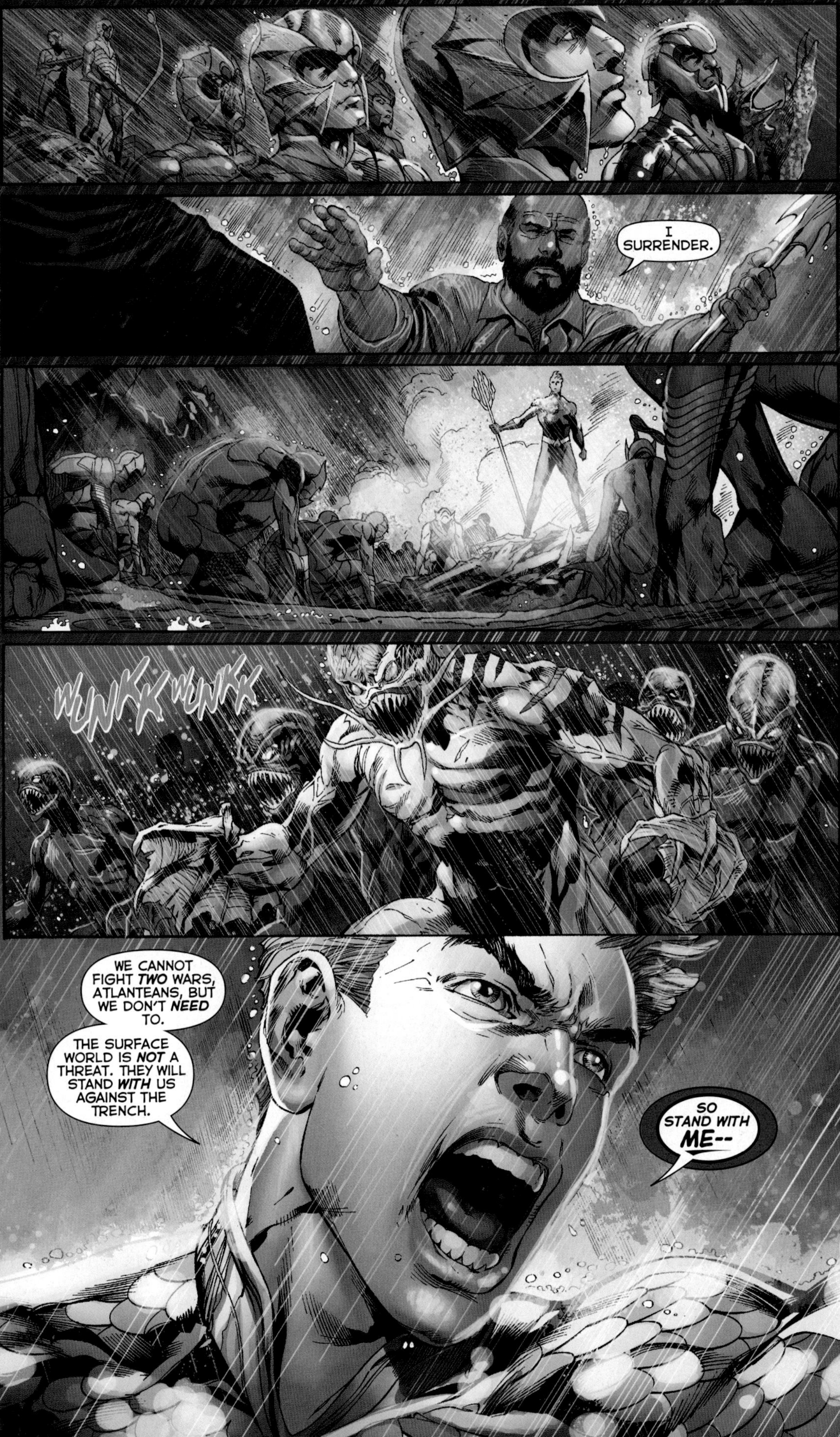

I SURRENDER.
WUNKK WUNKK
WE CANNOT FIGHT TWO WARS, ATLANTEANS, BUT WE DON'T NEED TO.
THE SURFACE WORLD IS NOT A THREAT. THEY WILL STAND WITH US AGAINST THE TRENCH.
SO STAND WITH ME--

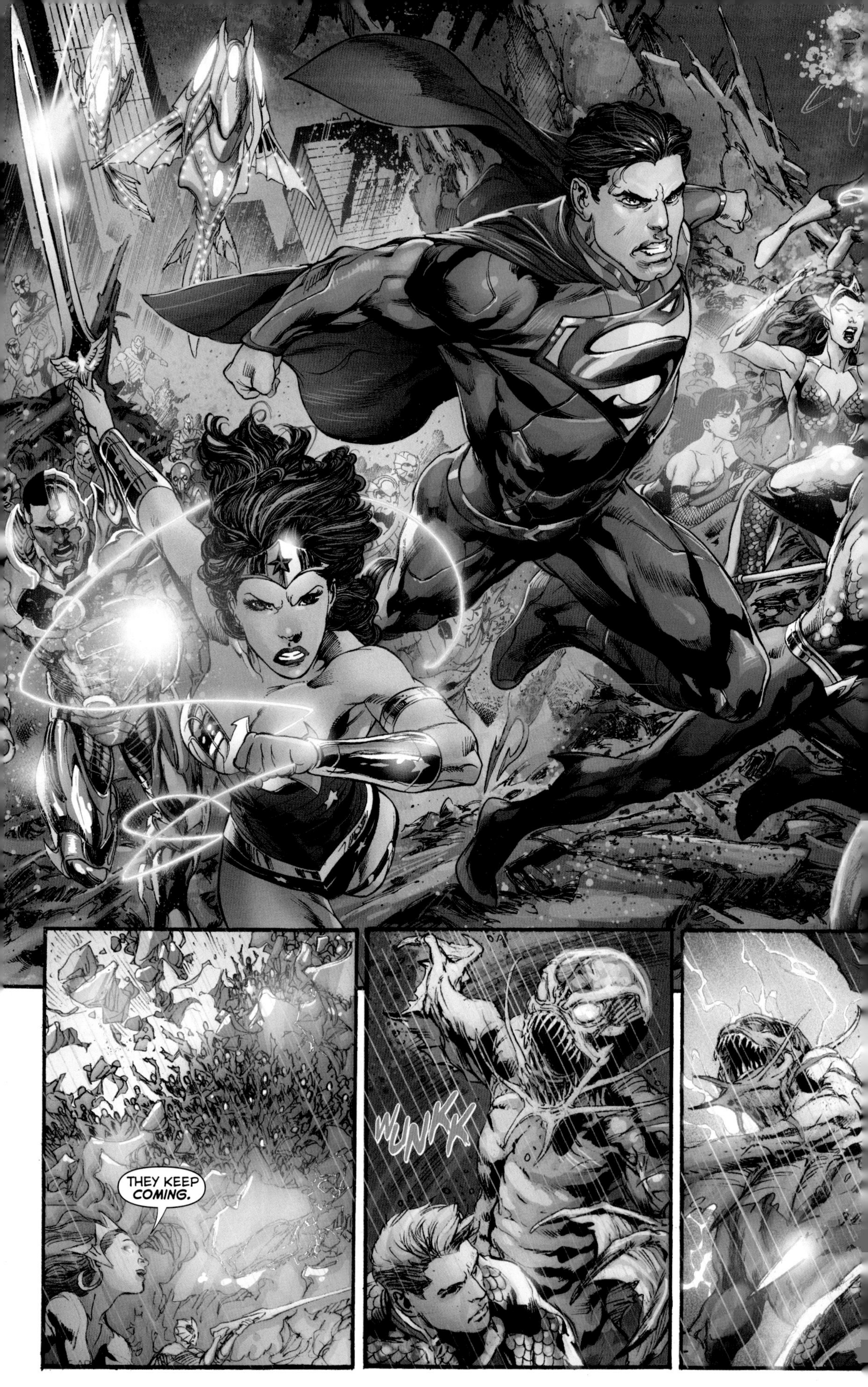
THEY KEEP COMING.
WUNKK

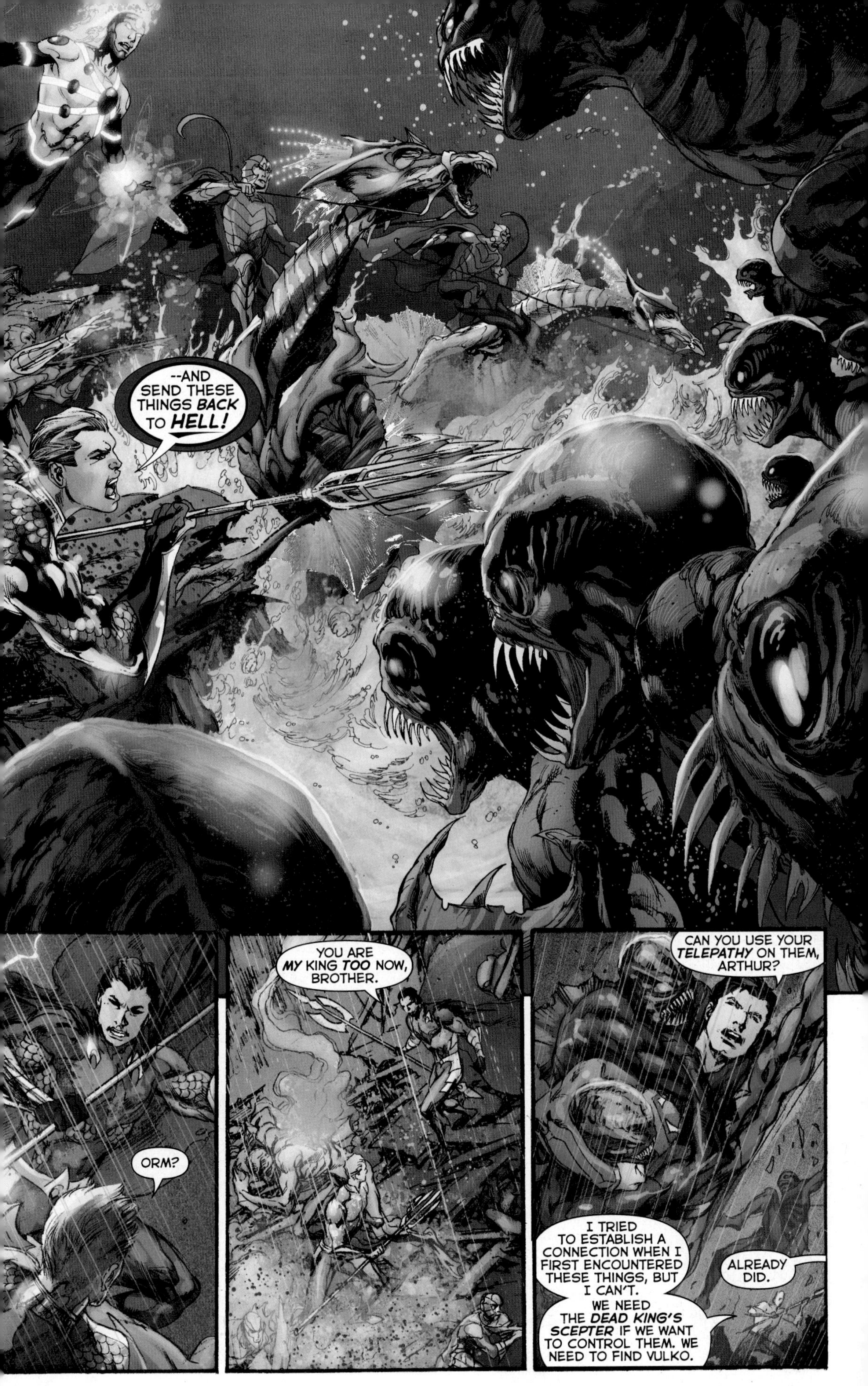
--AND SEND THESE THINGS BACK TO HELL!
ORM?
YOU ARE MY KING TOO NOW, BROTHER.
CAN YOU USE YOUR TELEPATHY ON THEM, ARTHUR?
ALREADY DID.
I TRIED TO ESTABLISH A CONNECTION WHEN I FIRST ENCOUNTERED THESE THINGS, BUT I CAN'T.
WE NEED THE DEAD KING'S SCEPTER IF WE WANT TO CONTROL THEM. WE NEED TO FIND VULKO.

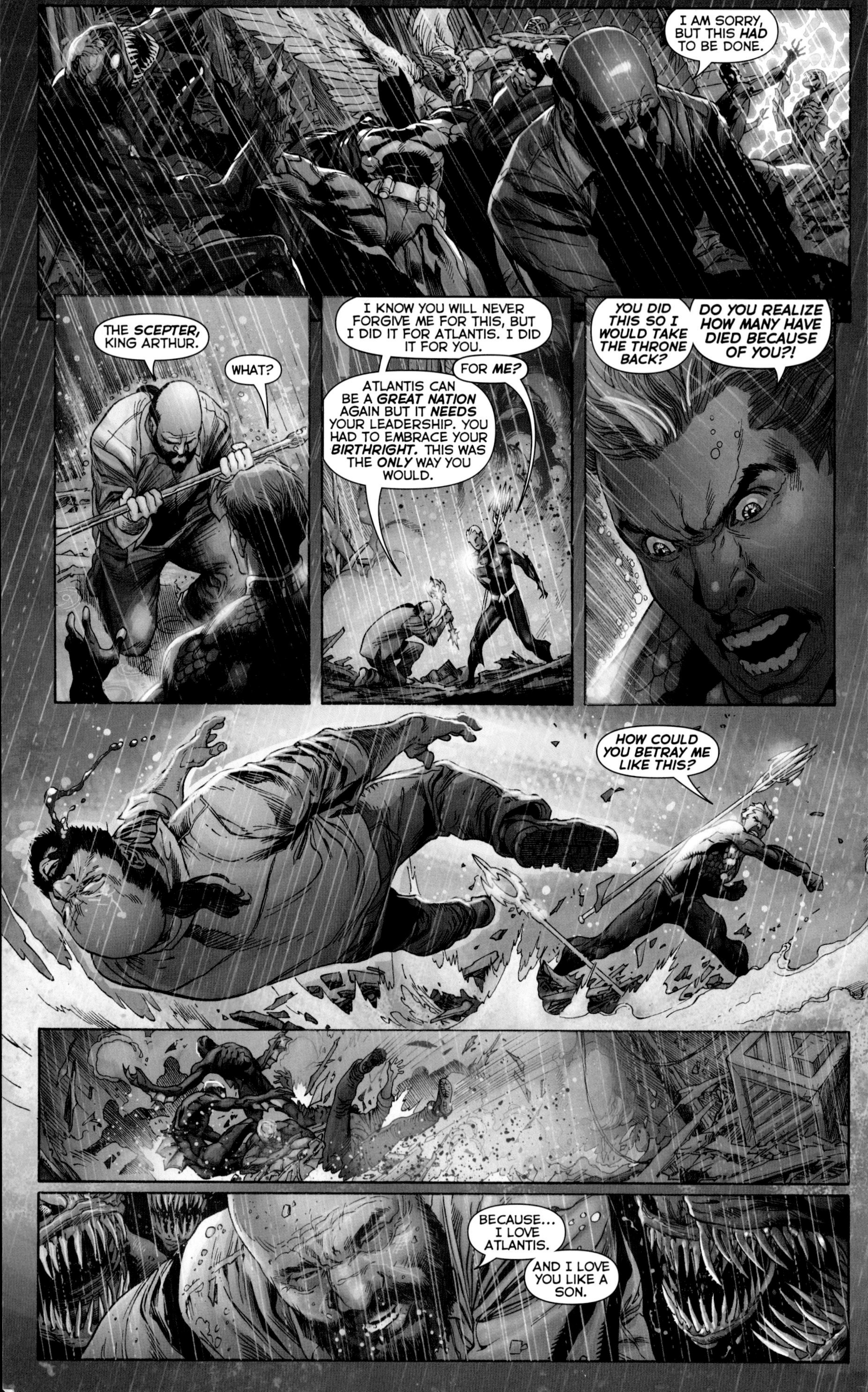

I AM SORRY, BUT THIS HAD TO BE DONE.
THE SCEPTER, KING ARTHUR.
WHAT?
I KNOW YOU WILL NEVER FORGIVE ME FOR THIS, BUT I DID IT FOR ATLANTIS. I DID IT FOR YOU.
FOR ME?
ATLANTIS CAN BE A GREAT NATION AGAIN BUT IT NEEDS YOUR LEADERSHIP. YOU HAD TO EMBRACE YOUR BIRTHRIGHT. THIS WAS THE ONLY WAY YOU WOULD.
YOU DID THIS SO I WOULD TAKE THE THRONE BACK?
DO YOU REALIZE HOW MANY HAVE DIED BECAUSE OF YOU?!
HOW COULD YOU BETRAY ME LIKE THIS?
BECAUSE... I LOVE ATLANTIS.
AND I LOVE YOU LIKE A SON.

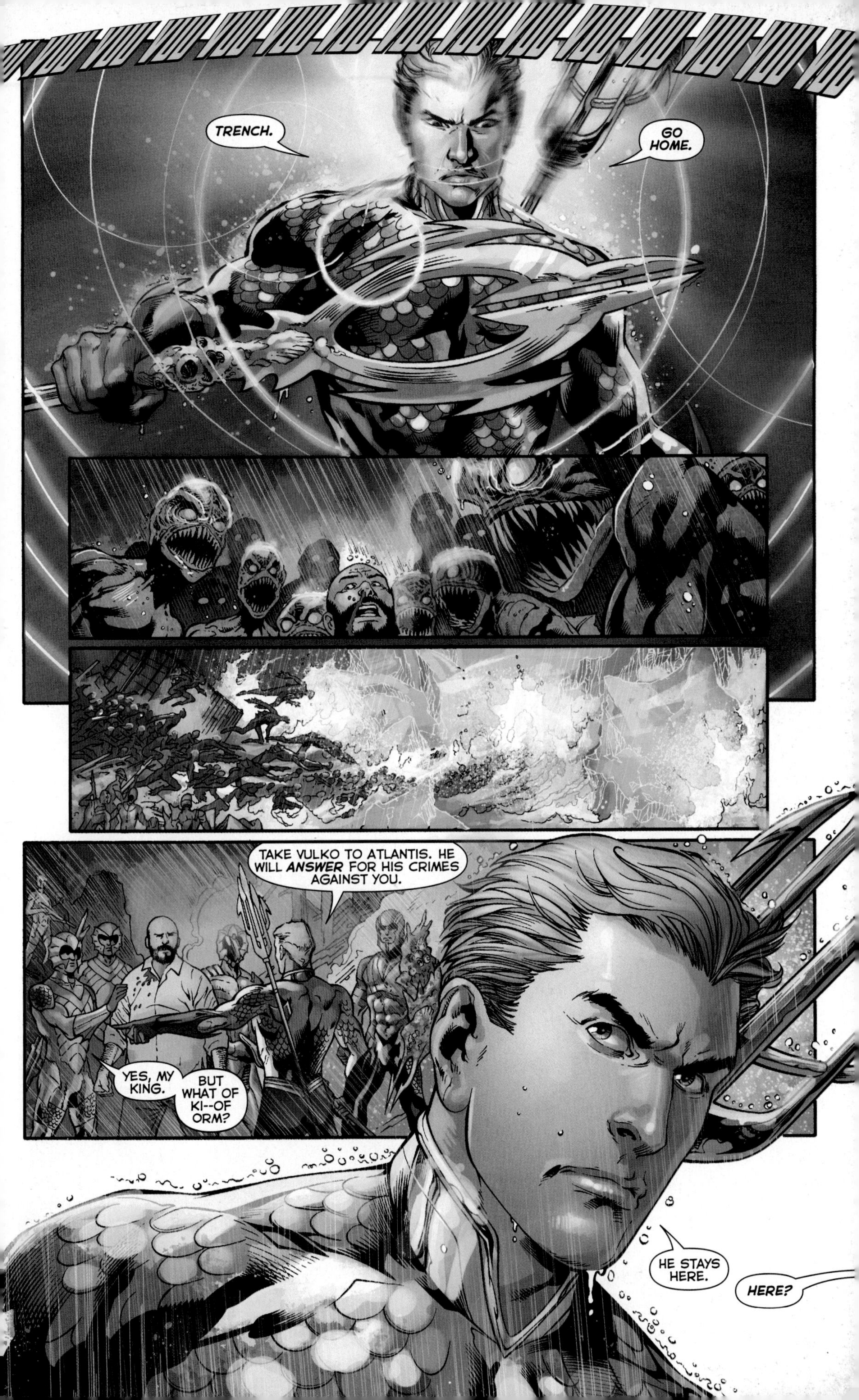
TRENCH.
GO HOME.
TAKE VULKO TO ATLANTIS. HE WILL ANSWER FOR HIS CRIMES AGAINST YOU.
YES, MY KING.
BUT WHAT OF KI--OF ORM?
HE STAYS HERE.
HERE?

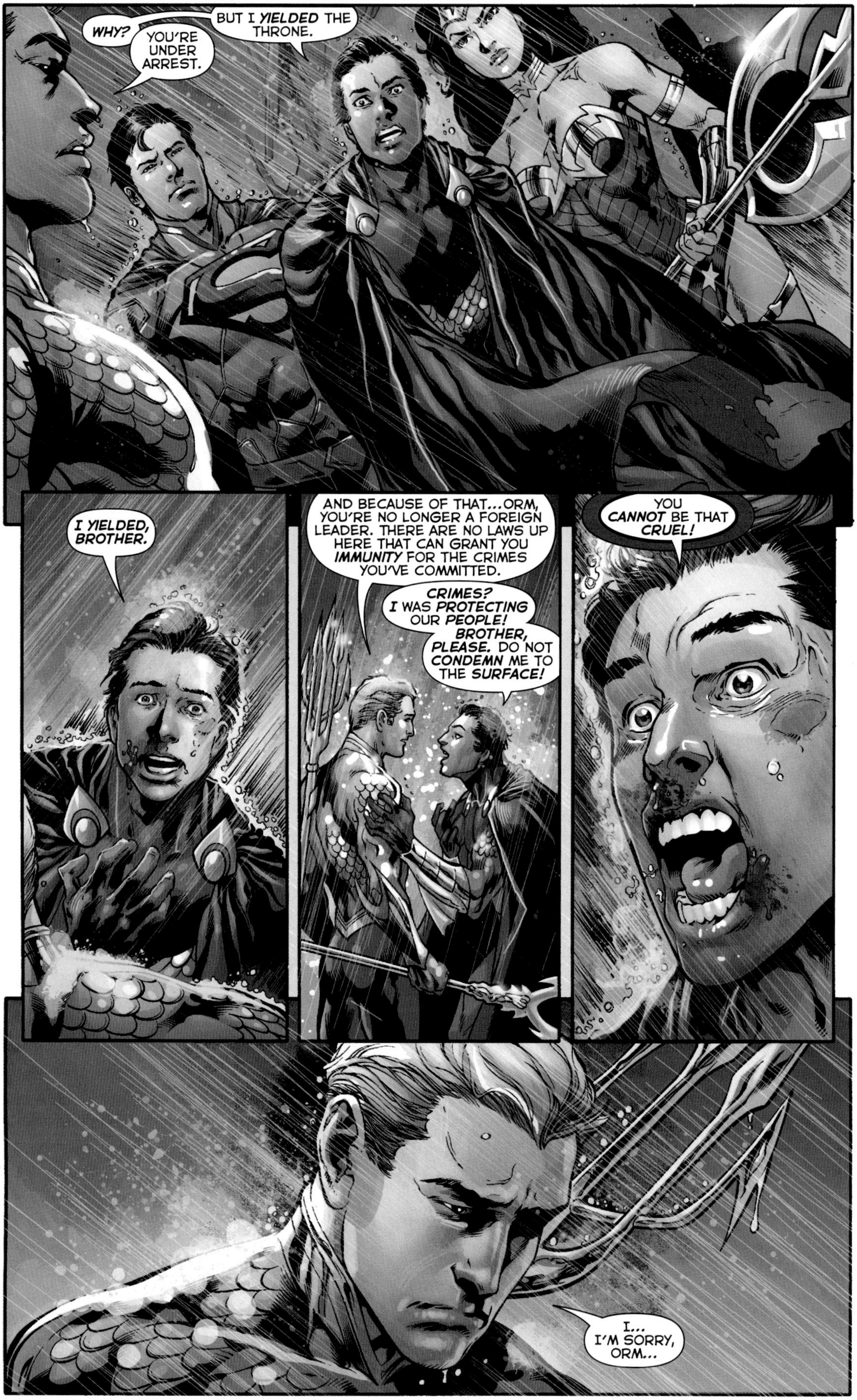

WHY?
BUT I YIELDED THE THRONE.
YOU'RE UNDER ARREST.
I YIELDED, BROTHER.
AND BECAUSE OF THAT...ORM, YOU'RE NO LONGER A FOREIGN LEADER. THERE ARE NO LAWS UP HERE THAT CAN GRANT YOU IMMUNITY FOR THE CRIMES YOU'VE COMMITTED.
CRIMES? I WAS PROTECTING OUR PEOPLE! BROTHER, PLEASE. DO NOT CONDEMN ME TO THE SURFACE!
YOU CANNOT BE THAT CRUEL!
I... I'M SORRY, ORM...

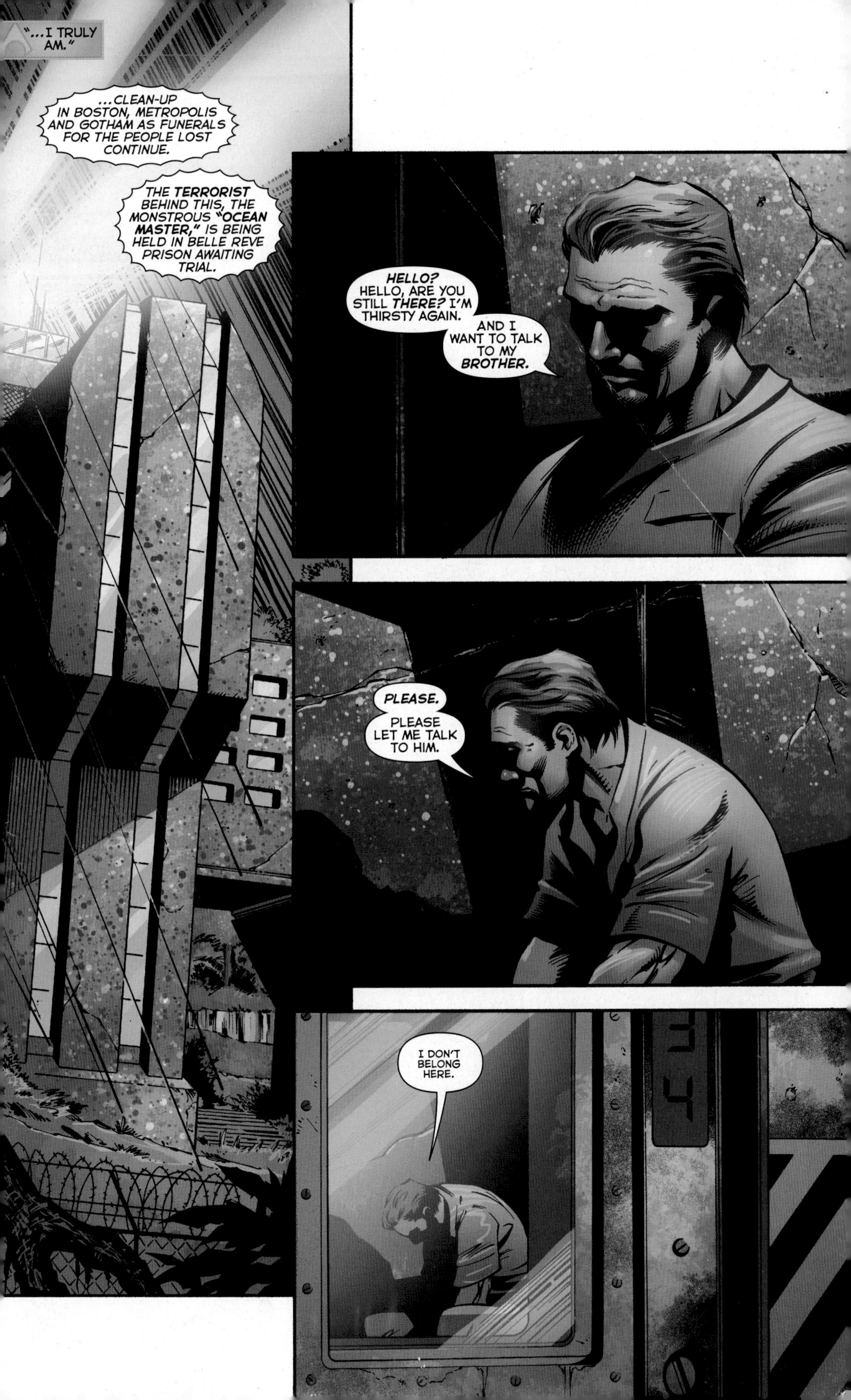
"...I TRULY AM."
...CLEAN-UP IN BOSTON, METROPOLIS AND GOTHAM AS FUNERALS FOR THE PEOPLE LOST CONTINUE.
THE TERRORIST BEHIND THIS, THE MONSTROUS "OCEAN MASTER," IS BEING HELD IN BELLE REVE PRISON AWAITING TRIAL.
HELLO? HELLO, ARE YOU STILL THERE? I'M THIRSTY AGAIN.
AND I WANT TO TALK TO MY BROTHER.
PLEASE.
PLEASE LET ME TALK TO HIM.
I DON'T BELONG HERE.

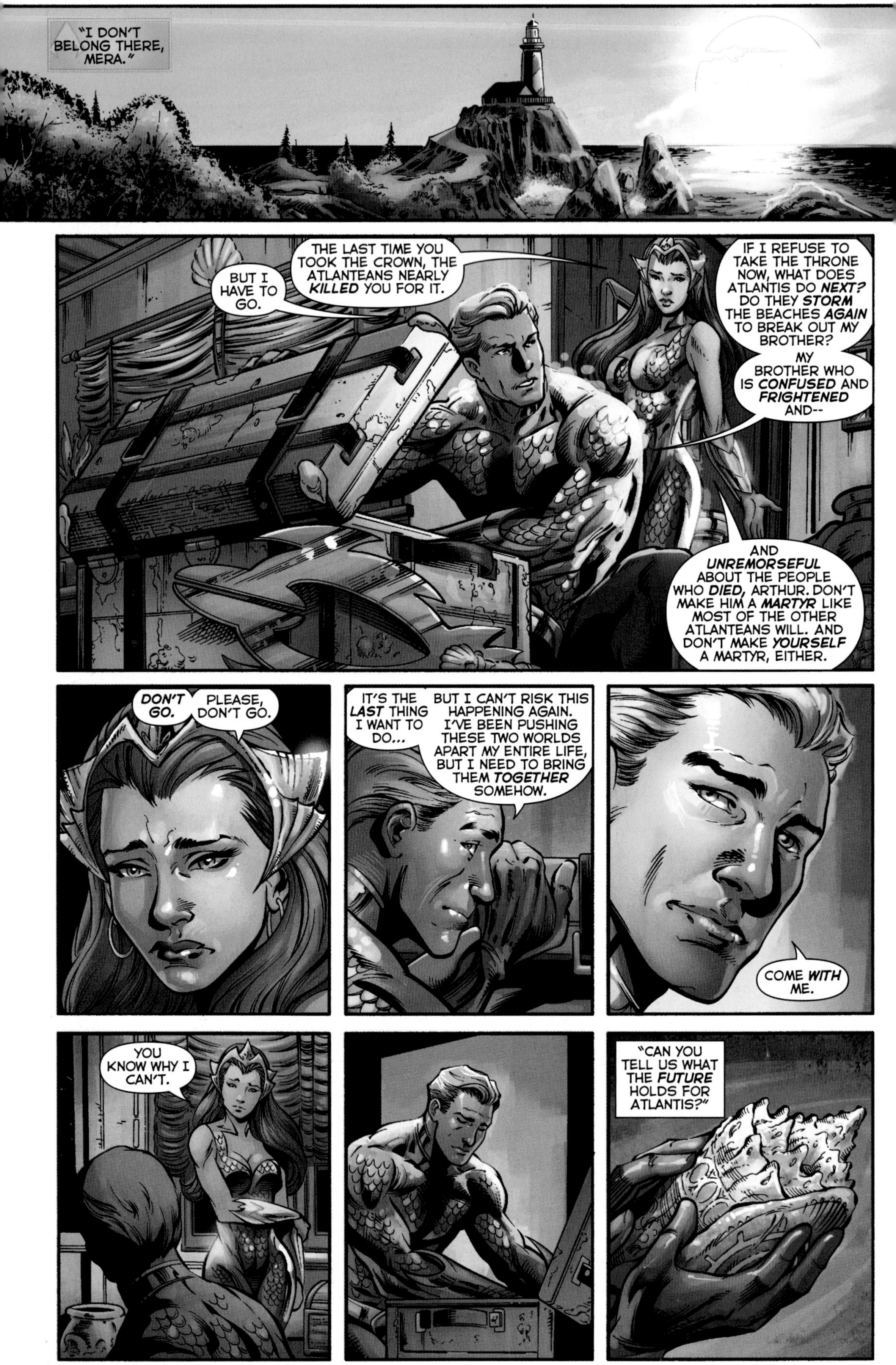

"I DON'T BELONG THERE, MERA."
BUT I HAVE TO GO.
THE LAST TIME YOU TOOK THE CROWN, THE ATLANTEANS NEARLY KILLED YOU FOR IT.
IF I REFUSE TO TAKE THE THRONE NOW, WHAT DOES ATLANTIS DO NEXT? DO THEY STORM THE BEACHES AGAIN TO BREAK OUT MY BROTHER?
MY BROTHER WHO IS CONFUSED AND FRIGHTENED AND--
AND UNREMORSEFUL ABOUT THE PEOPLE WHO DIED, ARTHUR. DON'T MAKE HIM A MARTYR LIKE MOST OF THE OTHER ATLANTEANS WILL. AND DON'T MAKE YOURSELF A MARTYR, EITHER.
DON'T GO.
PLEASE, DON'T GO.
IT'S THE LAST THING I WANT TO DO...
BUT I CAN'T RISK THIS HAPPENING AGAIN. I'VE BEEN PUSHING THESE TWO WORLDS APART MY ENTIRE LIFE, BUT I NEED TO BRING THEM TOGETHER SOMEHOW.
COME WITH ME.
YOU KNOW WHY I CAN'T.
"CAN YOU TELL US WHAT THE FUTURE HOLDS FOR ATLANTIS?"

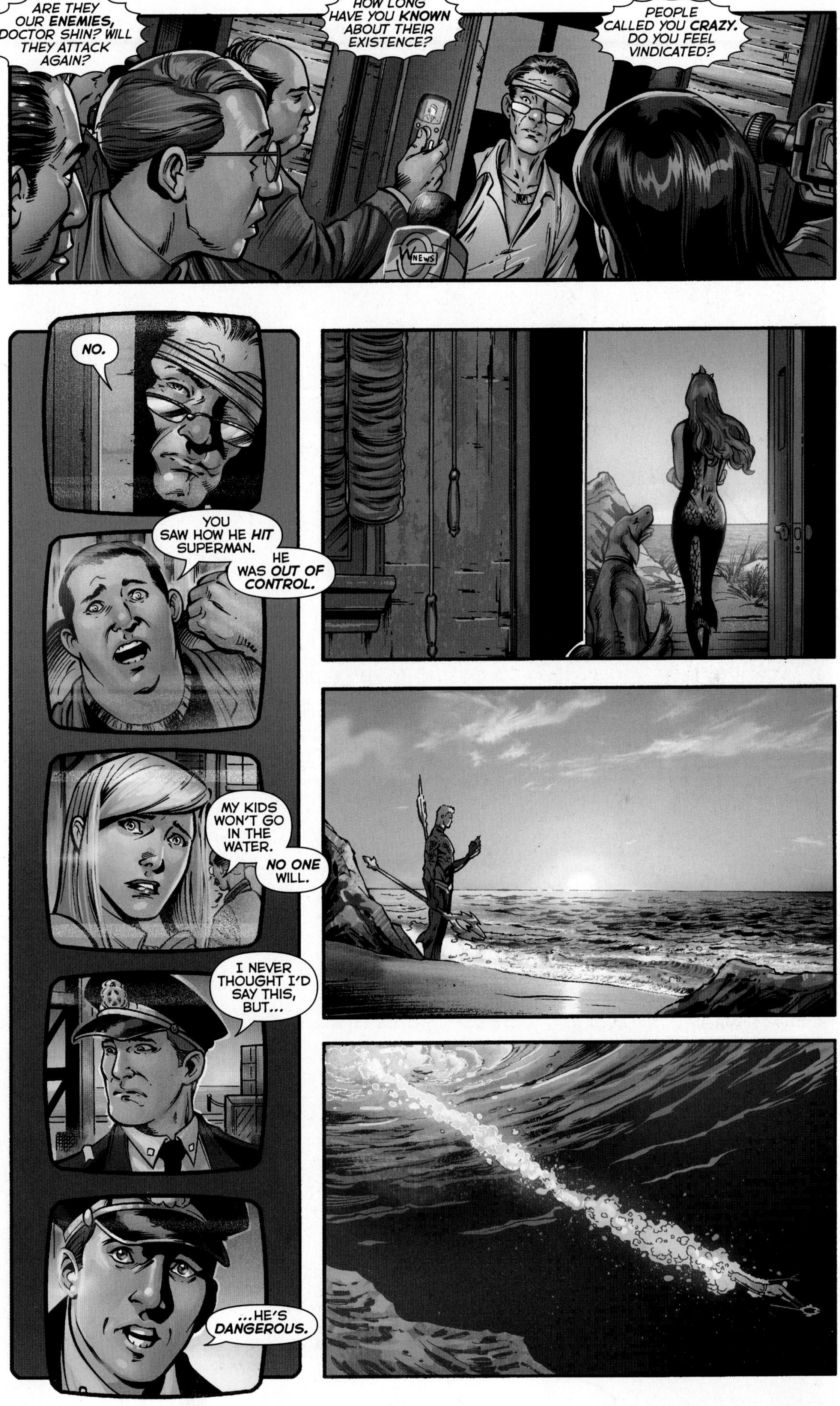
ARE THEY OUR ENEMIES, DOCTOR SHIN? WILL THEY ATTACK AGAIN?
HOW LONG HAVE YOU KNOWN ABOUT THEIR EXISTENCE?
PEOPLE CALLED YOU CRAZY. DO YOU FEEL VINDICATED?
NEWS
NO.
YOU SAW HOW HE HIT SUPERMAN.
HE WAS OUT OF CONTROL.
MY KIDS WON'T GO IN THE WATER.
NO ONE WILL.
I NEVER THOUGHT I'D SAY THIS, BUT...
...HE'S DANGEROUS.

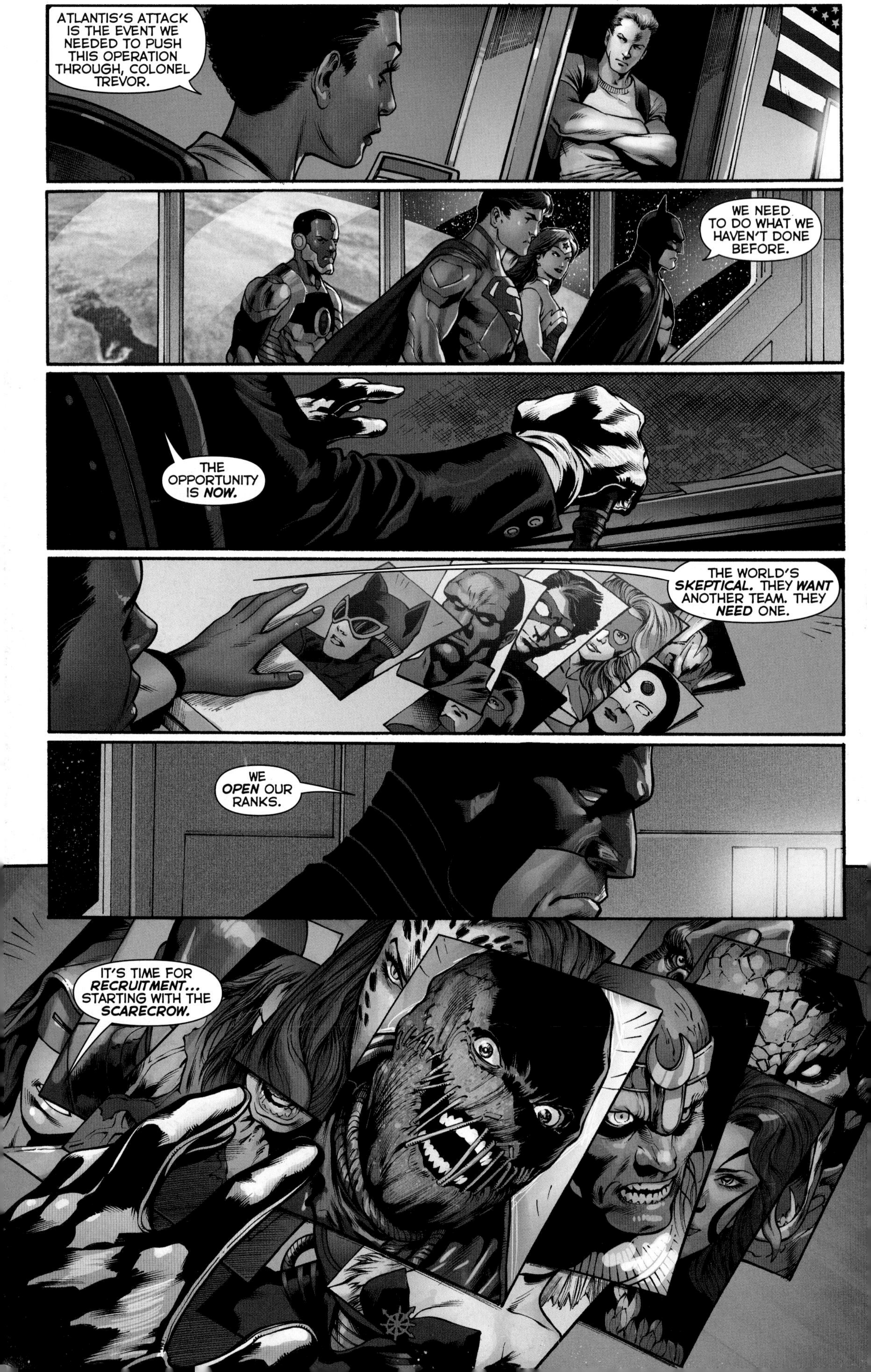
ATLANTIS'S ATTACK IS THE EVENT WE NEEDED TO PUSH THIS OPERATION THROUGH, COLONEL TREVOR.
WE NEED TO DO WHAT WE HAVEN'T DONE BEFORE.
THE OPPORTUNITY IS *NOW.*
THE WORLD'S *SKEPTICAL.* THEY *WANT* ANOTHER TEAM. THEY *NEED* ONE.
WE *OPEN* OUR RANKS.
IT'S TIME FOR *RECRUITMENT...* STARTING WITH THE *SCARECROW.*

VARIANT COVER GALLERY

AQUAMAN 15
By Jim Lee, Scott Williams & Alex Sinclair

JUSTICE LEAGUE 15
By Jim Lee, Scott Williams & Alex Sinclair

JUSTICE LEAGUE 15
By Billy Tucci & Hi-Fi

JUSTICE LEAGUE 16
By Langdon Foss & Jose Villarrubia

JUSTICE LEAGUE 17
By Steve Skroce & Alex Sinclair

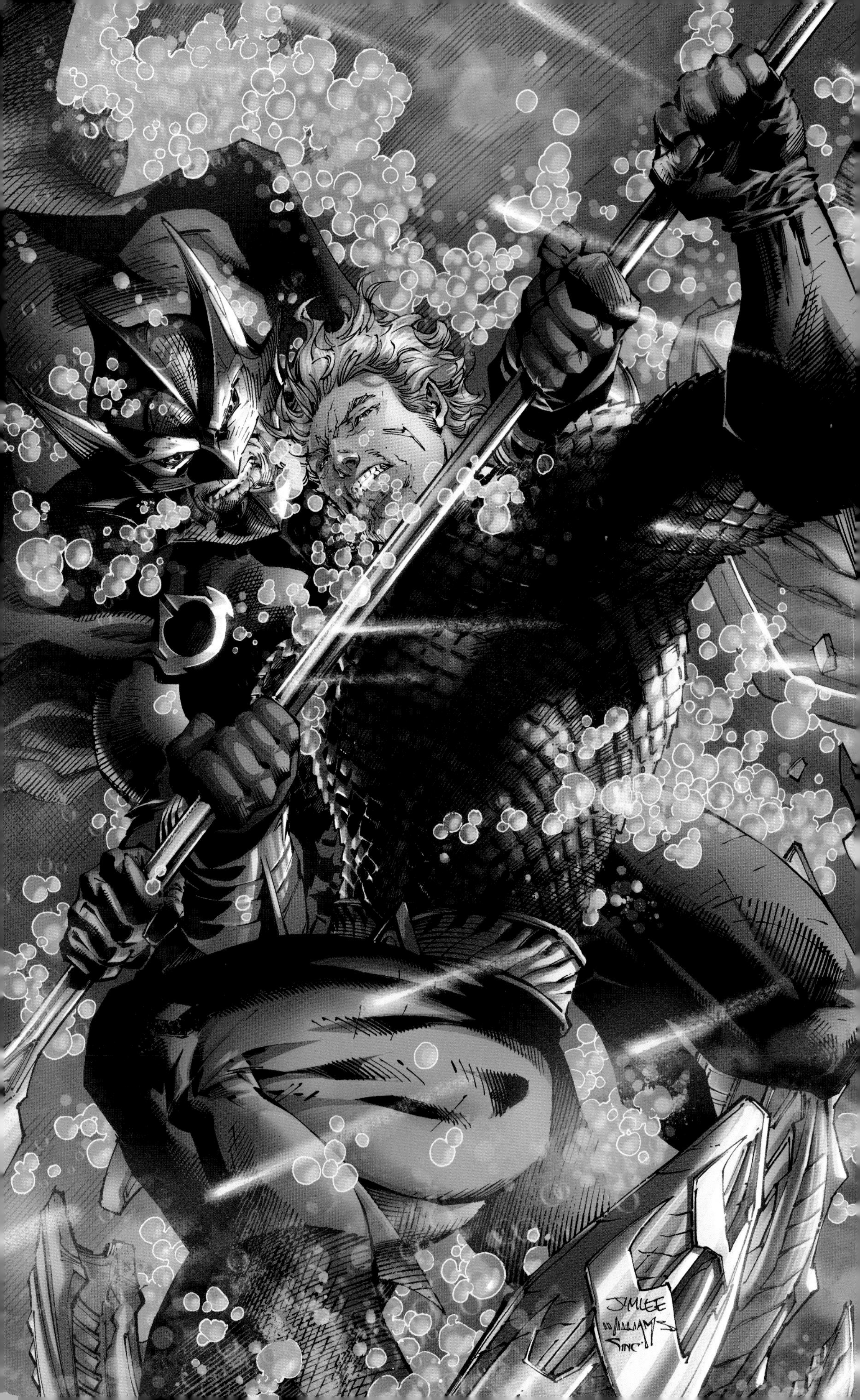

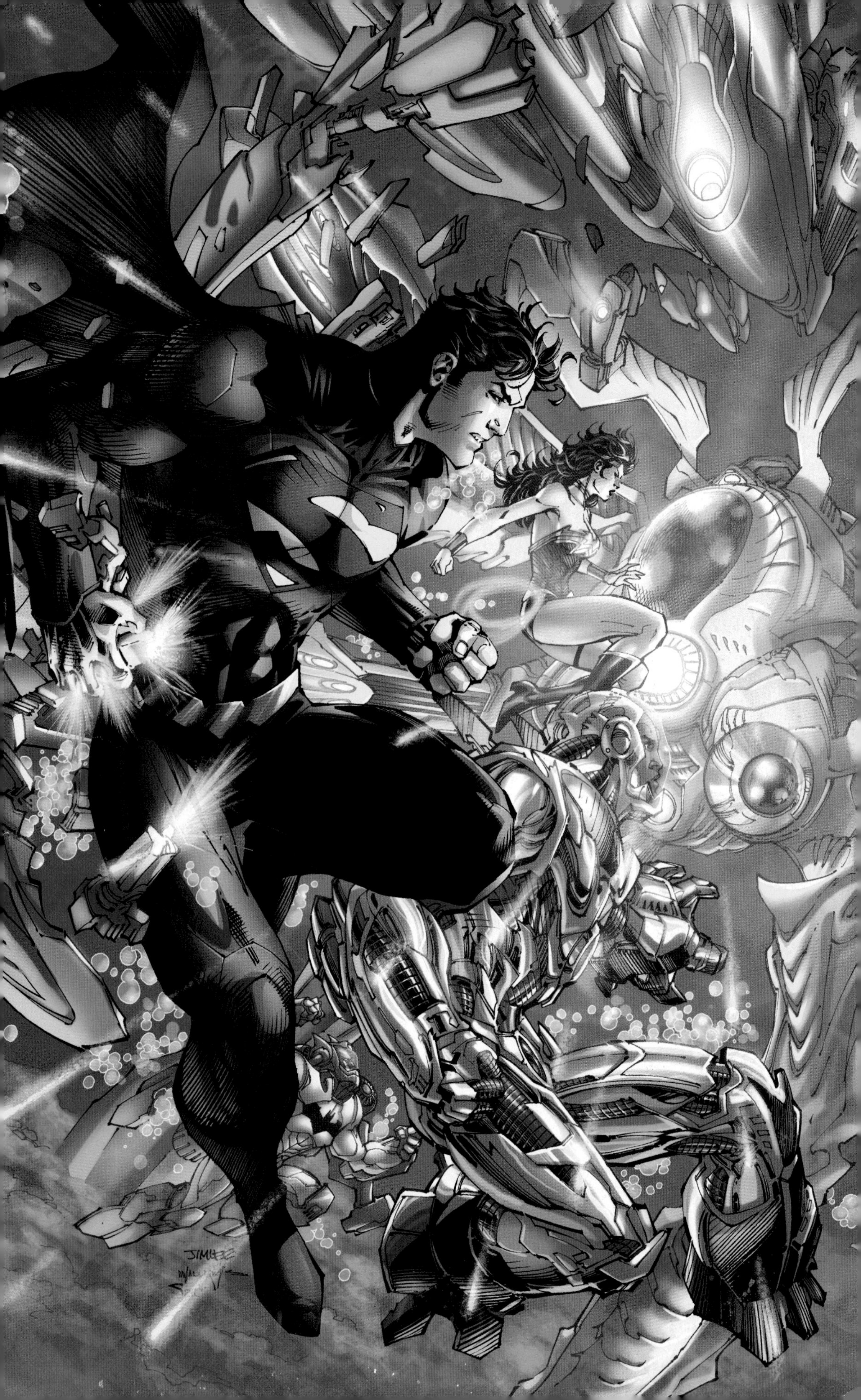

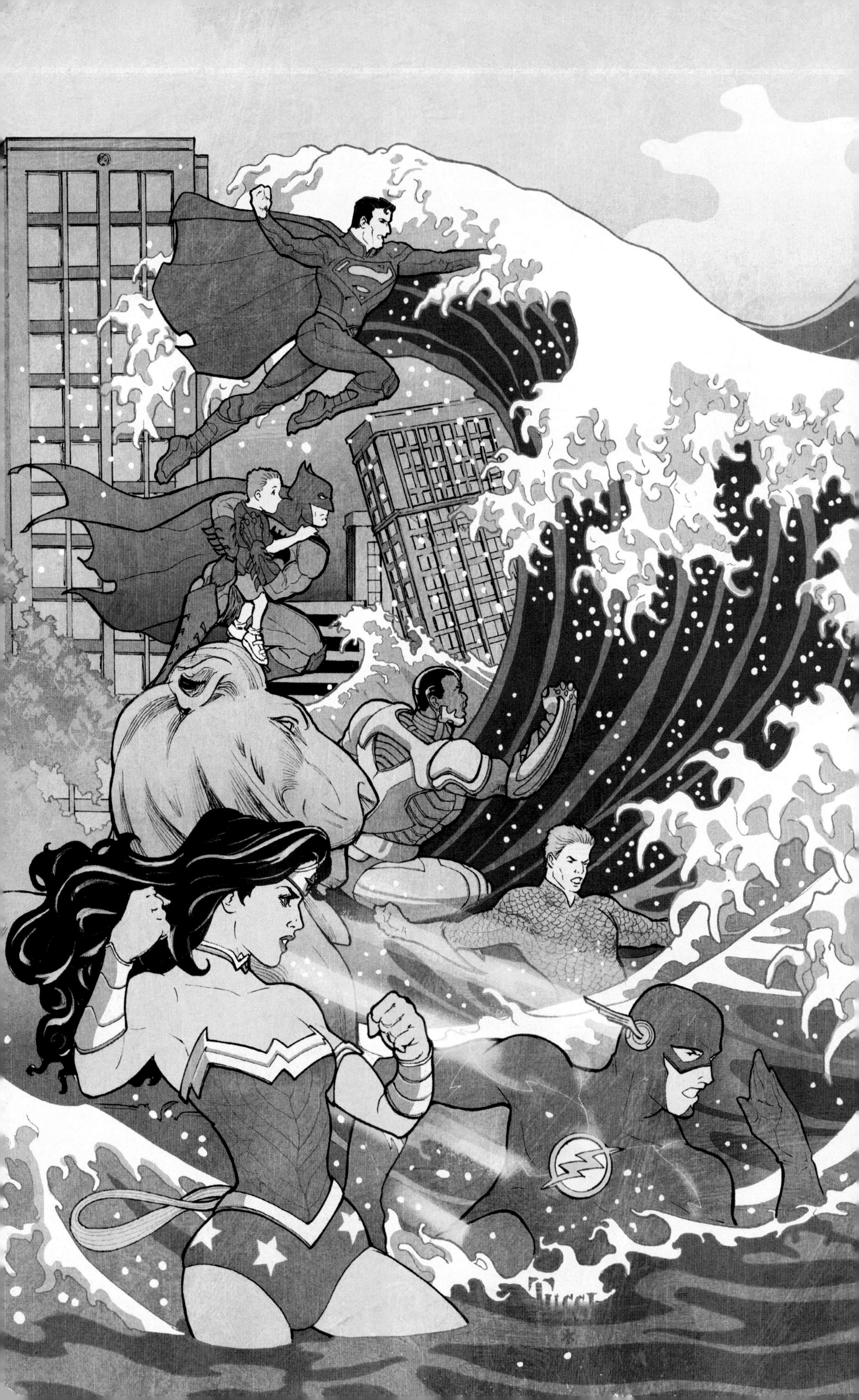

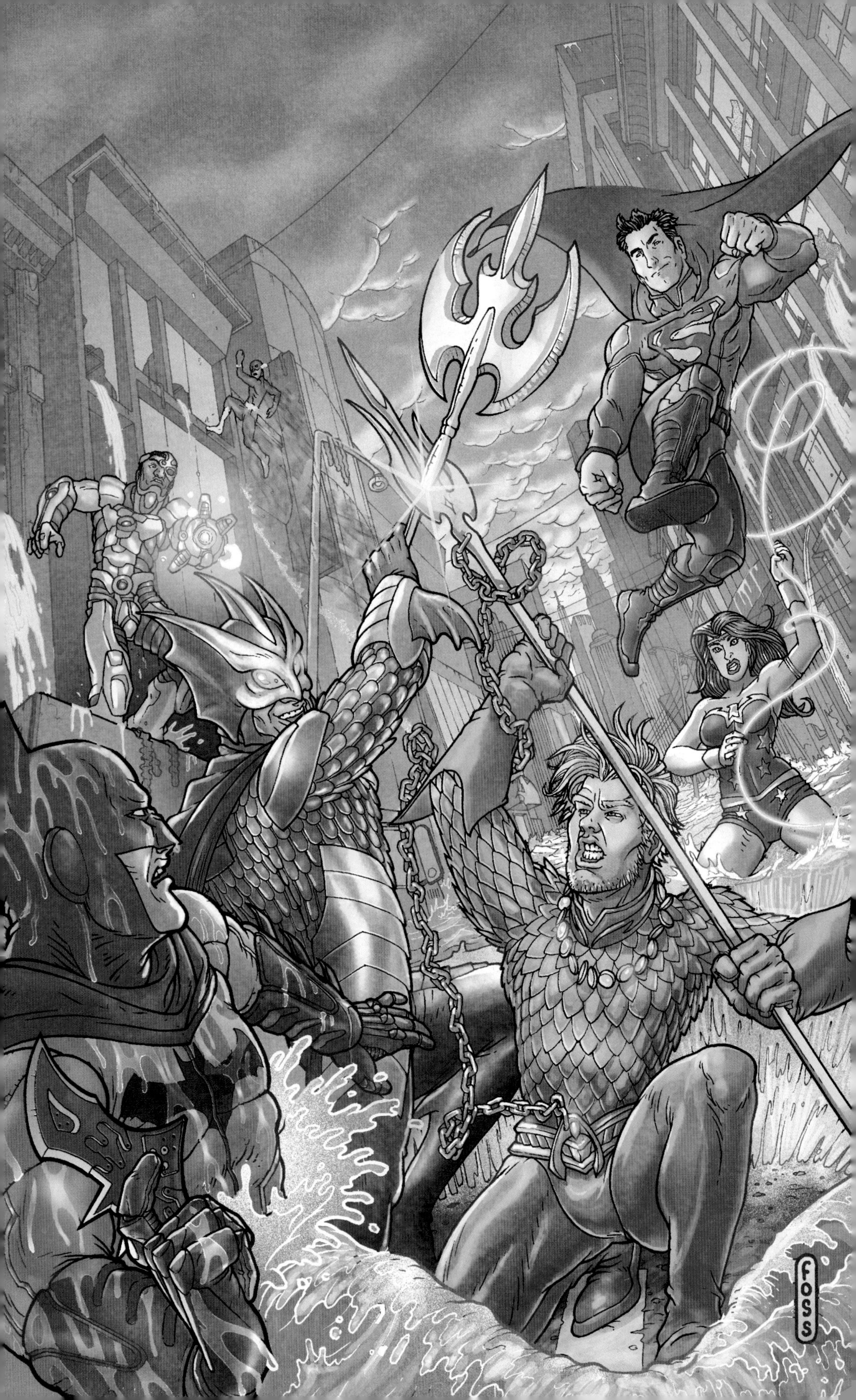
FOSS

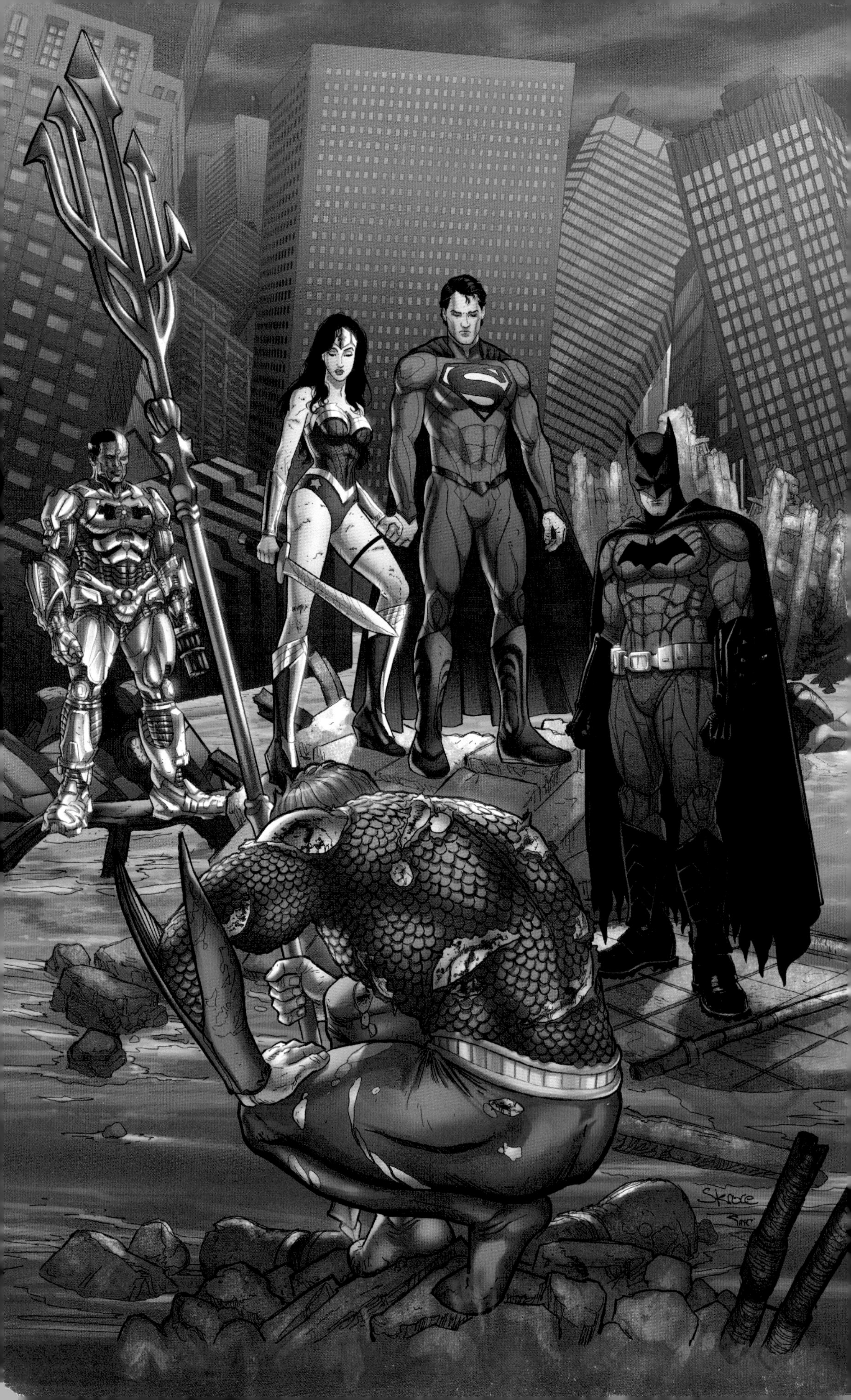

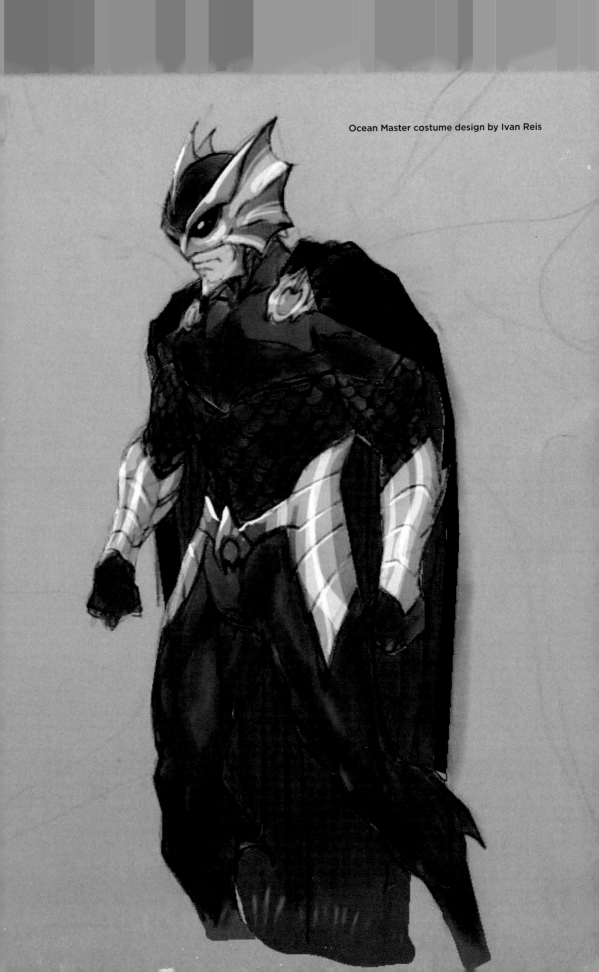

Ocean Master costume design by Ivan Reis

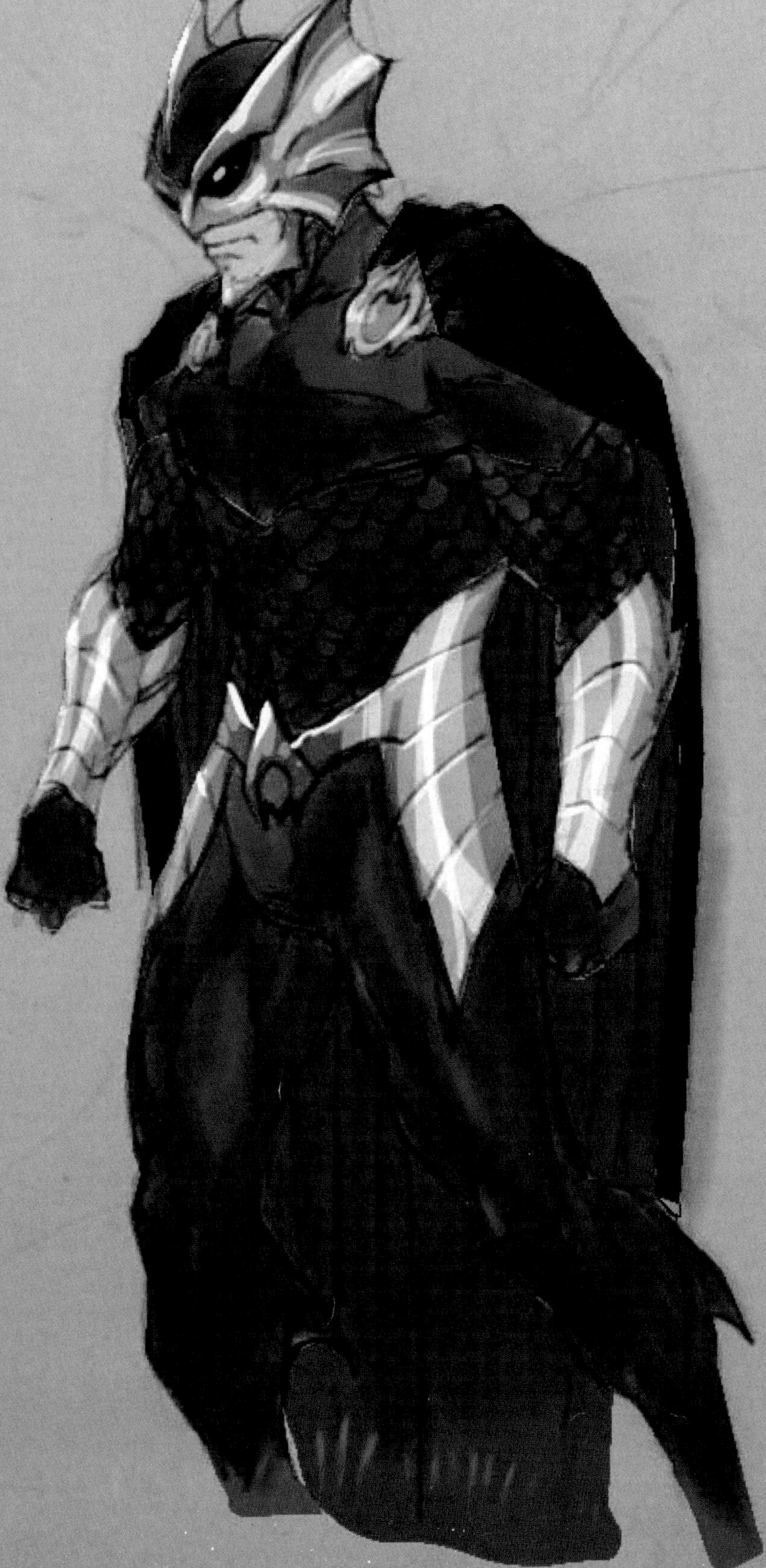

Mera costume update by Ivan Reis

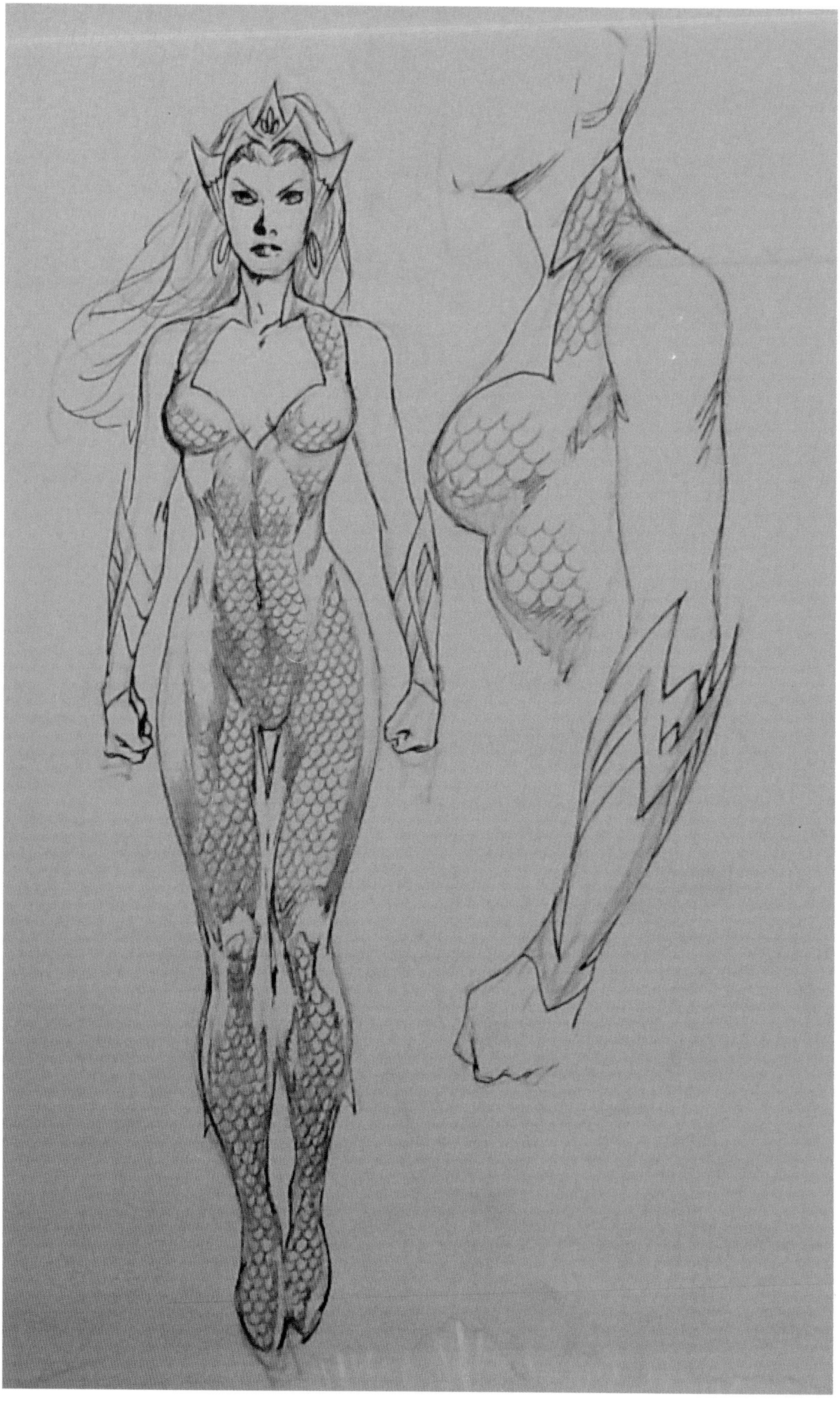

Step-by-step progression of New York Comic Con AQUAMAN promo piece by Paul Pelletier, Art Thibert & Gabe Eltaeb.

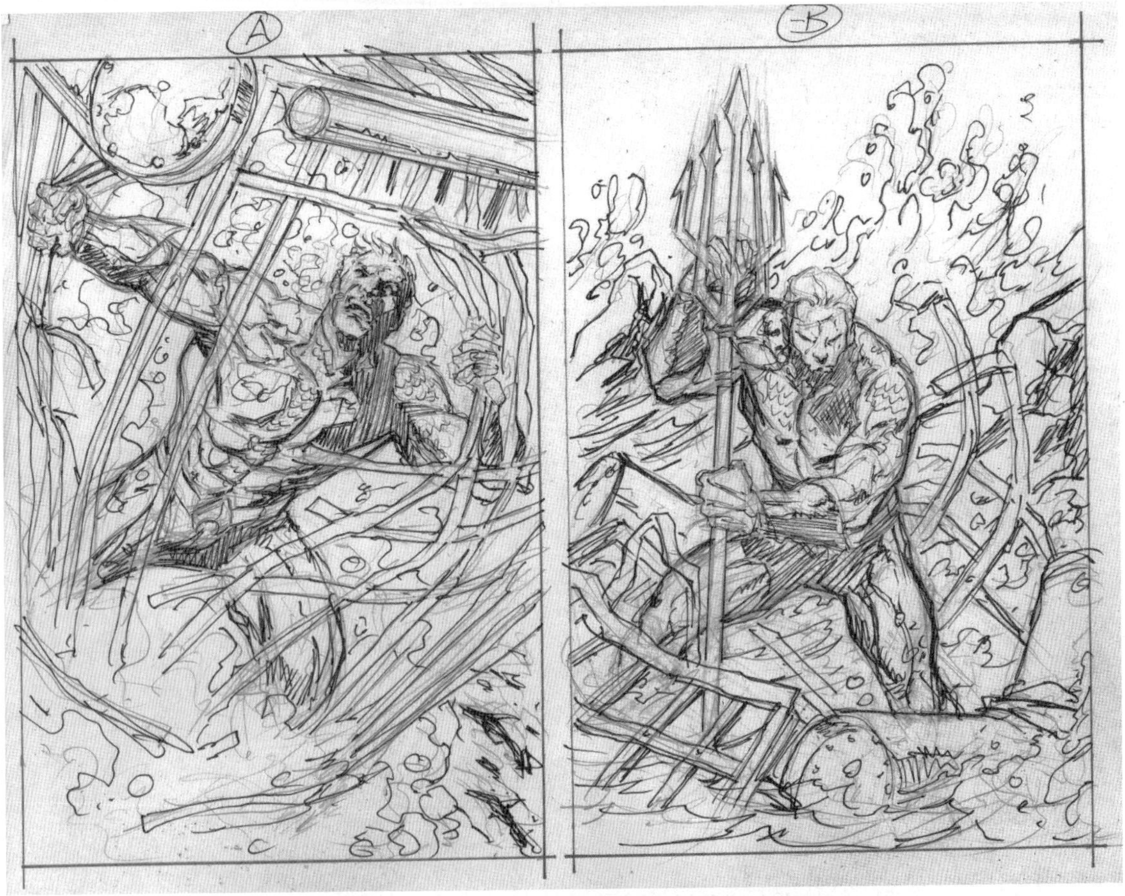
A
B

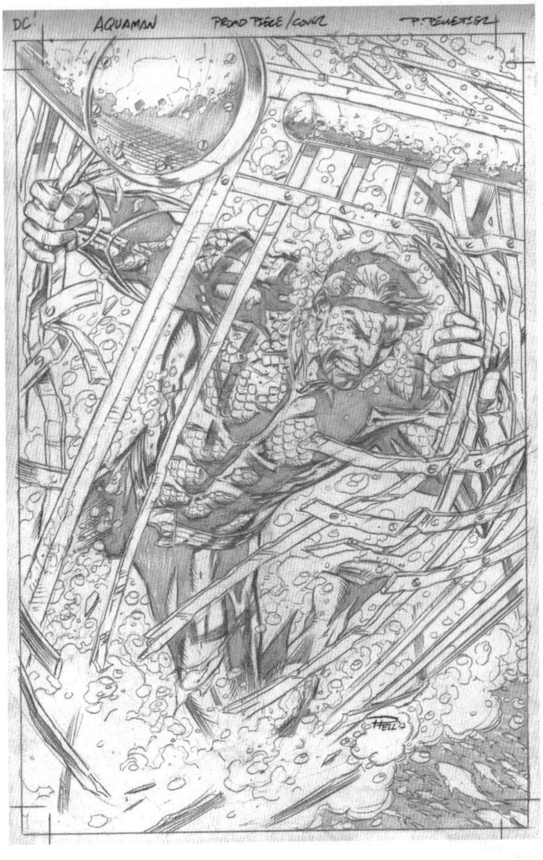
DC
AQUAMAN

AQUAMAN #15 cover sketches by Pete Woods

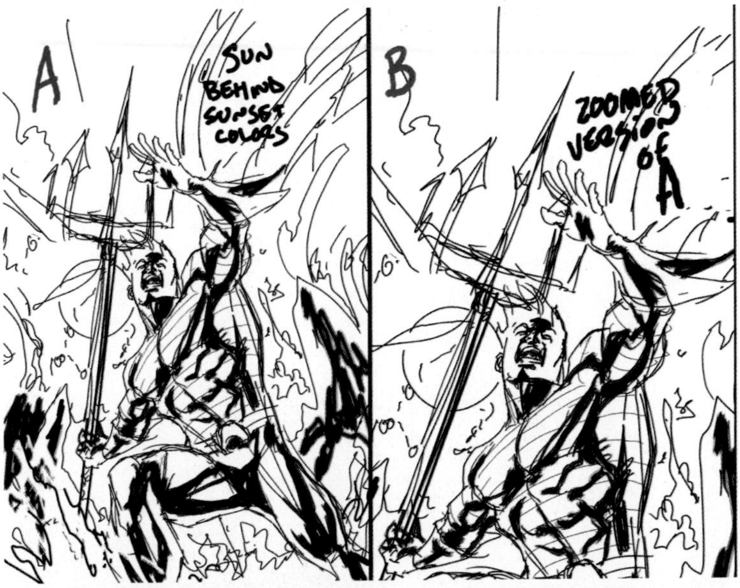
A
SUN BEHIND SUNSET COLORS
B
ZOOMED VERSION OF A

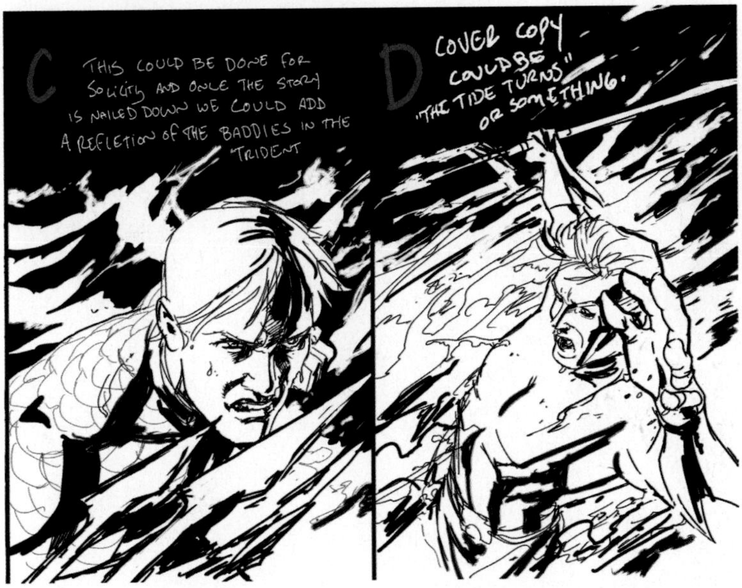
C
THIS COULD BE DONE FOR SOLICITS AND ONCE THE STORY IS NAILED DOWN WE COULD ADD A REFLETION OF THE BADDIES IN THE TRIDENT
D
COVER COPY COULD BE "THE TIDE TURNS" OR SOMETHING.

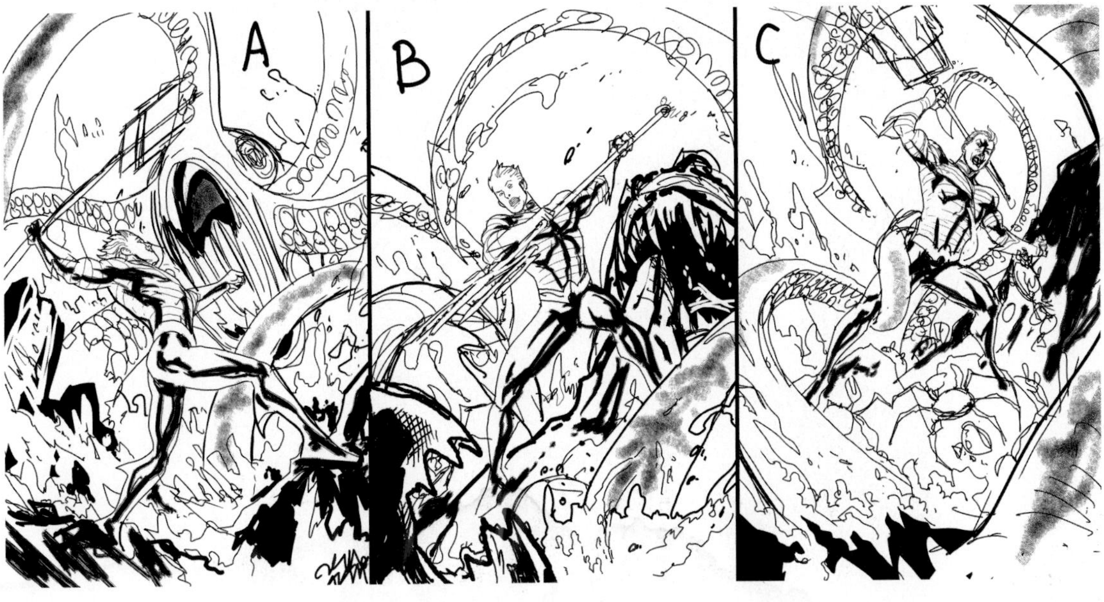
A
B
C

Pencils for AQUAMAN #15 variant cover by Jim Lee

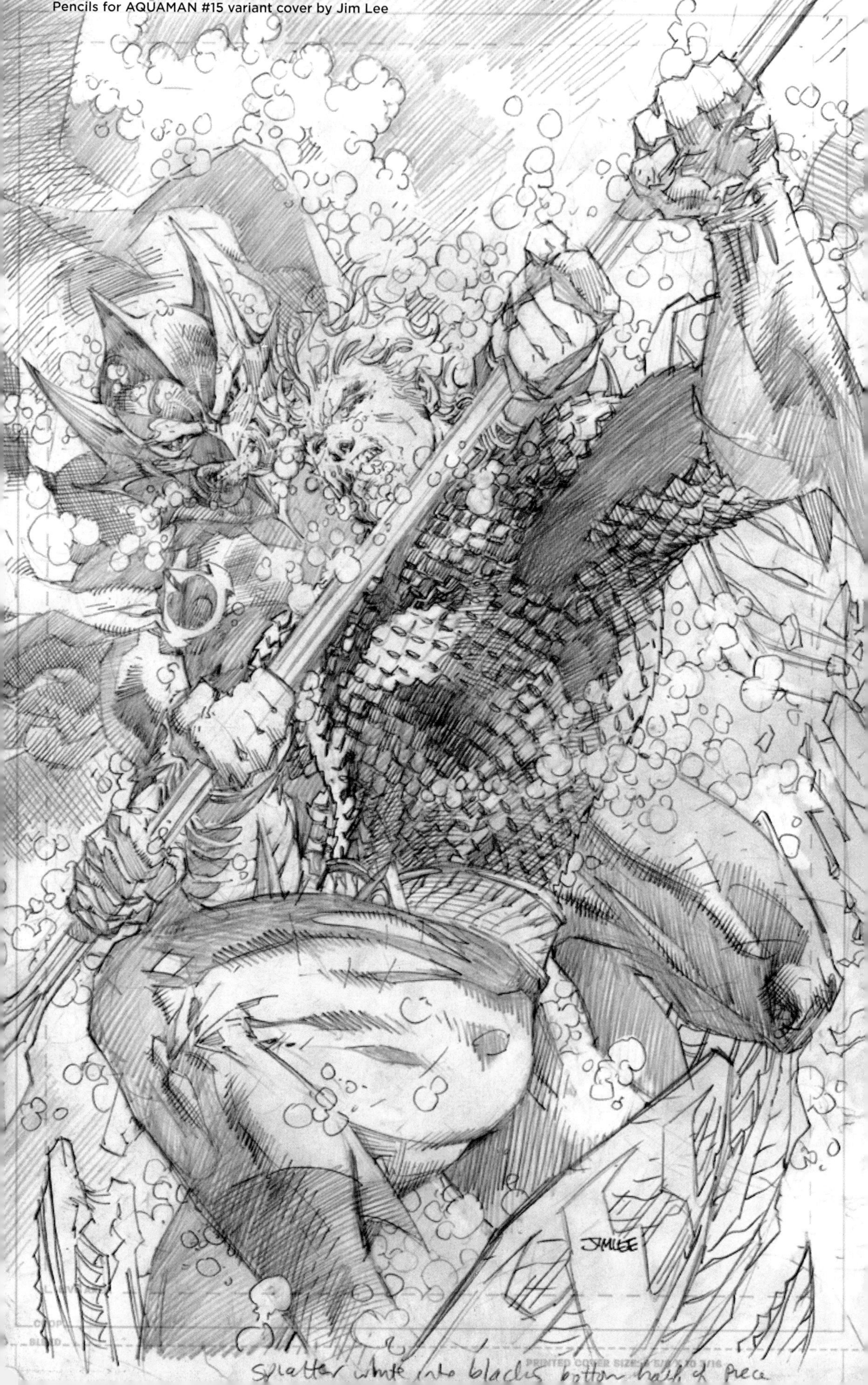
TITLE
ISSUE #
MONTH
TITLE CODE
COVER
JIMLEE
Splatter white into blacks bottom half of piece

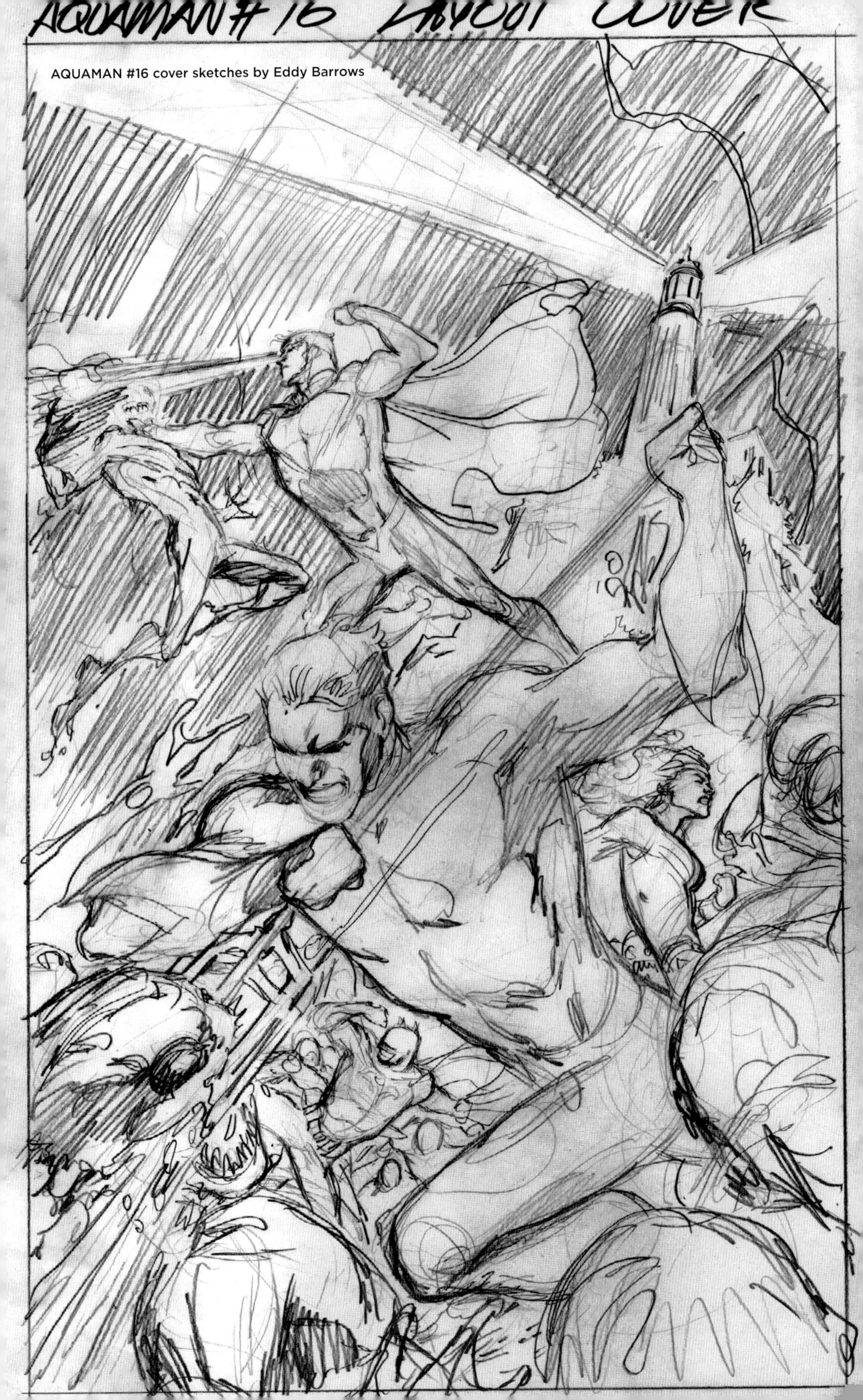
AQUAMAN #16 LAYOUT COVER

AQUAMAN #16 cover sketches by Eddy Barrows

AQUAMAN #16 VARIANT COVER (B)

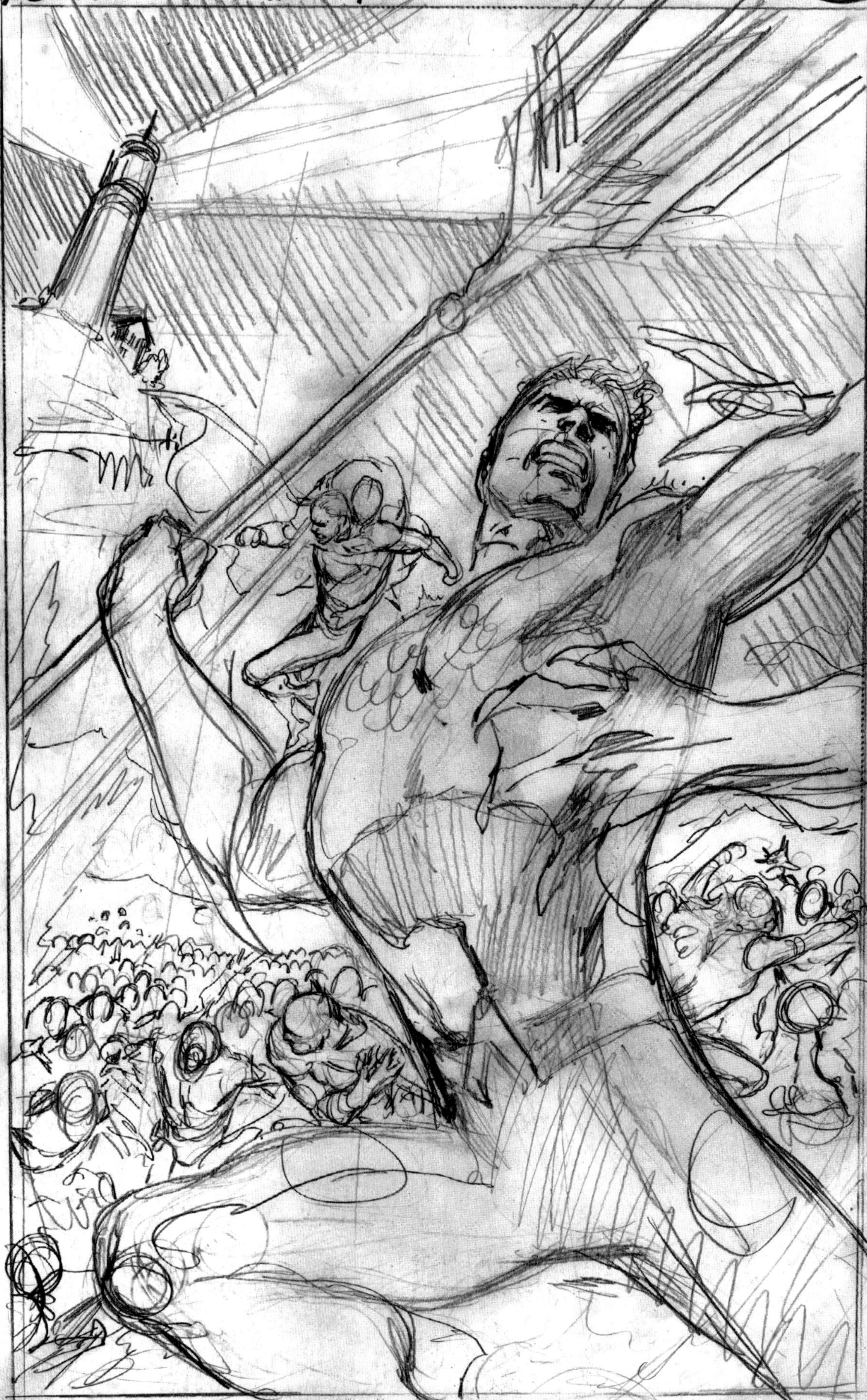

AQUAMAN #16 LAYOUT COVER

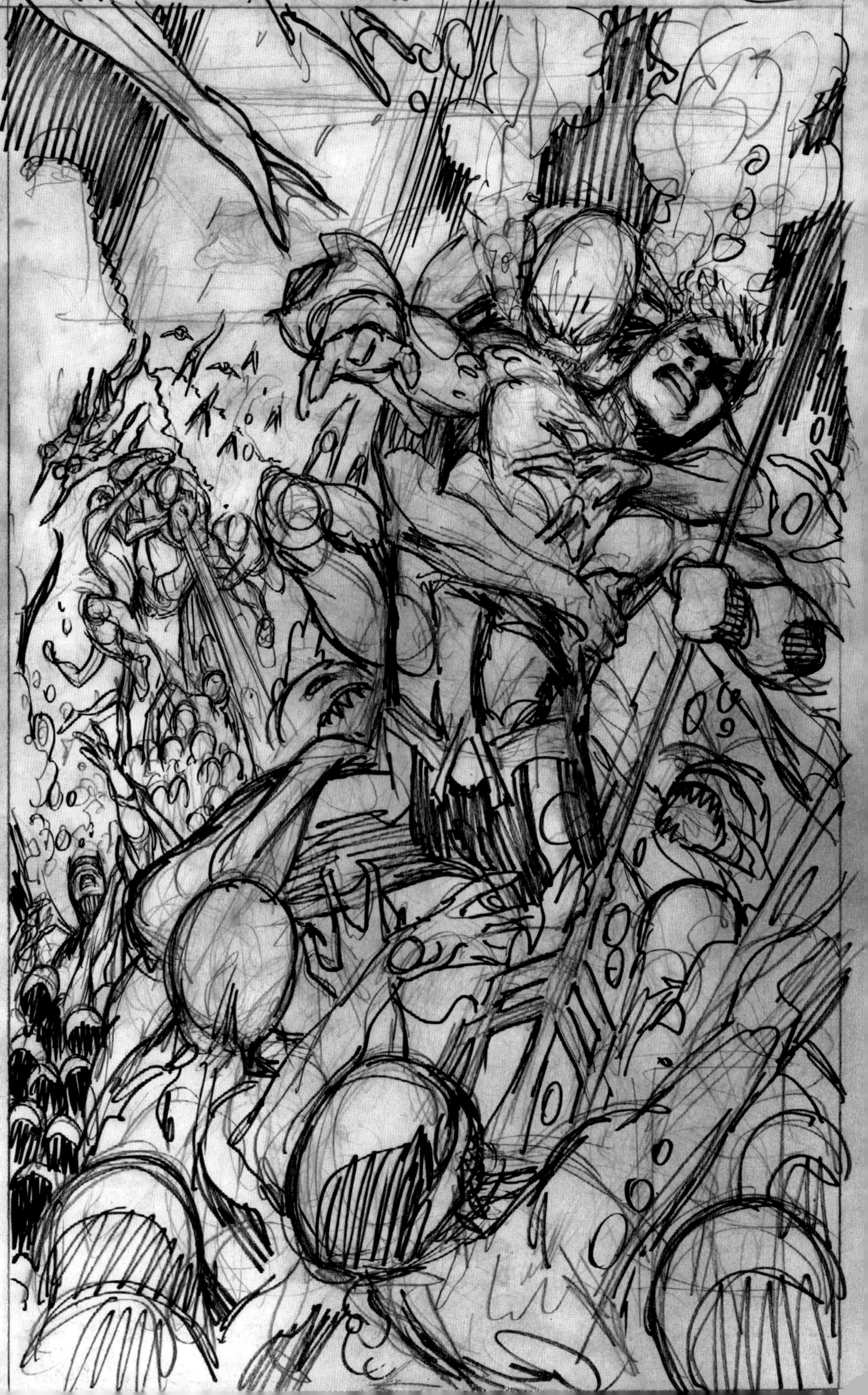

"Welcoming to new fans looking to get into superhero comics for the first time and old fans who gave up on the funny-books long ago."
—SCRIPPS HOWARD NEWS SERVICE

START AT THE BEGINNING!

JUSTICE LEAGUE
VOLUME 1:ORIGIN

**AQUAMAN
VOLUME 1:
THE TRENCH**

**THE SAVAGE
HAWKMAN VOLUME 1:
DARKNESS RISING**

**GREEN ARROW
VOLUME 1:
THE MIDAS TOUCH**

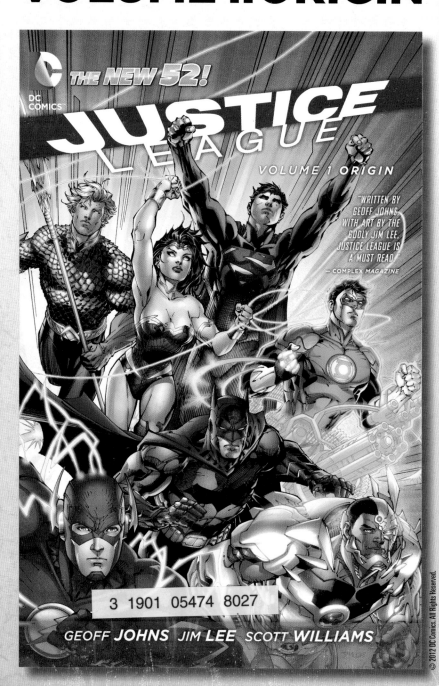

3 1901 05474 8027

GEOFF **JOHNS** JIM **LEE** SCOTT **WILLIAMS**